United Nations Economic Commission for Europe/
Food and Agriculture Organization of the United
Nations

UNECE

Timber Branch, Geneva, Switzerland

GENEVA TIMBER AND FOREST STUDY PAPER 20

EUROPEAN FOREST SECTOR OUTLOOK STUDY

MAIN REPORT

UNITED NATIONS
Geneva, 2005

Note

The designations employed and the presentation of material in this publication do not imply the expression of any opinion whatsoever on the part of the secretariat of the United Nations concerning the legal status of any country, territory, city or area, or of its authorities, or concerning the delimitation of its frontiers or boundaries.

Abstract

The European Forest Sector Outlook Study presents long term trends for supply and demand of forest products (roundwood, sawnwood, panels, pulp, paper, non-wood products) and services and outlook to 2020, in western and eastern Europe and four major CIS countries, including Russia. It reviews trends for the forest resource, trade, markets and recycling. It stresses the future shift in the balance of the sector to the east, and the importance of cross-sectoral issues, notably consequences for the forest sector of energy, environment and trade policies, which are examined in some detail. The study is based on a major collaborative effort by experts in the countries covered by the study, under the auspices of the UNECE Timber Committee and the FAO European Forestry Commission. The study identifies a number of major policy issues and proposes some policy recommendations, as a basis for future debate.

ECE/TIM/SP/20

UNITED NATIONS PUBLICATIONS
ISSN 1020 2269

TABLE OF CONTENTS

LIST OF TABLES

LIST OF FIGURES

LIST OF BOXES

PREFACE

Governments, forest owners, industries and civil society around the world rely on credible and current information to develop forest management plans, policies and strategies that respond to emerging issues and trends. Nowhere is the need for reliable data more greatly felt than in Europe where the forest sector must come to terms with new realities that are bringing about fundamental change. Major challenges include the need to determine 1) whether the production of raw materials should give way to recreation and the conservation of biological diversity in the post-industrial society of Western Europe or 2) the extent to which the forest sector can contribute in a sustainable way to overall economic development in Eastern Europe and Russia. How international trade and the rapid growth of markets in other parts of the world affect the European forest sector is another question to which answers must be found.

This edition of the European forest sector outlook studies (EFSOS) is the latest in a series which have supported policy making for half a century. While the basic objectives remain unchanged, each study focuses on different aspects of a complex dynamic. In 2005, we chose to address the supply and demand outlook of forest services and non-wood forest products. For the first time, the study provides quantitative projections for the Commonwealth of Independent States while continuing to give detailed estimates of wood demand and supply – a core component of earlier publications. In addition, an in-depth analysis of the interactions of forestry with other sectors demonstrates the clear need to take a broad and comprehensive approach when seeking lasting solutions.

The study, prepared jointly by our two organisations, is part of the series of outlook studies produced by the Food and Agriculture Organization of the United Nations. It is based on scientific analysis and includes key contributions from experts and national correspondents to whom we are grateful.

It is hoped that EFSOS will help draw further attention to emerging policy issues and stimulate debate on the region's response to challenges identified. UNECE, FAO and partners, notably the Ministerial Conference on the Protection of Forests in Europe, look forward to using the findings of this study as a basis for wider policy discussion in the coming years.

Hosny El-Lakany	Brigita Schmögnerová
Assistant Director-General	Executive Secretary
Forestry Department, FAO	United Nations Economic Commission for Europe

ABBREVIATIONS USED IN THE REPORT

CAP	Common Agricultural Policy
CEEC	Central and Eastern European Countries
CIS	Commonwealth of Independent States
COFORD	National Council for Forest Research and Development (in Ireland)
COMTRADE	UN Commodity Trade Statistics Database
CUM	cubic metres
EFI	European Forest Institute
EFISCEN	European Forest Information Scenario Model
EFSOS	European Forest Sector Outlook Study
EFTA	European Free Trade Area
ETTS	European Timber Trends Study
ETTS V	Fifth European Timber Trends Study
EU	European Union
FAO	Food and Agriculture Organization of the United Nations
FAOSTAT	FAO statistical database
FAWS	forest available for wood supply
FOWL	forest and other wooded land
FRA	Forest Resource Assessment
FSC	Forest Stewardship Council
FTE	full-time equivalents
GDP	gross domestic product
ha	hectare(s)
ICP Forests	International Co-operative Programme on the Assessment and Monitoring of Air Pollution Effects on Forests
IRF	International Road Federation
ISIC	International Standard Industrial Classification
MCPFE	Ministerial Conference on the Protection of Forests in Europe
MDF	medium density fibreboard
MT	metric tonnes
NAI	net annual increment
NOBE	Independent Centre for Economic Studies
o.b.	overbark
OSB	oriented strand board
PEFC	Programme for the Endorsement of Forest Certification
TFYR Macedonia	The former Yugoslav Republic of Macedonia
UNECE	United Nations Economic Commission for Europe
USSR	Union of Soviet Socialist Republics
WRI	World Resources Institute
WRME	wood raw material equivalent

EXECUTIVE SUMMARY

Introduction

This is the sixth major study in the European outlook study series. The aim of the study is to provide decision makers in the forest sector with information and analysis about long-term trends in the sector and projections of future developments. In particular, the study focuses on the interactions between the forest sector and society and attempts to describe how these are changing over time.

The study covers 38 countries, including all of the major European countries and seven of the countries from the former-USSR (the three Baltic States - Estonia, Latvia and Lithuania - plus Belarus, Republic of Moldova, Russian Federation and Ukraine). For the purpose of sub-regional analysis, countries are grouped into **Western Europe, Eastern Europe** and **CIS sub-regions** (see Figure 1 on page 3). Most of the results of the historical analysis are presented for the period from 1961 to 2000, while projections are presented for the period 2000 to 2020.

The forest sector has been defined to cover forest resources and the production, trade and consumption of forest products and services. Due to the limitations of available data, much of the analysis focuses on the markets for wood products, but advances have also been made in the analysis of the following: forest resources; policies affecting the forest sector; non-wood forest products; and forest services.

The statistics and information used in the study have come from FAO and ECE databases, supplemented with additional information supplied by national correspondents. National correspondents and outlook study experts were also involved in the design, implementation and peer review of different sub-components of the analysis. Supporting studies and analyses have been produced on the following topics: historical trends in forest resources; historical trends in forest product markets; the outlook for forest sector employment; the outlook for the Russian forest sector; policies affecting the forest sector; projections of economic growth in Europe; projections of forest product supply, demand and trade; and the outlook for forest resources. These studies have been produced separately as FAO-ECE discussion papers.

Following the introduction, the study is divided into four main sections. Section 2 presents the analysis of historical trends in the European forest sector. This section presents an extensive and comprehensive analysis of many different aspects of the sector, starting with forest resources and management, followed by market trends for forest products and finishing with a brief analysis of the trends in some of the linkages between the forest sector and society. Section 3 examines the "driving forces" or exogenous factors affecting the sector and presents qualitative and quantitative statements about likely future changes in many of these variables. Section 4 presents the outlook for the European forest sector and Section 5 presents a summary of the major results and conclusions of the study, including the main implications of the results for all stakeholders.

Trends and current status

Up until recently, the long-term trends in most aspects of the European forest sector have been generally stable. However, in the last decade, there have been some significant changes. Most of these have been due to the political and economic reforms in Eastern Europe and the CIS sub-region. However, other rapid changes have also occurred recently due to the effects of increased globalisation, technological change and changes in policies within and outside the sector.

Forest resources

Long-term trends in forest resources have been generally stable and show that the forest area, growing stock and increment have consistently increased in Europe over recent decades. Furthermore, this expansion of the forest resource can be observed at the European and sub-regional level (and also in most countries).

For example, the total area of forest and other wooded land has increased by three percent since 1980 (or about 36 million ha) and the area of forest available for wood supply has similarly expanded in most countries. For the European countries where long-term historical trends are available, growing stock has increased by 17 percent and annual increment has risen by 33 percent in total since 1950 (see Section 2.1 on page 13).

Another notable point is that Europe's forests are growing faster than the annual level of fellings and that this gap between fellings and increment has increased since 1960 (see Figure 9 on page 21). Currently the fellings to increment ratio is around 75 percent in Eastern Europe and 70 percent in Western Europe, but only 25 percent in the Russian Federation (with an average of about 45 percent for Europe as a whole).

It is difficult to measure qualitative aspects of Europe's forests, but the little information that exists suggests that the quality of forest resources and forest management in Europe has probably been quite stable and may have increased in some respects. However, significant problems still exist in many countries (e.g. defoliation, forest fires and outbreaks of pests and diseases). Most recently there has been increased concern about illegal activities in the sector, but it is not currently possible to reliably assess the extent of this problem or its impact on forest resources.

It is also worth noting that the management of forests in Europe has followed a gradual and long-term trend towards management for objectives other than wood production (see Section 2.2 on page 21). This may have led to improvements in the "quality" of forest management, but it has also led to higher expectations of performance from the sector.

Forest products and services

In forest products markets, the most notable trend in recent years has been the collapse of production and consumption in Eastern Europe and the CIS sub-region in the early 1990s, followed by the gradual recovery in most of these countries. The figures vary by country and product but, on the whole, production and consumption fell by between one-third and two-thirds in most of these countries up until the mid-1990s (see Section 2.3 on page 27). Since then, recovery has been mixed, with the most rapid and dramatic recoveries in markets taking place in the Baltic States, followed by most of the rest of Eastern Europe and then the CIS sub-region. Although recovery in the Russian Federation has, perhaps, been the slowest to start, there is now considerable growth in the forest sector in the Russian Federation and, due to its size, developments in this one country are likely to have the most profound impact on the sector in the future at the European and global levels.

Another important trend in Europe has been the structural change in the markets for solid wood products observed over the last four decades. Reconstituted panels have gradually increased in importance, as their rates of growth in production and consumption have been higher than the rates of growth in sawnwood and plywood markets. Furthermore, this shift appears to have increased over the last decade, perhaps due to the introduction of new types of panel product such as medium density fibreboard and other engineered wood products (see Figure 25 on page 41).

Historical trends in the markets for paper and paperboard show that these markets have generally grown more rapidly than the markets for solid wood products. The one exception to this is newsprint, where growth has been quite modest. In contrast, rates of growth in the markets for printing and writing paper and other paper and paperboard have been dramatic and have generally exceeded the rates of growth in all other forest product sectors (see Figure 26 on page 42).

The structural changes in solid wood products markets plus the rapid growth in paper and paperboard markets have led to a significant change in the structure of demand for wood raw materials and the availability of different types of wood and fibre. In particular, the relative importance of sawlog demand has declined over the last 40 years. In addition, at the same time that demand has increased most rapidly for small-sized roundwood, the availability of alternative sources of wood and fibre has also increased (e.g. wood residues and recovered paper, which can substitute for small-sized industrial roundwood in many applications). This increase in availability has largely been driven by the changes in demand noted above and improvements in technology, but environmental policies have also played an important role in this respect, particularly in the 1990s (see Sections 2.4 and 2.5 on pages 42-72).

The net effect of these changes has been a gradual decline in the importance of industrial roundwood for the manufacturing of forest products in Europe. For example, in Western Europe, the direct use of industrial roundwood now only accounts for about one-half of all wood and fibre used to produce forest products. Industrial roundwood accounts for about 90 percent of all wood and fibre used in the other two sub-regions, but the average for Europe as a whole has declined consistently over the last four decades and is currently around 60 percent (see Figure 47 on page 67). Future developments in environmental policies and forest processing in the other two sub-regions may result in them following a similar path to the trends experienced in Western Europe.

Reliable information about the production and consumption of non-wood forest products and forest services is extremely difficult to obtain. However, there is a general perception that the importance of these forest outputs is increasing in Europe relative to the importance of wood production. What little information is available would seem to confirm this perception.

For example, depending on which products are included, non-wood forest products could account for between around 10 percent to 25 percent of the total value of forestry production in Europe (i.e. the value of production of roundwood and non-wood forest products). The value of forest services is even more difficult to assess, but it seems likely that they are at least as important as non-wood forest products and could be more important than wood production (depending on the country). The relative importance of wood, non-wood forest products and forest services will vary significantly from country to country, but it seems likely that forest services are probably more important in Western Europe that in the other two sub-regions. Similarly, non-wood forest products are probably more important in Eastern Europe than elsewhere in Europe (see Sections 2.9 and 2.10 on pages 93-112).

International trade is another area where there have been some dramatic changes in trends in recent years (see Section 2.6 on page 72). Across all categories of forest products, the proportion of production that is exported has increased over the last four decades. This trend appears at the global, European and sub-regional level. Furthermore, this proportion has increased much more rapidly during the 1990s than in the previous three decades. This is due to the increased globalisation of forest products markets in the 1990s. Within Europe, it is also due to the rapid development of forest products exports and low growth in domestic demand in Eastern Europe and the CIS sub-region in recent years.

At the global level, Europe remains an important exporter of forest products, accounting for about half of global forest products exports (by total value). In contrast, the importance of Europe as an importer of forest products has declined, due to more rapid growth in imports into other regions (particularly Asia). This has led to the situation where Europe is now a small net exporter of forest products (by total value).

The value of European imports and exports of sawnwood and wood based panels are now roughly in balance, but Europe is a significant importer of wood pulp and an even more significant exporter of paper and paperboard. The trade balances for each product vary by sub-region (see Figure 57 and Figure 58 on page 78) but, in general, exports have increased by more than imports for most products over the last four decades.

One final trend worth noting is the decline in forest product prices that has been recorded in recent years. In real terms, since 1970, the international trade prices of processed forest products have either remained stable or fallen (depending on the product). In some cases (e.g. coniferous sawnwood, particleboard, plywood and veneer sheets and paper and paperboard) the long-term decline in prices has been dramatic (e.g. a fall of almost 50 percent in the real prices of sawnwood and plywood since 1970). However, real price levels in Eastern Europe and the CIS sub-region have increased in the last decade, as their international trade has expanded and their prices have started to converge with those in Western Europe. Only partial information is available about stumpage prices, but this information suggests that stumpage prices have followed the trends noted above and may have declined by as much as 50 percent in real terms since 1970.

Other developments

Two other major developments have been observed in the historical analysis of the European forest sector, particularly in the last decade. The first of these is the changing policy environment.

To various extents, government policies in Europe have changed to reflect the increased public interest in sustainable development. Thus, there has been an increase in support for recycling in many European countries. More recently, renewable energy has also been promoted as a major component of environmental policies. Within the forest sector, forestry policies have encouraged the production of non-market benefits and, particularly in Western Europe, forestry development has been promoted as an alternative to agriculture.

Another notable development has been institutional and administrative changes in the way that governments act within the sector. Some countries have partially privatised state forest assets and, in Eastern Europe, the restitution of forests to their previous owners has created a vast number of small private forest owners. Furthermore, where significant areas of forest remain in public ownership, many governments have encouraged their public forest managers to act more like private forest owners by setting clear commercial targets and more clearly separating the different roles of the forestry administration (i.e. policy formulation, policy implementation and the management of public forests).

At the same time that these changes have taken place, there has also been a gradual decline in the economic viability of forest management. This second major development has been due to factors such as: an increase in the potential wood supply; increased supply of alternative sources of wood and fibre; increased global competition from low-cost suppliers (along with increased competition within Europe from low-cost countries in the east); and declining product prices. These factors have combined to create a situation where forest managers are increasingly expected to meet higher management standards and produce a broader range of products and services at the same time that their main source of income (revenue from wood production) is lower than ever before. This is clearly one of the most important challenges for the European forest sector at the moment that all stakeholders must address.

Driving forces

At the broadest level, the driving forces that will shape the European forest sector in the future can be divided into two groups. First, there are the exogenous factors that will drive the sector in one direction or another (i.e. socio-economic and environmental trends). Linked to these are the future changes in demands placed upon the sector that can be expected in response to these trends (see Sections 3.1 and 3.2 on pages 127-140). Secondly, there are changes in policies and market frameworks that may be implemented by those working in the sector in an attempt to steer the sector in a particular direction. These have been investigated by creating a number of alternative scenarios for future developments and examining what impact they might have on the sector (see Sections 3.3 and 3.4 on pages 141-151).

Exogenous factors

The two main exogenous factors that are likely to have most impact on the forest sector in the future are changes in forest products prices and future rates of economic growth. For the baseline outlook scenario, it has been assumed that forest product prices will remain constant in real terms over the next 20 years. This assumption has been adjusted slightly in the alternative scenarios (see below) to reflect, in a very simple way, what might happen to forest products markets under the alternative scenarios.

For economic growth, the analysis of historical trends has suggested that Gross Domestic Product will grow more slowly in the future in Western Europe (compared to the past and compared to the other European sub-regions). For Eastern Europe and the CIS sub-region, it is expected that economic growth will not change markedly from current levels, but will gradually slow down as levels of Gross Domestic Product per capita start to converge with those in Western Europe. This is based on an assumption that educational levels and the employment of technology will gradually converge across most of Europe.

This analysis of economic trends was used to produce the projections of economic growth used in the baseline outlook scenario (see Table 1). As above, the lower and higher economic growth projections were also used in the investigation of alternative scenarios.

Table 1   ***Projections of average annual economic growth in Europe from 2000 to 2020 under three different growth scenarios***

Region/sub-region	Economic growth scenario		
	Low	**Baseline**	**High**
Western Europe	1.1%	1.3%	2.6%
Eastern Europe	2.6%	4.2%	5.3%
CIS sub-region	2.4%	4.0%	5.3%
Europe	1.5%	2.2%	3.5%

Source: NOBE (2002).

Another important driving force is the gradual ageing of the European population. Over the next 20 years, this will be felt mostly in Western Europe. However, this change will also start to appear in the other two sub-regions after 2010. The impact of this trend will be felt in two ways. Firstly, labour is likely to become more scarce and expensive. This will encourage the greater substitution of capital for labour in end-use markets (e.g. construction), which is likely to lead to greater demand for engineered wood products as opposed to simpler sawnwood and panel products. The second impact of this will be changes in the broader demands placed upon the sector. As populations age and become wealthier, it is likely that the demands for non-wood goods and services will increase relative to the demands for forest products. Thus, the historical trend towards greater public interest in forest services is likely to continue and strengthen in the future.

The main environmental driving force will be the continued abundance of potential wood supply in Europe in the foreseeable future. Even with a significant increase in wood production, the potential availability of wood in Europe's forests is likely to continue to increase over the next 20 years, due to the area, increment and age-structure of existing forest resources. Combined with similar trends in several regions outside Europe, this makes it very unlikely that roundwood prices will increase in the near future. However, it does also present an opportunity to expand the area of forests in Europe that are managed for objectives other than wood supply. The extent to which forest management is redirected towards non-wood management objectives will depend upon the economic viability (for forest owners) of different forest management options. This is closely linked to the issue of public subsidies for the sector and the ability of forest owners to commercialise non-wood forest outputs in the future.

Alternative future scenarios for the sector

The analysis of policies affecting the sector included an assessment of historical trends in policies and an inquiry of expert opinion on future trends in policies and their likely impact on important variables such as: forest area; production; trade; and consumption. This resulted in the elaboration of a number of possible future scenarios, of which the following three scenarios were explored in the analysis.

Baseline scenario: the baseline scenario assumes that the long-term historical relationships in forest products markets will remain the same in the future. In terms of forest resources, it assumes that future developments in the bio-physical characteristics of Europe's forests will be largely determined by the existing status of forest resources. Constant prices and the baseline economic growth projections were used to produce the forest product market forecasts under this scenario.

Conservation scenario: the conservation scenario assumes that there will be an accelerated shift towards environmental enhancement and conservation of forest resources in the future. This will be driven by an increase in public awareness of and demand for environmental benefits and will be supported by policies that will move society in this direction. Under this scenario, it has been assumed that forest products prices may increase slightly and that economic growth will be slightly slower in the future.

Integration scenario: this scenario assumes that there will be more rapid economic integration and market liberalisation across all of Europe. This will result in higher economic growth, so the higher economic growth projections have been used to produce the forest product market projections under this scenario. These will tend to exert downward pressure on forest prices, so an assumption of a small decline in forest product prices has also been used to produce the market projections.

Outlook

Processed wood products

Consumption and production of wood products is expected to show stable growth in Western Europe over the next 20 years, with growth rates similar to those in recent years. However, market growth may gradually decline towards the later part of the period. In Eastern Europe and the CIS sub-region, markets will expand considerably and grow much faster than in the west (see Section 4.1 on page 153.

Annual growth in production in Eastern Europe will be about twice the level of growth in Western Europe across all product categories and growth in the CIS sub-region will be as much as three times higher (see Table 2). Nevertheless, Western Europe will remain the largest producer of all forest products in Europe.

Table 2   ***Average annual projected growth rates in production and consumption of forest products from 2000 to 2020 under the baseline scenario***

Product	Europe	EFSOS sub-regions		
		Western Europe	Eastern Europe	CIS
Production				
Sawnwood	2.3%	0.9%	2.3%	5.2%
Wood based panels	2.7%	1.9%	3.6%	6.0%
Paper and paperboard	2.6%	2.0%	5.0%	6.1%
Consumption				
Sawnwood	1.8%	0.8%	2.4%	5.0%
Wood based panels	2.6%	1.8%	4.0%	6.2%
Paper and paperboard	2.9%	2.3%	5.4%	6.0%

The rapid market growth expected in the east is due to the higher rates of economic growth expected in these sub-regions and their higher elasticities of supply and demand (i.e. supply and demand in Eastern Europe and the CIS sub-regions will increase by more than in Western Europe for a given increase in GDP). These higher elasticities of supply and demand reflect the generally lower levels of personal income in these countries and their need for forest products for reconstruction, investment and general development.

Likewise, trade patterns will change, with a significant absolute and relative increase in exports from the east. This will occur as the Russian Federation and other countries succeed in redeveloping their forest sectors to supply the world's expanding markets in Asia as well as the traditional European markets. Because of the sheer size of the forest resource in the Russian Federation and its potential to increase exports significantly, developments in that country will strongly influence the global supply and demand balance for forest products. For example, the CIS sub-region's share of total European production of all forest products (measured in WRME) will increase from 10 percent at present to 20 percent by 2020.

Trade patterns will also change as net exports increase strongly, in particular from the CIS sub-region. Net exports from Eastern Europe will increase less rapidly and even decline in some cases, because the domestic market will grow as fast as or faster than domestic production. The main developments in European net exports in the future will come from the Russian Federation (see Table 3).

Table 3   ***Net trade by European sub-region in 2000 and 2020 (in millions)***

Product	Western Europe		Eastern Europe		CIS	
	2000	2020	2000	2020	2000	2020
Sawnwood (in CUM)	-8.8	-8.2	+8.4	+12.5	+7.9	+23.5
Wood based panels (in CUM)	-1.7	-1.2	+0.9	+0.2	+1.2	+3.3
Paper and paperboard (in MT)	+9.3	+6.1	-1.9	-7.1	+1.6	+5.3

Note: positive values are net exports and negative values are net imports.

Roundwood and fibre

The forecast expansion of production, consumption and trade will require a higher level of fellings in all European countries (see Section 4.3 on page 176). For Europe as a whole, production and consumption of industrial roundwood are forecast to increase by slightly more than 40 percent from 2000 to 2020 (see Figure 118 on page 183). The ratio of fellings to net annual increment, which is a crude indicator of the sustainability of wood supply, is expected to rise in all countries, but it is not expected to exceed 100 percent. Furthermore, European production and consumption are expected to remain roughly in balance, with exports from east to west in 2020 at levels that are similar to at present.

The greatest increase in production is expected in the CIS sub-region, where production in 2020 could be double the level recorded in 2000. In Western Europe, production and consumption will expand at the same rate as in the past (or maybe slightly higher, due to maturing forest plantations in some countries). In Eastern Europe, production and consumption growth will slow down compared to recent years (i.e. since 1990) as some countries start to reach the limits of available wood supply. However, the forecast rate of growth will be similar to the long-term historical trend for this sub-region.

Production and consumption of recovered paper in Europe are expected to double over the next 20 years and annual net exports of recovered paper are expected to increase from about 3 million MT to 8 million MT (see Section 4.2 on page 168). Furthermore, the importance of wood and fibre from sources other than industrial roundwood is expected to continue to increase as it has in the past (see Table 4).

Table 4   ***The European wood raw material balance in 2020***

Component	Europe	Sub-regions		
		Western Europe	Eastern Europe	CIS
Derived demand for wood raw materials				
Other industrial roundwood	27.7	6.9	10.1	10.7
Sawnwood, plywood and veneer sheets	383.9	191.8	72.1	119.9
Reconstituted panels	141.8	85.2	32.1	24.4
Net pulp exports	52.1	21.5	3.0	27.7
Paper and paperboard	604.1	465.1	69.9	69.1
Total derived demand	**1,209.7**	**770.6**	**187.2**	**251.8**
Consumption of wood raw materials				
Industrial roundwood	659.4	337.4	130.0	192.0
Recovered paper	315.4	246.5	38.3	30.7
Net pulp imports	83.1	72.3	9.2	1.6
Other	151.8	114.5	9.8	27.6
- net imports of chips, particles and residues	*0.1*	*5.9*	*-4.0*	*-1.8*
- utilisation of wood residues	*151.7*	*108.5*	*13.8*	*29.4*
Total consumption	**1,209.7**	**770.6**	**187.2**	**251.8**

Note: the above figures are expressed in million m³ WRME. For trade in chips, particles and residues, imports are shown as a positive number and exports are shown as negative numbers.

Non-wood forest products

Quantitative forecasts for non-wood forest products and forest services could not be produced, due to problems of measuring many of these outputs and a general lack of information about some of these outputs. However, a qualitative assessment of the outlook for some of these outputs was produced (see Section 4.5 on page 186) and the main features of this analysis are presented below.

Production of non-wood forest products: in Western Europe, commercial collection of non-wood forest products is likely to continue to decline, due to the labour intensive nature of these activities and the relatively high labour costs in Western Europe. However, in many cases, collection is more of a recreation activity, so total collection may increase in the future. In Eastern Europe and the CIS sub-regions, relatively low labour costs will continue to give these sub-regions a comparative advantage in commercial non-wood forest product production, so production will probably continue to increase in the future.

Demand for edible non-wood forest products: in Western Europe, it is possible that demand for many edible non-wood forest products will increase in the future (in particular, for some of the higher value products such as mushrooms and honey).

Demand for medicinal plants: an increase in demand for medicinal plants might be expected in Western Europe in the future. However, if such an increase were to arise, it would probably be only a gradual increase.

Markets for cork: stable and moderate growth appears to have returned to the market for cork bottle stoppers and it seems unlikely that producers of high quality wines will switch to alternative materials, so long as the product remains price competitive and reliable. Thus, it is expected that this market will continue to grow in line with recent historical trends.

Decorative foliage and Christmas trees: both of these products are luxury items, so it is likely that demand will increase in the future, particularly in Western Europe. Furthermore, it may be possible to raise prices in Western Europe, with innovative marketing and advertising.

Tree nuts: the historical statistics for tree nut production and consumption show quite strong trends, indicating level consumption with declining production in Western Europe and increasing consumption and production in the other two sub-regions. It would be reasonable to assume that these trends will continue.

Forest services and employment

Protection of soil, water and infrastructure: historical statistics have shown that demand for this forest function is quite small overall, but very high in specific locations. It seems likely that the importance of this function will remain unchanged in the future.

Demand for recreation: demand for forest recreation is already probably very high in Western Europe, so high growth in visitor numbers seems unlikely given the expected changes in population. In the future, it seems more likely that demand will increase for a higher quality of forest recreation experience. In contrast, high growth in demand for forest recreation (i.e. visitor numbers) can be expected in the other two sub-regions.

Demand for biodiversity conservation: demand for biodiversity conservation will probably increase in all countries, due to the projected changes in socio-economic driving forces. Again, the largest increases in demand might occur in the future in Eastern Europe and the CIS sub-region, where economic growth will be most rapid.

Supply of recreation and biodiversity: the supply of these forest services in the future will very much depend upon government policies. Some forest owners will probably develop commercial forest recreation businesses, but supplying forest recreation services (as well as biodiversity conservation) will remain a loss-making activity (in a financial sense) for the majority of forest owners and managers. Therefore, the future supply of these services will depend upon the level of public support for these activities.

Mitigation of climate change: Europe's forests are almost certainly going to continue to increase in volume over the next 20 years, so increased "supply" of carbon storage in the future is virtually guaranteed. On the demand-side, much will depend on future policies and the incentive mechanisms that are developed to encourage reductions in net carbon emissions. Mechanisms for controlling net carbon emissions that could affect the forest sector are as follows:

- measures to maintain or increase carbon stocks in forest ecosystems;
- incentives for the use of wood energy as part of renewable energy policies; and
- measures to encourage the use of forest products instead of less "carbon-friendly" materials.

The scope for encouraging the establishment of new fast-growing plantations (some for the supply of wood energy and some for carbon sequestration) will vary across Europe. In Western Europe and parts of Eastern Europe, the scope is likely to be limited by competing land uses. But in the rest of Europe there is considerable development potential.

Employment: over the last few decades, labour productivity has been rising faster than the volume of production, so total employment in the forest sector has been steadily falling. It is expected that this trend will continue, Regarding employment quality, wage levels in the pulp and paper sector compare favourably with those in the other two forestry sub-sectors and with average manufacturing wages, but wages in forestry and the wood industries are typically lower than average. Ageing populations may reverse this trend. The health and safety situation has improved in the forest processing industry but continues to be a major problem in forestry in many countries. In some regions and for some groups, the situation has actually deteriorated significantly over the past decade (most notably for the self-employed and private forest owners in Eastern Europe). This situation may persist unless remedial action is taken.

Summary of main policy relevant forecasts

Recycling and residue use will continue to expand

In all future scenarios, it is projected that wood and wood products will continue to be used in an efficient way, resulting in minimum waste and high use of recycled and recovered sources of wood and fibre. By 2020, it is expected that the direct use of industrial roundwood will account for only 44 percent of wood raw material consumption in Western Europe (compared with just under 50 percent in 2000). In contrast, recovered paper will account for 32 percent of wood and fibre inputs (compared with 27 percent in 2000).

Renewable energy policies will increase the demand for wood

Over the next 20 years, it is considered very likely that more policies will be put in place to promote the production and use of renewable energy. It is expected that one of the likely consequences of renewable energy promotion could be the creation of a major new market for small-sized roundwood. This could encourage more active forest management, as well as raise pulpwood prices.

Europe's forest resource will continue to expand

The total forest area in Europe is expected to increase by around five percent between 2000 and 2020. This will occur due to a mixture of afforestation and natural processes and will occur both on former agricultural land as well as along the tree margin in mountain and boreal areas. However, the area available for wood supply might decrease, due to increasing demands to set-aside forests for other functions, such as: biodiversity conservation; recreation; and protective functions.

Average increment will continue to increase over the next two decades, but this increase will slow down markedly by 2020. There are also studies that indicate that the productivity of European forest sites is increasing. Although the evidence is not very strong at the moment, this could lead to further increases in increment in the future.

Fellings will remain below annual increment in Europe

At the moment, about 45 percent of the annual increment on forest and other wooded land is harvested in Europe. This proportion will increase in the future, due to the forecasts of increased in fellings. However, the expected increases in European roundwood production can be covered by the potential roundwood supply, without threatening the sustainability of forest resources.

The gap between fellings and increment, plus the increases in increment expected in the future, will result in a significant increase in the growing stock volume over the next two decades. This presents a range of opportunities to increase fellings and/or set-aside forest areas for purposes other than roundwood production.

Forest products trade will intensify further

International trade, both within Europe and between Europe and the rest of the world, is expected to increase in the future. Intensified trade is expected between Western Europe and the other two sub-regions. Furthermore, the European forest sector is also expected to face increasing competition from producers outside the region (especially from countries with extensive areas of fast-growing forest plantations). On the other hand, foreign export markets will also increase dramatically in some countries.

Economic viability of forest management will remain threatened

Recent downward trends in roundwood prices and the generally low harvesting intensities in much of Europe all indicate that the income from forest operations is declining at the same time that costs may be rising. There are few possibilities to increase profitability (e.g. by reducing costs or increasing prices). Furthermore, the potential to develop markets for previously non-marketed goods and services is probably quite limited. Therefore, without appropriate policy intervention to address this situation, it appears that the economic viability of European forest management will remain threatened.

Forest sector institutions will continue to evolve rapidly

In recent years, many forest sector institutions and legal frameworks have adapted to changing circumstances (e.g. separation of "authority" and "management" functions for public forests, increased emphasis on extension services, national forest programmes, etc.). Future developments will continue to place greater demands and a wider range of demands on forest sector institutions and policies. This will force them to adapt to ever-changing circumstances and open decision making processes to many specialists who are not conventionally trained foresters. To some extent, it will also require a redirection of skills and capacities in the sector to deal with these new challenges.

Policy recommendations

This section presents, on the responsibility of the secretariat, some recommendations for policy and indications of the main stakeholders that should consider these recommendations. It is suggested that these should be discussed at the European level as a follow-up action to this study.

General policy development

Necessity of a cross-sectoral approach (governments, all stakeholders): forest sector stakeholders should intensify the policy dialogue, proactively drawing the attention of other policy areas (such as agriculture, trade, environment and energy) to the social and environmental benefits of sustainable forest management, as one component of the overall sustainable development of society.

Forestry, wood and climate change (governments, research institutions): forest sector institutions should be proactive in analysing the consequences of climate change policy decisions for the sector and urgently take measures to reconcile the provisions of climate and energy policies, strategies and commitments with national forest programmes and other forest sector planning documents.

Monitoring environmental and social benefits from forests and forestry (governments, international organisations, research institutions): there are still rather few reliable quantitative and policy relevant data on the environmental and social benefits of forests available to policy makers. The situation in this respect has improved notably over recent years, notably through the pan-European indicators of sustainable forest management, but is still not satisfactory. It will require political will and resources to provide satisfactory instruments for well informed policy discussions and for careful coordination of efforts and good communication between all actors.

Forest law enforcement and governance (governments, all stakeholders): governments should work together, first to ensure that domestic forest law enforcement and governance are at an acceptable level, and then to help other countries, inside and outside the region, to improve the situation in this respect. It should be stressed that sustainable forest management in all countries is threatened by bad governance in a few.

Market policies

Need for policies to stimulate the sound use of wood (governments, forest industries, forest owners): governments and EU institutions should develop a policy and legislative framework to support and promote the sound use of wood as an integral part of overall sustainable development and considering the long-term sustainable development of forest resources. All major forest sector stakeholders should identify and implement new financial mechanisms to support these actions.

Balanced implementation of wood energy policies (governments): governments should promote wood energy production and use. They should fund research and development into wood energies and create the necessary infrastructure for a modern and competitive wood energy sector

Developing the region's comparative advantages (forest industries, governments): in the increasingly competitive global markets, the European industry and its raw material suppliers (the forest owners of Europe) have been put on the defensive in many areas. Stakeholders, led by Governments, should identify, region by region, what are Europe's areas of comparative advantage and disadvantage in the forest/timber field and how they should be developed.

Sustainable forest management

Improve the economic viability of forest management in Europe (governments, forest industries, research community): the EFSOS analysis confirms the perception that there is a significant structural threat to the economic viability of forest management. This is now widely recognised and at the Vienna Ministerial conference the ministers committed to implement a series of measures, Governments should attach sufficient political priority to implementing the commitments made in Vienna.

Employment and the work force (governments, employers, unions): in spite of the decline in employment volumes, the sector is likely to be faced with difficulties in finding adequate employees with relevant qualifications in the future. This issue would appear to merit closer scrutiny at the national and local level. Improvements in employment quality such as wages, training and career prospects, as well as working environment and safety, will be critical to maintain adequate levels of new workers, in particular women.

Need to control forest fires and to intensify international cooperation in this area (governments, forest owners): the highest political authorities of southern Europe and the Russian Federation should attach sufficient priority to preventing and controlling forest fires National strategies for forest fire control should also address international co-operation.

International co-operation

Urgent need to address threats to sustainability in south-eastern Europe and the CIS sub-region (governments, donors): the situation in some countries in Eastern Europe and the CIS sub-region is not well understood by the international community. However, it is clear that poverty, civil disturbance or war, with weak institutions, have put some of these countries in an unsustainable situation with excessive forest fires, increasing wood demand, notably for fuel wood, overgrazing, illegal logging leading to forest depletion, shortages of forest products, erosion and deforestation, even desertification. A special problem concerns the management of forests contaminated by radioactivity, notably, but not exclusively, as a result of the Chernobyl catastrophe. Governments of these countries should give more priority to forest policy issues and the international community should work together to support them.

Need to devote policy attention to the consequences of the dynamic developments in Eastern Europe and the CIS sub-region (governments): the likely future developments in Eastern Europe and the CIS sub-region will have a significant impact on forest products trade and production (also in Western Europe and Asian markets). Further policy analysis is needed of the consequences of these trends, and the dialogue between East and West should be intensified in order to assist with the sustainable development of the forest sector and to avoid any undesirable outcomes.

Institutional change in countries in transition (governments, international institutions): there have been profound and rapid changes in the forest sector institutions of many of the advanced reform countries in Eastern Europe, which have left them much better equipped than in the past to face the challenges of the future. Yet many countries are only just starting on the complex processes, and could benefit from the experience accumulated up to now. Mechanisms should be strengthened to share this experience.

The European forest sector in the global context (all stakeholders): In a period of general globalisation, one of the principal questions is: How can forest policy making - still focused at the national level - respond to the changing global environment? European forest sector stakeholders should strengthen their efforts on an international level. The European experiences in sustainable forest management need to be promoted more actively on a global level.

1 INTRODUCTION

1.1 Aims and objectives

Since the early 1950s, the United Nations Economic Commission for Europe (UNECE) and Food and Agriculture Organization of the United Nations (FAO) have been working with countries to produce outlook studies for the European forest sector. The objective of these studies has been to provide decision makers in the forest sector with information and analysis about long-term trends in the sector and projections of future developments. This is the sixth major study in the European outlook study series.

The earlier outlook studies were called *"European Timber Trends Studies"* (ETTS) and focused very much on the supply and demand of wood products and the implications of market developments for roundwood supply. However, since the 1980s, the scope of these studies has been enlarged to cover all of the main products and services supplied by forests. Although the analysis of non-wood forest products and services has never been of the same depth and focus as that for wood (due to the limited availability of data and methodologies), the more recent outlook studies have attempted to provide a more holistic outlook for the sector and the current study continues in this direction. In addition, the study has been re-named the *"European Forest Sector Outlook Study"* (EFSOS) to reflect this change.

The previous European outlook study (ETTS V) was published in 1996 and work started on the current study in 2000. The study follows most of the main lines of investigation pursued in previous outlook studies, but with an additional effort to improve the analysis in the following three areas:

- a more detailed analysis of the outlook for the former centrally planned countries in Eastern Europe and the former-USSR (countries in transition), where the transition towards market economies has progressed significantly since the preparation of ETTS V;

- an expansion in the scope of the analysis to cover other aspects of sustainable forest management, including non-wood forest products and services and developments in forest resources, forest management and policy; and

- an examination of cross-sectoral policy linkages, to demonstrate how the sector is affected by policies in other sectors and how the sector can contribute to the broader objectives of sustainable development.

In addition to the main objective of analysing long-term trends and preparing the outlook for the sector, two other objectives of the outlook study are:

- to identify long term structural trends in the past; and

- to provide a comprehensive data set of historical trends and outlook scenarios for decision makers to use in their own analyses.

1.2 Scope of the study

1.2.1 Time horizon

The time horizon for the analysis of past trends is based on the availability of data. In most cases, historical statistics were available back to the year 1961 (e.g. forest products statistics), so the results are presented for the period from 1961 to 2000. Where longer time-series were available, some parts of the analysis have looked back as far as 1950 (e.g. the development of forest resources). In other cases, the analysis of historical trends has only looked at the last 20 to 30 years.

The year 2000 was used as the base-year for the outlook study projections and the projections cover the period 2000 to 2020. A 20-year time horizon was used because of the uncertainty of making projections for a longer time period. For example, projections of some of the underlying variables used in the outlook (e.g. Gross Domestic Product or GDP) become increasingly unreliable over longer time periods. Furthermore, policies, technology and socio-economic variables can change very rapidly and in ways that are difficult to foresee and this reduces the reliability of projections over a longer time period. Given these challenges, the analysis also describes some of the main factors that could affect the reliability of the outlook study projections.

1.2.2   Definition of the forest sector

As in previous studies, the forest sector has been defined to cover both forest resources and the production trade and consumption of forest products and services. The analysis of forest resources includes an analysis of biological variables (e.g. forest area, growing stock, increment, fellings and removals) as well as an analysis of forest management and policy related variables. The analysis of forest products and services focuses mostly on market trends, although changes in technology and some policy related variables have also been examined.

Forest products include all of the primary wood products manufactured in the forest processing sector (sawnwood, wood-based panels, paper and paperboard) and the main inputs or partly processed products used in the sector (roundwood, wood pulp, wood residues and recovered paper). Secondary or value-added forest products (such as wooden doors, widow frames and furniture) are not covered, although trends in these markets have been taken into consideration. In addition, the use of wood for energy has been partly covered in the analysis, but the analysis has been limited due to the poor quality of existing data.

Non-wood forest products (NWFPs) and forest services are also included in the study, but the analysis is limited by the lack of quantitative statistics about the production and consumption of these outputs over a long period.

1.2.3   Geographical scope

The UNECE region comprises 55 member countries from Europe (including Turkey and Israel), North America (United States of America and Canada) and the former-USSR. This study covers 38 of these countries (see Figure 1), including all of the major European countries (including Turkey, but excluding Israel) and seven of the countries from the former-USSR (the three Baltic States - Estonia, Latvia and Lithuania - plus Belarus, Republic of Moldova, Russian Federation and Ukraine).

The other countries from the former-USSR were excluded from the study, due to a lack of data and because these countries are geographically closer to Asia than they are to Europe. In addition, they will be covered in a separate outlook study for West and Central Asia, which FAO has just started to prepare.

Some of the very small countries in Europe[1] are excluded from the study because they have very few forest resources and small markets and the UNECE and FAO have few statistics for these countries. Their exclusion is unlikely to detract from the analysis for the region as a whole.

---

[1]   Note: wherever "Europe" is mentioned in this report, it refers to the countries listed below, unless otherwise specified.

For the purpose of the sub-regional analysis, countries were grouped as follows:[2]

- **Western Europe:** Austria; Belgium; Denmark; Finland; France; Germany; Greece; Iceland; Ireland; Italy; Luxembourg; Netherlands; Norway; Portugal; Spain ; Sweden; Switzerland; and United Kingdom (18 countries);

- **Eastern Europe:** Albania; Bosnia and Herzegovina; Bulgaria; Croatia; Czech Republic; Estonia; Hungary; Latvia; Lithuania; Poland; Romania; Serbia and Montenegro; Slovakia; Slovenia; The former Yugoslav Republic of Macedonia (TFYR Macedonia); and Turkey (16 countries); and

- **CIS sub-region:** Belarus; Republic of Moldova; Russian Federation; and Ukraine (4 countries).

Figure 1   Geographical scope and sub-regions used in the outlook study

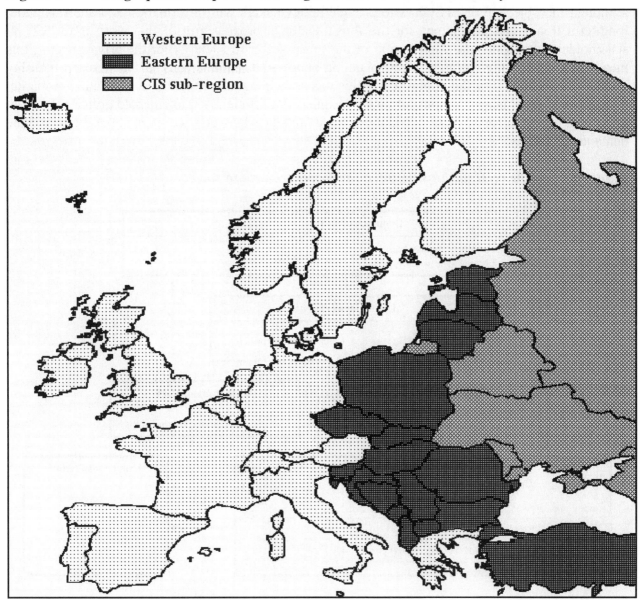

Any grouping of countries is likely to be unsatisfactory in some respects, but it was felt that these three sub-regions would reflect the similarities between countries in each sub-region and many of the main differences between each of the sub-regions in terms of their forest resources, markets and levels of economic development. One disadvantage of the above groupings is that it is not possible to identify the EU as a single unit, either before or after the expansion in 2004. However the EU has now become so large, that variations within the EU are now at least as large, in some respects, as between EU and some non-EU countries. Another disadvantage is the loss of a specific perspective for southern Europe, the Nordic countries, or the Balkans. The secretariat is happy to supply the country level data to any analyst wishing to reconstruct the trends for different country groups than those presented here.

1.3 Methodology

1.3.1 Interactions between the forest sector and society

Although the objective of EFSOS is to provide policymakers with information and analysis about long-term trends and projections for the forest sector, a broader aim of this work is to help all stakeholders to enhance the contribution of the forest sector to society. For the private-sector, this means helping to improve investment, planning and marketing decisions, to increase profitability and wealth creation. For the public-sector this means helping governments to translate non-market demands and other considerations into well designed and efficiently implemented policies. In order to do this, it is necessary to understand the complex linkages between activities in the sector and the demands of society.

Figure 2   The relationships between the forest sector and society

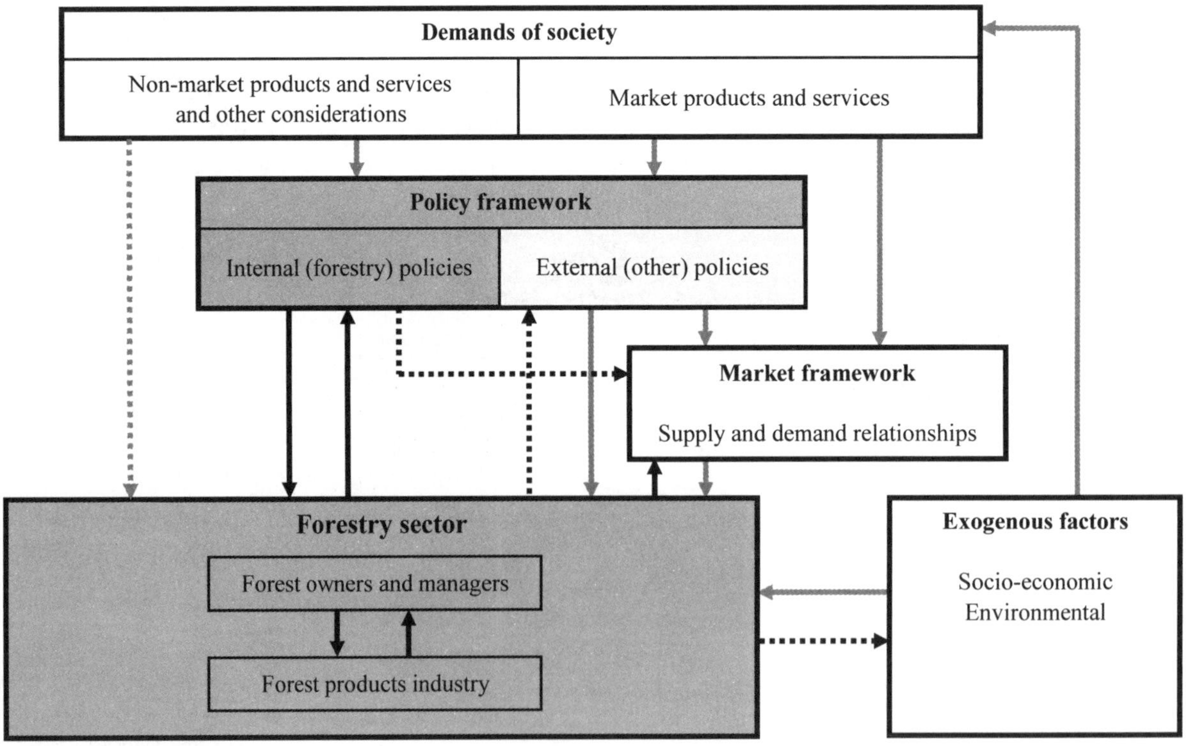

Source: based on Thoroe et al (2004).

Figure 2 presents a simplified picture of some of the main interactions between the forest sector and society. The shaded boxes represent areas that are largely under the control of individuals working in the forest sector, while the unshaded boxes represent areas that are outside the control of the sector. Similarly, black lines represent relationships and interactions that can be controlled by the sector, while grey lines represent external forces (dashed lines indicate a weak relationship).

The underlying forces that drive developments in the forest sector are the exogenous factors shown in the bottom right-hand corner of the figure. These include socio-economic trends (e.g. changes in income, technology, population and human preferences), which mostly influence the demands placed on the sector. Environmental factors (e.g. rates of tree growth, climate change and natural disasters) tend to have more of an influence on forest resources and the supply of products and services. Although the forest sector can do little to influence these exogenous factors, there are some actions that may have an impact. For example, improved information about the sector can influence society's perception of the sector and forest research can improve technology or alter some of the environmental factors that affect the sector.

The main way in which these exogenous factors affect the sector is by changing the demands that society places on the sector (shown in the box at the top of the figure). These include demands for marketed products and services from the sector as well as demands for non-marketed products and services. In addition to these demands, society also raises other considerations that are becoming increasingly important in the sector. For example, in recent years, people have become more interested in how forest products and services are produced as well as how much is produced.

Most of the interactions between society and individuals working in the forest sector take place within two different frameworks. Demands for marketed products are largely expressed within a market framework, whereas most of the other demands placed on the sector are translated into government policies and regulations (the policy framework) (Schmithüsen, 2004). In addition to this, there are some direct linkages between society and the forest sector (e.g. as expressed in corporate social responsibility statements), but these linkages are currently quite weak.

The policy framework includes the set of policies, laws and regulations that are implemented by forestry administrations (internal policies), plus other government policies that have an impact on the sector (external policies). All of these policies can have a direct effect on the sector or an indirect effect through their effects on the markets for forest products and services.

Internal (forestry) policies are under the control of forestry administrations and are largely established through a dialogue between society and individuals working in the sector. The linkages between the forest sector and forestry policies are generally strong and operate in both directions (i.e. forestry policies have a major impact on the sector and individuals in the sector can usually influence these policies). The majority of forestry policies are directed at forest resources and, in particular, at the way that forests are managed.

External policies (e.g. in sectors such as the environment, agriculture, energy, industry and trade) also have an impact on the forest sector. Environmental policies affect both forest resources and the markets for forest products and services. Agricultural policies affect the demand for land and the profitability of alternative land uses. Energy policies affect the demand for wood energy, while policies in trade and industry affect the forest products industry in many ways. Although these policies can have a major impact on the forest sector, individuals working in the forest sector currently tend to have less of an influence on these policies.

Most of the demands for marketed forest products and services fall within the market framework. This is where demands are translated into market transactions and commercial relationships are established between customers and suppliers of outputs from the sector and inputs to the sector. These relationships may be self-regulated, but are often governed by rules and regulations established by law (e.g. contract law).

Markets are not under the control of any institution or group of individuals, but individuals working in the forest sector can have an influence on markets through their marketing activities. Governments also have a significant impact on markets through their economic policies (e.g. fiscal and monetary policies, trade regulations and exchange rate policies) and policies such as building codes and safety regulations. In contrast, forestry policies generally have less of an impact on the market framework and are mostly concerned with technical issues such as phytosanitary regulations.

The text above has briefly described the main interactions between society and the forest sector and described where individuals working in the sector can have an influence. Some of the forces affecting the sector can not be easily influenced. In these cases, the outlook study provides information about the historical and future directions of these forces, so that the sector can adapt to these changes. In areas where the sector does have an influence (e.g. forestry policies), the outlook study can be used as an analytical tool to assess alternative courses of action. In this way, the outlook study can be used to assist with the preparation of policies, plans and programmes that will enhance the future contribution of the forest sector to society. It may also serve as a means of communication to the "non-forest" sectors, helping them to appreciate the consequences of their policies on the forest sector.

1.3.2 Major components of the outlook study

The outlook study comprises four main components, covering: exogenous factors; forest resources; markets; and policies. The analytical work implemented in each of these four areas has attempted to examine the main trends and relationships within the sector (as portrayed in Figure 2) and, where possible, make projections of future developments. This work included a mixture of quantitative analysis (e.g. statistical analysis of past trends, development of models and projections for the future) and qualitative analysis. Details of the methodologies used in each component can be found in the Discussion Papers produced in support of this study.

Exogenous factors. The major piece of analytical work on exogenous factors was carried out by the Independent Centre for Economic Studies (NOBE) in Poland (NOBE, 2002). The NOBE study analysed trends in GDP in all European countries and produced projections of GDP growth that were used in the outlook. The NOBE study focused in particular on economic growth in the countries in transition and presented three alternative future scenarios of economic growth for all countries in the region.

In addition to the NOBE study, trends in some of the other main exogenous factors were also analysed as part of the preparation of this report. The results of this analysis are presented in various part of the report, particularly in Section 1.

Forest resources. An historical analysis of forest resources was produced by Gold (2003). The main objective of this study was to describe how market forces and policy decisions have affected the development of forest resources in the past. An additional aim was to describe some of the main driving forces that will affect forest resources in the future.

The study was implemented by collecting historical statistics on forest resources from national correspondents, harmonising the statistics to comparable measurement units (where possible) and producing simple trends showing the changes in the most important variables (i.e. area, growing stock and increment). Historical statistics were collected for 18 out of the 42 countries in the region and the results were validated by national correspondents, who also provided interpretations of the historical trends in their countries

The outlook for forest resources was produced by researchers from Alterra in the Netherlands and the European Forestry Institute (Schelhaas *et al*, in prep). The objective of this study was to describe the future development of forest resources in Europe (in terms of forest area, growing stock and increment) under each of the three future scenarios produced in the outlook study.

The analysis used forest inventory statistics and information about forest management regimes (e.g. rotation periods, intensity of thinning, etc.) provided by national correspondents. This information was received from nearly all countries in the region. The information was input into the European Forest Information Scenario (EFISCEN) Model, which is an age-class simulation model. The EFISCEN Model was then used to show how different projections of future roundwood production would affect the future growth and development of European forest resources.

Markets. An historical analysis of the markets for wood products was produced by Solberg (in prep). The objectives of this analysis were to gather and analyse information about historical trends in forest products markets in Europe, to identify the major structural changes that have taken place and to describe some of the main reasons behind these changes. Some of the trends in markets were also analysed in greater depth during the preparation of this report. All of this analysis was based on the UNECE and FAO forest products statistics (e.g. FAOSTAT) as well as a number of macroeconomic statistics from various sources.

The outlook for wood products markets was produced by Kangas and Baudin (2003). The objective of their study was to quantify the relationships between changes in exogenous factors (e.g. GDP and product prices) and the production, consumption and trade of processed wood products. Statistical (econometric) techniques were used to estimate these relationships. Following this, these relationships were then used to make projections of future production and consumption under each of the scenarios used in the study.

Following the work of Kangas and Baudin (2003), the raw material balance was analysed to show how different sources of wood and fibre supply have been used in the past (and will be used in the future) to satisfy the raw material needs of the forest processing sector. The approach used in ETTS V was repeated in the EFSOS. Projections of the production of processed forest products were converted to the amounts of wood required to manufacture those product (wood raw material equivalent or WRME) using technical conversion factors. These results were then compared with trends in the production of different types of wood and fibre used in the sector and it was assumed that international trade would bring supply and demand into equilibrium.

In addition, to the analysis of markets for wood products, some information was collected about the production, consumption and trade of non-wood products and forest services. This analysis was limited by the lack of statistics and information available about these outputs from forests. However, despite the lack of information, it is possible to make some tentative suggestions about the trends and outlook for these outputs and these are presented in the report.

Policies. Historical changes in policies within and outside the forest sector were described as part of the studies already mentioned above. In addition to this, information was also collected about some of the other major policy changes that have affected the sector in the recent past and this information is presented in various parts of the report.

For the outlook, a survey and analysis of likely future policy developments was undertaken by a group of forestry policy experts (Thoroe *et al*, 2004). The main objective of this study was to identify specific internal and external policy changes that might have a significant impact on the forest sector in the future. The work started with research and analysis of all available publications and policy documents, from which possible future policy developments were organised into 19 different policy areas. After consultation with a wider group of policy experts, the number of areas was reduced to 13 and a "Delphi inquiry" was used to solicit expert opinions about the likely future changes in each of these areas and the possible impact of these changes. One important part of this analysis was an examination of cross-sectoral policy issues (in areas such as: energy; environment; trade; and agriculture), which were shown to be significant.

Many of the results of the policy analysis could not be integrated into the quantitative statistical modelling of the outlook for the sector, but the results of this analysis provide important additional qualitative information about likely future developments in the sector.

1.3.3 Additional outlook study analyses

In addition to the main components described above, a number of other studies were either commissioned as part of the EFSOS or were used in the preparation of this report.

Russian outlook study. The Russian Federation has one of the largest forest sectors in Europe and, as a country in transition, has seen tremendous changes in the forest sector over the last decade. In order to obtain detailed and up-to-date information about the current status and outlook for the forest sector in this country, an outlook study for the Russian forest sector was produced by Russian experts as part of the EFSOS. The information from this study was incorporated into the results presented here and further information can be found in OAO NIPIEIlesprom (2003).

Employment outlook study. An analysis of the trends and outlook for employment in the forest sector was produced by the International Labour Office (ILO). Employment is one of the important social dimensions of sustainable forest management and the results of this study have been included here in the sections on the contribution of the forest sector to national economies. Further details of the study can be found in Blombäck *et al* (2003).

FAO global trends and outlook studies. In order to place the European outlook in a global context, a number of FAO's global trends and outlook studies were used during the preparation of this report. Specifically, the global outlook for forest plantations (Brown, 2003) was used to assess the future production of roundwood, the global outlook for woodfuel was used for wood energy projections (Broadhead *et al*, in prep) and information is presented here from FAO's recent study of the contribution of the forest sector to national economies (Lebedys, in prep). More generally, many of the developments discussed here are also occurring at the global level and a number of the trends identified in FAO's global outlook studies have been incorporated into this report.

1.3.4 Scenario development

As noted above, the future is determined by a mixture of variables. Some of these can be easily influenced, while others can not. Trends in the variables that can not be easily influenced present a number of constraints on future courses of action. Given these, the purpose of scenario analysis is identify where society might want the forest sector to go in the future and the actions (i.e. policy measures) that are feasible and would lead the sector in this direction.

The EFSOS policy analysis identified five main scenario "packages" that could each be considered as a group of policy measures that would lead the forest sector towards one overall aim or objective.

The five packages included policy measures that would influence the development of the forest sector in the following areas:

- biodiversity, including nature conservation;
- globalisation, innovation and market structures;
- countries with economies in transition;
- regional development; and
- energy and environment.

These alternative scenarios should not be considered as mutually exclusive, as some of the measures included in one package would also contribute to the aims of some of the other packages. Furthermore, it is possible that a country or group of countries might try to move the sector towards more than one of these objectives at the same time. However, for the purpose of this analysis, a more limited set of scenarios was used to see what might happen if the sector was steered in very different directions in the future. One scenario (a baseline or "change nothing" scenario) assumed a continuation of past trends, with no attempt to shift the sector in one way or another. In addition to this, three of the scenarios listed above (the first, second and fifth) were considered as alternatives for further investigation. A lack of information about wood energy prevented an in-depth analysis of the fifth scenario (energy and environment), so, in addition to the baseline scenario, the two alternative scenarios that were finally used in the outlook study were the "conservation" and "integration" scenarios.

The translation of alternative scenarios into quantitative projections of the future is difficult, because of the limitations of the available analytical models. For example, in most previous outlook studies, alternative scenarios have been simply defined in terms of different assumptions about future rates of growth in population and GDP and changes in forest products prices. The scenarios developed for EFSOS contain a richer description of the differences between the alternatives and some of the more subtle impacts of different courses of action. Unfortunately, however, the models developed for EFSOS are still largely driven by changes in GDP growth, prices of forest products and forest resource variables (e.g. forest area). The information about these variables contained in the alternative scenarios was used to produce the results presented later on, but it should be noted that these projections present only some of the differences that may occur under each of the different scenarios.

1.4 Data sources, definitions and measurement conventions

Unless otherwise specified, the statistics used in the EFSOS come from the statistical databases of the UNECE and FAO (e.g. FAOSTAT). These databases contain statistics that are supplied by national correspondents or estimates produced by UNECE and FAO (where national statistics are not available). The terms, definitions and measurement units used in these statistics have been developed over many years in collaboration with national experts and they are standardised across all countries. Further technical information about the statistics can be found in other UNECE and FAO publications, such as the Timber Bulletin (UN, 2003) and the Forest Resource Assessment (FRA) (UN, 2000).

The UNECE and FAO statistical databases are regularly updated, as part of a continuous dialogue with countries about how to improve the quality of these statistics. The statistics used in the analyses presented here are those that were available and the time each study was implemented. Therefore, some of the statistics may not correspond exactly with those quoted in other UNECE and FAO publications.

1.4.1   Forest resources

Most of the basic data on forest resources was taken from the current FRA (UN, 2000) and earlier versions of the FRA. Forest fire statistics were taken from the UNECE on-line database on forest fires and earlier published versions of these statistics. Other information about forest resources was obtained from a variety of sources noted in the text.

For the analysis of historical trends in forest resources in Europe, statistics were collected for the following three variables: forest area; growing stock volume; and annual volume increment. These statistics were collected from national correspondents, supplemented by information from existing databases and literature such as the FRA (UN, 2000).

The statistics provided by national correspondents were mostly taken from the results of national forest inventories as far back as the mid-1940s. The majority of countries supplied three or four historical estimates of each of the three variables listed above and trends in these statistics were derived by interpolating between the different estimates. From this, a consolidated data set was produced, covering the period 1950 to 2000.

For each of the three variables, countries were asked to supply statistics related to the area of forest available for wood supply (FAWS). In most cases this was possible, although a few countries supplied statistics using a different definition of forest area. In particular, the statistics for the Russian Federation relate to the area of forest and other wooded land (FOWL). In addition, for the increment statistics, countries were asked to provide net annual increment (NAI), but a few countries supplied statistics using a different definition of annual increment.

The statistics collected for this analysis covered all of the countries in Western Europe. In Eastern Europe, statistics were obtained for all countries except the Baltic States (Estonia, Latvia and Lithuania) and four of the five countries of the former Yugoslavia (Bosnia and Herzegovina, Croatia, Slovenia and TFYR Macedonia). For the CIS countries, historical statistics about the forest resource could only be obtained for the Russian Federation. For the comparison between fellings and increment (see Section 2.1.5), production in the Russian Federation until 1992 was estimated as a proportion of production from the former-USSR, based on production statistics from all of the former-USSR countries since 1992. The conversion from production (or removals) to fellings was based on statistics from the FRA.

A detailed analysis of these trends is published in Gold (2003), where further explanations of the data collection process and definitions of the different statistics supplied by countries can also be found.

1.4.2   Forest products

Forest products statistics only record the amounts of production and trade in forest products. In many places, the historical analysis refers to the amount of forest products consumed. It should be noted that this is "apparent consumption", which is calculated as the sum of production plus imports minus exports.

It should also be noted that the sub-regions include countries that did not exist before the early-1990s. For the historical analysis of trends in forest products markets, historical statistics for these new countries were estimated as a proportion of the recorded amounts for the previous geographical units. Thus, for example, the historical statistics for Yugoslavia were used to produce historical statistics for the five new countries that have replaced Yugoslavia. The proportions that were used were based on the relative shares of each new country in the old geographical unit, using the more recent statistics produced by each of the new countries. This is a simplistic assumption that is of little importance at the sub-regional level except in the case of the three Baltic States (formerly in the USSR, but now included in Eastern Europe) and the CIS sub-region (which includes only four countries of the former USSR).

1.5   Structure of the report

The remainder of this report is in four main sections. Section 1 presents the analysis of historical trends in the forest sector in Europe. This section presents an extensive and comprehensive analysis of many different aspects of the sector, starting with forest resources and management, followed by market trends for forest products and finishing with a brief analysis of the trends in some of the linkages between the forest sector and society.

Sections 1, 4 and 5 can all be considered as the "outlook" part of the study. Section 1 examines the "driving forces" or exogenous factors affecting the sector and presents qualitative and quantitative statements about likely future changes in many of these variables. It also includes further details of the EFSOS policy analysis.

Section 4 presents the projections for the future production, consumption and trade of forest products and services. Due to the lack of data and difficulty in modelling the supply and demand of some forest outputs, the majority of this section focuses on the markets for wood products.

Section 5 presents a summary of the major results and conclusions of the study and the main implications for all stakeholders in the forest sector in Europe. This is based on the discussion contained in the EFSOS policy analysis, after modification to take into account the outlook study projections (presented earlier) and consultation with national correspondents.

1.6   European network of outlook study experts and contributors

The production of EFSOS was a collaborative effort between UNECE, FAO and numerous individuals in countries. Official national correspondents were nominated by UNECE member states and, in addition, a number of other experts and representatives of different stakeholder groups were involved in the production of this study. A list of all of the participants known to UNECE and FAO is given in Box 1 and their participation in this exercise is gratefully acknowledged.

Box 1   ***National correspondents and outlook study experts involved in the production of the European Forest Sector Outlook Study***

Martti Aarne, Camille Artiges, Oscar Barreiro Mouriz, Anders Baudin, Staffan Berg, David Brooks, Aija Budreiko, Nikolai Burdin, Valeri Caisin, Alain Chaudron, Bernard Chevalier, Roger Cooper, Bernard Cugnet, Bernard De Galembert, Francois de Sars, Louk Dielen, Irene Durbak, Sandra Eglaja, Jean Fahys, Stefan Gold, Thomas Grünenfelder, Marja Gustafsson, Karl Gustafsson, , Johannes Hangler, Vladimir Henzlik, Peter Hofer, Natalie Hufnagl, Rino Jans, Lionel Jayanetti, Alastair Johnson, Lars Jordan, Kari Kangas, Kokul Kasirov, Edgar Kastenholz, Edgar Kaufmann, Rolf Kevin, Albert Knieling, Margers Krams, Christian Küchli, Andrei Laletin, Ludwig Lehner, António Leite, Graudums Martins, Peter Mayer, Alexander Moiseyev, Beatriz Molero, Martin Moravcik, Sanna Myrttinen, Gert-Jan Nabuurs, Sten Nilsson, Heiner Ollmann, Witold Orlowski, Heikki Pajuoja, François Pasquier, Tim Peck, Susan Phelps, Duncan Pollard, Peter Poschen, Erik Poulstrup, Snezana Prokic, Ewald Rametsteiner, Mart-Jan Schelhaas, Jörg-Peter Schmitt, Wolfgang Schöpfhauser, Peter Schwarzbauer, Pat Snowdon, Birger Solberg, Erik Sollander, Wladyslaw Strykowski, Sverre Thoresen, Carsten Thoroe, Jukka Tissari, Gerard Van Dijk, Marie-Anne Vautrin and Jeremy Wall.

The UNECE and FAO will continue to work with countries on improving the statistical databases and analysis presented in this study as well as with identifying follow-up activities to enhance the performance of the European forest sector in the light of these results. In this respect, comments on any aspect of the EFSOS would be most welcome and can be directed to Kit Prins (christopher.prins@unece.org), Volker Sasse (volker.sasse@fao.org) or Adrian Whiteman (adrian.whiteman@fao.org).

2   TRENDS AND CURRENT STATUS OF THE FOREST SECTOR

This first major chapter of this report presents information about the trends and current status of a number of different aspects of the forest sector in Europe. It starts by describing the European forest resource, both in terms of the quantity and quality of the resource and the way that it is managed. Following this, a number of sections describe some of the main trends in the markets for forest products (wood products and raw materials, non-wood forest products, forest services and wood energy). It finishes by briefly describing how the sector interacts with society, both in terms of government policies within and outside the sector and the contribution that the forest sector makes to society.

2.1   Forest resources

A major factor affecting the development of the forest sector is the quantity and quality of forest resources and the way that those resources are managed to provide benefits for society. The following text describes some of the main quantitative trends in European forest resources over the last few decades.

2.1.1   Total forest area

Recent historical trends in the total area of forest and other wooded land (FOWL) in Europe are shown in Figure 3. As this figure shows, the area has increased slightly at the European level (by 3.4 percent or 36 million ha) over the last 20 years and in all three sub-regions. The CIS sub-region accounted for most of the increase during the 1980s, while Western Europe accounted for most of the increase in the 1990s.

Figure 3   *Trends in the total area of forest and other wooded land in Europe since 1980*

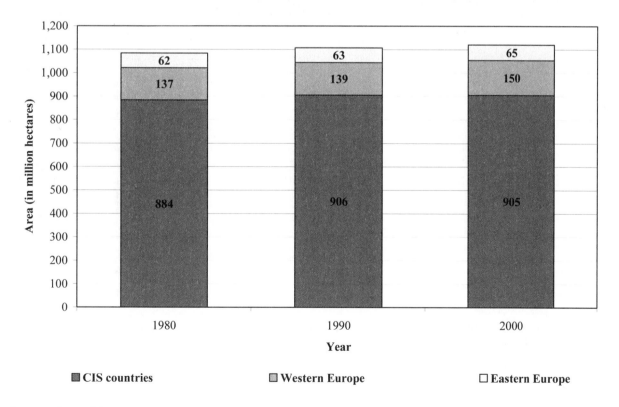

Source: derived from UN (1992) and UN (2000). Note: figures for the Eastern Europe and CIS sub-regions before 1992 have been estimated from statistics for the USSR (see Section 1.4.2).

2.1.2   Area of forest available for wood supply

For the purpose of analysing the productive capacity of Europe's forest resources, changes in the area of forest available for wood supply (FAWS) are more relevant than the trends in total forest area. The study by Gold (2003) produced long-term historical trends in forest area for the majority of European countries and these are shown in Figure 4. As noted above, with the exception of the Russian Federation, this figure is based on the area of FAWS in most countries, so it also shows how the potential wood supply in Europe has changed over the last 50 years.

Figure 4   *Trends in forest area in selected European countries from 1950 to 2000*

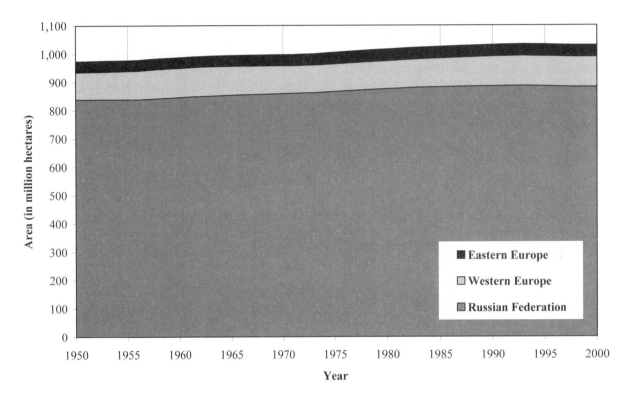

Source: derived from Gold (2003), Annex 5.1. Note: the Eastern Europe region excludes the Baltic States and four of the five countries of the former Yugoslavia. The forest area shown here is FAWS, except for a few countries where statistics were provided for other definitions of forest area. See Section 1.4.1 for further details and explanation.

Overall, the FAWS area in these countries has increased by about 57 million ha (or six percent), from 973 million ha in 1950 to 1,030 million ha in 2000. At the sub-regional level, the area has also increased over the last 50 years in all three EFSOS sub-regions. The highest rate of growth has occurred in Western Europe, where the area has increased by 11 percent (or 11 million ha) since 1950. In the selected countries of Eastern Europe, forest area has increased by six percent (or 2 million ha) and the area of FOWL in the Russian Federation has increased by five percent (or 43 million ha). In addition, of the 27 countries covered in this analysis, the area has expanded in all but four countries.

These trends in forest area can be explained by three different driving forces: policy decisions; management decisions and natural causes. These driving forces have differed between countries and sub-regions, have changed over time and have acted in different directions. However, over the last 50 years, the most important driving forces have probably been changes in policies within and outside the forest sector. Changes in policy and management will be discussed in more detail later in this chapter (Sections 2.2 and 2.11), but a summary of the main driving forces behind these trends is given here below.

Agricultural policies: changes in agricultural policies have reduced the demand for agricultural land in some countries and encouraged the conversion of agricultural land to other land uses. In Western Europe, agricultural subsidies have resulted in an intensification of agriculture and a concentration of agricultural production on more productive land. In more recent years, agricultural policies in this region have deliberately encouraged the conversion of agricultural land to other uses and one of the main alternative uses has been the establishment of forest plantations.

Industrial policies: in Eastern Europe, the conversion of agricultural land to forest has occurred for slightly different reasons. In many of these countries, industrialisation has been a major policy goal over the last 50 years. This has resulted in urbanisation and rural depopulation, leading to abandonment of agricultural land and conversion of some of this land to forests.

Afforestation policies: in addition to agricultural policies, another major driving force has been forestry policies that deliberately encouraged afforestation for a variety of reasons. Such policies have been particularly important in Western Europe, where many of the countries with the highest growth in forest area are also countries where the establishment of forest plantations has been given most support (e.g. Belgium, Denmark, France, Ireland, Portugal and the United Kingdom). Afforestation has also been supported in some East European countries (e.g. Poland in the 1950s and 1960s) and was supported in Russia during the 1960s and 1970s.

Land restitution: in many of the countries in transition, land that was nationalised has been returned to the original land owners or their heirs. In some places, forest has been returned and has been converted to agricultural land. In most countries, this has probably not outweighed the forces acting in the opposite direction. However, it may provide an explanation for the slight reduction in forest area (FOWL) in the Russian Federation recorded at the end of the period (1993 - 1998).

Over-harvesting: over-harvesting of forest resources has been a problem in some Mediterranean countries, particularly in the earlier part of the period. Combined with grazing in forest areas and some deliberate conversion of forest to agricultural land, this has led to reductions in forest area in a few countries.

Illegal activities: illegal harvesting of forest resources is a more recent problem, which mostly affects some of the countries in transition. Statistics on the extent of this problem are not available, but it is believed that this has led to forest clearance in some areas. Illegal forest clearance to obtain land for commercial and tourism enterprises has also been mentioned as a problem in some Mediterranean countries. However, it appears that these two problems have generally not outweighed the forces encouraging forest expansion.

Inadequate funding: historically, clear cutting was the main harvesting system used in many parts of the Russian Federation. Inadequate funding for replanting and other activities to support regeneration has been noted as a problem since the 1980s. However, this does not appear to have resulted in a loss of forest area, although it has probably led to some forest degradation.

Natural causes: as noted above, natural regeneration has resulted in the conversion of some abandoned agricultural land back to forest. This has been suggested as an explanation for some of the increase in forest area in Scandinavian countries in the 1950s and 1960s. Regeneration of low quality trees and shrubs also partly explains the increase in forest area in the Russian Federation up until the early 1990s. Acting in the opposite direction, forest fires remain a major problem in Mediterranean countries and some parts of the Russian Federation and have led to some reductions in forest area.

It is not possible to compare the changes in the FAWS area with changes in the area of FOWL over this long time period, but an analysis of this for the last decade is given in the FRA (UN, 2000). This shows that, in general, both areas have increased over the last decade, except in a very small number of countries where the area of FAWS has declined while the area of FOWL has increased. These net figures show an increase of forest not available for wood supply in all but a very few countries, and in general the increase in "non-FAWS" is greater than the increase in FAWS. Thus, it is generally true to say that the area of forest reclassified from "available for wood supply" to "not available for wood supply" over the last decade (e.g. for nature conservation reasons) is less than the total increase in forest area. Unfortunately it is not possible at present to track with any accuracy the shifts between these categories, despite the undeniable policy interest of these trends.

2.1.3 Growing stock of forest available for wood supply

The historical trend in growing stock in selected European countries is shown in Figure 5. For this figure, the growing stock statistics in each country refer to same forest areas that are presented above (i.e. mostly FAWS, but including other definitions of forest area in a few cases). Thus, the two data sets are comparable and the trends in growing stock per hectare have also been calculated (see Figure 6).

Figure 5   ***Trends in growing stock in selected European countries from 1950 to 2000***

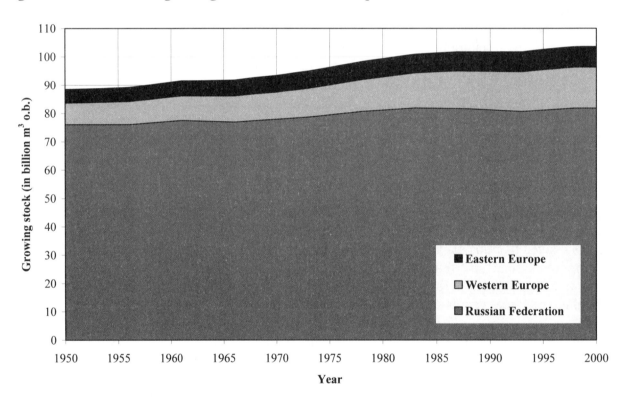

Source: derived from Gold (2003), Annex 5.2. Note: the Eastern Europe region excludes the Baltic States and four of the five countries of the former Yugoslavia. The growing stock shown here is for FAWS, except for a few countries where statistics were provided for other definitions of forest area. See Section 1.4.1 for further details and explanation.

The figure shows that the growing stock in these countries has increased by about 17 percent or 15 billion cubic metres overbark (o.b.), from 88 billion m^3 o.b. in 1950 to 104 billion m^3 o.b. in 2000. Within Europe, growing stock has also increased in all three EFSOS sub-regions and in all of the selected countries except one (Albania).

The highest rate of growth has occurred in Western Europe, where growing stock has increased by 91 percent (or 7 billion m^3 o.b.) since 1950. In the selected countries of Eastern Europe, growing stock has increased by 51 percent (or 2 billion m^3 o.b.) and growing stock in the Russian Federation has increased by eight percent (or 6 billion m^3 o.b.). These changes in growing stock volume have mostly occurred due to changes in forest management (supported by changes in forestry policy) and, to a lesser extent, natural causes.

In most of Western Europe, the intensity of forest management has increased over the last 50 years, leading to higher levels of growing stock and increment. The main example of this is the expansion of forest plantations throughout much of the 1960s and 1970s. Apart from the increase in forest area, this has also led to higher levels of growing stock in the last two decades, as these plantations have reached the age when the trees start to grow very fast. Another example of increased management intensity is the conversion of coppice and coppice with standards to high forest in Belgium , France and other countries since 1970. In addition, an EFI study by Spieker et al. showed an "unexplained" increase in site productivity on sample plots all over Europe. This has been attributed among other things to the fertilising effect of nitrogen immissions.

In other parts of Western Europe, there have been trends towards less intensive forest management since the 1950s. However, this has also led to the same result. For example, in Italy during the 1950s, new forest policies were adopted that eliminated large-scale clear cutting. This led to reduced harvesting levels and increased growing stock. More generally, because harvesting levels have always been less than increment over the last 50 years (see Figure 9), this has led to an increase in growing stock across the whole of Europe.

Figure 6   ***Trends in growing stock per hectare in selected European countries from 1950 to 2000***

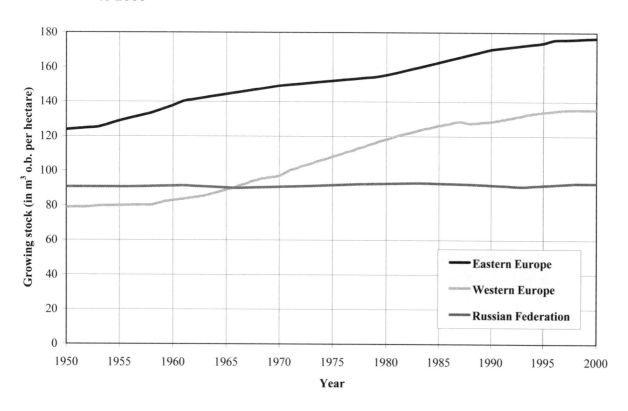

Source: derived from Gold (2003), Annexes 5.1 and 5.2. Note: the Eastern Europe region excludes the Baltic States and four of the five countries of the former Yugoslavia. The growing stock shown here is for FAWS, except for a few countries where statistics were provided for other definitions of forest area. See Section 1.4.1 for further details and explanation.

In Eastern Europe, changes in growing stock have probably occurred due to natural causes more than changes in management intensity. Growing stock in Eastern Europe is higher (per hectare) than in Western Europe and has increased consistently throughout the period. However, forest area and increment have not increased significantly since 1970. This suggests that fellings and other losses (e.g. due to pests, disease and other disasters) have increased significantly since the 1970s at the same time that the forest estate has matured (i.e. middle-aged forest stands with high increment have grown into mature stands with lower increment). Much of the current forest area was planted in the late 1940s to 1960s, so it appears that the trend in growing stock in Eastern Europe has largely been driven by a shift in the age structure of forests.

The trend in growing stock in the Russian Federation indicates a modest rate of growth but also displays some volatility in the last two decades. This volatility is probably due to problems with data quality rather than changes in the forest resource. However, some qualitative indications of recent trends in growing stock were provided for this analysis by the national correspondents for the Russian Federation and these are presented below.

Recent trends in growing stock have varied between the different regions of the Russian Federation, with slight increases in the western parts of the country and decreases in Siberian regions. The main reasons for decreases in growing stock in Siberian regions have been intensive fellings in the 1980s, forest fires and attacks by insects. The greatest increase in growing stock has occurred in the Central Region, where felling has been reduced and the forests grow quite quickly.

Currently, mature and over-mature stands account for 54 percent of the total growing stock in the Russian Federation. Coniferous species (e.g. larch, spruce, pine and cedar) predominate, with a share of 78 percent of the growing stock. However, the growing stock of mature and over-mature stands (mainly conifers) has fallen by 9 billion m^3 o.b. in recent years. On the other hand, the growing stock of broadleaved species has increased by 1.7 billion m^3 o.b. This is largely due to the preference of the forest processing industry towards the utilisation of softwoods.

In general, the main reason for the increase in growing stock in the Russian Federation is that fellings have always been far below increment. For example, since 1950, annual increment has varied from 850 million m^3 o.b. to 970 million m^3 o.b., while the volume of fellings has varied from 500 million m^3 o.b. to 250 million m^3 o.b. (in more recent years). As in Eastern Europe, this shortfall combined with the gradual maturation of many stands has led to the trend displayed in Figure 5.

The volume of wood harvested per hectare amounts to only 0.22 m^3 o.b. across the whole of the Russian Federation, with amounts as low as 0.11 m^3 o.b. in the West Siberian Region, 0.15 m^3 o.b. in the East Siberian Region and 0.05 m^3 o.b. in the Far Eastern Region. For comparison, annual harvesting per hectare in countries with more developed forest industries often exceeds 2.5 m^3 o.b.

2.1.4   Annual increment of forest available for wood supply

The historical trend in annual increment in selected European countries is shown in Figure 7. In most cases, countries provided statistics for NAI, but a few countries provided statistics using alternative measures of increment. This figure presents totals for Europe and each sub-region, based on all of these statistics. Again, these statistics are comparable with the forest area statistics given earlier, so the trends in annual increment per hectare have also been calculated and are shown in Figure 8.

Figure 7 shows that annual increment in Europe has increased since 1950 by 33 percent or 411 million m^3 o.b., from 1,246 million m^3 o.b. in 1950 to 1,657 million m^3 o.b. in 2000. Western Europe accounts for the majority of this increase, where annual increment has risen by 87 percent or 234 million m^3 o.b. over the period. Annual increment has increased over the last 50 years by 45 percent (57 million m^3 o.b.) in Eastern Europe and 14 percent (120 million m^3 o.b.) in the Russian Federation.

In terms of annual increment per hectare, the increase in forest growth in Western Europe is also remarkable, having risen from 2.8 m^3 o.b. to 4.7 m^3 o.b. over the same period. Annual increment per hectare in Eastern Europe increased in the earlier part of the period to 4.3 m^3 o.b. in 1970, but has increased very little since then. In the Russian Federation, forest growth has remained at around 1 m^3 o.b. per hectare per year over the whole period.

Figure 7   Trends in annual increment in selected European countries from 1950 to 2000

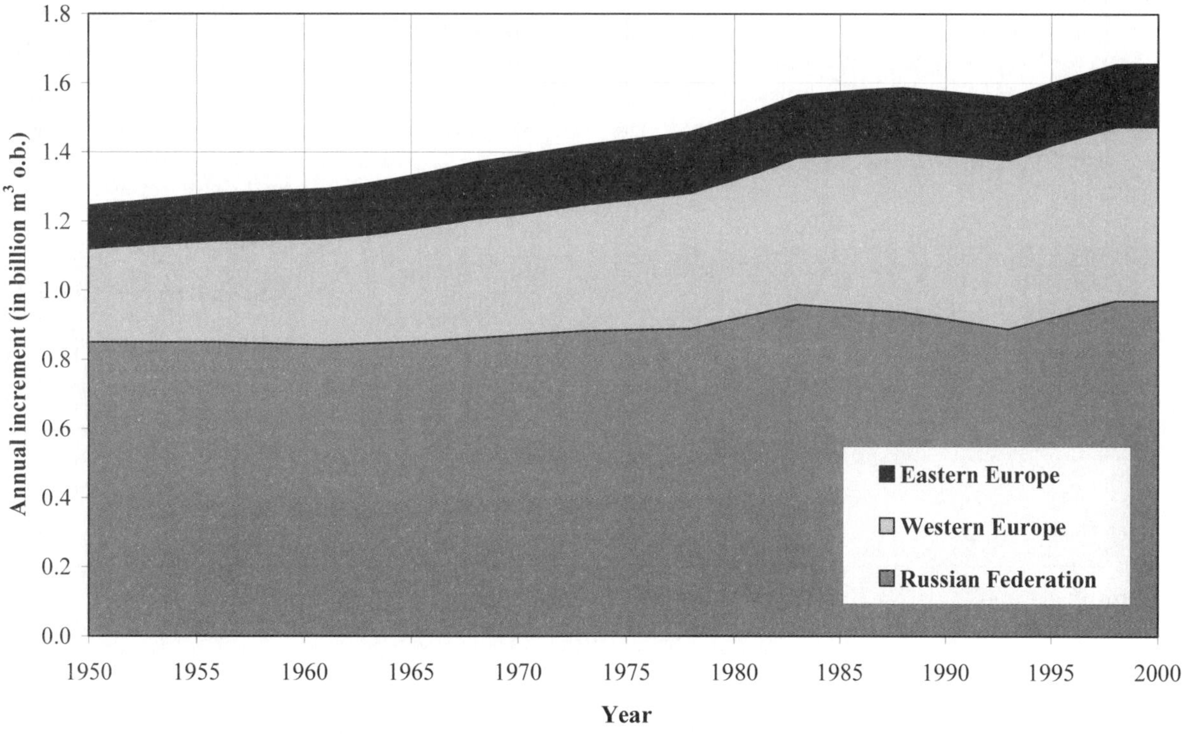

Source: derived from Gold (2003), Annex 5.3. Note: the Eastern Europe region excludes the Baltic States and four of the five countries of the former Yugoslavia. The annual increment shown here is for FAWS, except for a few countries where statistics were provided for other definitions of forest area. See Section 1.4.1 for further details and explanation.

The remarkable increase in increment in Western Europe can largely be explained by a number of changes in forest management regimes. The most obvious of these is the establishment of forest plantations in the western and southern parts of Europe. The growth rates in these forest plantations are generally higher than in other types of forest and this has led to an increase in the average increment in Western Europe as a whole.

In addition, in northern parts of Western Europe, changes in forest management from selective cutting regimes to clear cutting regimes in the 1950s has led to the conversion of older slow growing stands to younger more vigorous stands. By the mid-1970s, many of these large areas of intensively managed semi-natural forest came into their fast growing phase, resulting in increases in annual increment. Other changes in forest management in Western Europe have also had an impact, such as the conversion of slow growing broadleaved forests into coniferous forests in the 1960s and 1970s in parts of Norway and the United Kingdom.

As explained above, the lack of a major increase in annual increment in Eastern Europe since the 1970s can be explained by natural losses, which increased in the mid-1970s until the mid-1980s. The reasons for this are complex, but are thought to include increases in air pollution, water pollution and man-made disturbance to the hydrology of the forest, which have all led to higher tree mortality. In addition, throughout many parts of Europe, the general increase in homogeneity and conversion of forests to even-aged stands have probably increased the susceptibility of forests to pathogens such as insects and fungi. These factors are made worse by natural events such as storms and forest fires, which can turn relatively minor problems into major natural losses. However, since the early-1990s, it is believed that forest health has started to improve in many East European countries.

Figure 8   Trends in annual increment per hectare in selected European countries from 1950 to 2000

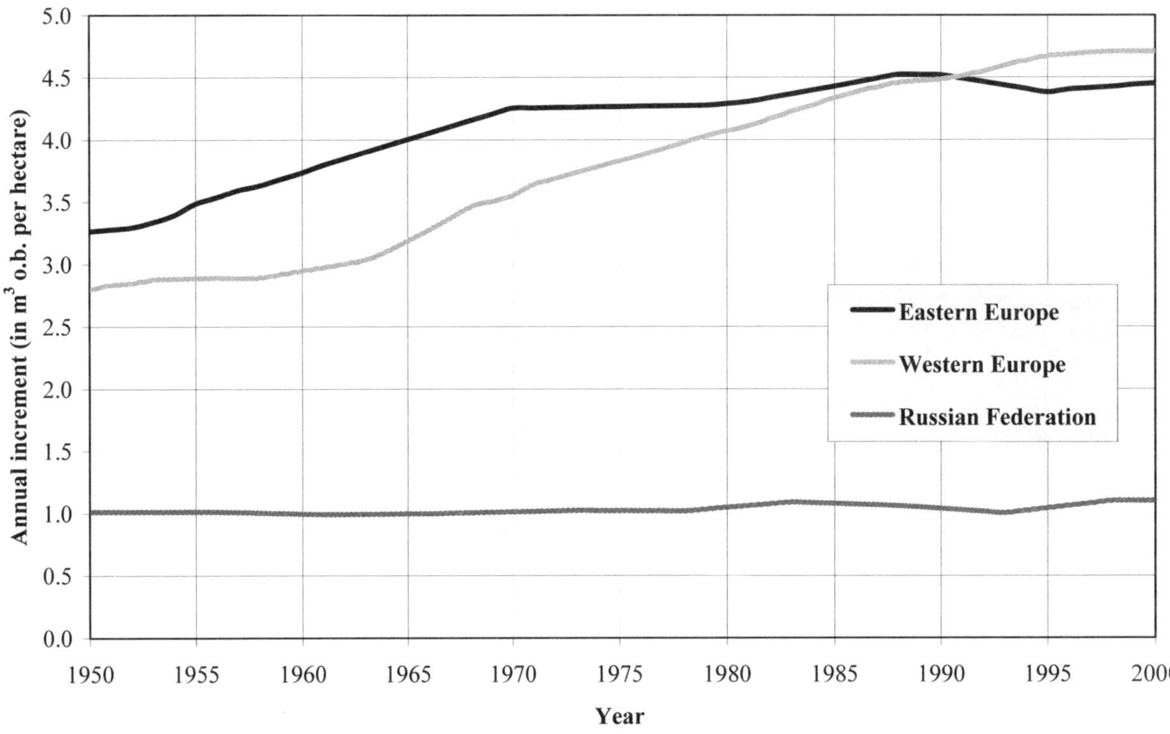

Source: derived from Gold (2003), Annexes 5.1 and 5.3. Note: the Eastern Europe region excludes the Baltic States and four of the five countries of the former Yugoslavia. The annual increment shown here is for FAWS, except for a few countries where statistics were provided for other definitions of forest area. See Section 1.4.1 for further details and explanation.

2.1.5   Comparison of removals and increment

One of the most important factors affecting the volume of growing stock and annual increment in the forest is the level of fellings from the forest. In addition, this is probably the most important human influence on the development of forest resources. Thus, it is interesting to see how the amount of fellings has compared with increment in the past and this is shown in Figure 9.

As this figure shows, the level of fellings in Europe and all three sub-regions has been persistently less than the annual increment in Europe's forests over the period from 1961 to 2000. Furthermore, the difference between these measures has increased over the last 40 years. The ratio of fellings to increment has fallen from around 90 percent in Western Europe in the 1960s to 70 percent in the last decade. Similarly, the ratio has fallen from 80 percent to 70 percent in Eastern Europe over the same period. As noted above, the level of harvesting in the Russian Federation has always been far below increment, at around 50 percent, but this has also fallen dramatically in the last decade to around 20 percent.

As already noted, investments in expanding the forest area (forest plantations) and more intensive silviculture have increased the capacity of Europe's forests to produce wood, both in the past and (probably) in the future. However, the increase in fellings over the last four decades has not kept up with this increase in potential production. This presents both challenges and opportunities for the long-term viability of forest management in Europe, which will be discussed in a later part of this report.

Figure 9   ***Trends in the comparison of fellings to increment in selected European countries from 1961 to 2000***

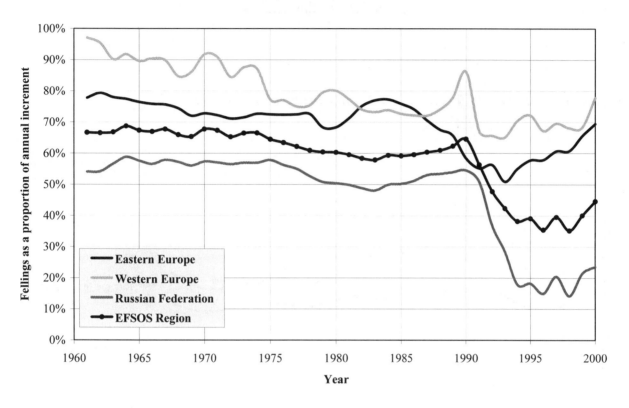

Source: increment is derived from Gold (2003), Annex 5.3 and the statistics for fellings come from FAOSTAT roundwood production statistics (http://faostat.external.fao.org) adjusted to fellings using conversion factors from the FRA (UN, 2003). Note: the Eastern Europe region excludes the Baltic States and four of the five countries of the former Yugoslavia. In addition, Turkey is excluded from the analysis due to the quality of woodfuel production statistics for that country. Fellings in the Russian Federation before 1992 have been estimated from statistics for the USSR (see Section 1.4.2).

2.2   Forest quality and forest management

The previous section described some of the quantitative trends in Europe's forests and briefly explained some of the underlying forces behind these changes. This section describes some of the qualitative changes in the forest resource that have taken place in recent years. Although many of these changes can not be quantified, the discussion presents some statistical information about selected issues.

2.2.1   Forest health

Many aspects of forest quality are difficult to measure and subjective in nature. However, one aspect of forest quality that can be measured is forest health. Forest health can be assessed using a number of measures or indicators of vitality, such as attacks by pests and pathogens, defoliation and foliage discolouration and forest fires. Historical information about defoliation and forest fires is available for most countries in Europe and trends in these figures are presented here below.

Defoliation. In the late 1970s, the condition of tree crowns was observed to deteriorate in several forest areas of Europe. As a result of this decline being originally ascribed mainly to air pollution, the UNECE established the International Co-operative Programme on the Assessment and Monitoring of Air Pollution Effects on Forests (ICP Forests) in 1985, under its Convention on Long-range Transboundary Air Pollution. In co-operation with other UNECE and European Union (EU) programmes, ICP Forests presents scientific information and analysis of the effects on forests of air pollution and other environmental factors and this work has contributed to the design and implementation of a number of policies on atmospheric pollution in the EU.

Currently, 36 European countries participate in this exercise (as well as Canada and the United States of America). The monitoring of forest health in the UNECE is one of the world's largest biomonitoring systems, with large-scale monitoring in more than 6,000 plots and intensive monitoring in more than 860 plots in participating countries.

Figure 10   *Trends in forest defoliation in Europe from 1992 to 2003*

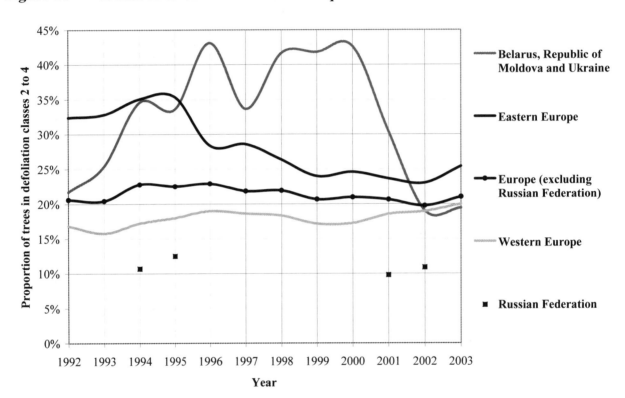

Source: derived from UN (2004).

Trends in forest defoliation in Europe are shown in Figure 10 for the period 1992 to 2003. The averages for each sub-region have been calculated by weighting the results for each country by their area of FOWL. Statistics for the Russian Federation are shown separately because only four observations are available for the period.

The extent of defoliation is divided into different defoliation classes and classes two to four represent defoliation of more than 25 percent of crown cover. Trees in these classes are generally referred to as "damaged", as they represent trees where considerable defoliation has taken place.

These trends show no increase or decrease in defoliation at the European level over the last decade, although a slight upward trend can be observed for Western Europe and a much larger trend downwards appears for Eastern Europe , attributable to the end of the massive emissions of pollutants from industry and energy plants in the former centrally planed economies. The few available observations for the Russian Federation also suggest that defoliation there has not changed much over the last decade, although the number of observations is very small.

These broad trends mask a number of important differences at the level of individual countries and species groups and further detailed information about the results of these surveys can be obtained in Lorenz *et al* (2004). However, at the broad level, these trends show that the problem of defoliation in Europe does not appear to be getting any worse. The evidence of increased defoliation in earlier years is only partial and anecdotal, so this suggests that if there was a trend towards increased defoliation in earlier years, this upward trend has probably been halted. The causes of defoliation, previously attributed by many to air pollution alone are still not clear. Increasingly, defoliation appears to be one symptom of a number of different syndromes involving multiple causes, whose inter-relationship is not well understood.

Forest fires. Statistics on the number of forest fires and area burned have been collected by UNECE and FAO since the early 1950s. However, the collection of these statistics on an annual basis did not start until 1970 and a reasonably complete set of data for the countries outside Western Europe is only available from 1982 onwards. Based on these statistics, the trends in the area of forest fires since 1950 have been produced and are shown in Figure 11.

Figure 11   *Trends in forest fires in Europe from 1950 to 2000*

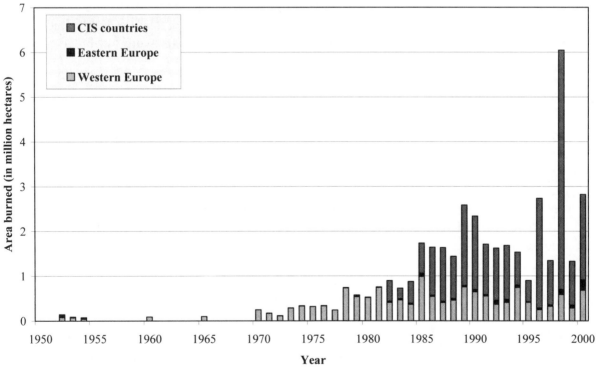

Source: UN (1999 and earlier).

At first glance, these statistics appear to show an upward trend in the area of FOWL affected by forest fires each year. However, this is largely due to the partial availability of forest fire statistics before 1982. Since 1982, there has been great variation in the area of forest fires in Europe each year, but no strong trend upwards or downwards.

At the sub-regional level there is also no strong trend upwards or downwards in these figures, although it is notable that the area burned in Western Europe is higher now than in earlier years. For instance, the average area burned in the 1970s was only 330,000 hectares per year, while that average area of forest fires since than has been around 520,000 hectares per year. This could be due to the greater use of forests by the public for recreation (i.e. fires started by humans), or it could simply be due to improvements in the monitoring and recording of forest fires.

Forest fires are caused by a mixture of human and natural factors and most of the variation from year to year can probably be attributed to short-term climatic changes that make forests more susceptible to fires. The importance of climate is also shown by the distribution of fires across Europe. Over the last decade, the warmer countries of Western Europe (Greece, Italy, Portugal and Spain) accounted for 95 percent of the area burned in Western Europe, while Bulgaria, Croatia and Turkey accounted for 52 percent of the forest fires in Eastern Europe.

Since 1982, the average annual area burned in Europe has been 1.9 million hectares, with 1.3 million hectares of forest fires in the CIS sub-region (mostly in the Russian Federation), 510,000 hectares in Western Europe and 60,000 hectares in Eastern Europe. These figures amount to only a very small fraction of the total forest area (generally much less than one percent), although forest fires are important in certain countries (e.g. Italy, where one percent has been burned each year on average over the last decade, or Portugal, where the figure is three percent).

To conclude, these figures suggest that forest fires are generally not getting any worse in Europe, but remain important in a few specific countries. However, when taking into consideration the greater public interest in forests in recent years (and their greater use of forests), it could be said that the public's perception of the problem has probably increased. There is also concern about the possible effect of climate change on the severity of forest fires, and on the relative lack of success in some countries of programmes to prevent forest fires e.g. by public education and by reducing the fuel load. Spectacular fires in Siberia and the Russian far East in 2003 were attributed to weather conditions as well as to illegal logging.

2.2.2   Forest management

Trends in forest management can not be easily assessed or quantified, as measurement of the quality of forest management is quite subjective and attempts to measure this have only been developed in recent years. The previous section referred to changes in the intensity of forest management that have probably taken place in the past, based on the observed changes in forest area, growing stock and increment. Two other qualitative aspects of forest management that can be measured are the purpose or objectives of forest management and the standards of management in forests used for wood production.

Management objectives. Europe has a long history of managing forests for multiple objectives. For example in the FRA 1990, the following seven functions of forests were listed: wood production; protection; water; grazing (range); hunting; nature conservation; and recreation (UN, 1993) and countries were asked to assess the areas of forest where each of these functions were of high, medium or low importance as a management objective. Broadly speaking, wood production, hunting and recreation were of relatively high importance in Europe, while the other objectives were of more limited importance. It is not possible to identify trends in the importance of all of these functions, because the methodology used to assess management objectives was not repeated in the FRA 2000. However, information is available about the trends and current status of forest management with respect to some of these functions.

The FRA 2000 (UN, 2003) presents information about the area of FOWL managed primarily for soil protection at two different points in time (i.e. years). This information is given for the majority of European countries, using a wide range of different years as the two reference points for measurement. By interpolating and/or extrapolating the results for each country, it is possible to estimate a trend in this variable over the period 1980 to 2000 and these results are shown in Figure 12.

In Western Europe, the importance of soil protection has not increased by very much and the average is relatively low because soil protection is generally not considered to be an important objective in a few countries with large forest areas (e.g. Finland and Sweden). Soil protection is important in Spain, but Spain is not included in the European average shown in Figure 12 because a figure is only given for one year. (If Spain was included, the average for Europe would be significantly higher). The trend for Eastern Europe reflects a large increase in the importance of FOWL managed for soil protection in Turkey and the trend for the CIS sub-region largely reflects developments in the Russian Federation. To summarise these results, the figure shows that this function is quite important and has probably increased in importance by a small amount over the last two decades.

Figure 12   Trends in the proportion of FOWL managed primarily for soil protection in selected European countries from 1980 to 2000

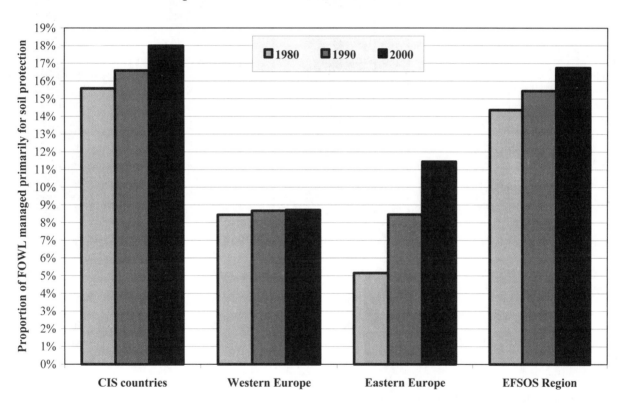

Source: derived from UN (2000). Note: the figures for Western Europe exclude Germany, Luxembourg, Norway, Spain and Switzerland; and the figures for Eastern Europe exclude Bosnia and Herzegovina and TFYR Macedonia.

The FRA 2000 also presents information about the area of FOWL where public access is legally allowed. Although this is not an indicator of where recreation is a forest management objective, it does give a more general indication of the importance of recreation as a use of Europe's forests.

Figure 13 shows the proportion of FOWL in Europe where access is legally allowed, using figures from a range of years (in each country) during the 1990s. This shows that access to forests is allowed across the majority of the forest resource in Europe, particularly in the case of publicly owned forests. It is not possible to present trends in this variable, but an analysis of the descriptive information presented by countries showed that the area of forest where access is legally allowed has probably been quite stable. The restitution of forests in Eastern Europe (i.e. transfer of public forests back to their previous private owners) does not appear to have had much of an impact on forest access. In the few cases where access has been reduced, this has often been because the public have been excluded from areas that are important for nature conservation.

Combining this information with the results of the FRA 1990, it seems likely that forest recreation remains an important forest management objective in Europe and that the level of importance has not changed by very much.

Figure 13   The proportion of FOWL in Europe where public access is legally allowed

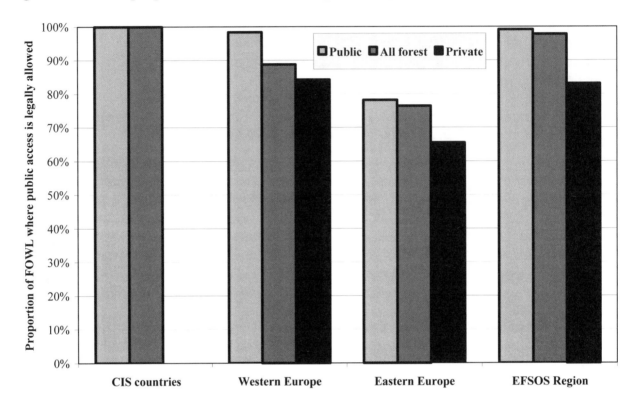

Source: derived from UN (2000). Note: the figures for Western Europe exclude Spain; and the figures for Eastern Europe exclude Serbia and Montenegro and Turkey.

The above text has described the trends and current status of two of the functions of forests in Europe. The FRA 2000 also presents some quantitative information about other forest functions, measured in terms of the volumes and/or values of outputs (e.g. values and volumes of wood and non-wood forest product production). Although it is not possible to assess this in terms of the relative importance of the different functions, it suggests that European forests are still managed for a wide variety of different objectives, depending on their ownership, location and type of forest.

Management for wood production. The quality of forest management in areas used for wood production is also difficult to assess. However, one indicator of this is the growth in the area of forests that have been certified by the two main certifying bodies operating in Europe (the Forest Stewardship Council or FSC and the Pan European Forest Certification Council or PEFC).

Figure 14 shows the proportion of the forest area in Europe that has been certified by the FSC and PEFC over the last decade. As this figure shows, the area of certified forests in Europe has increased significantly over the last decade, particularly in Western Europe and, to a lesser extent, in Eastern Europe.

These trends can not be used to suggest that the quality of forest management in Europe has increased over the last decade. However, these trends do suggest that it has been relatively easy for forest owners and managers to obtain certification over a significant part of the European forest estate. This, in turn, implies that the quality of forest management in Europe is generally quite high.

Figure 14   ***Recent trends in forest certification in Europe***

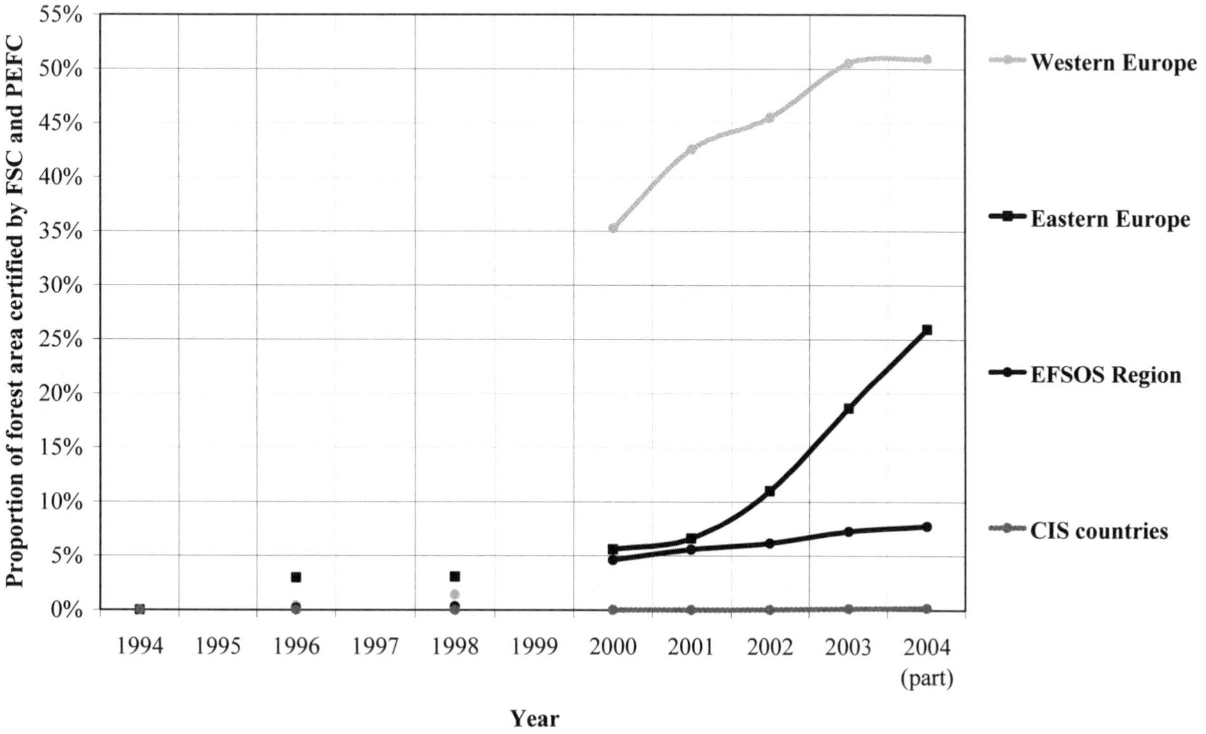

Source: derived from WRI (2004) and PEFC (2004 and earlier).

2.3   *Production and consumption of processed wood products*

Processed wood products are those products that are produced by the forest processing industry and are consumed by other industries outside the sector or consumers. At the broad level, these include: sawnwood; wood based panels; and paper and paperboard.[3] Trends in the production and consumption of each of these products are described below and this section finishes with a description of some of the changes in the relative importance of these products over the last 40 years.

2.3.1   Sawnwood production and consumption

Trends in coniferous sawnwood production and consumption in Europe are shown in Figure 15. This figure shows a number of interesting changes that have taken place in the markets for coniferous sawnwood in Europe over the last 40 years.

---

[3]   Note: the analysis here does not go beyond these products. There are a range of further processed wood products (e.g. wooden furniture) that could be considered as part of the forest sector, but information is not readily available about the trends in production and consumption of these products.

Figure 15 ***Trends in production and consumption of coniferous sawnwood from 1961 to 2000***

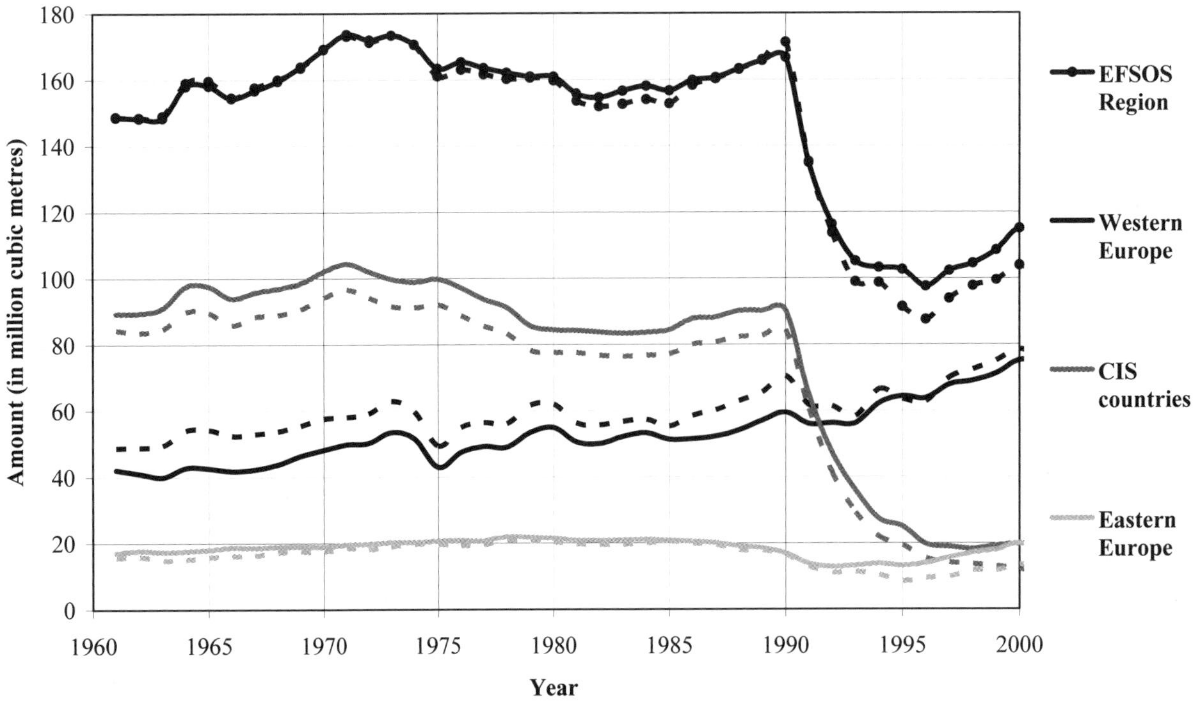

Solid lines represent production and dashed lines represent apparent consumption

Source: derived from FAOSTAT production and trade statistics (http://faostat.external.fao.org). Note: totals for the Eastern Europe and CIS sub-regions before 1992 have been estimated from statistics for the USSR (see Section 1.4.2).

The first and probably most important feature of these trends is that Europe has changed from a situation of approximate balance in production and consumption over the period 1960 to 1990 to a situation of net exports from the region (to the rest of the World) over the last ten years. In 1990, European consumption exceeded production slightly and Europe was a net importing region. By 2000, the situation had changed to one where European production exceeded consumption by just over 10 million m^3 (or around 10 percent of production). Furthermore, the level of net exports from Europe has continued to increase to around 15 million m^3 in 2002.

Two main changes lie behind this development in production and consumption. First, production of coniferous sawnwood in Western Europe has increased more rapidly than consumption over the last ten years, significantly reducing net imports into the sub-region (from around 12 million m^3 in 1990 to 4 million m^3 in 2000 and approximately zero in 2002). Countries that have contributed most to this increase in production are the traditionally important producers in Western Europe such as: Austria; Finland; Germany; and Sweden. However, another notable development has been the increase in production in some countries with significant forest plantation resources (e.g. Ireland and the United Kingdom). Secondly, Eastern Europe has moved from a position of approximate balance in production and consumption (until 1990) to one where production exceeds consumption by 7 million m^3 (or about one-third of production). The three Baltic States account for much of the growth in production in this sub-region. The CIS sub-region has always been a net exporter of coniferous sawnwood (at a level of just under 10 million m^3) and this has not changed over the period.

The second interesting feature of this figure is that it shows the dramatic fall in production and consumption in the Eastern Europe and CIS sub-regions in the early-1990s and the degree to which they have recovered since then. In the case of Eastern Europe, production and consumption fell by about one-third in the early-1990s. Since then, production has recovered to a level of 20 million m^3 in 2000 (around the same level as in 1990), but consumption in 2000 was only 13 million m^3. In the CIS sub-region, the fall in production and consumption was even more dramatic (a fall of around three-quarters). However, production and consumption in both Eastern Europe and the CIS have been growing strongly in the first years of the twenty-first century.

These recent trends have led to changes in the relative importance of the three different sub-regions in the European market for coniferous sawnwood. Historically, Western Europe accounted for around 35 percent of European consumption and 30 percent of production, but now accounts for 65 percent and 75 percent of production and consumption respectively. Eastern Europe's share of European consumption has remained relatively unchanged at around 12 percent, but the importance of production in this region has risen from around 12 percent of total European production in the period before 1990 to about 17 percent in 2000. The greatest change has occurred in the CIS sub-region, which used to account for the majority of production and consumption in Europe (around 60 percent of production and 55 percent of consumption up until 1990). In 2000, this sub-region accounted for 17 percent of production and 13 percent of consumption, which is about the same as the Eastern Europe sub-region.

The dramatic changes in the latter two sub-regions make it difficult to present useful information about historical growth rates in the markets for coniferous sawnwood in Europe. However, the trends in Western Europe have been more stable and it is possible to give an indication of recent growth trends in the other two sub-regions.

In Western Europe, production of coniferous sawnwood has grown consistently over the last 40 years at a rate of about 1.3 percent per year (or roughly 800,000 m^3 per year). Average growth in consumption has been about 0.9 percent per year (or roughly 700,000 m^3 per year). Other than short-term fluctuations, the trend in production and consumption in Western Europe appears quite stable. In Eastern Europe, growth in production and consumption was negligible over the period until 1990. Since 1995, production has grown by 5.3 percent per year (600,000 m^3 per year), while consumption has grown by 6.4 percent per year (300,000 m^3 per year). It seems likely that the positive trends in production and consumption in this sub-region will continue into the future. In the CIS countries, there was neither a positive or negative trend in production and consumption before 1990. The trends since 1995 still appear to be changing and it looks like the decline in production is starting to reverse and the trend in consumption may also reverse in the near future.

Figure 16 presents the trends in non-coniferous sawnwood production and consumption in Europe over the same period. This figure is similar in many respects to the previous figure, but also shows some subtle differences in the markets for this product.

The first notable feature of the non-coniferous sawnwood market is that Europe has always been a net importer of non-coniferous sawnwood and that the level of net imports has increased in recent years. This is mostly due to net imports of non-coniferous sawnwood into Western Europe (Eastern Europe is a small net exporter and the production and consumption are roughly in balance in the CIS sub-region).

One of the reasons for the increase in net imports is that production of non-coniferous sawnwood has declined in Western Europe while consumption has remained roughly constant. Net exports from Eastern Europe have increased in recent years (due to increased production) and have probably substituted for some production in Western Europe. However, this increase in net exports has not affected the position for Europe as a whole.

Figure 16   ***Trends in production and consumption of non-coniferous sawnwood from 1961 to 2000***

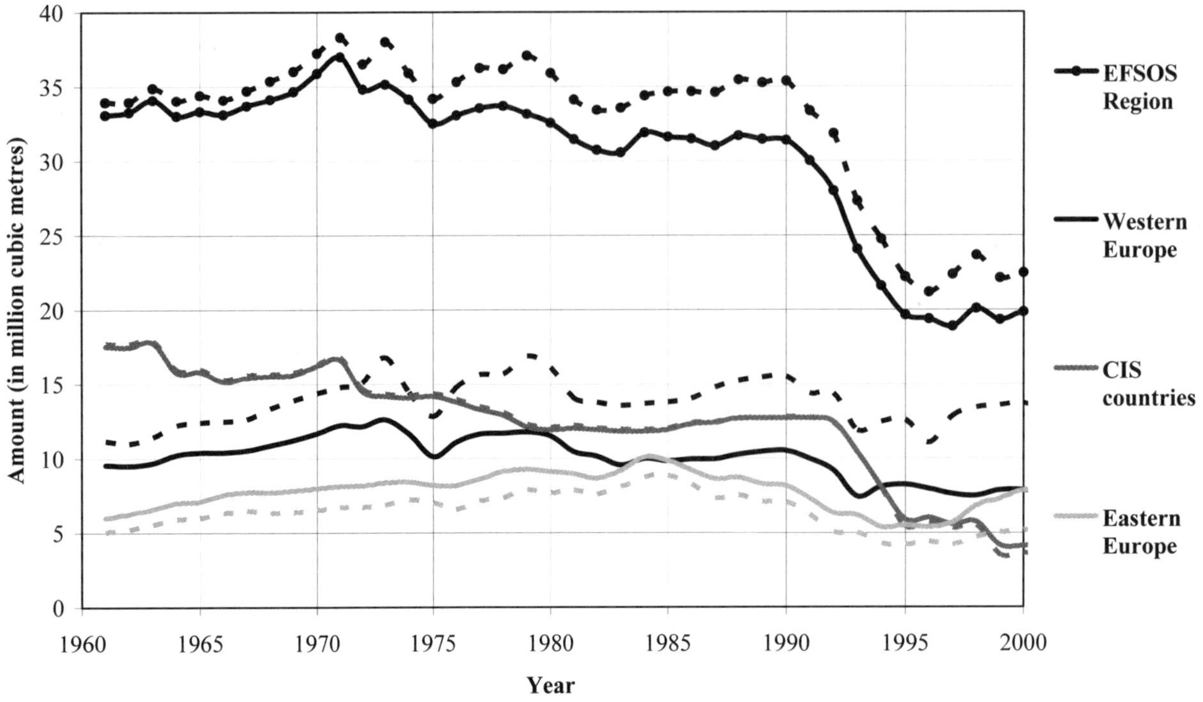

Solid lines represent production and dashed lines represent apparent consumption

Source: derived from FAOSTAT production and trade statistics (http://faostat.external.fao.org). Note: totals for the Eastern Europe and CIS sub-regions before 1992 have been estimated from statistics for the USSR (see Section 1.4.2).

One of the reasons for net imports into Europe is the variety of species demanded in the markets for non-coniferous sawnwood. Consumption of non-coniferous sawnwood includes consumption of tropical non-coniferous sawnwood as well as sawnwood made from North American tree species. Although some of this demand is satisfied by importing roundwood and manufacturing the sawnwood in Europe, it seems likely that Europe will remain a net importer of sawnwood made from these species for the foreseeable future.

A second notable feature of Figure 16 is that the distribution of production and consumption across all three sub-regions is more even. Production in the CIS sub-region has declined from about half of the total in 1961 to one-quarter in 2000. Production in the rest of Europe in 2000 was divided equally between Western and Eastern Europe. Western Europe accounted for about half of all consumption in 2000, with the remainder shared equally between the Eastern Europe and CIS sub-regions.

As before, the figure shows the decline in production and consumption in the Eastern Europe and CIS sub-regions since 1990, although the longer trends in all three sub-regions show a long-term decline in the markets for this product. Broadly speaking the trends in production and consumption in the three sub regions are as follows.

In Western Europe, production of non-coniferous sawnwood has fallen over the last 40 years by about 0.9 percent per year (or roughly 60,000 m^3 per year) on average, while consumption has grown by about 0.1 percent per year (or roughly 20,000 m^3 per year). The trend appears to have changed slightly over time, with a higher decline in production and little or no growth in consumption in more recent years.

In Eastern Europe, there was steady positive growth in production and consumption of non-coniferous sawnwood up until 1985. By 1995, production and consumption had fallen by half, to levels lower than in 1961. However, since 1995, production and consumption have risen at an average annual growth rate of 6.9 percent and 5.2 percent respectively (equal to an annual increase of about 400,000 m^3 and 200,000 m^3).

In the CIS sub-region, the trend in production and consumption of non-coniferous sawnwood shows a persistent decline in this market, with the exception of a levelling-off of the trends in the 1980s. On average, production and consumption have declined each year by 3.1 percent and 3.3 percent respectively (equal to falls of about 330,000 m^3 and 350,000 m^3 respectively). Statistics from the most recent years suggest that production and consumption may be starting to level-off, but this is far from certain.

2.3.2   Wood based panel production and consumption

The wood based panels sector covers a variety of panel products that can be divided into the following three main types of product: fibreboard; particleboard; and plywood and veneer sheets. Fibreboard and particleboard can also be further sub-divided into panels with different properties and uses, such as: hardboard; medium density fibreboard (MDF); chipboard; and orientated strand board (OSB).

One of the most important differences between the various wood panels is the types of wood raw materials that can be used to manufacture each product. Fibreboard and particleboard are reconstituted panels and are manufactured from wood chips that can come from a variety of sources. Plywood and veneer sheets are manufactured from industrial roundwood and are usually made from larger sizes of roundwood (i.e. sawlogs and veneer logs).

Figure 17 shows the trend in fibreboard production and consumption in Europe over the last 40 years. In general, production in Europe has slightly exceeded consumption over most of the period, leading to a small amount of net exports. Production and consumption are currently in balance in Western Europe, although there have been years when consumption exceeded production. Eastern Europe has always been a small net exporter of fibreboard, while production and consumption in the CIS sub-region have been in balance or with a slight surplus of production over consumption. In total, the markets for fibreboard in Europe have expanded quite significantly over the last 40 years, from a level of production and consumption of around 2 million m^3 in 1961 to production of 13 million m^3 and consumption of 12 million m^3 in 2000.

At the sub-regional level, production and consumption in Europe has been concentrated in Western Europe over much of the period, although the shares of all three sub-regions were quite even in the mid-1970s and 1980s. In the last decade, the fibreboard market in Western Europe has increased dramatically and the market in the CIS sub-region has declined. The market in Eastern Europe fell in the early-1990s, but has since recovered.

Figure 17   Trends in production and consumption of fibreboard from 1961 to 2000

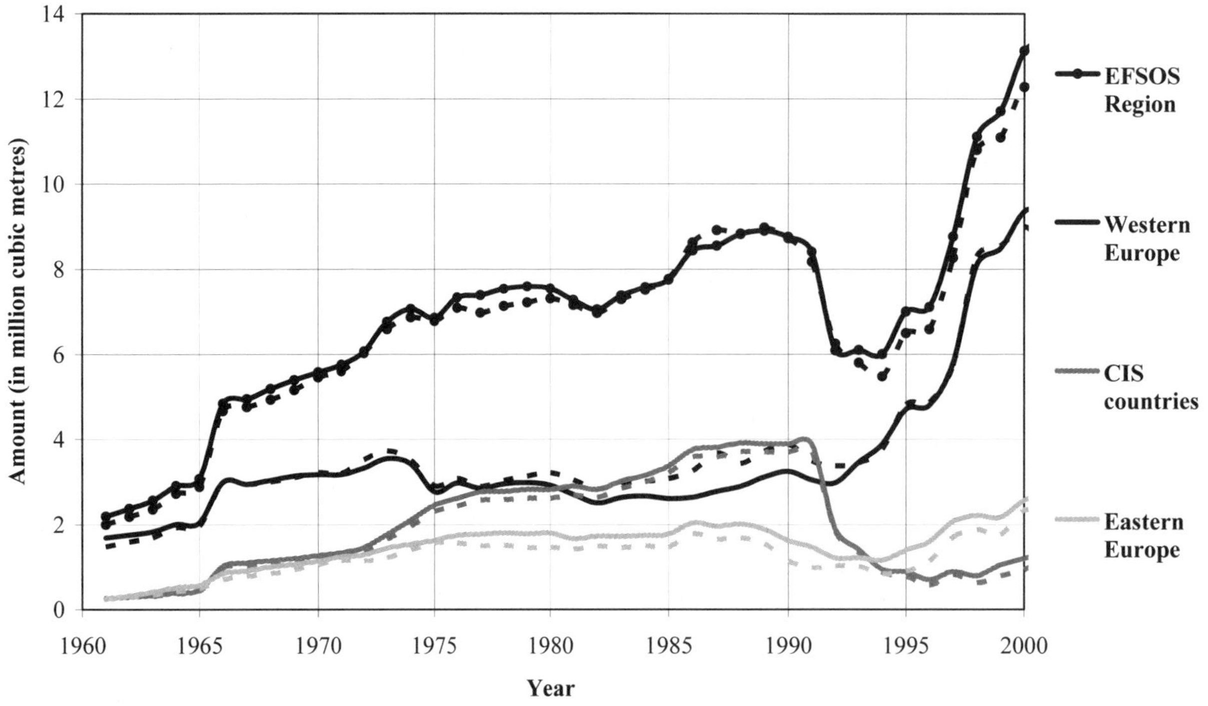

Solid lines represent production and dashed lines represent apparent consumption

Source: derived from FAOSTAT production and trade statistics (http://faostat.external.fao.org). Note: totals for the Eastern Europe and CIS sub-regions before 1992 have been estimated from statistics for the USSR (see Section 1.4.2).

In Western Europe, production and consumption since 1961 have increased by 2.8 percent and 2.9 percent on average each year (equal to increases of around 210,000 m³ and 180,000 m³ respectively). However, there has been a structural change in this trend, with extremely rapid growth in the last few years. From 1992 to 2000, both production and consumption trebled from a level of 3 million m³ in 1992 to just over 9 million m³ in 2000.

In Eastern Europe, the long-terms trends in production and consumption have been similar to those in Western Europe, except that both fell during the early 1990s. Since 1992, the markets for fibreboard in this region have recovered and have been growing at an annual rate of 11.0 percent or 190,000 m³ (production) and 12.6 percent or 200,000 m³ (consumption).

In the CIS sub-region, the markets for fibreboard grew rapidly up until 1990, at which point this sub-region accounted for almost half of all fibreboard production and consumption in Europe. Since 1990, production and consumption fell by three-quarters, although a slight upward trend has appeared since 1995.

One of the main reasons behind the recent changes in the trends in Western Europe (and, to a lesser extent, Eastern Europe) has been the development of MDF. Large-scale production of MDF started in the mid-1980s in North America and Europe and this has developed to become one of the fastest growing wood product sectors in recent years. As Figure 17 shows, there was very little growth in fibreboard production and consumption in both of these sub-regions throughout the 1970s and 1980s. However, since 1990, there has been a renewed and rapid expansion of fibreboard markets and much of this new growth can be attributed to MDF. Statistics on MDF production and trade are only available from 1995 onwards, but they show quite clearly that most of the growth in the fibreboard sector has come from growth in this product category (see Figure 18). MDF currently only accounts for a modest share of fibreboard production and consumption in the CIS sub-region, but it can be expected that it will start to have an impact there as well in coming decades.

Figure 18   Changes in the composition of fibreboard production from 1995 to 2002

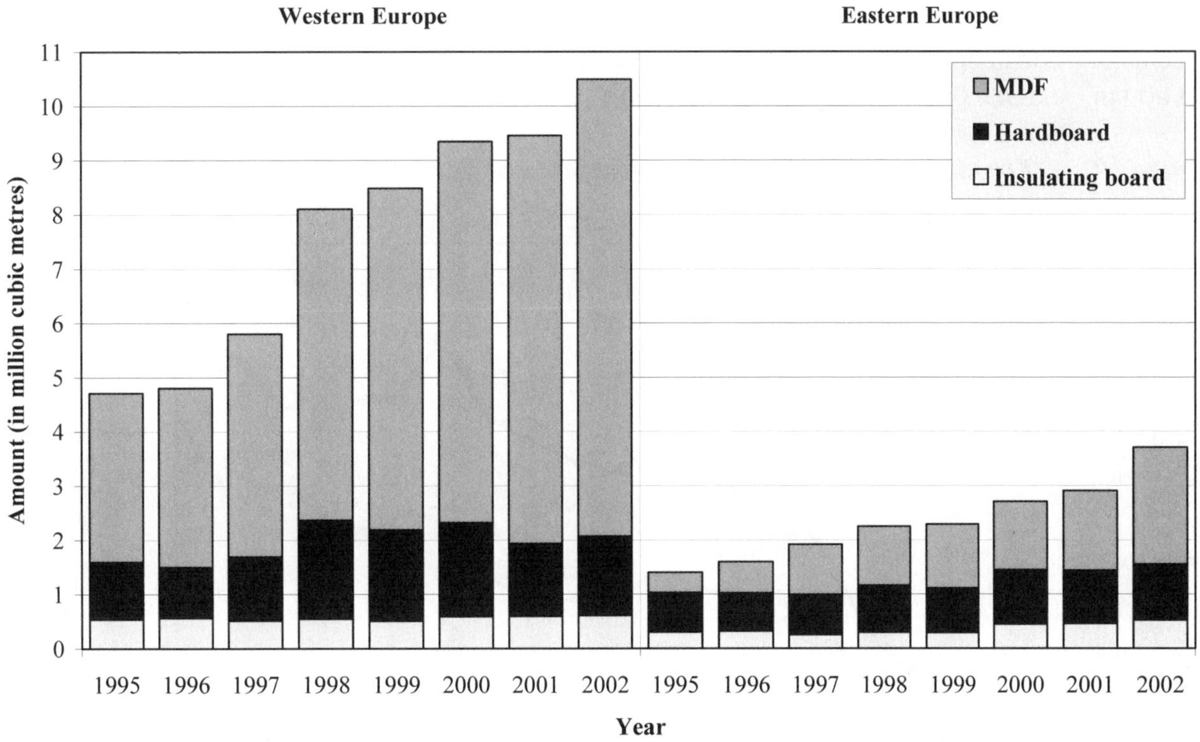

Source: derived from FAOSTAT production and trade statistics (http://faostat.external.fao.org).

Historical trends in the production and consumption of particleboard are shown in Figure 19. To some extent, many of the main features of these trends are the same as those described above for fibreboard.

Production and consumption of particleboard in Europe as a whole has been roughly in balance until the last decade, when production has started to exceed consumption, leading to a small amount of net exports from the region (slightly more than 2 million m^3 per year in 2000). Within Europe, Western and Eastern Europe are small net exporters, while production and consumption are roughly in balance in the CIS sub-region. Western Europe has always been the major producer and consumer of particleboard in Europe, accounting for almost 100 percent of the European market in 1961, falling to about 75 percent of the market in 2000. Overall, the market has grown from levels of consumption and production of around 3 million m^3 in 1961 to production of 42 million m^3 and consumption of 40 million m^3 in 2000, making this the largest component of the wood based panel sector.

In Western Europe, apart from short-term fluctuations, the market for particleboard has grown persistently and with a relatively high growth rate. Since 1961, production and consumption have grown on average each year by 4.7 percent and 4.8 percent respectively (equal to increases of around 690,000 m^3 and 620,000 m^3 respectively), although growth may have slowed slightly in more recent years.

In Eastern Europe, the particleboard sector has also grown strongly at an average annual growth rate of 5.7 percent or 180,000 m^3 (production and consumption). In contrast to many other components of the forest processing sector, the economic changes in the early-1990s did not have much of an impact on the particleboard sector in Eastern Europe, which suffered only slight falls in production and consumption in 1990.

The trend in the CIS sub-region matches that for the fibreboard sector, with strong growth up until 1990, when production and consumption fell by about three-quarters until 1995. Since 1996, recovery has been very strong in this sector, with production growing at an annual rate of 10.9 percent and consumption growing by 15.1 percent per year (equal to annual increases of about 260,000 m^3 and 380,000 m^3 per year respectively).

Figure 19   Trends in production and consumption of particleboard from 1961 to 2000

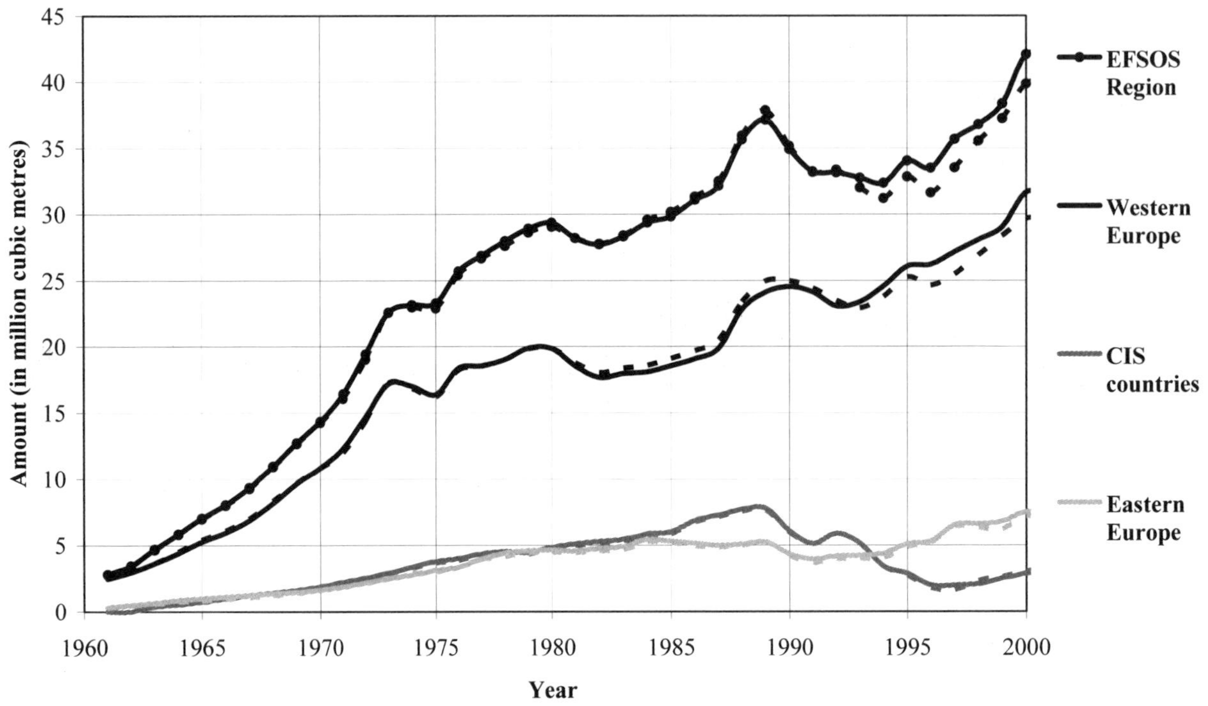

Solid lines represent production and dashed lines represent apparent consumption

Source: derived from FAOSTAT production and trade statistics (http://faostat.external.fao.org). Note: totals for the Eastern Europe and CIS sub-regions before 1992 have been estimated from statistics for the USSR (see Section 1.4.2).

Trends in the production and consumption of plywood and veneer sheets since 1961 are shown in Figure 20. On average, veneer sheet production accounts for about 30 percent of total production of plywood and veneer sheets and this proportion has not changed over the period 1961 to 2000.

The production of veneer sheets is the first stage in the manufacturing of plywood, but the statistics for veneer sheet production exclude the production of veneer sheets carried-out as part of the plywood manufacturing process in a country. A proportion of the veneer sheets traded between countries could be used in plywood production (i.e. veneer sheets imported into a country could be used in that country's plywood industry), but it is suspected that the amount of veneer sheets used in this way is very low. In stead, most veneer sheets are probably used in the furniture industry or to provide facing materials for other types of wood panel. Consequently, the amount of double-counting of production is believed to be quite low.

Figure 20 shows that plywood and veneer sheet consumption in Europe exceeds production by a considerable amount and that net imports of these products have grown over the last 40 years to about 1.7 million m^3 in 2000. Over most of the last 40 years, production in Europe was divided as follows: 50 percent in Western Europe; 30 percent in CIS countries; and 20 percent in Eastern Europe. However, over the last decade, Western Europe's share of production has increased slightly, while the shares held by the other two sub-regions has declined slightly. Western Europe has always accounted for the majority of plywood and veneer sheet consumption in Europe and Western Europe's share of consumption has risen in recent years to 80 percent in 2000.

Figure 20   Trends in production and consumption of plywood and veneer sheets from 1961 to 2000

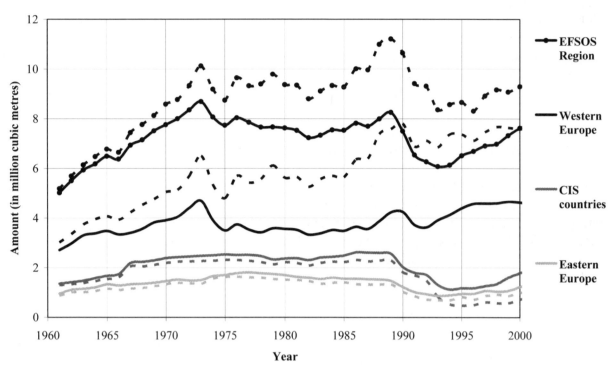

Solid lines represent production and dashed lines represent apparent consumption

Source: derived from FAOSTAT production and trade statistics (http://faostat.external.fao.org). Note: totals for the Eastern Europe and CIS sub-regions before 1992 have been estimated from statistics for the USSR (see Section 1.4.2).

The high level of net imports into Europe is also due to Western Europe, which is a significant net importing region. Eastern Europe is and has always been a small net exporter of plywood and veneer sheets. In addition, the CIS sub-region has always been a net exporter, with net exports increasing significantly over the last few years, as consumption has fallen dramatically in this sub-region. As in the market for non-coniferous sawnwood, part of the reason for the high level of net imports of plywood and veneer sheets into Europe is the market's demand for products made from tropical tree species.

In Western Europe, the long-term trends in production and consumption of plywood and veneer sheets are as follows. Production has risen at an annual rate of 0.7 percent per year (equal to an annual increase of about 50,000 m^3), while consumption has increased by 1.9 percent or 110,000 m^3 per year. Over the last decade, growth in consumption appears to have slowed slightly, but growth in production may have increased slightly.

In Eastern Europe, the long-term trends in production and consumption show little or no growth over the last 40 years. The market for plywood and veneer sheets in Eastern Europe has declined steadily since the mid-1970s and fell significantly in the early-1990s. There has been a slight recovery since then, but at a very low growth rate.

The long-term trends in the CIS sub-region also show little or no growth in this product category over the last four decades. Furthermore, in the period 1989 to 1995, production fell by half and consumption fell by three-quarters, which led to a significant increase in net exports from this sub-region. Since then, there has been strong growth in production and, to a lesser extent, consumption. Since 1995, production has grown by 11.1 percent per year (equal to about 180,000 m^3 per year) and consumption has grown by 10.2 percent per year (80,000 m^3 per year). Given that plywood and veneer sheets are usually made from large-sized roundwood and that this region has an abundance of large-sized trees, this indicates that the CIS sub- region may have a comparative advantage in the production of these products.

2.3.3   Paper and paperboard production and consumption

The paper and paperboard sector covers a wide variety of types and grades of paper. However, for the purpose of this analysis, the sector is divided into the following three main categories: newsprint; printing and writing paper; and other paper and paperboard. The first two categories are self-explanatory, while the last covers a mixture of different products such as: wrapping paper; tissue paper; paper used in the manufacturing of other industrial and consumer goods; and paper used to make boxes and sacks.

Figure 21 shows the historical trend in newsprint production and consumption over the last 40 years. As the figure shows, production of newsprint in Europe has exceeded consumption over most of the last 40 years, leading to a small amount of net exports from Europe. Furthermore, in recent years the level of net exports has increased slightly, amounting to between 0.5 million metric tonnes (MT) and 1.0 million MT per year.

Western Europe accounts for the majority of production and consumption of newsprint in Europe (80 percent of production and 84 percent of consumption in 2000) and has been a small net exporter of newsprint over most of the period. The CIS sub-region has been the next most important producer and consumer of newsprint, although consumption fell dramatically in the early 1990s, leading to a significant increase in net exports. Eastern Europe accounts for only a very small share of production and consumption in Europe. Eastern Europe has always been a net importer of newsprint and the level of net imports has increased slightly in recent years.

The long-term trends in production and consumption in Western Europe show persistent and sustained growth in this sector over the last 40 years. Production and consumption have both grown at an average annual growth rate of 2.4 percent or about 140,000 MT per year.

In Eastern Europe, growth in the newsprint sector has also been sustained and was not affected very much by the economic changes in the early 1990s. Over the last 40 years, production and consumption have grown at an annual rate of 2.3 percent and 2.7 percent respectively (both equal to an increase of around 20,000 MT per year).

Figure 21   Trends in production and consumption of newsprint from 1961 to 2000

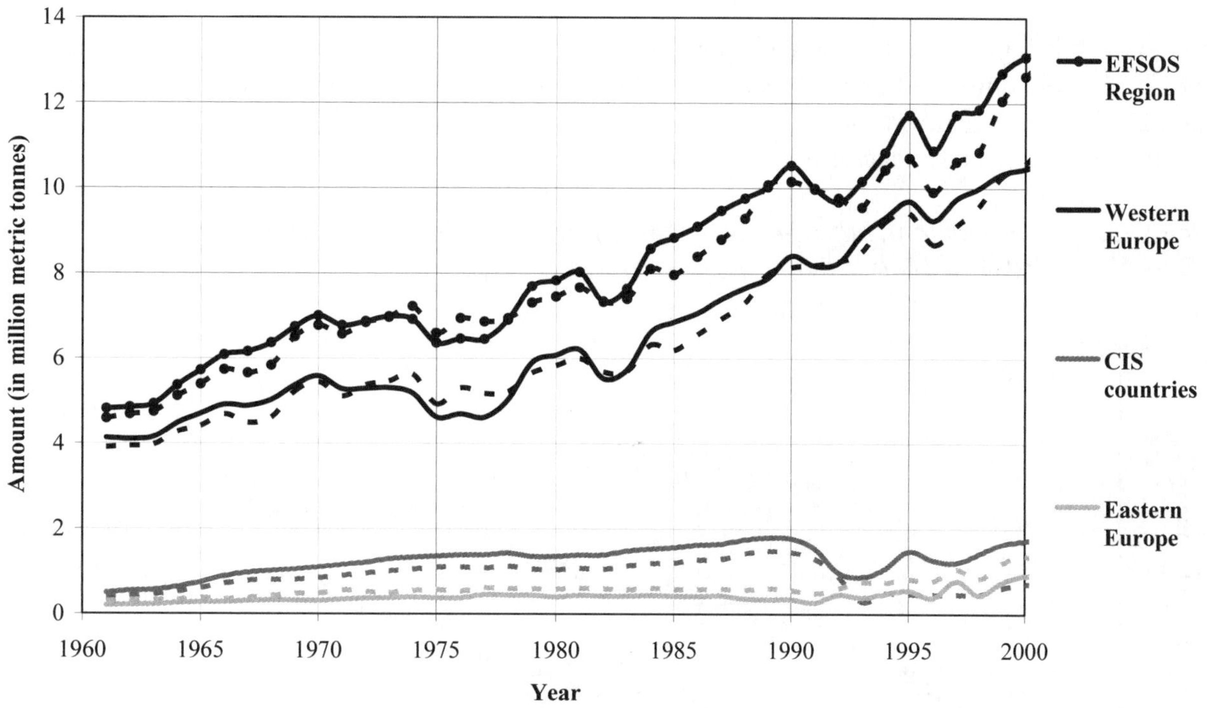

Solid lines represent production and dashed lines represent apparent consumption

Source: derived from FAOSTAT production and trade statistics (http://faostat.external.fao.org). Note: totals for the Eastern Europe and CIS sub-regions before 1992 have been estimated from statistics for the USSR (see Section 1.4.2).

As in many other sectors, the trends in production and consumption of newsprint in the CIS sub-region show sustained growth until the early 1990s, when production fell by half and consumption fell by three-quarters. Since 1995, there has been a rapid recovery in production, although consumption is still far below the level in 1990. From 1993, production has increased by 7.1 percent per year and consumption has increased by 8.3 percent per year (equal to average annual increases of 100,000 MT and 50,000 MT respectively). Given the large investments required for paper processing and the level of existing capacity in the CIS sub-region, it is perhaps not surprising that production has recovered quite quickly in this sector.

Figure 22 shows the trends in production and consumption of other paper and paperboard in Europe since 1961. Again, Western Europe accounts for the majority of production and consumption (around 85 percent of the total), although the other two sub-regions were growing in importance until 1990. Production and consumption have been in balance throughout most of the last 40 years, although production has exceeded consumption and led to some net exports from the region over the last decade. In 2000, these net exports amounted to 3 million MT. Western Europe is the major net exporter of other paper and paperboard, because production and consumption in the other two sub-regions are (and have always been) more or less equal.

In Western Europe, the long term trends in production and consumption of other paper and paperboard show sustained and relatively high rates of growth over the last 40 years. Production has increased at an average annual rate of 2.8 percent (or about 800,000 MT per year), while consumption has grown by 2.6 percent per year (equal to around 740,000 MT per year).

Production and consumption in Eastern Europe grew steadily until 1989, but then fell by about one-third from 1989 to 1991. Since 1991, production and consumption have returned to their previous levels of growth, with production growing by 3.5 percent per year (about 160,000 MT per year) and consumption growing by 4.8 percent per year (or 200,000 MT per year).

In the CIS sub-region, production and consumption both increased at a sustained and relatively high level of growth until 1990. Since 1990, both have fallen by around three-quarters and have only started to increase again in the last few years. The most recent statistics from 2002 suggest that a sustained recovery in this sector is now taking place.

Figure 22   **Trends in production and consumption of other paper and paperboard from 1961 to 2000**

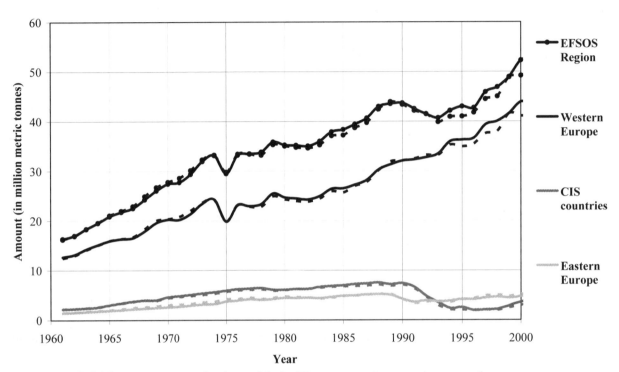

Solid lines represent production and dashed lines represent apparent consumption

Source: derived from FAOSTAT production and trade statistics (http://faostat.external.fao.org). Note: totals for the Eastern Europe and CIS sub-regions before 1992 have been estimated from statistics for the USSR (see Section 1.4.2).

Figure 23 shows the trends in production and consumption of printing and writing paper in Europe since 1961. There are two very notable features of these trends compared with the trends for the rest of the paper and paperboard sector. Firstly, the historical growth in production and consumption of printing and writing paper has been much higher than growth in the other two sectors. Although this sector is not the largest component of the total paper and paperboard sector (it is second in importance after other paper and paperboard), it may soon become the most important if it continues to grow so rapidly.

The second notable point is that Europe is (and has always been) a significant net exporter of printing and writing paper, with production exceeding consumption by 5.5 million MT in 2000. All of this is due to Western Europe, which accounts for 95 percent of production and 90 percent of consumption in the region as a whole. Western Europe has always been a significant net exporter of printing and writing paper, while production and consumption in the other two regions have been roughly equal (although Eastern Europe has started to become a slight net importer in recent years).

The long-term trends in production and consumption of printing and writing paper in Western Europe show high levels of sustained growth over the last four decades, with production growing by

4.7 percent per year on average (around 700,000 MT per year) and consumption growing by 4.3 percent per year (or around 520,000 MT per year). These growth rates are far higher than those experienced in the other two sub-regions and exceed the long-term growth rates for other types of paper and paperboard.

In Eastern Europe, production and consumption of printing and writing paper grew modestly until 1989 when, as in many other sectors, there was a slight decline for three years. Since 1993, production and, in particular, consumption have recovered and started to grow very rapidly. The short-term trend in production and consumption since 1993 shows average annual growth in production of 10.3 percent (or about 140,000 MT per year) and very high growth in consumption of 11.9 percent per year (or 190,000 MT per year).

Figure 23   Trends in production and consumption of printing and writing paper from 1961 to 2000

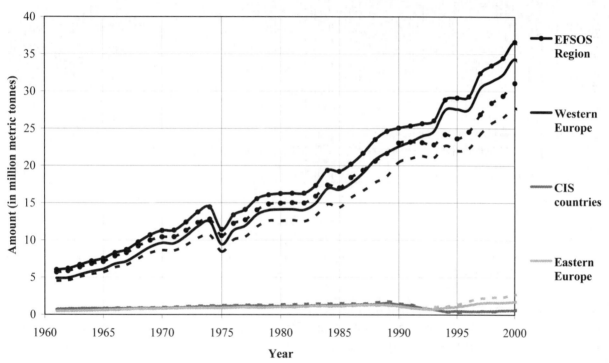

Solid lines represent production and dashed lines represent apparent consumption

Source: derived from FAOSTAT production and trade statistics (http://faostat.external.fao.org). Note: totals for the Eastern Europe and CIS sub-regions before 1992 have been estimated from statistics for the USSR (see Section 1.4.2).

The trends in production and consumption of printing and writing paper in the CIS sub-region are similar to those described above. After a period of modest growth up until 1990, production and consumption fell by three quarters from 1990 to 1995 and have only just started to recover. Of all of the three paper and paperboard sectors, this appears to be the sector that has had the slowest recovery in the CIS sub-region after the economic changes of the early 1990s.

2.3.4   Structural changes in the markets for processed wood products

Previous parts of this section have examined the trends in individual product categories by sub-region and for Europe as a whole. This final part examines how these trends have affected the relative importance of different types of processed wood product across the region.

For the solid wood products (sawnwood and wood based panels), the different rates of growth in the various product categories show that wood based panels are becoming increasingly important, while sawnwood is declining in importance.

Figure 24   Trends in the consumption of sawnwood and wood based panels in Europe from 1961 to 2000

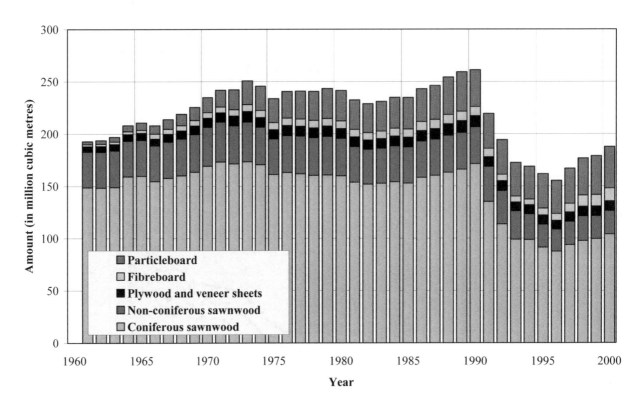

Source: derived from FAOSTAT production and trade statistics (http://faostat.external.fao.org). Note: totals for the Eastern Europe and CIS sub-regions before 1992 have been estimated from statistics for the USSR (see Section 1.4.2).

Figure 24 shows the trend in consumption of solid wood products over the last 40 years for the whole of Europe. It also shows how the composition of consumption has changed over time in terms of the relative importance of different products. Broadly speaking there have been two changes.

Firstly, within the sawnwood sector, the relative importance of coniferous sawnwood has increased slightly, while non-coniferous sawnwood has declined (i.e. the share of non-coniferous sawnwood in total sawnwood consumption has fallen over time). In the region as a whole, the increased importance of coniferous sawnwood has been only slight, with coniferous sawnwood accounting for 81 percent of all sawnwood consumption in 1961 and 83 percent of consumption in 2000. However, at the sub-regional level, the change has been more noticeable in Western Europe, where the share of coniferous sawnwood in total sawnwood consumption has increased from 80 percent to 85 percent over the same period.

Conversely, the relative importance of coniferous sawnwood has declined in the other two sub-regions. In Eastern Europe, there appears to have been a steady and gradual long-term shift from coniferous sawnwood to non-coniferous sawnwood (but by only relatively small amounts). In the CIS sub-region, the trend was also towards more consumption of coniferous sawnwood until the early-1990s when production and consumption in this sector fell by much more than in the non-coniferous sawnwood sector.

Given that Europe is a net importer of non-coniferous sawnwood and that non-coniferous sawnwood accounts for less than 20 percent of total sawnwood consumption, this indicates that production of non-coniferous sawnwood is of only limited and declining importance. It is difficult to say whether this trend will continue in the future, but given the much longer time period generally required to produce non-coniferous sawlogs, it suggests that the prospects for this particular component of the sector are quite limited.

Figure 25 **Trends in the importance of reconstituted panels from 1961 to 2000**

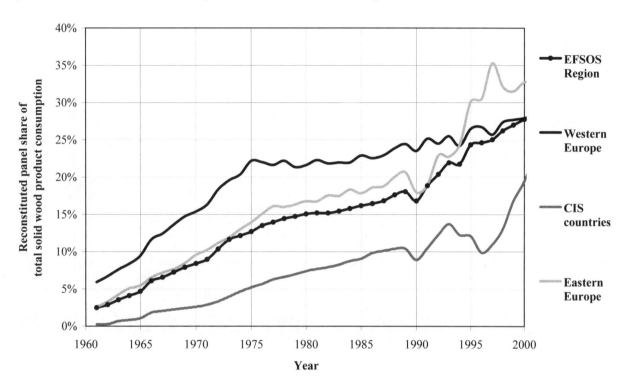

Source: derived from FAOSTAT production and trade statistics (http://faostat.external.fao.org). Note: totals for the Eastern Europe and CIS sub-regions before 1992 have been estimated from statistics for the USSR (see Section 1.4.2).

The second and more noticeable feature of these trends is the rising importance of wood based panels and, in particular, the reconstituted panels (fibreboard and particleboard). Figure 25 shows reconstituted panel consumption as a proportion of total solid wood product consumption from 1961 to 2000. This figure shows quite clearly that growth in the consumption of reconstituted panels has exceeded growth in the other components of this sector (sawnwood, plywood and veneer sheets) and that reconstituted panels have increased their share of the solid wood product market from around three percent in 1961 to 28 percent in 2000.

To some extent, reconstituted panels can substitute for sawnwood and plywood in many main end-uses (e.g. construction and furniture manufacturing). Therefore, it is likely that some of the growth in reconstituted panel consumption has come at the expense of sawnwood consumption. Given the different raw material requirements for reconstituted panels (as opposed to sawnwood, plywood and veneer sheets), this trend has had a profound impact on the demand for wood raw materials and is likely to continue to do so in the future.

In the paper and paperboard sector, substitution between the three different product categories is much more limited, so changes in the relative importance of each of them is due more to the different ways that they respond to changes in economic growth and other socio-economic variables.

Figure 26 shows the trend in consumption of paper and paperboard in Europe from 1961 to 2000 and the distribution of consumption across thee three main product categories. This figure shows that consumption of paper and paperboard has grown consistently over the last 40 years and at a relatively high rate of growth. It also shows the growing importance of printing and writing paper referred to earlier.

Figure 26   Trends in the consumption of paper and paperboard in Europe from 1961 to 2000

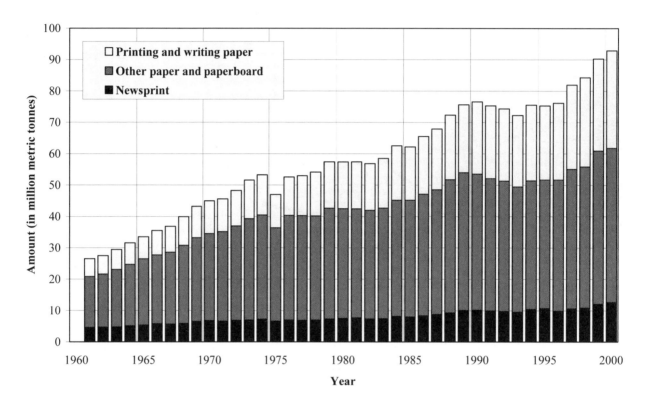

Source: derived from FAOSTAT production and trade statistics (http://faostat.external.fao.org). Note: totals for the Eastern Europe and CIS sub-regions before 1992 have been estimated from statistics for the USSR (see Section 1.4.2).

The figure above reflects the trends in Western Europe, because this sub-region accounts for the majority of paper and paperboard consumption in Europe. However, at the sub-regional level, the trends in the other two sub-regions are quite similar to this. The main difference is that consumption of other paper and paperboard is relatively more important in Eastern Europe and CIS countries, while consumption of printing and writing paper is less important. However, in the last decade, consumption of printing and writing paper in Eastern Europe has started to increase dramatically and the pattern of consumption in this sub-region is starting to look similar to that in Western Europe.

2.4   Production and consumption of raw materials and intermediate products

The materials used to manufacture processed wood products comprise a wide variety of raw materials, including industrial roundwood (in various forms) and recycled materials (such as wood residues and recovered paper). In addition, as part of the production of paper and paperboard, wood pulp is produced as an intermediate product, usually as part of an integrated pulp and papermaking operation. Although analyses of trends in forest products markets tend to focus mainly on the production and consumption of raw materials and processed products, it is also important to analyse the production and consumption of wood pulp, because there is significant international trade in this intermediate product.

Figure 27   The flow of raw materials and intermediate products in the forest processing sector

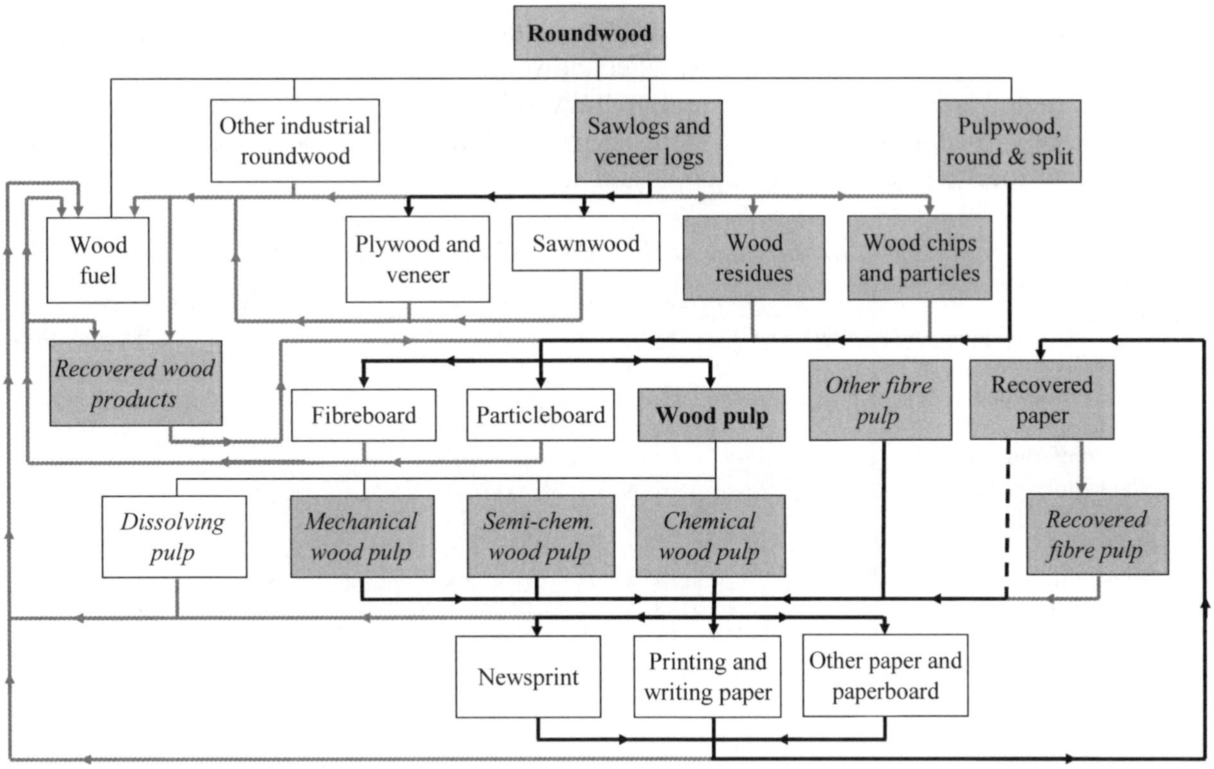

Note: raw materials and intermediate products are shown in shaded boxes. The thin lines represent disaggregation of a broader product category (shown in bold) into its components (e.g. wood pulp is further subdivided into four different types of wood pulp). The thick lines represent flows of materials through the system. The black lines represent flows where data is readily available, while the grey lines represent flows where information is less reliable. Product categories shown in italics are products that will not be included in the analysis due to lack of information or their relatively low importance. The flow of recovered paper back into the papermaking process is shown as a broken line, because this product is not used directly in the production of paper, but the statistics on recovered fibre pulp production are weak. It should also be noted that all of these products are traded internationally and that the flows into each box reflect the production of each product, while the flows out of each box represent consumption of each product. Thus, for example, it is possible for a country that imports a lot of paper, to produce more recovered paper than original paper production in that country.

The complexity of the flows of raw materials from the forest (and elsewhere) into the wood processing sector is shown in Figure 27. In this figure, raw materials and intermediate products are shown in shaded boxes. Due to the limitations of data, the analysis here focuses on three main raw materials and intermediate products, namely: industrial roundwood (which comprises sawlogs and veneer logs, pulpwood and other industrial roundwood); wood pulp (including the three main types of wood pulp used for papermaking) and recovered paper.

Wood residues and wood chips and particles[4] are very important components of the raw material supply in Europe, but information about the production of these materials has only been collected in recent years (see Table 5) and is very partial. An analysis of the utilisation of these materials will be presented in Section 2.5, where the wood raw material balance will be examined. Another source of raw materials for the wood processing sector is recovered wood products, but this is also excluded from the analysis here due to a lack of information.

---

[4]   It should be noted that the definition of wood chips and particles used for production now only includes the production of these materials from industry processing waste and does not include the production of wood chips and particles made from roundwood. The latter should be included as part of pulpwood, round and split. . In trade statistics, it is of course not possible to record the origin (forest or industry, even recovered wood) of the chips which cross a frontier.

2.4.1   Industrial roundwood

At the broadest level, roundwood is subdivided into industrial roundwood and wood fuel (which will be examined in a later section). Industrial roundwood is further subdivided into sawlogs and veneer logs, pulpwood and other industrial roundwood.[5] The first two subdivisions cover the roundwood that is used in the forest processing sector. Each of these product categories can also be subdivided into species groups (e.g. coniferous and non-coniferous).

Table 5   ***Availability of production and trade statistics for wood raw materials***

Product category	Production statistics			Trade statistics	
	1961 - 1991	1992 - 1997	1998 and after	1961 - 1989	1990 and after
Roundwood	x	x	x	x	x
Industrial roundwood	x	x	x	x	x
Coniferous	x	x	x		x
Non-coniferous tropical	n.a.	n.a.	n.a.		x
Non-coniferous other	x	x	x		x
Sawlogs and veneer logs	x	x	x	x	
Coniferous	x	x	x	x	
Non-coniferous	x	x	x	x	
Pulpwood and particles	x	x			
Coniferous	x	x			
Non-coniferous	x	x			
Pulpwood, round and split			x	x	
Coniferous			x		
Non-coniferous			x		
Other industrial roundwood	x	x	x	x	
Coniferous	x	x	x		
Non-coniferous	x	x	x		
Wood fuel	x	x	x	x	x
Coniferous	x	x	x		
Non-coniferous	x	x	x		
Other solid wood raw materials					
Chips and particles			x	x	x
Wood residues		x	x	x	x

Note: "x" indicates that statistics for a product category are available for a specific time period, "n.a." = not applicable. "Other solid wood raw materials" is not a standard definition, but is used here to indicate the sum of chips and particles plus wood residues.

Although statistics have been collected for many of the different subdivisions of industrial roundwood (e.g. product type and species group), there have been a number of changes in definitions over the last 40 years (see Table 5) that make it difficult to analyse the trends in individual components of industrial roundwood production and consumption. For example, production of pulpwood was combined with the production of wood particles (chips) until 1998, when these two products were clearly separated in production statistics. In particular, the changes in trade statistics (in 1990) - from subdivisions of industrial roundwood based on product type to subdivisions based on species groups - make it impossible to analyse consumption in any detail. Therefore, this section analyses trends in production and consumption of all industrial roundwood and trends in production (only) of the individual components of industrial roundwood.

---

[5]   Other industrial roundwood is roundwood that is used without further processing and includes products such as: utility poles; fence posts; and roundwood used in the mining industry as pit props.

Figure 28   Trends in production and consumption of industrial roundwood from 1961 to 2000

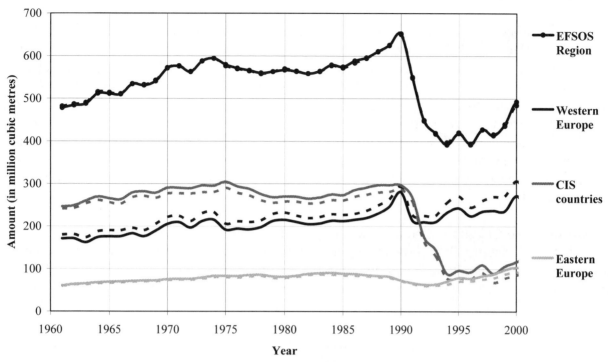

Solid lines represent production and dashed lines represent apparent consumption

Source: derived from FAOSTAT production and trade statistics (http://faostat.external.fao.org). Note: totals for the Eastern Europe and CIS sub-regions before 1992 have been estimated from statistics for the USSR (see Section 1.4.2).

The historical trend in production and consumption of industrial roundwood in Europe is shown in Figure 28. As the figure shows, production and consumption across the whole of Europe has been roughly in balance for the last 40 years, with differences between production and consumption generally amounting to no more than 5 million m^3 or around one percent of the total market size.

At the sub-regional level, Western Europe has always been a small net importer of industrial roundwood, while the CIS countries have always been small net exporters. However, this does not imply that all net exports from CIS countries were sent to Western Europe, because Western Europe imports a relatively small amount of tropical industrial roundwood and the CIS countries (notably the Russian Federation) also export industrial roundwood to Asia. Net imports into Western Europe have increased in recent years, with the majority of this increase coming from CIS countries and Eastern Europe (where production and consumption were in balance until the early 1990s).

Until 1990, the CIS sub-region accounted for about half of all production and consumption of industrial roundwood, Western Europe accounted for about 35 percent and Eastern Europe accounted for the remaining 15 percent. Since the economic changes in the early 1990s, the share of production and consumption in CIS countries has fallen dramatically, such that Western Europe now accounts for about 60 percent of European production and consumption, while the remaining 40 percent is divided roughly equally between the other two sub-regions.

The long-term trends in production and consumption in Western Europe show persistent and sustained growth over the last 40 years, with average annual growth in production of 0.9 percent (or an increase of about 1.8 million m^3) and growth in consumption of 1.0 percent per year (equal to about 2.4 million m^3). The trends in production and consumption have been fairly stable over the period, although there have been some sudden changes due to natural events (e.g. the sudden increase in production in 1990 due to the salvaging of storm-damaged roundwood). It also appears that the rate of growth may have increased slightly in more recent years, perhaps due to the maturation of forest plantations in some West European countries.

In Eastern Europe, the long-term trends in production and consumption match those in Western Europe, with growth of about one percent per year. However, as in other sectors, the trends in production and consumption of industrial roundwood in Eastern Europe display three distinctly different phases. Firstly, from 1960 to 1985, growth was stable but at a relatively modest rate of increase. From 1985 to 1992, production and consumption declined as these countries started the process of economic reform. Since 1992, production and consumption have grown much more rapidly, with annual growth in production of 5.7 percent (or an increase of about 4.6 million m^3) and growth in consumption of 5.2 percent per year (equal to about 3.8 million m^3). The industrial roundwood sector was the first part of the forest sector to recover in these countries and continues to grow very strongly.

The trends in the CIS sub-region are also similar to the trends in other parts of the forest sector in this sub-region. The trends in production and consumption were quite flat until 1990, when both production and consumption fell by two-thirds over the period 1990 to 1994. Since 1994, there appears to have been a modest recovery in industrial roundwood production but little growth in consumption, leading to an increase in net exports of industrial roundwood from the CIS sub-region.

For Europe as a whole, the trends in the overall composition of industrial roundwood production are shown in Figure 29. Currently, sawlogs and veneer logs account for about 55 percent of all industrial roundwood production (with coniferous sawlogs and veneer logs accounting for 45 percent of the total), pulpwood accounts for about 40 percent of production and other industrial roundwood accounts for the remaining five percent.

The trends in the composition of industrial roundwood production over the last 40 years are as follows. Firstly, the production of other industrial roundwood has declined significantly, both in relative and absolute terms. In 1960, other industrial roundwood production amounted to about 100 million m^3 per year or about 20 percent of total production. By 2000, it had declined to only 30 million m^3 per year. This decline is mostly due to the fall in production in the CIS sub-region, although production of other industrial roundwood has also declined in both of the other two sub-regions. These declines in production can probably be attributed, in some part, to the reduction in deep mining and the substitution of other devices for wooden pit props in most countries in the region.

In contrast, pulpwood production has increased dramatically over the period, both in relative and absolute terms. In 1960, annual production of pulpwood amounted to about 90 million m^3 or roughly 18 percent of total production: less pulpwood was produced than "other industrial wod" such as pitprops (a strategic material at the time). By the year 2000, this production had doubled to 180 million m^3, making this the fastest growing component of industrial roundwood production.

Coniferous sawlog and veneer log production accounts for the majority of sawlog and veneer log production in Europe and the trend in this sector largely reflects the trend in the CIS sub-region. Production of coniferous sawlogs and veneer logs in Europe increased slowly up until the early 1990s then fell by about one-third in the early 1990s. More recently, production in this sector has started to recover. In contrast, production of non-coniferous sawlogs and veneer logs has been fairly stable over the period, at around 50 million m^3 per year to 60 million m^3 per year over most of the period.

Figure 29   Trends in the composition of industrial roundwood production in Europe from 1961 to 2000

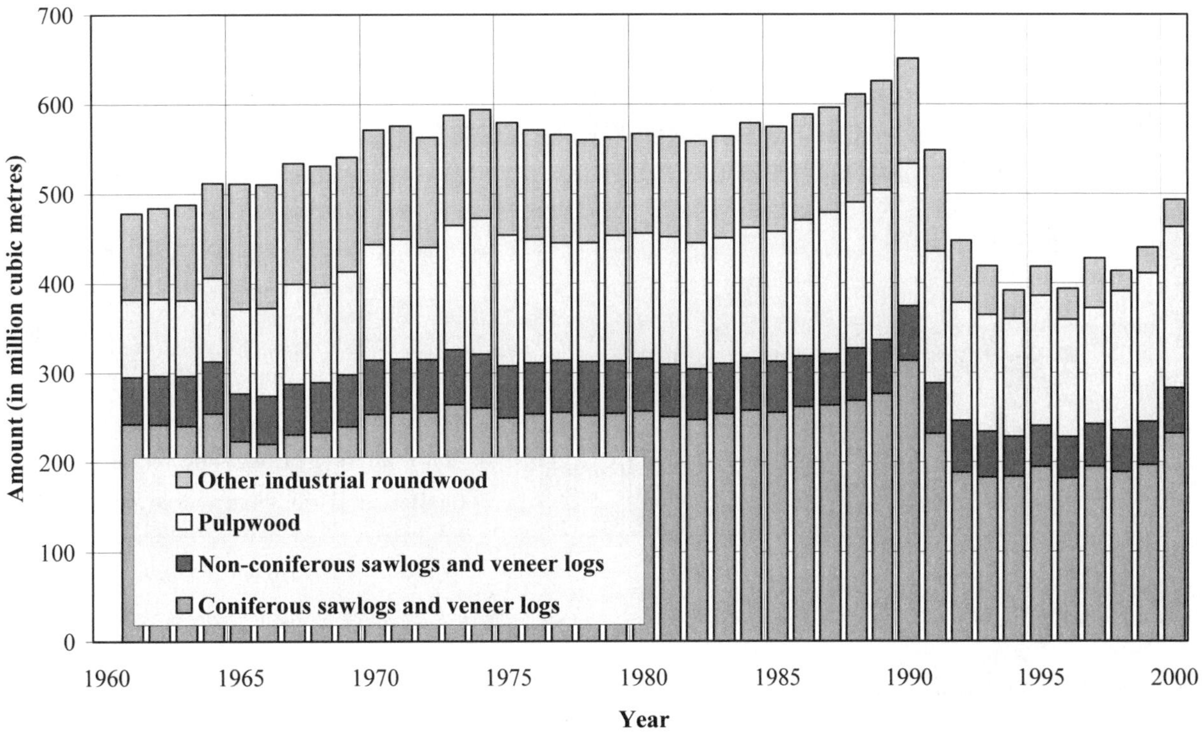

Source: derived from FAOSTAT production and trade statistics (http://faostat.external.fao.org). Note: totals for the Eastern Europe and CIS sub-regions before 1992 have been estimated from statistics for the USSR (see Section 1.4.2).

The figure above masks a number of subtle differences in the trends in industrial roundwood production in each of the three different European sub-regions, so the same information is presented and analysed for each of the three sub-regions below.

Figure 30 shows the trends in industrial roundwood production in Western Europe from 1961 to 2000. The first noticeable feature of this figure is that pulpwood production accounts for a significant share of total production, which is compatible with the forest management and harvesting practices that are common throughout most countries in this sub-region.

Figure 30 **Trends in the composition of industrial roundwood production in Western Europe from 1961 to 2000**

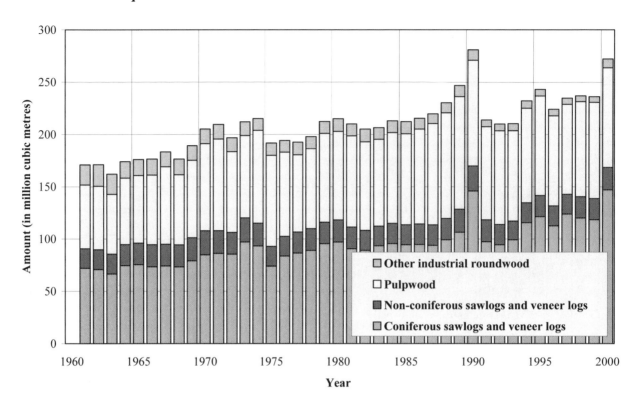

Source: derived from FAOSTAT production and trade statistics (http://faostat.external.fao.org).

In terms of growth, production of coniferous sawlogs and veneer logs has increased by about 1.5 percent per year, leading to a doubling of production over the period, from 72 million m^3 in 1960 to 147 million m^3 in 2000. Production of pulpwood has increased at a slightly lower rate of one percent per year, from 61 million m^3 in 1961 to 95 million m^3 in 2000. As noted above, production of non-coniferous sawlogs and veneer logs has remained roughly constant in Western Europe at around 20 million m^3 per year, while production of other industrial roundwood has fallen by about half from 19 million m^3 in 1960 to 8 million m^3 in 2000.

Figure 31 shows the trends in industrial roundwood production in the CIS sub-region from 1961 to 2000. In this region, it is noticeable that pulpwood production accounts for a much smaller share of total production, averaging about 16 percent of total production over the last four decades.

The figure shows that most of the fall in total production in the early 1990s was due to falls in production of coniferous roundwood and other industrial roundwood. Until 1990, coniferous industrial roundwood accounted for slightly over half of all industrial roundwood production, at around 140 million m^3 to 150 million m^3. From 1994 onwards, this has fallen to under 50 million m^3. Similarly, other industrial roundwood accounted for about 30 percent of total production until the early 1990s, since when it has only accounted for around 10 percent of total production.

Production of non-coniferous roundwood has always been less important in the CIS sub-region, accounting for about 10 percent of total production. Production of non-coniferous roundwood also fell in the early 1990s, but only by about 50 percent. In contrast to this, the importance of pulpwood production has actually increased in recent years in absolute and relative terms. In 1961, pulpwood production was around 17 million m^3 or seven percent of total production. The importance of pulpwood production increased gradually until 1990 then fell by about half until 1994. Since 1994, there has been a rapid increase in the production of pulpwood, which amounted to around 49 million m^3 or 42 percent of total production in 2000.

Figure 31   Trends in the composition of industrial roundwood production in the CIS sub-region from 1961 to 2000

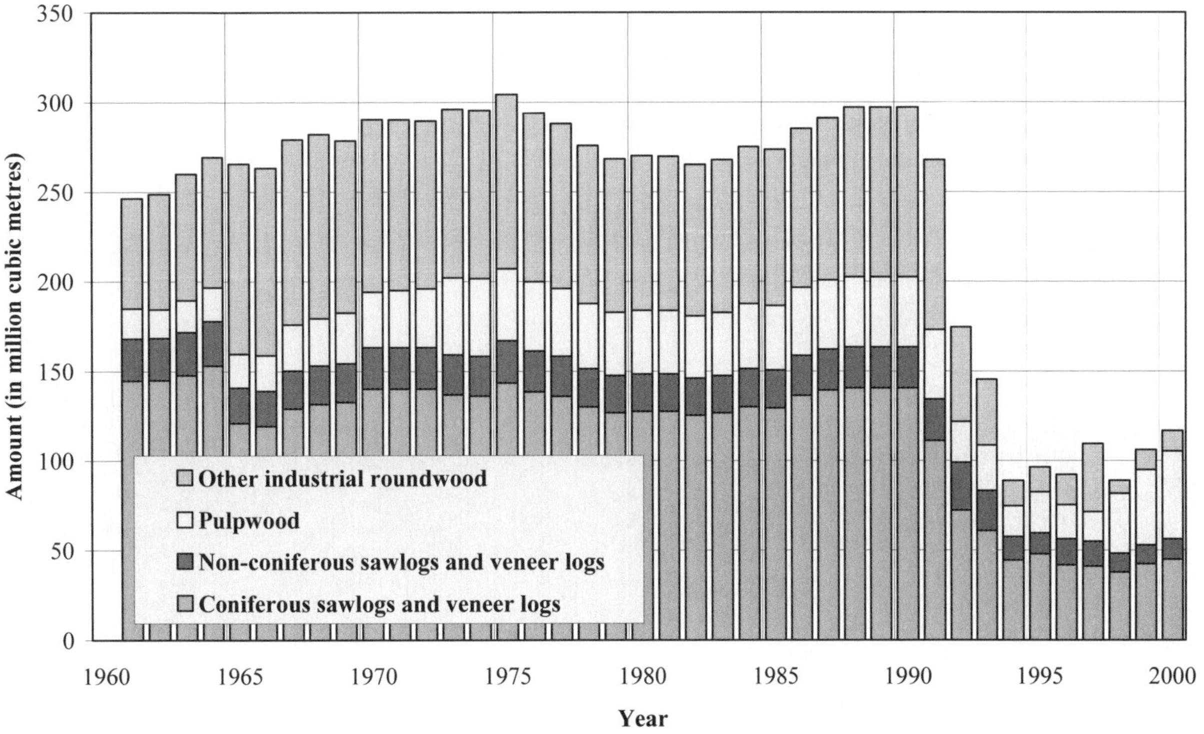

Source: derived from FAOSTAT production and trade statistics (http://faostat.external.fao.org). Note: totals for the CIS sub-region before 1992 have been estimated from statistics for the USSR (see Section 1.4.2).

Figure 32 shows the trends in industrial roundwood production in Eastern Europe from 1961 to 2000. Here, the most noticeable feature of these trends is how rapidly the production of industrial roundwood has recovered after the economic reforms of the early 1990s. To some extent, the increases in production at the end of the 1990s can be attributed to two countries, namely Estonia and Latvia.

Another feature of these trends is that the balance in production between sawlogs and veneer logs and pulpwood has shifted over the period from a greater emphasis on sawlog and veneer log production at the start of the period towards a higher proportion of pulpwood production in more recent years. Indeed, in 2000, pulpwood production amounted to 35 million m^3 (34 percent of total production), while coniferous sawlog and veneer log production amounted to 40 million m^3 (38 percent of total production).

In contrast to the other European sub-regions, the production of non-coniferous roundwood has also increased over the period, from 10 million m^3 (17 percent of the total) in 1960 to 19 million m^3 (18 percent of the total) in 2000. However, as in the other sub-regions, the importance of other industrial roundwood has declined, from 15 million m^3 (25 percent of the total) in 1960 to 10 million m^3 (10 percent of the total) in 2000.

Figure 32   ***Trends in the composition of industrial roundwood production in Eastern Europe from 1961 to 2000***

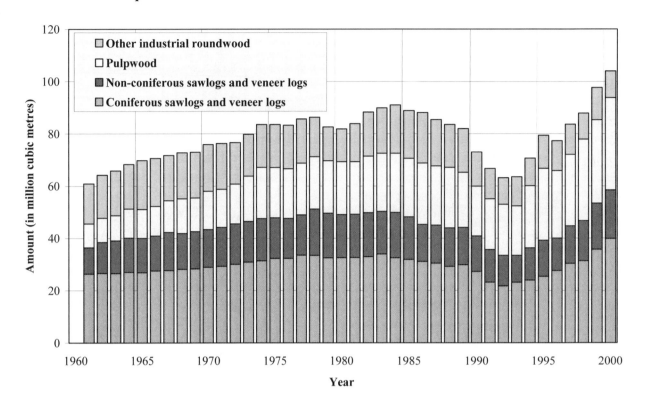

Source: derived from FAOSTAT production and trade statistics (http://faostat.external.fao.org). Note: totals for Eastern Europe before 1992 have been estimated from statistics for the USSR (see Section 1.4.2).

2.4.2   Wood and other fibre pulp

The total production of wood pulp encompasses the production of a number of different types of wood pulp with different properties and characteristics. These are blended in the papermaking process to produce different types, grades and qualities of paper. In addition, some types of wood pulp are not used for papermaking and, conversely, some other types of pulp are used to make paper. At the broadest level, wood pulp can be divided into four main types: dissolving wood pulp; mechanical wood pulp; semi-chemical wood pulp; and chemical wood pulp. The latter three are used for papermaking. In addition, other fibre pulp (made from non-wood fibres such as grasses, agricultural waste and cotton) is used to produce some types of paper.

Figure 33 shows the historical trend in production and consumption of wood pulp in Europe from 1961 to 2000. As the figure shows, consumption has always exceeded production in Europe (leading to net imports into the region) and this difference has increased throughout the last four decades. Western Europe accounts for most of these net imports, accounting for 80 percent of total production and 84 percent of total consumption in the region and net imports of over 6 million MT in 2000. Eastern Europe is a very small net importer of wood pulp, with production of 3.4 million MT and consumption of 4.1 million MT in 2000. The CIS sub-region is a very small net exporter, with production of 5.9 million MT and consumption of 4.4 million MT in 2000.

The significance of these trends is that, although Europe is not a major importer of industrial roundwood, a proportion of the wood fibre used to manufacture forest products in Europe is imported in the form of wood pulp.

Figure 33   ***Trends in production and consumption of total wood pulp from 1961 to 2000***

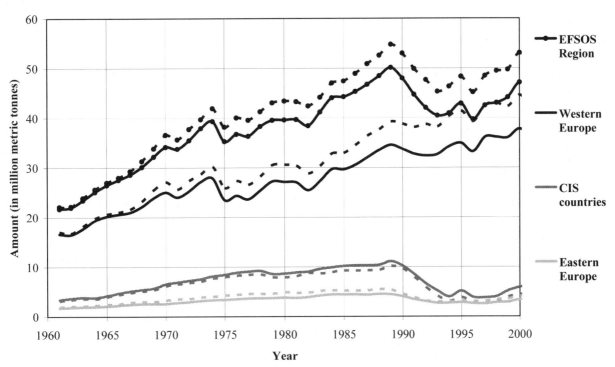

Solid lines represent production and dashed lines represent apparent consumption

Source: derived from FAOSTAT production and trade statistics (http://faostat.external.fao.org). Note: totals for the Eastern Europe and CIS sub-regions before 1992 have been estimated from statistics for the USSR (see Section 1.4.2).

At the regional level, production and consumption increased over the period 1961 to 1989, but have not shown a sustained positive growth trend since then. However, this is largely due to recent declines in production and consumption in Eastern Europe and the CIS sub-region offsetting continued growth in Western Europe.

In Western Europe, production and consumption of wood pulp has growth consistently over the last four decades, with average annual growth rates of 1.8 percent for production (900,000 MT) and 2.2 percent for consumption (1 million MT). Thus, production has doubled over the last four decades and consumption has more than doubled. Visual inspection of Figure 33 suggests that the trend in production growth may have declined very slightly over the last decade, but the trend in consumption growth does not appear to have changed.

In Eastern Europe, production and consumption grew at much more modest growth rates from 1961 to 1990, at around one percent per year. From 1990 to 1994, production and consumption fell by around half, but both have since recovered to the levels of 1990. Considering the trends in pulpwood production shown above, there are certainly sufficient raw material supplies to maintain a high rate of growth in wood pulp production in the future, although much will depend on the cost-competitiveness of wood pulp production in this sub-region and the competition for this small sized roundwood from other sectors.

In the CIS sub-region, there was very strong growth in production and consumption of wood pulp from 1961 to 1989, with both growing at around four percent per year. In the early 1990s, both production and consumption fell by around two-thirds. Since 1994, production has returned to a high growth rate of 6.2 percent per year, but consumption has not increased at all.

The trends in total pulp production and consumption are largely determined by the two most important types of pulp, which are mechanical wood pulp and chemical wood pulp. Production and consumption of dissolving wood pulp and other fibre pulp have never been very important and have declined over the last four decades to less than one million MT in 2000. In simple terms, the wood fibre that is used to make dissolving wood pulp (and thus, does not go into papermaking) is replaced by the other fibres (from outside the forest sector) used to make other fibre pulp. Similarly, the semi-chemical wood pulp sector is quite insignificant, accounting for less than five percent of wood pulp production and less than five percent of the pulp used to make paper. Europe is a small net importer of semi-chemical wood pulp, but production and consumption of this product have been constant at around two million MT since 1970. Thus, the trends in these three product categories have almost no impact on the raw material balance within the forest sector.

Figure 34   ***Trends in production and consumption of mechanical wood pulp from 1961 to 2000***

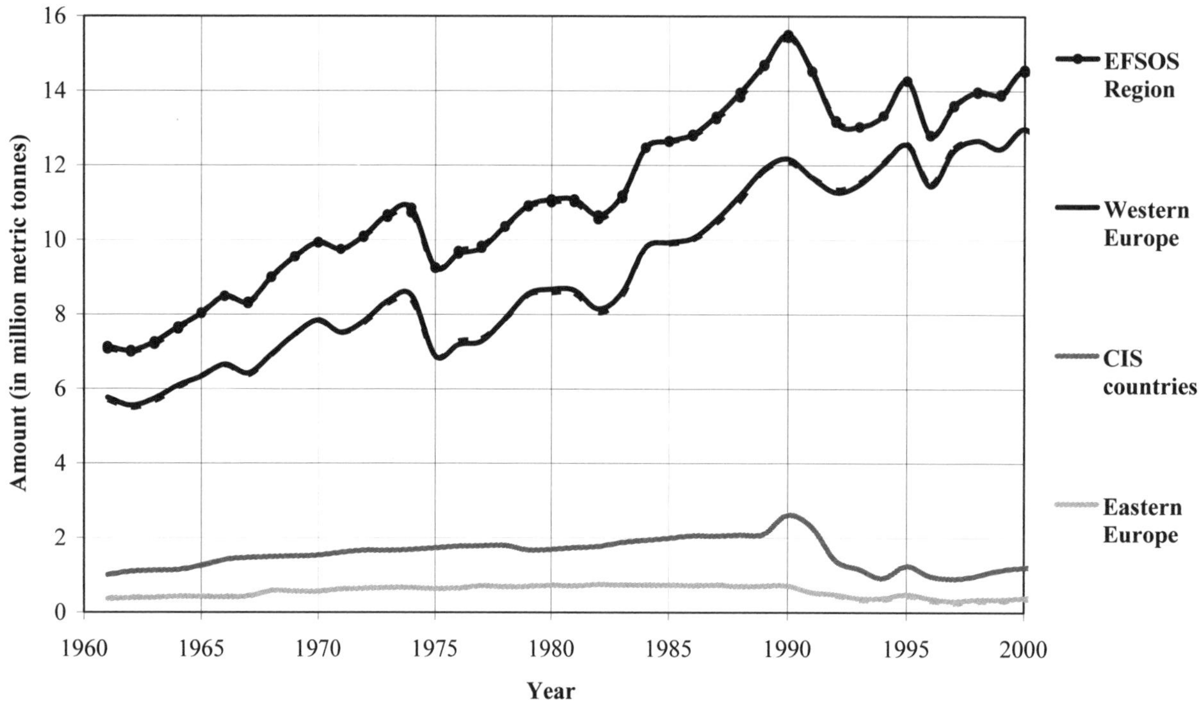

Solid lines represent production and dashed lines represent apparent consumption

Source: derived from FAOSTAT production and trade statistics (http://faostat.external.fao.org). Note: totals for the Eastern Europe and CIS sub-regions before 1992 have been estimated from statistics for the USSR (see Section 1.4.2).

The trends in the production and consumption of mechanical wood pulp in Europe are shown in Figure 34. This shows that production and consumption in Europe have always been roughly in balance. It also shows that Western Europe accounts for the majority of production and consumption (around 90 percent). In Europe as a whole, the same trend as before is visible, with strong growth until 1990, then no visible upward growth trend thereafter. As before, this is due to declines in the CIS and Eastern Europe sub-regions offsetting continued upward growth in Western Europe.

In Western Europe, production and consumption of mechanical wood pulp have grown by 2.1 percent per year on average (equal to an increase of about 200,000 MT per year) since 1961. Again, it appears that growth may have reduced significantly over the last decade. There has been almost no growth in this sector in Eastern Europe. In the CIS sub-region, growth in production and consumption matched that in Western Europe until 1990, but production and consumption have not recovered since the fall of 50 percent in the early 1990s.

Figure 35   Trends in production and consumption of chemical wood pulp from 1961 to 2000

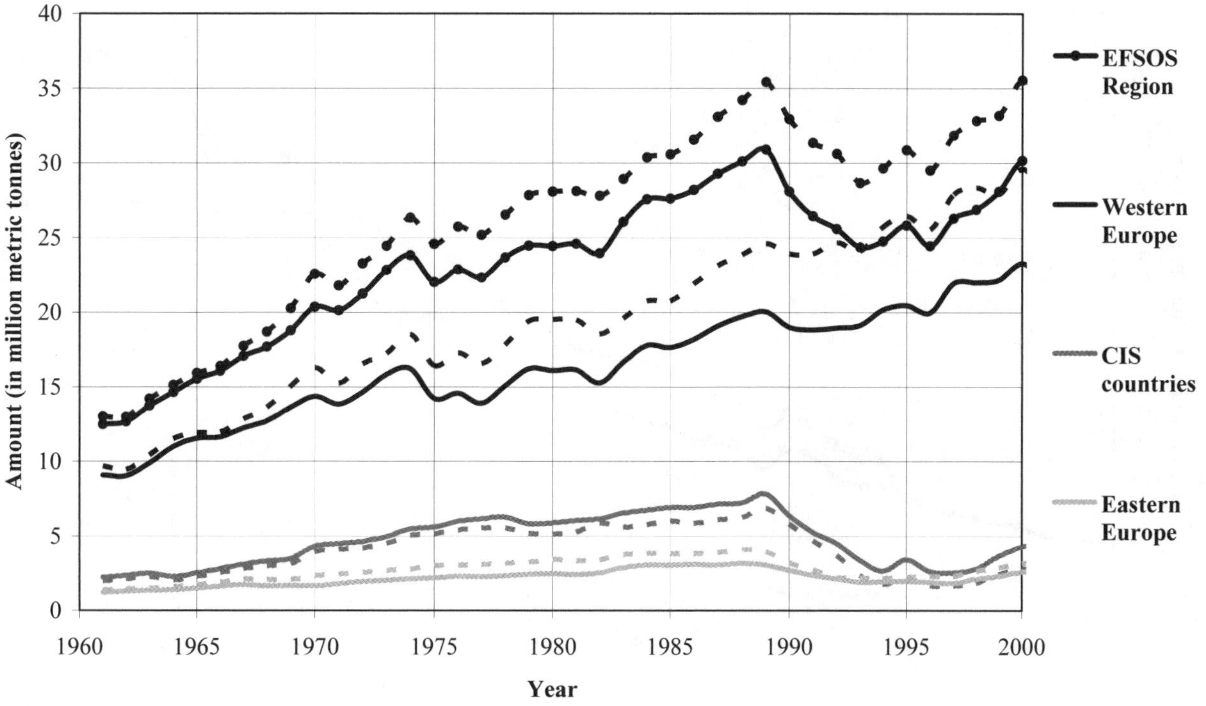

Solid lines represent production and dashed lines represent apparent consumption

Source: derived from FAOSTAT production and trade statistics (http://faostat.external.fao.org). Note: totals for the Eastern Europe and CIS sub-regions before 1992 have been estimated from statistics for the USSR (see Section 1.4.2).

The trends for chemical wood pulp production and consumption are shown in Figure 35. This is by far the largest component of total wood pulp production and consumption and this product is largely responsible for the net imports of wood pulp into Europe. Again, Western Europe accounts for the majority of production and consumption of this product, with a 77 percent share of total European production and an 83 percent share of consumption.

In Western Europe, production has increased by 2.0 percent per year (about 400,000 MT) or more than doubled from 1961 to 2000. Consumption has increased by 2.5 percent (about 500,000 MT), leading to a trebling of consumption over the same period. In contrast to mechanical pulp, these strong growth trends have continued throughout the whole of the period.

These differences in production and consumption growth have led to the situation where net imports now account for 20 percent of consumption in Western Europe (or about 6 million MT), with an increase in net imports of around 100,000 MT every year.

The trends for Eastern Europe and the CIS sub-region are similar to those described previously, with very little growth in Eastern Europe and strong growth followed by collapse in the CIS sub-region. However, growth in production and consumption in both of these sub-regions appears to have recovered somewhat in recent years.

2.4.3   Recovered paper

The other major source of fibre used for papermaking is recovered or recycled paper and the trends in production and consumption of this product are shown in Figure 36.

Figure 36   ***Trends in production and consumption of recovered paper from 1961 to 2000***

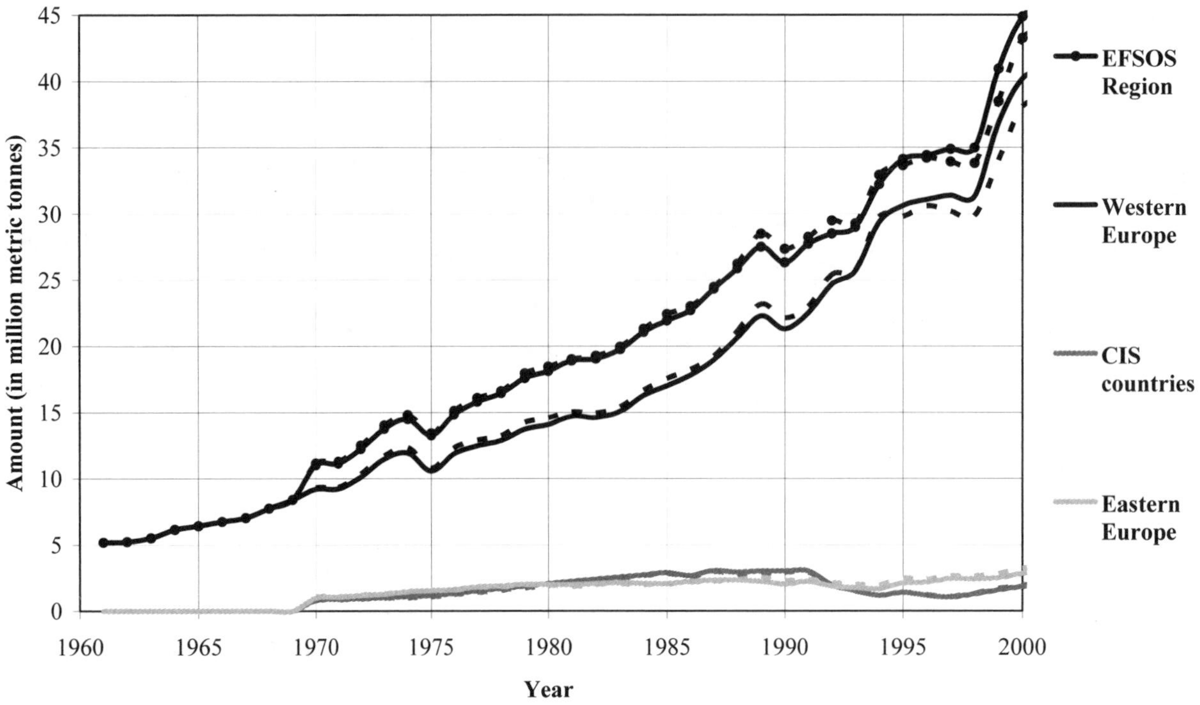

Solid lines represent production and dashed lines represent apparent consumption

Source: derived from FAOSTAT production and trade statistics (http://faostat.external.fao.org). Note: totals for the Eastern Europe and CIS sub-regions before 1992 have been estimated from statistics for the USSR (see Section 1.4.2).

This figure shows that, of all the sources of fibre used for papermaking, recovered paper is the largest (by weight) and has increased the most over the last 40 years. However, high levels of collection and utilisation of recovered paper only exist in Western Europe (which accounts for around 90 percent of production and consumption in Europe as a whole). In the other two sub-regions, the relative importance of recovered paper is much less and the papermaking industry in these countries still relies largely on wood pulp for their raw material needs.

In Western Europe, production and consumption of recovered paper have increased by around five percent on average each year. Production has increased by slightly more than consumption in the last five years, resulting in a very small amount of net exports of recovered paper. In addition, it appears that growth in production and consumption of recovered paper may have increased very slightly over the last decade.

In Eastern Europe and the CIS sub-region, statistics on recovered paper are only available from 1970 onwards. Since 1970, production of recovered paper increased by 2.3 percent per year in Eastern Europe and consumption increased by 2.8 percent. This growth has been sustained over the period and was not affected very much by the economic changes in the early 1990s. In the CIS sub-region, growth was slightly higher, but both production and consumption fell by half in the early 1990s. However, since 1995, production and consumption appear to have returned to their previous growth rates of around three percent per year.

2.5   Technology and the raw material balance

The two previous sections have described the trends in the production and consumption of processed forest products (i.e. the outputs of the processing sector) and the raw materials and intermediate products used to produce them (i.e. the inputs to the processing sector). These two major components of the forest sector are linked through the processing technologies that are used to convert the latter into the former.

The raw material balance compares the derived demand for inputs to the processing sector with the production of those inputs. It can be used to show how changes in the markets for outputs lead to changes in the derived demand for inputs and how the mixture of inputs has altered over time due to these changes and changes in resource availability. It can also be used to show how changes in technology have altered the relationship between inputs and outputs in the past, or to explore the effect of such changes in the future.

The following text examines the trends in the raw material balance in Europe over the last 40 years. It starts with a brief discussion of processing technology and the impact of changes in technology on the raw material balance. It then presents the derived demand for inputs, based on the production of processed forest products in Europe and expressed in WRME. Finally, the production and consumption of inputs is compared with the derived demand for inputs, showing how the importance of different types of input has changed over time.

2.5.1   Forest product processing technology, conversion factors and recycling

Improvements in technology can have a significant impact on the sustainability and economic viability of the forest sector. Technology affects all stages of the production chain, from the forest to the end-user. Thus, for example, there can be technological improvements in tree breeding, silviculture, harvesting, processing, or in the utilisation of the final product. Technological improvements can also benefit the sector in different ways, such as: reducing costs or labour inputs; increasing the amount or value of product that can be made from a given level of inputs; altering the composition of required inputs from high-cost to low-cost sources; or expanding the range of products that can be made from wood.

Improvements in all of these areas have probably occurred in the forest sector in most European countries over the last 40 years. However, the analysis here will focus on two main aspects of technological change in the sector, notably changes in the conversion factors (amount of wood raw material required to produce one unit of output) and changes in the composition of inputs used in the sector.

FAO-UNECE surveys of conversion factors in Europe were stopped in the mid-1980s, due to the difficulties of collecting this information. Therefore, it is not possible to examine trends in conversion factors directly. However, it is possible to examine the conversion factors for some products indirectly, by comparing the trends in raw material consumption and processed product production.

Figure 37 shows the trends in product recovery for sawnwood and plywood production in Europe from 1961 to 1989. These were calculated by dividing sawnwood and plywood production by the apparent consumption of sawlogs and veneer logs in each year of the period. The trends shown in the figure stop at 1989, because sawlogs and veneer logs are not identified in international trade statistics after this year (and, hence, apparent consumption could not be calculated).

Firstly, the figure shows one of the problems with this approach to estimating conversion factors. The sudden increase in product recovery in the CIS sub-region in 1965 occurs because a greater share of industrial roundwood production was suddenly classified as "other industrial roundwood" rather than "sawlogs and veneer logs" in that year, but sawnwood and plywood production (and industrial roundwood trade) did not change by very much. Given this sudden unexplained shift, it seems likely that the figures for the CIS sub-region are not a very reliable indicator of the trend or level of product recovery (although the figures from the 1980s seem more reasonable).

Figure 37   Trends in product recovery in the sawnwood and plywood sectors from 1961 to 2000

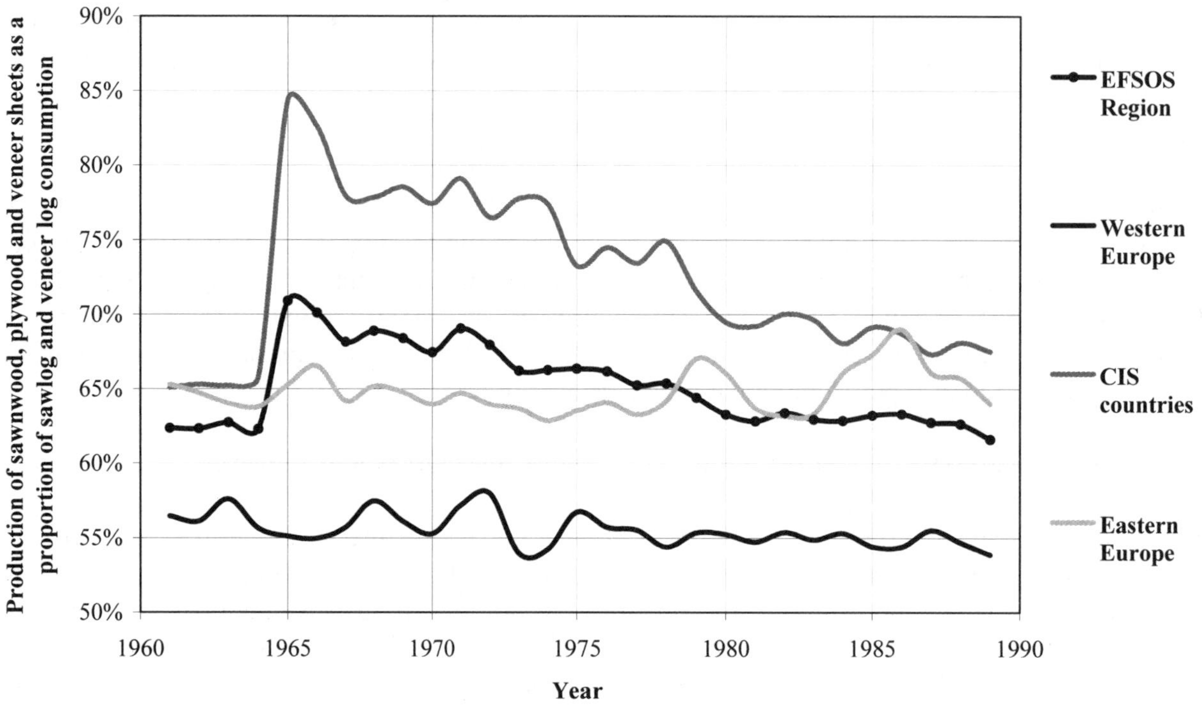

Source: derived from FAOSTAT production and trade statistics (http://faostat.external.fao.org). Note: totals for the Eastern Europe and CIS sub-regions before 1992 have been estimated from statistics for the USSR (see Section 1.4.2).

For Western and Eastern Europe the trends look more plausible. In Western Europe, the trend shows that product recovery has stayed roughly the same or, maybe, declined slightly over the period. Although this might suggest that technology has not led to any improvements in product recovery, it should be noted that the average size (i.e. diameter) of logs used in the sawnwood and plywood sectors has probably fallen over the same period, due to a reduction in the rotation ages commonly used in intensively managed forests and an increase in the proportion of wood production coming from intensively managed forests (as opposed to more "natural" forests). Thus, it is likely that there have been technological improvements, but that the benefits of these changes have resulted in a lowering in the quality (i.e. size) of logs required by the industry rather than an increase in product recovery. Similarly, it appears that product recovery in Eastern Europe has not changed over the period, possibly for the same reasons explained above.

Comparing between the sub-regions, product recovery in the late 1980s was 54 percent in Western Europe, 68 percent in the CIS sub-region and 64 percent in Eastern Europe (and 62 percent for Europe as a whole). Alternatively, these figures can be expressed as the amount of wood raw material input required to produce one unit of output, to give the figures: 1.86; 1.48; 1.56; and 1.62 respectively.

The relatively low product recovery rate in Western Europe is probably due to the relatively small log size. This reflects the predominance of production from Nordic countries in this sub-region and the relatively high share of production from forest plantations in the total. Relatively small log sizes might be expected in the Nordic countries (where trees grow slowly) and from forest plantations (where investment costs tend to encourage early clear-felling).

Until recently, forest management in Eastern Europe tended to favour longer rotation ages and less intensive management, which would tend to result in larger log sizes at the time of harvesting. Although technology in the processing sector is likely to be behind that in Western Europe, larger average log sizes would offset this effect and could explain the relatively higher rates of product recovery in this sub-region. The same reasoning could apply to the CIS sub-region, where harvesting in natural or "old-growth" forests would probably result in relatively large log sizes.

Unfortunately it is not possible to perform this type of analysis for pulpwood, because pulpwood is used to manufacture a range of very different products (reconstituted panels, pulp and paper) and other non-forest materials are used in the production of these products. However, there have been technological advances in these industries over the last 40 years that have probably led to improvements in product recovery (e.g. the development of closed-cycle pulping technology).

In the reconstituted panel and pulp and paper industries, a more important technological development over the last 40 years has been the increased use of residues and recycled materials in the production process. These non-forest sources of raw materials reduce the dependence of the industry on pulpwood and enable the same piece of wood or fibre to be used several times over. Implicitly, this increases product recovery (in terms of the pulpwood needed to produce a given amount of product) and increases the sustainability of production.

Information about the production of residues has only been collected recently and the available statistics are still partial and probably unreliable. However, statistics about wastepaper recovery are available from the early 1960s for Western Europe and from 1970 for the rest of Europe and they have been used to produce Figure 38. This shows the rate of wastepaper recovery in Europe, calculated as the production of recovered paper (i.e. the amount of wastepaper recovered) divided by total paper and paperboard consumption.

For Europe as a whole, wastepaper recovery has increased from around 25 percent of consumption in 1970 to just under 50 percent of consumption in 2000. In particular, there has been a more rapid increase in the recovery of wastepaper in the last ten years compared with the earlier part of the period. This can be attributed to environmental (i.e. recycling) policies introduced in many countries in the 1990s, which have subsidised and encouraged the collection and re-use of wastepaper.

The trend in wastepaper recovery in Western Europe accounts for most of the trend for the region as a whole, due to the size of the paper market in this sub-region. In Western Europe, wastepaper recovery remained at around 25 percent for most of the 1960s and then gradually increased to 35 percent in 1990. In the last decade it has increased to reach over 50 percent by the year 2000. The high level of wastepaper recovery in Western Europe is no doubt due to the environmental policies in this sub-region, but it also reflects the huge demand for wastepaper from the paper industry in this sub-region. Thus the expansion of waste paper use is both due to "supply push" (by environment policies and other policy encouragements) and "demand pull" (recovered fibre is a cheap raw material, increasingly acceptable for a wide variety of technical uses)

In Eastern Europe, wastepaper recovery increased slightly in the 1970s, but has remained at between 30 percent and 35 percent for most of the last 20 years. This lower level of wastepaper recovery probably reflects the relatively low level of demand for wastepaper in this sub-region, due to the quite small number of pulp mills there.

The trend for wastepaper recovery in the CIS sub-region is most interesting of all. It shows that wastepaper recovery increased from less than 15 percent in 1970 to around 30 percent in the late 1980s. Since 1990, it has increased significantly to reach about 42 percent in 2000. This increase has occurred because, while the consumption of paper in this sub-region has declined dramatically over the last decade (by about three-quarters), the production of recovered paper has fallen by much less than this. This suggests that the demand for wastepaper from pulp mills has not been strongly affected by the decline in domestic consumption. Given the general economic downturn in this sub-region, it also implies that the business of collecting wastepaper has remained quite attractive, possibly due to the relatively low capital costs generally required in the recycling sector.

Figure 38   Trends in wastepaper recovery 1961 to 2000

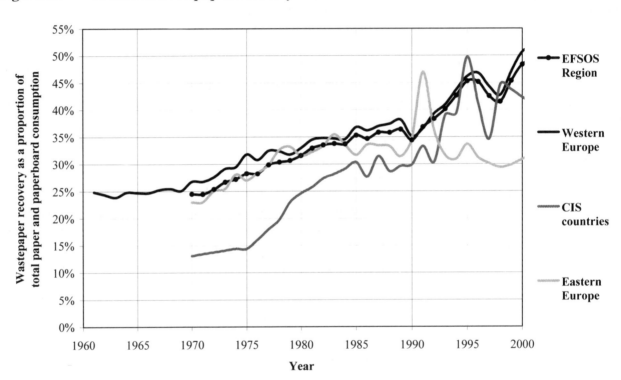

Source: derived from FAOSTAT production and trade statistics (http://faostat.external.fao.org). Note: totals for the Eastern Europe and CIS sub-regions before 1992 have been estimated from statistics for the USSR (see Section 1.4.2).

There is a limit to the proportion of paper and paperboard consumption that can be recycled. This is because certain types of paper (e.g. household and sanitary papers) are not easy to collect. However, it appears that this limit has not been reached yet, although it must be near in some countries, such as the Netherlands which has an urban, environmentally aware population, and supportive policies in place. Furthermore, with the increasing importance of printing and writing papers and packaging materials in total paper and paperboard consumption, it seems likely that wastepaper recovery could continue to increase in future years.

Another factor that limits the potential for wastepaper recovery is the degree of urbanisation in a country. With higher rates of urbanisation, the costs of wastepaper recovery are generally lower and higher rates of recovery can usually be achieved. This analysis shows that there is considerable scope to increase wastepaper recovery in Eastern Europe and this may be supported by the gradual economic development and urbanisation that is expected to take place in some of these countries in the future.

2.5.2   Wood raw material demand by sector

The total wood raw material demand in Europe has been calculated by multiplying the production of processed forest products in different sectors by the amount of wood required to produce those products (WRME). The conversion factors used to convert from the amount of production to the amount of wood required were based on the results of the last FAO-UNECE conversion factor survey (in the mid-1980s), supplemented by other information (e.g. the results of the analysis shown in Figure 37 and reference sources such as Ollmann, 2001). The range of conversion factors used for each country in the analysis is shown in Table 6, by product and sub-region.

Table 6   Conversion factors used in the wood raw material balance analysis

Product	Sub-region		
	Western Europe	**Eastern Europe**	**CIS**
Coniferous sawnwood	1.42 - 2.10	1.50 - 2.00	1.60 - 2.00
Non-coniferous sawnwood	1.46 - 3.52	1.40 - 2.10	1.45 - 2.00
Particleboard	1.20 - 1.80	1.40 - 1.80	1.40 - 1.60
Fibreboard	1.50 - 1.94	1.80 - 3.30	2.80 - 3.00
Plywood	1.50 - 3.10	1.80 - 2.90	2.50 - 2.70
Veneer sheets	1.20 - 3.10	1.70 - 2.90	2.00 - 2.90
Mechanical pulp	2.16 - 2.60	1.20 - 2.90	1.20 - 2.50
Chemical pulp	4.48 - 4.70	4.50 - 6.40	4.48 - 5.21
Semi-chemical pulp	2.20 - 2.90	2.30 - 3.20	2.86 - 2.90
Newsprint	3.20	3.20	3.50
Printing and writing paper	4.00	4.00	4.20
Other paper and paperboard	3.39 - 3.40	3.40 - 4.70	3.80
Recovered paper	3.80	3.80	3.80

Note: the above conversion factors show the amount of industrial roundwood (cubic metres underbark) required to produce one unit of output (one metric tonne of pulp or paper or one cubic metre of sawnwood or panels).

The above factors were then applied to the production statistics for every country in Europe from 1961 to 2000. It should be noted that this does not take into account the possibility of changes in the conversion factors over the period. If product recovery has increased over the last 40 years (due to improvements in technology), this would suggest that any increases in wood raw material requirements shown in these trends are over-stated. It should also be noted that these figures present a very "gross" figure for wood raw material demand, because they do not take into account the fact that wood may be re-used several times.

The trends produced in this analysis are shown in Figure 39. This shows how much wood and fibre would have been required over the last four decades to supply the European forest processing sector. It also shows how this has varied across the different components of the forest processing sector.[6]

---

[6]   Note that, for pulp trade, countries have been divided into two groups for each year: net exporters and net importers. The wood required to produce net pulp exports is shown here only for those countries that are net pulp exporters. For the countries that are net importers of pulp, the wood raw material equivalents of these imports are shown in the later figures (i.e. as a source of fibre rather than a demand for fibre).

Figure 39   Trends in wood raw material demand in Europe from 1961 to 2000

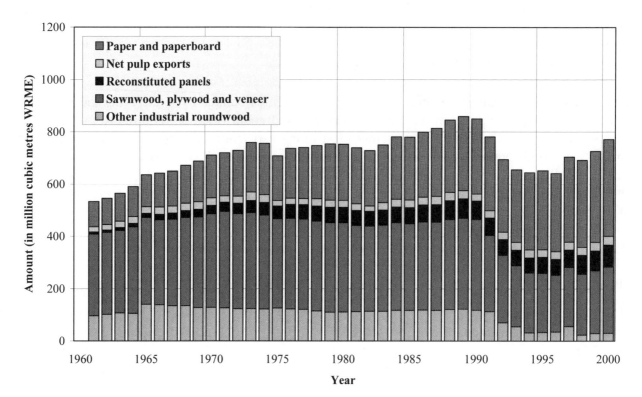

Source: derived from FAOSTAT production and trade statistics (http://faostat.external.fao.org). Note: totals for the Eastern Europe and CIS sub-regions before 1992 have been estimated from statistics for the USSR (see Section 1.4.2).

Figure 39 shows that total wood and fibre consumption in Europe has increased from 534 million m³ WRME in 1961 to 771 million m³ WRME in 2000, giving a total increase in consumption of around 45 percent (or 0.9 percent per year).

It also shows that the structure of wood and fibre demand has changed. In 1961, the production of other industrial roundwood, sawnwood, plywood and veneer sheets accounted for 77 percent of total wood and fibre demand. By the year 2000, these same products accounted for only 37 percent of total demand. For the other forest products, demand for wood from the reconstituted panels sector has increased almost ten times over the period (or 6.2 percent per year), while demand for net pulp exports and paper and paperboard production has increased by 67 percent and 282 percent (equal to 1.3 percent per year and 3.5 percent per year) respectively.

As before, the trends for the three sub-regions of Europe are quite different compared to the trends for Europe as a whole, so the trends for Western Europe, the CIS sub-region and Eastern Europe are shown in Figure 40 to Figure 42.

Figure 40   **Trends in wood raw material demand in Western Europe from 1961 to 2000**

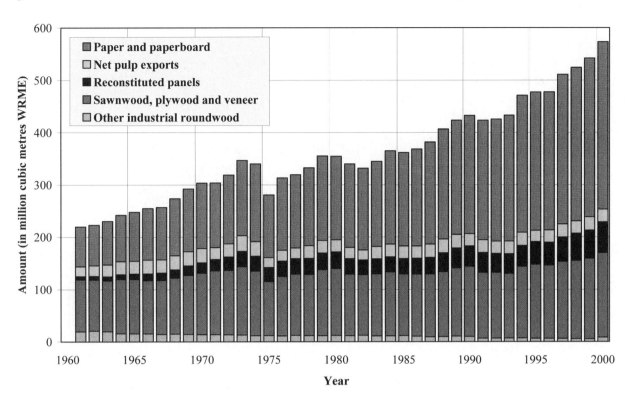

Source: derived from FAOSTAT production and trade statistics (http://faostat.external.fao.org).

In Western Europe, wood and fibre demand has increased almost three-fold over the last four decades, from 220 million m³ WRME in 1961 to 575 million m³ WRME in 2000. As Figure 40 clearly shows, most of this increase has occurred in the reconstituted panels and paper and paperboard sectors. Consumption of wood by the reconstituted panels sector has increased from 6 million m³ WRME to 76 million m³ WRME (equal to average annual growth of 6.0 percent). Similarly, consumption of wood and fibre for paper and paperboard production has increased from 60 million m³ WRME to 320 million m³ WRME over the same period (or 3.8 percent per year). In contrast, the demand for sawlogs and other industrial roundwood has only increased by about 0.9 percent per year, from 119 million m³ WRME in 1961 to 170 million m³ WRME in 2000.

Figure 41   Trends in wood raw material demand in the CIS sub-region from 1961 to 2000

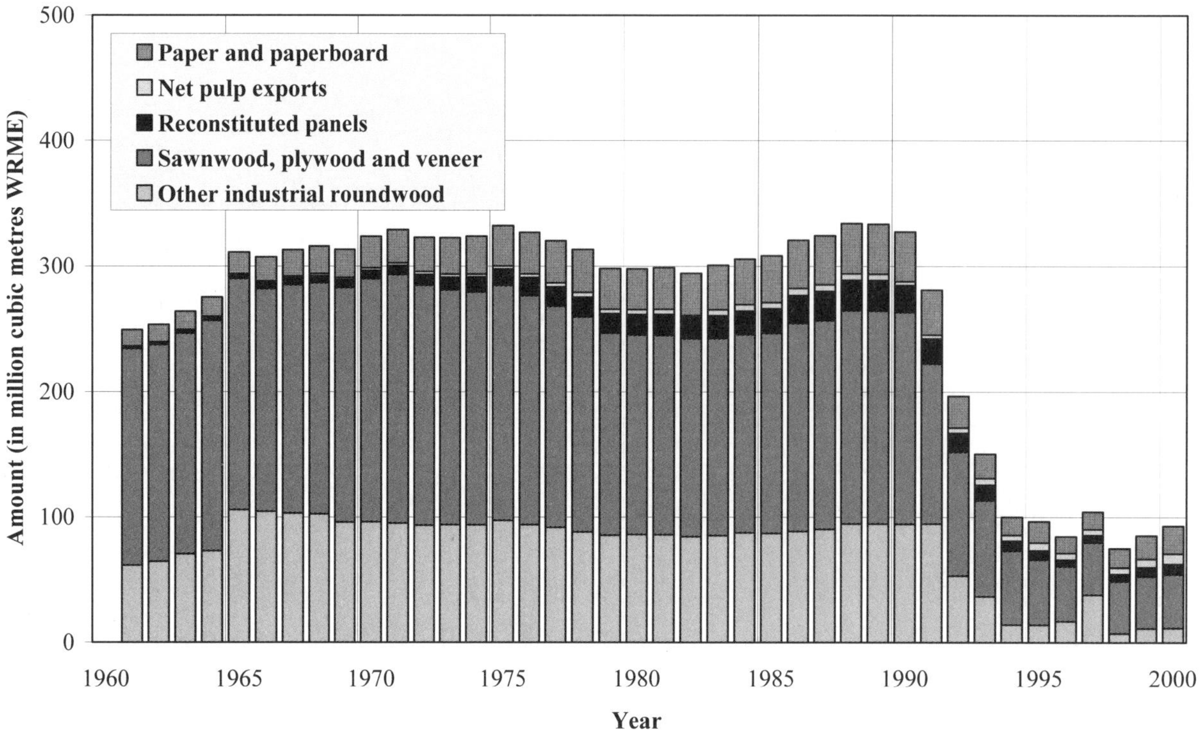

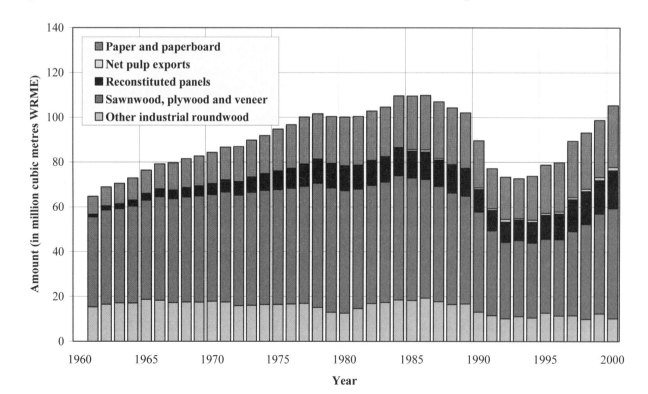

Source: derived from FAOSTAT production and trade statistics (http://faostat.external.fao.org). Note: totals for the CIS sub-region before 1992 have been estimated from statistics for the USSR (see Section 1.4.2).

Figure 42   Trends in wood raw material demand in Eastern Europe from 1961 to 2000

Source: derived from FAOSTAT production and trade statistics (http://faostat.external.fao.org). Note: totals for Eastern Europe before 1992 have been estimated from statistics for the USSR (see Section 1.4.2).

In the CIS sub-region, the total demand for wood and fibre remained relatively static over the period 1965 to 1990 at around 300 million m³ WRME and then fell by about two-thirds in the early-1990s to under 100 million m³ WRME. Since then, there has been no increase in total wood and fibre demand.

The demand for wood and fibre in this sub-region has always been heavily concentrated on the production of other industrial roundwood, sawnwood, plywood and veneer sheets. However, the dominance of these sectors has fallen, as they now account for only 58 percent of total wood raw material demand compared with 95 percent in 1961. Since the economic disruptions of the early-1990s, only the pulp and paper sectors have shown some recovery in production. They now account for around 30 million m³ WRME or one-third of the total wood and fibre demand of 91 million m³ WRME in 2000.

In Eastern Europe, the trend in wood raw material demand follows the pattern of growth, collapse and recovery demonstrated in the trends in processed product markets. Staring from total wood and fibre demand of 65 million m³ WRME in 1961, demand increased to 110 million m³ WRME in 1986, fell by about one-third in the early-1990s and has since recovered to about 105 million m³ WRME in 2000. Almost all of this variation can be attributed to changes in demand for the production of sawnwood, plywood and veneer sheets. The demand for wood and fibre for reconstituted panel, pulp and paper production has generally shown strong and consistent growth over the period, although it did also fall slightly in the early-1990s. Again, the latter have also increased in relative importance over the period, accounting for 43 percent of total wood raw material demand in 2000, compared with a figure of only 14 percent in 1961.

2.5.3   Wood raw material supply by source

On the other side of the wood raw material balance, there have also been significant changes in the relative importance of different sources of wood and fibre supply. Figure 43 shows the trends in consumption of the three main sources of wood and fibre in Europe over the last 40 years. The solid line represents the total requirement or derived demand in WRME (taken from the previous analysis). The differences between the tops of the bars and the solid line represent the utilisation of other sources of supply that are not recorded in FAO-UNECE statistics. Most of this is probably wood residues, but it also possibly includes the utilisation of recovered wood products (other than wastepaper) and unrecorded production and trade flows (i.e. inaccuracies in the FAO-UNECE statistics).

Figure 43   **Trends in wood raw material consumption in Europe from 1961 to 2000**

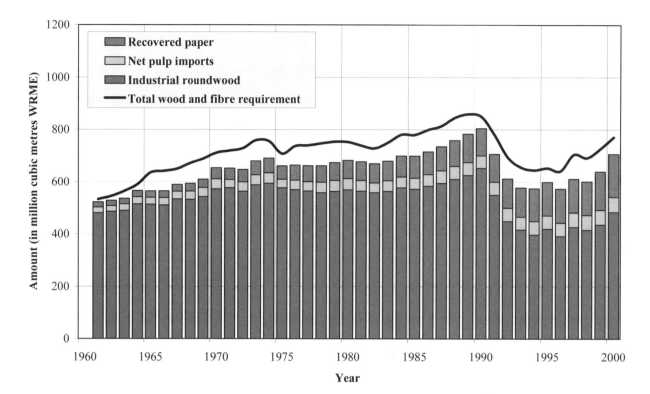

Source: derived from FAOSTAT production and trade statistics (http://faostat.external.fao.org). Note: totals for the Eastern Europe and CIS sub-regions before 1992 have been estimated from statistics for the USSR (see Section 1.4.2).

Figure 43 shows that the composition of wood raw materials consumed in Europe has changed over the last 40 years, with a decline in the relative importance of industrial roundwood compared with other types of wood and fibre. In 1961, industrial roundwood accounted for 90 percent of all wood and fibre consumed in Europe, with the remaining ten percent divided equally between the other types of wood and fibre. By the year 2000, the importance of industrial roundwood had fallen to only 63 percent of total consumption. Consumption of all of the other types of wood and fibre have increased over the period, but the most significant increase by far has been in the use of recovered paper, which accounted for 21 percent of wood and fibre consumption in 2000.

Again, the relative importance of these different wood and fibre supply sources varies between the three sub-regions, so the trends in each of the sub-regions are shown in Figure 44 to Figure 46.

Figure 44   ***Trends in wood raw material consumption in Western Europe from 1961 to 2000***

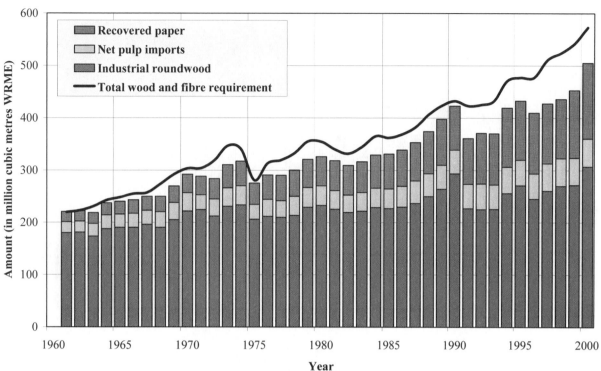

Source: derived from FAOSTAT production and trade statistics (http://faostat.external.fao.org).

As noted above, in Western Europe the total consumption of wood and fibre has increased almost three-fold over the last 40 years. However, consumption of industrial roundwood has increased by only 70 percent over the same period (from 180 million m^3 in 1961 to 307 million m^3 in 2000). Thus, the relative importance of industrial roundwood as a source of wood and fibre supply has fallen dramatically and now accounts for only 54 percent of total wood and fibre consumption compared with a figure of 82 percent in 1961.

The greatest increase in importance has occurred in the use of recovered paper, which accounted for 20 million m^3 WRME (or nine percent of the total) in 1961, rising to 145 million m^3 WRME (or 25 percent of the total) in 2000. In addition, the use of net pulp imports has more than doubled to 53 million m^3 WRME, although the relative importance of this source of supply has declined slightly to nine percent of total wood and fibre consumption in the year 2000.

The other noticeable feature of these trends is the increase in the gap between raw material requirement (or derived demand) and the known consumption of wood and fibre sources that has taken place over the last four decades. In 1961, this gap was negligible, but by the year 2000 it had increased to 12 percent, making this the third most important supply source. The use of residues from the sawmilling and plywood sectors probably fills most of this gap, although the recycling and re-use of wood products (other than paper) has probably increased in recent years. Currently, very little information is available about the latter (see Box 8 on page 148), but there is strong evidence for some countries, including Germany, that environmental measures (such as landfill taxes) are increasing the supply of wood and fibre from the recycling of other (i.e. non-paper) wood products, notably used pallets and crates, and demolition waste.

Figure 45   Trends in wood raw material consumption in the CIS sub-region from 1961 to 2000

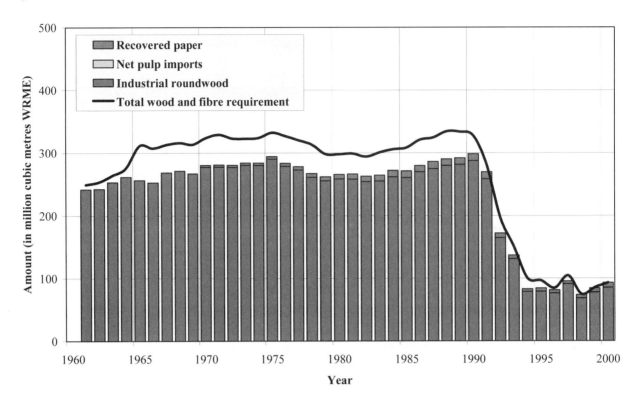

Source: derived from FAOSTAT production and trade statistics (http://faostat.external.fao.org). Note: totals for the CIS sub-region before 1992 have been estimated from statistics for the USSR (see Section 1.4.2).

Figure 46   Trends in wood raw material consumption in Eastern Europe from 1961 to 2000

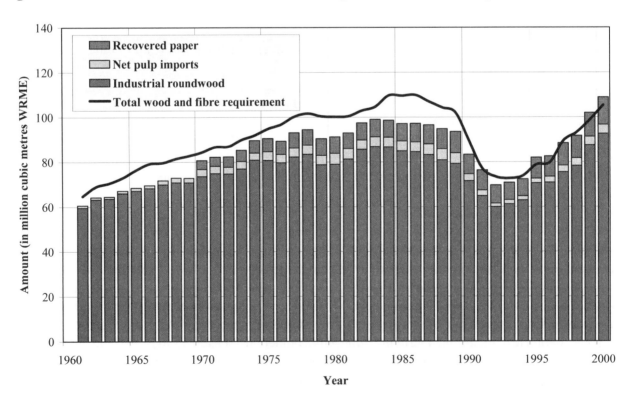

Source: derived from FAOSTAT production and trade statistics (http://faostat.external.fao.org). Note: totals for Eastern Europe before 1992 have been estimated from statistics for the USSR (see Section 1.4.2).

In Eastern Europe and the CIS sub-regions, the first noticeable feature is the almost complete reliance on industrial roundwood as a source of wood and fibre supply. In both sub-regions, industrial roundwood has accounted for between 80 percent to 90 percent of total wood and fibre consumption in nearly every year over the last four decades. This contrasts strongly with the trend in Western Europe, where the importance of industrial roundwood has declined dramatically (see Figure 47).

Figure 47   Trends in the importance of industrial roundwood as a source of wood raw material supply from 1961 to 2000

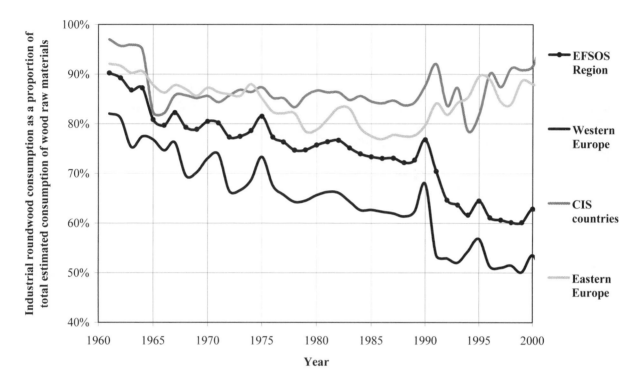

Source: derived from FAOSTAT production and trade statistics (http://faostat.external.fao.org). Note: figures for the Eastern Europe and CIS sub-regions before 1992 have been estimated from statistics for the USSR (see Section 1.4.2).

The only other source of raw materials that is significant in these sub-regions is the use of recovered paper. In the CIS sub-region, recovered paper accounts for about eight percent of total wood and fibre consumption (or 7 million m^3 WRME in 2000), while in Eastern Europe it accounts for about 12 percent of total consumption (12 million m^3 WRME in 2000).

The gap between total wood and fibre requirements and total consumption from known supply sources has shrunk to almost zero during the 1990s. In fact, in Eastern Europe, the most recent statistics show greater consumption of raw materials than requirement (i.e. the bars are higher than the line in Figure 46). Apart from the fact that the conversion factors used in this analysis could be incorrect, this implies that the use of wood residues has fallen in recent years. However, it also suggests that there may be some problems in the forest product statistics (see below).

The dominance of industrial roundwood in these sub-regions can be partly explained by the structure of the forest processing sectors in most of these countries, which are strongly focused on sawnwood and panel production. It does also suggest though, that there may scope for substitution of recycled materials and wood residues for industrial roundwood or increased exports of such materials in the future.

Trends in the importance of recovered paper as a source of raw material supply to the European pulp and paper industry are shown in Figure 48. These have been calculated by dividing recovered paper consumption by the production of paper and paperboard (plus net pulp exports), with all figures converted to WRME.

Figure 48   *Trends in the importance of recovered paper as a source of raw material supply for the pulp and paper industry from 1961 to 2000*

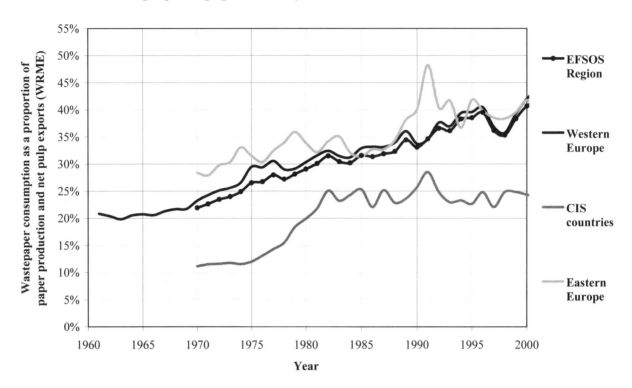

Source: derived from FAOSTAT production and trade statistics (http://faostat.external.fao.org). Note: figures for the Eastern Europe and CIS sub-regions before 1992 have been estimated from statistics for the USSR (see Section 1.4.2).

The trends in this figure show that the consumption of recovered paper has increased in importance in Europe (as an input to pulp and paper making), although less so in the CIS sub-region. In Western Europe, the utilisation of recovered paper now accounts for around 40 percent of the wood and fibre used to produce pulp and paper, compared with a figure of only 20 percent in 1961. In Eastern Europe, the trend in utilisation has been similar to this, although it started from a slightly higher level. In the CIS sub-region, the importance of recovered paper increased significantly in the 1970s, to account for 25 percent of the total wood and fibre requirements in the pulp and paper industry in 1982. However, it has not increased in importance since then.

As with the rate of wastepaper recovery, there are some technical limits to how much recovered paper can be used in the pulp and paper making process. For example, certain types of paper require fibre properties that are extremely difficult to find in recovered paper. Similarly, the quality of recovered paper declines as paper is recycled again and again. For example, it is currently estimated that paper can only be recycled a maximum of six times on average (CPI, 2004). However, it is unlikely that these limits will be reached in most countries in the foreseeable future.

Figure 49 shows the trends in the importance of net pulp imports as a source of fibre for the European paper making industry. Pulp imports remain an important source of fibre in Western and Eastern Europe, accounting for about 15 percent of the fibre used for this purpose. In Western Europe, the importance of net pulp imports has declined slightly over the last 40 years, but their importance in Eastern Europe has not changed very much over the period. The CIS sub-region was not a net pulp importer until very recently, when one of the countries there started to import a very small amount of wood pulp.

Combining the information in Figure 48 and Figure 49, it can be seen that industrial roundwood and wood residues account for about 45 percent of the wood and fibre used in pulp and paper production in Western and Eastern Europe and 75 percent of the wood and fibre used for this purpose in the CIS sub-region. Again, this highlights the radically different structure of wood raw material inputs used in the different sub-regions of Europe.

Figure 49 ***Trends in the importance of net pulp imports as a source of raw material supply for the pulp and paper industry from 1961 to 2000***

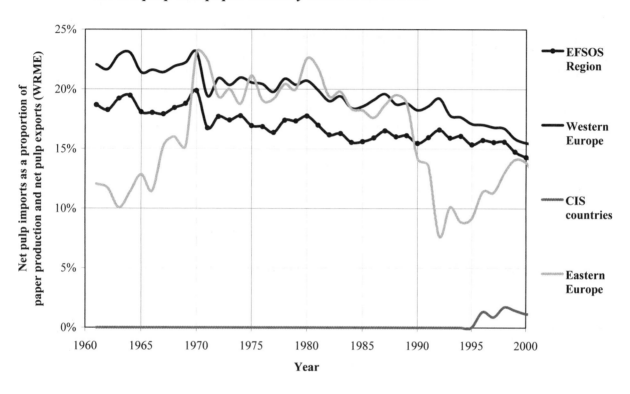

Source: derived from FAOSTAT production and trade statistics (http://faostat.external.fao.org). Note: figures for the Eastern Europe and CIS sub-regions before 1992 have been estimated from statistics for the USSR (see Section 1.4.2).

Up until now, the analysis has focused on the trends in the known wood raw material supply sources. The major unknown factor in the European wood raw material balance is the availability and utilisation[7] of wood residues. However, from the statistics presented earlier, it is possible to estimate what these figures might look like.

Figure 50 shows the estimated potential availability of wood residues in Europe from 1961 to 2000. This has been calculated by subtracting the total volume of sawnwood, plywood and veneer sheets produced from the derived demand (in WRME) of the wood raw materials required to support that level of production (shown in Figure 39). This calculation gives only an approximate estimate, as it assumes that all residues could be used by the forest processing sector. Furthermore, a problem with the interpretation of these figures is that some of this wood is probably used as wood fuel. In some cases, this could be significant. However, these figures do present some information about the last major component of the wood raw material supply

---

[7]   To avoid confusion between the availability of residues and the production of residues, the word "utilisation" is
        used here rather than production. This means the use of wood residues either for domestic consumption or export.

Figure 50   Estimated potential availability of wood residues from 1961 to 2000

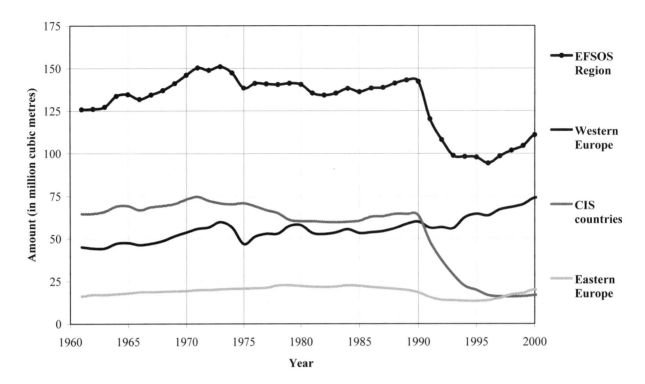

Source: derived from FAOSTAT production and trade statistics (http://faostat.external.fao.org). Note: totals for the Eastern Europe and CIS sub-regions before 1992 have been estimated from statistics for the USSR (see Section 1.4.2).

Figure 51   Estimated utilisation of wood residues from 1961 to 2000

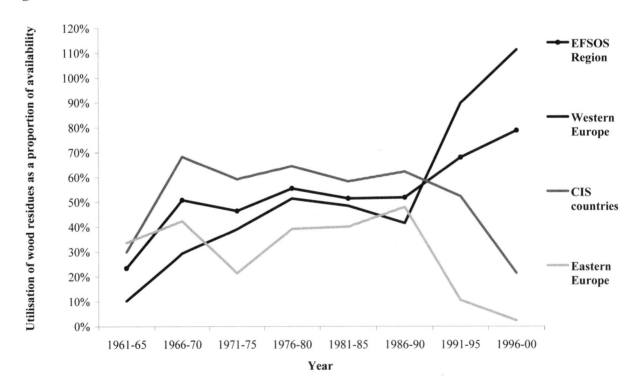

Source: derived from FAOSTAT production and trade statistics (http://faostat.external.fao.org). Note: figures for the Eastern Europe and CIS sub-regions before 1992 have been estimated from statistics for the USSR (see Section 1.4.2).

For Europe as a whole, Figure 50 shows that just over 110 million m³ WRME of residues were potentially available in 2000, which is slightly less than at the start of the period. The trends in these estimates match the trends in sawnwood, plywood and veneer sheet production presented earlier, so they show a gradual increase in Western Europe throughout the period, a fluctuation in production in Eastern Europe and a decline in production in the CIS sub-region in the early 1990s. In general, the availability of wood residues has not increased very rapidly over the period, because growth in production in these product sectors has also been relatively low.

A potentially more interesting piece of information is the proportion of these residues that are actually used by the forest products sector and some estimates of this are shown in Figure 51. (Because these results are extremely erratic, 5-year averages are shown in the figure for the period 1961 to 2000).

These figures were calculated by first estimating the domestic consumption of residues in each country. This was done by taking the gaps between WRME demand and consumption of known supply sources (i.e. the gaps shown in Figure 43 to Figure 46). These figures were then adjusted for net trade in chips, particles and wood residues (i.e. exports were added and imports were subtracted from the figures). This gave estimates of the total utilisation of residues, which were then divided by the estimated residue availability (Figure 50). This calculation assumes that wood residues are the only other (unknown) source of wood raw material supply.

For Europe as a whole, the figure shows that the utilisation of wood residues has increased significantly over the last four decades from around 20 percent to around 80 percent of potentially available residue supply. At the sub-regional level, there was not much difference in residue utilisation until the 1990s, as all of the sub-regions showed some growth in residue utilisation from 1961 to 1990. However, since 1990, the figures have changed dramatically, casting doubt on the reliability of these estimates (and, implicitly, the reliability of the forest product statistics more generally).

The problem highlighted by this figure is one of the consistency of the European forest product statistics. Problems of consistency arise when a country appears to be consuming far too many wood raw materials compared to its level of product production or, more often, when a country produces far more forest products than the consumption of raw materials would suggest. There has always been a slight problem of inconsistency in European forest products statistics, but this appears to have worsened in the 1990s. Furthermore, at the individual country level, the problems of inconsistency are even greater than those shown here.

There are a number of possible explanations for these results. First, if the conversion factors that have been used in this analysis are incorrect, this could account for the problem. However, this would not explain why consistency suddenly becomes a problem in the 1990s. A second explanation would be the development of another new (and unrecorded) source of wood raw material supply. Recycling of other (i.e. non-wood) forest products has already been noted as a possibility, but it is unlikely that this could account for all of the changes.

The weight of the evidence suggests that the European production and trade statistics may have declined in quality in the 1990s. This could be due to factors such as the relaxation of customs controls in the European Union and the transition from public to private control of many parts of the forest sector in the East. For Europe as a whole, the trend in residue utilisation looks quite plausible, but it is conspicuous that estimated residue utilisation in Western Europe increases dramatically (to over 100 percent) in the last decade, while the opposite occurs in the other two sub-regions. Not only does this suggest that the quality of statistics has declined, but it also implies that unrecorded or mis-classified wood raw material trade flows may have started to appear in the last decade.

Of course, by including the possible inaccuracies in statistics in the residue sector (which is a relatively small component of total wood and fibre supply) this magnifies the appearance of the problem. However, the preceding analysis does suggest that there are some statistical issues that should be examined in the future.

Table 7   *The European wood raw material balance (average of the years 1996 to 2000)*

Component	Europe	Sub-regions		
		Western Europe	Eastern Europe	CIS
Derived demand for wood raw materials				
Other industrial roundwood	34.3	6.3	11.1	16.9
Sawnwood, plywood and veneer sheets	234.2	150.5	41.5	42.2
Reconstituted panels	71.7	50.8	14.5	6.4
Net pulp exports	31.7	24.5	1.1	6.0
Paper and paperboard	335.2	293.3	25.0	16.9
Total derived demand	**707.1**	**525.4**	**93.3**	**88.4**
Consumption of wood raw materials				
Industrial roundwood	431.4	270.8	81.0	79.7
Recovered paper	139.6	123.7	10.4	5.5
Net pulp imports	55.6	51.9	3.3	0.3
Other	80.6	79.1	-1.4	2.9
- net imports of chips, particles and residues	*0.1*	*2.6*	*-1.8*	*-0.6*
- utilisation of wood residues	*80.4*	*76.5*	*0.4*	*3.5*
Total consumption	**707.1**	**525.4**	**93.3**	**88.4**

Note: the above figures are expressed in million m³ WRME and show average annual demand and consumption. For trade in chips, particles and residues, imports are shown as a positive number and exports are shown as negative numbers.

Drawing together all of the previous analysis, Table 7 shows the current European wood raw material balance in terms of the average annual demand for and consumption of wood raw materials over the years 1996 to 2000. This clearly shows the structural differences between Western Europe and the other two sub-regions, in particular the greater demand for wood and fibre from the pulp and paper industry in Western Europe and the lower dependence on industrial roundwood and a fibre supply source. As the other two sub-regions in Europe continue their transition to developed market economies, it can be expected that the structure of their forest sectors will also start to alter to look more similar to the Western European forest sector.

2.6 *International trade in wood products*

Based on the trends in production and consumption, previous sections have already described some of the changes in net trade that have taken place in Europe over the last four decades. This section expands upon the analysis, by showing how international trade has become relatively more important in much of Europe (especially in the last decade) and by describing the structure of trade across the region. It also briefly discusses the competitiveness of European wood products in global markets.

2.6.1   Growth in international trade in wood products

International trade in wood products has increased in importance across most regions of the World over the last four decades. International trade within Europe and between Europe and the rest of the World has followed this pattern, as is demonstrated by the rates of growth in imports and exports in Europe over the last four decades (shown in Figure 52 and Figure 53).

Since 1961, imports and exports of sawnwood have increased by 1.7 percent 2.3 percent per year respectively, while imports and exports of wood pulp have increased at an average annual rate of 2.7 percent and 1.8 percent respectively. International trade in wood based panels and paper and paperboard has increased even more rapidly than this. Average annual growth in imports and exports of wood based panels has amounted to 6.6 percent and 6.7 percent respectively, while the corresponding figures for paper and paperboard are 6.1 percent and 6.2 percent.

Behind these broad trends there have been some interesting developments for different products in different sub-regions and during different time periods in the recent past. In the sawnwood sector, growth in international trade was relatively modest up until the 1990s and, in the case of Eastern Europe and the CIS sub-region, actually declined for parts of the period 1961 to 1990. In the 1990s, European trade in sawnwood increased dramatically at both the European and sub-regional level, with a particularly high rate of growth in Eastern Europe and the CIS sub-region. A similar pattern in the growth of European trade in wood based panels also occurred over the last four decades, with relatively slow growth during the 1970s and 1980s and a remarkable increase in international trade in the 1990s.

European trade in wood pulp has increased only modestly over the last 40 years and has, in general, grown more slowly than production and consumption. However, as in the solid wood products sector, trade with Eastern Europe and the CIS sub-region has increased more rapidly during the 1990s.

The paper and paperboard sector is the one major component of the forest products sector where there has been strong and sustained growth in European trade throughout most of the region over the last four decades. However, again, very little growth in trade occurred in some parts of Eastern Europe and the CIS sub-region until the 1990s, when both imports and exports increased significantly.

The importance of international trade to the forest sector can be shown by the proportion of production (or consumption) that is exported (or imported). For each of the four main forest products categories, the trends in the ratio of exports to production since 1961 are shown in Figure 54 and Figure 55. With the exception of wood pulp, these figures show how the importance of exports has gradually and consistently increased in Western Europe with, for example, exports accounting for almost 60 percent of paper and paperboard production in the late 1990s. In the case of wood pulp, the importance of exports in Western Europe has declined over the last 40 years, although this decline levelled-out over the latter half of the period.

For the other two sub-regions, the figures present an even more dramatic picture of the changes in international trade that have taken place in the last decade. As the domestic economies in these sub-regions have shrunk over the last decade, production has become more export-oriented and the importance of exports to the forest processing industry has increased several-fold. For example, exports of sawnwood accounted for only around 10 percent of production in Eastern Europe in 1990, but accounted for over 45 percent of production in 2000.

Figure 52   ***Growth in European trade in solid wood products from 1961 to 2000***

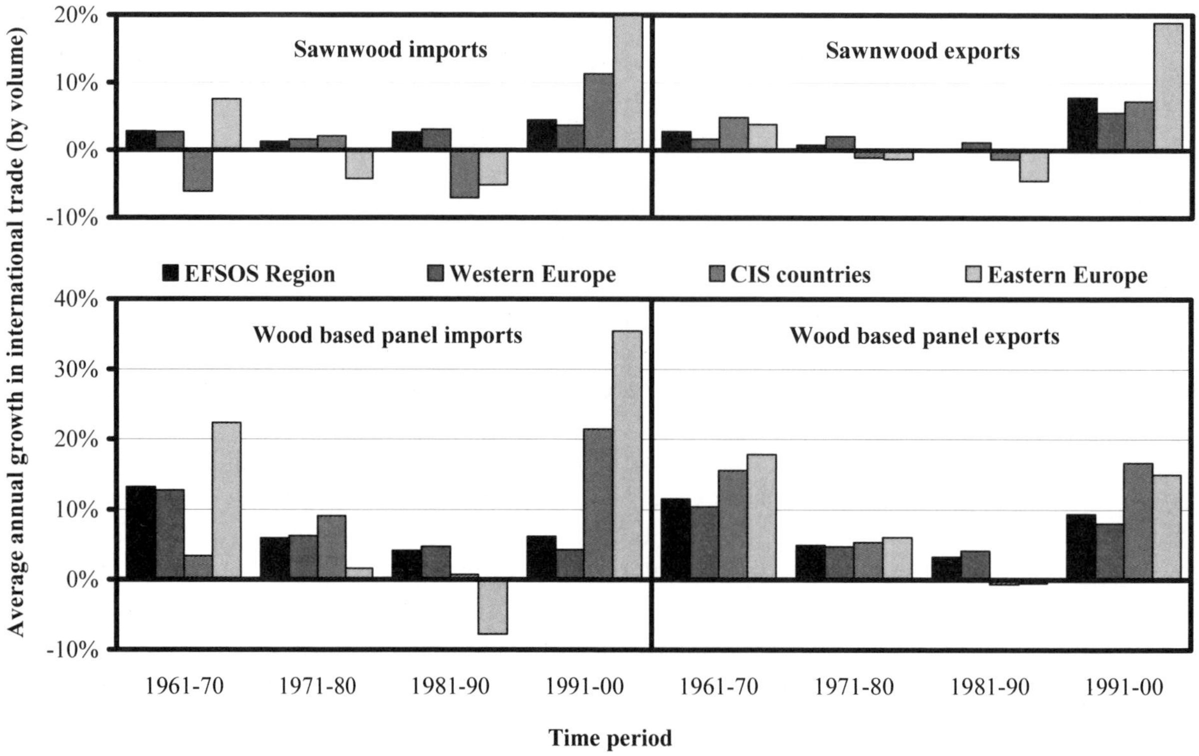

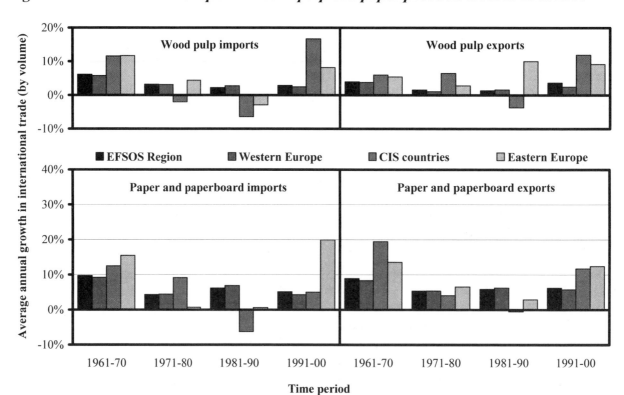

Source: derived from FAOSTAT production and trade statistics (http://faostat.external.fao.org). Note: figures for the Eastern Europe and CIS sub-regions before 1992 have been estimated from statistics for the USSR (see Section 1.4.2).

Figure 53   ***Growth in European trade in pulp and paper products from 1961 to 2000***

Source: derived from FAOSTAT production and trade statistics (http://faostat.external.fao.org). Note: figures for the Eastern Europe and CIS sub-regions before 1992 have been estimated from statistics for the USSR (see Section 1.4.2).

Figure 54   *Exports as a share of solid wood product production from 1961 to 2000*

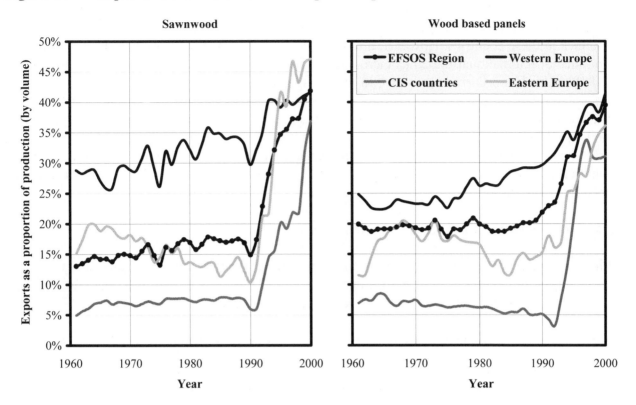

Source: derived from FAOSTAT production and trade statistics (http://faostat.external.fao.org). Note: figures for the Eastern Europe and CIS sub-regions before 1992 have been estimated from statistics for the USSR (see Section 1.4.2).

Figure 55   *Exports as a share of pulp and paper product production from 1961 to 2000*

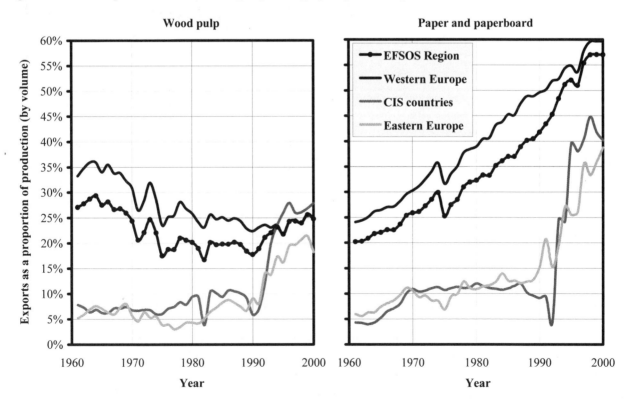

Source: derived from FAOSTAT production and trade statistics (http://faostat.external.fao.org). Note: figures for the Eastern Europe and CIS sub-regions before 1992 have been estimated from statistics for the USSR (see Section 1.4.2).

As noted in earlier sections, the fluctuations in trade with Eastern Europe and the CIS sub-region can be explained by the replacement of the trading systems of the formerly planned economies by free-market trade. These changes have occurred as part of the transition towards market-based economies in these countries. However, a more interesting observation from these trends is that the importance of international trade has increased more generally across all parts of the region during the 1990s. This has occurred partly due to the changes in transition countries, but it also reflects a more general trend towards the globalisation of forest products markets. For example, at the global level, the importance of forest products exports (measured as a proportion of production) increased during the 1990s by as much as in the previous three decades. Furthermore, this increase in international trade occurred across all major categories of forest products. This trend towards globalisation is one of the major driving forces that has affected forest products markets in recent years and will be discussed in more detail in Section 3.3.6 of this report.

2.6.2   The position of Europe in global markets

As in most other sectors, Europe's position in the global markets for wood products is largely determined by the relative size of the European economy. Figure 56 shows the trends in Europe's share of total global wood products imports and exports (by value) since 1961.

Figure 56   The European share of global trade in wood products from 1961 to 2000

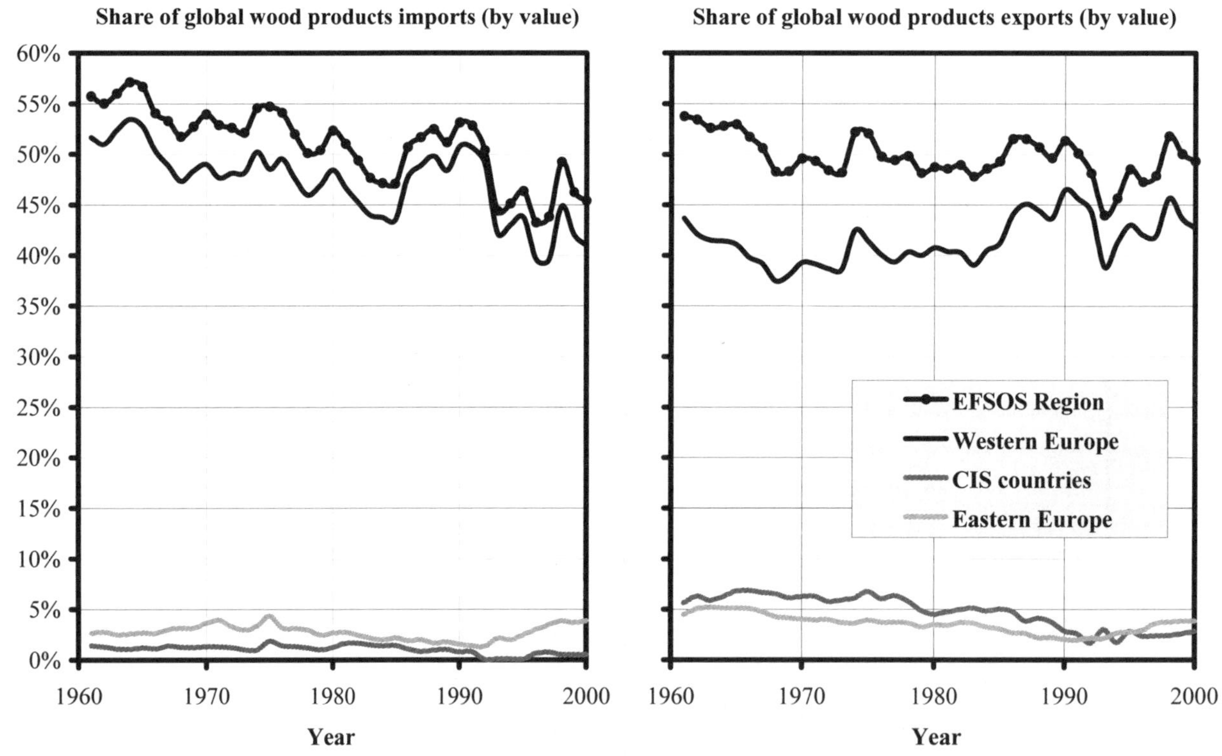

Source: derived from FAOSTAT production and trade statistics (http://faostat.external.fao.org). Note: figures for the Eastern Europe and CIS sub-regions before 1992 have been estimated from statistics for the USSR (see Section 1.4.2).

Europe's relative importance as an importer of wood products has declined gradually over the last 40 years. Western Europe has always accounted for the majority of imports into Europe, so this trend has occurred largely because imports into other regions, most notably East Asia (e.g. Japan, Korea and China), have grown much more rapidly than in Western Europe. Another minor feature of this figure is the increase in the importance of imports into Eastern Europe that has occurred in the last decade. This is due to the rapid economic growth in this region, which has stimulated the demand for all types of wood products in this sub-region from both domestic and foreign sources.

The importance of Europe as an exporter of wood products has also declined over the last four decades, although by less than in the case of imports. The decline in the importance of European exports is mostly attributable to the low growth and decline (in some periods) of exports from Eastern Europe and the CIS sub-region. As noted above, these trends have started to reverse, but the longer-term effect of this has been to reduce the contribution of these two sub-regions to global wood products exports. In contrast, the value of wood products exports from Western Europe has increased at about the same rate as in the rest of the World. Thus, Western Europe has consistently accounted for about 40 percent to 45 percent of global wood products exports over the last four decades.

Another interesting feature of Figure 56 is that it shows that Europe is now a small net exporter of wood products (by value) at the regional and sub-regional level.[8] A more detailed picture of the trends in net trade is given by the trends in the Normalised Trade Balances for the main product categories and these are shown in Figure 57 and Figure 58.

The Normalised Trade Balance is a measure of net trade, which is calculated by dividing the total value of net trade in each sub-region (i.e. total value of exports minus total value of imports) by the total value of trade (i.e. total value of exports plus total value of imports). The figure varies from +100 percent (in locations with exports only) to -100 percent (in locations with imports only), with a figure of zero indicating that the value of imports and exports are equal.

Figure 57 shows that European net trade in sawnwood and wood based panels has shifted over the period to a position where the value of imports and exports are approximately equal. In sawnwood markets, Eastern Europe and the CIS sub-region have always been significant net exporters, with almost no imports of sawnwood into the CIS sub-region and exports roughly four times higher than imports into Eastern Europe. The main shift in the net trade position at the European level has occurred due to changes in Western Europe, particularly in the last decade. The value of sawnwood imports into Western Europe is currently less than one-and-a-half times the value of exports, leading to a normalised trade deficit of less than 20 percent. This compares with a normalised trade deficit of 30 percent to 40 percent in the 1960s, when the value of imports was more than twice the value of exports in Western Europe.

Trends in the net trade balance for wood based panels show similar features to the trends for sawnwood, although the surplus of exports over imports in the CIS sub-region is relatively smaller and net trade in Eastern Europe has changed from a position of significant net exports to one of a small amount of net imports. Again, a significant change has occurred in Western Europe in the last decade, with a shift towards equality in the value of imports and exports.

The Normalised Trade Balance for wood pulp shows how Western and Eastern Europe remain significant net importers of this product, while the CIS sub-region is a significant net exporter (see Figure 58). The deficit in European wood pulp trade has increased over the last four decades due to an increase in the deficit in Western Europe. This can be attributed to strong growth in paper and paperboard production in Western Europe, combined with a redirection of pulp production away from export markets towards domestic processing into paper.

---

8 The value of forest products exports from Western Europe was slightly less than the value of imports in 2000, but the Western European share of global exports exceeded the Western European share of global imports. This is due to the different measurement conventions used for export and import values (i.e. FOB versus CIF).

Figure 57   Historical trends in the Normalised Trade Balance for solid wood products

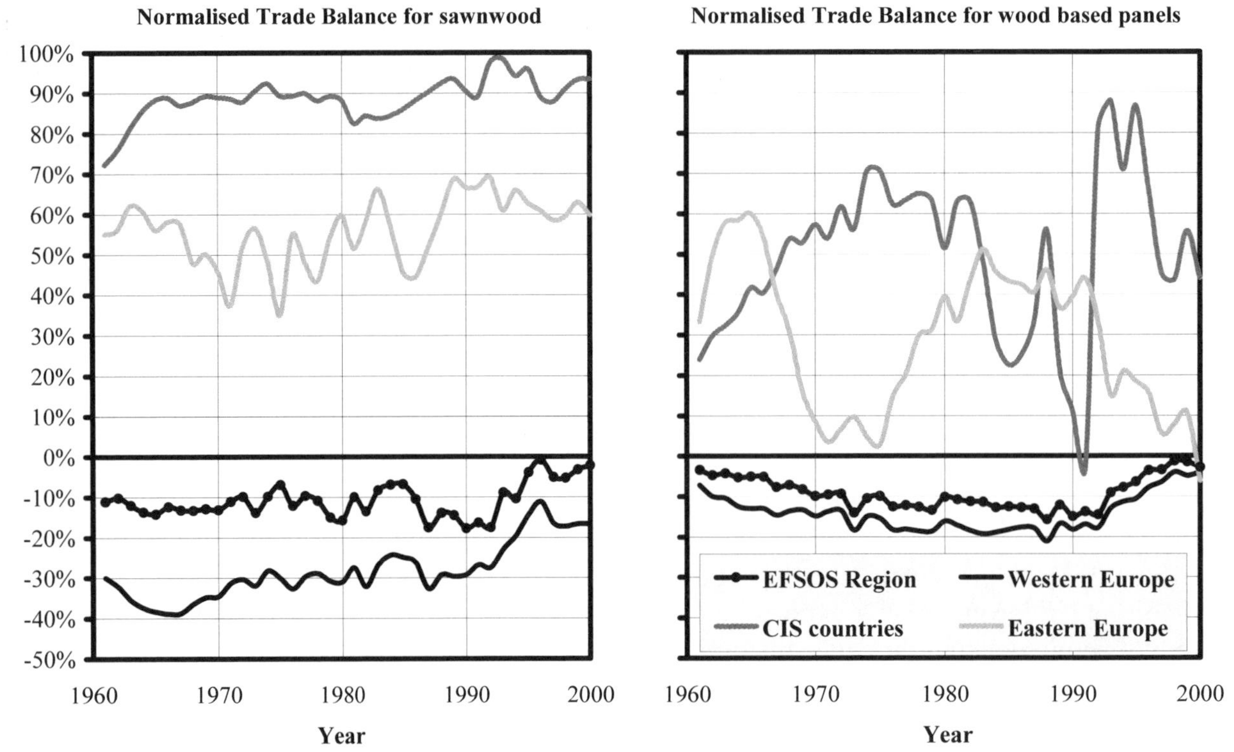

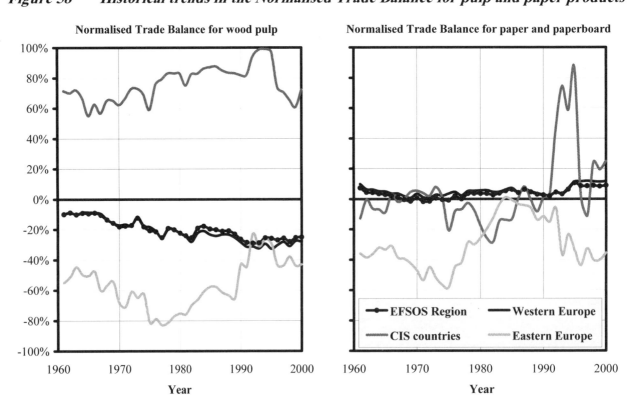

Source: derived from FAOSTAT production and trade statistics (http://faostat.external.fao.org). Note: figures for the Eastern Europe and CIS sub-regions before 1992 have been estimated from statistics for the USSR (see Section 1.4.2).

Figure 58   Historical trends in the Normalised Trade Balance for pulp and paper products

Source: derived from FAOSTAT production and trade statistics (http://faostat.external.fao.org). Note: figures for the Eastern Europe and CIS sub-regions before 1992 have been estimated from statistics for the USSR (see Section 1.4.2).

Figure 58 also shows how the balance of trade in paper and paperboard has shifted over the last 40 years, with a consistent and gradual strengthening of net exports (largely from Western Europe). Although the Normalised Trade Balance appears quite small (+10 percent) the value of this trade is huge, amounting to more than the value of trade in the other three major product categories combined.

In addition to the growth in Western Europe, the CIS sub-region has become a modest net exporter of paper and paperboard in the last decade. Eastern Europe remains in a position where the value of paper and paperboard imports are about two-and-a-half times higher than the value of exports, leading to a Normalised Trade Balance of around -40 percent. However, this does little to affect the position of Europe as a whole, as the contribution of both of these sub-regions to European trade is quite small.

Another interesting feature of European trade in forest products is that a high proportion of the international trade in Europe takes place within the continent itself. In part, this is because Europe contains countries with significant forest resources and relatively small markets as well as countries with large markets and few forest resources.

Thus, for example, 80 percent of European forest products exports (by value) were exported to other European countries in 2000 (EUR 60 billion out of EUR 75 billion - see Table 8). Furthermore, 80 percent of the trade within Europe was between the countries of Western Europe. Western Europe is the largest European exporter of forest products to the rest of the World (EUR 12.4 billion of exports in 2000), but the CIS sub-region is the most exposed to external forest products markets, with exports to non-European countries accounting for almost 45 percent of exports in 2000.

Table 8   *Value of exports of wood products to and from Europe in 2000 (in billion Euros)*

Exporting region	**Importing region**					
	Western Europe	Eastern Europe	CIS	**Europe**	Rest of World	**World total**
Western Europe	48.4	3.5	0.5	**52.3**	12.4	**64.7**
Eastern Europe	3.9	1.1	0.2	**5.2**	0.7	**5.9**
CIS	1.5	0.7	0.3	**2.5**	1.9	**4.4**
Europe	**53.8**	**5.3**	**0.9**	60.0	15.0	75.0
Rest of World	11.8	0.4	0.0	**12.2**	69.9	**82.1**
World total	**65.6**	**5.7**	**0.9**	**72.2**	84.9	**157.0**

Note: the above figures are all export values (i.e. FOB) converted from USD to EUR at the exchange rate in 2000 of EUR 1.09 per USD 1.00.

An indicator of the strength of the trading relationships between countries, regions and sub-regions is the Trade Intensity Index. This is used to determine whether the value of trade between two locations in a particular good is greater or smaller than would be expected on the basis of their importance in world trade of that good. It is defined as the share of one location's exports going to a partner location divided by the share of world exports going to the partner location.[9] An index of more (or less) than one indicates a bilateral trade flow that is larger (or smaller) than expected, given the partner location's importance in world trade (Hoekman *et al*, 2003).

---

[9] $T_{ij} = (x_{ij}/X_{it})/(x_{wj}/X_{wt})$; where T_{ij} is the Trade Intensity Index between location i and j; x_{ij} and x_{wj} are the values of location i's exports and of world exports to location j; and X_{it} and X_{wt} are location i's total exports and total world exports respectively.

EUROPEAN FOREST SECTOR OUTLOOK STUDY

The Trade Intensity Index was calculated for wood products exports for every country in Europe and the results at the regional and sub-regional levels are shown in Table 9. As would be expected, due to the costs of transport and other socio-economic factors, the Trade Intensity Index is higher for trade flows within each European sub-region than for trade between each sub-region and the other two European sub-regions. However, the table does provide some insights into the integration in European wood products markets that has already taken place. For example, there are very strong linkages in trade between Eastern Europe and the CIS sub-region, showing that each of these sub-regions is important as a source of exports to the other. The linkages between the CIS sub-region and Western Europe are currently not as strong.

Trade within Eastern Europe is stronger than trade with the other two sub-regions, but the CIS sub-region is almost as important as a source of imports into Eastern Europe as countries from within the sub-region, Furthermore, the intensity of trade from Eastern Europe to Western Europe is almost as strong as the intensity of trade within Western Europe.

Table 9   *Intensity of European trade in wood products in 2000 (Trade Intensity Index)*

Exporting region	Importing region				
	Western Europe	Eastern Europe	CIS	**Europe**	Rest of World
Western Europe	1.79	1.48	1.25	**1.76**	0.35
Eastern Europe	1.59	5.28	4.51	**1.92**	0.22
CIS	0.82	4.53	10.34	**1.23**	0.80
Europe	**1.72**	**1.95**	**2.04**	1.74	**0.37**
Rest of World	0.34	0.13	0.05	**0.32**	1.58

Note: a Trade Intensity Index value of one indicates a trade flow of "average" importance given the total level of exports from a region and imports into an importing region. A value of less than one indicates a weaker trading relationship (minimum bound is zero), while a value greater than one indicates a stronger relationship.

The Trade Intensity Index shows that considerable progress has already been made towards integrating the forest products sectors in the different European sub-regions, particularly in terms of the integration of Western and Eastern Europe. Another important highlight of this table is the weakness of trading links between the rest of the World and Europe, particularly in terms of exports to Europe. The only notable trading relationship is between the CIS sub-region and the rest of the World, although this is still less than would be expected given the magnitude of exports from the CIS sub-region and imports into the rest of the World.

2.6.3   The potential for growth in exports of wood products from Europe

International trade statistics can also be used to indicate the potential for growth in exports, by comparing trends in exports of wood products with trends in the exports of all goods from a country or region. The index of Revealed Comparative Advantage[10] measures the potential for export growth in different product sectors, by assuming that a country or region will increase exports of products in which it has a comparative advantage.

It can also provide useful information about potential trade prospects with other partners. Countries or regions with similar indices are unlikely to have high bilateral trade intensities (unless intra-industry trade is involved, which is frequently the case), but trade may be expected to increase between countries or regions with very different indices.

---

[10]   The Revealed Comparative Advantage for product j in country i is measured by the product's share in total exports compared with the country's share of total world trade: $RCA_{ij} = (x_{ij}/X_{it})/(x_{wj}/X_{wt})$; where RCA_{ij} is the comparative advantage of product j in country i; x_{ij} and x_{wj} are the values of country i's exports of product j and world exports of product j; and X_{it} and X_{wt} refer to the country's total exports and world total exports.

Indices of Revealed Comparative Advantage have been used to help assess the export potential of different types of products from a country or region. Trends in the Revealed Comparative Advantage in forest products in Europe are given in Figure 59 and Figure 60 for the period 1980 to 2000. A value of less than one implies that a sub-region has a revealed comparative disadvantage in the product, whereas a value of greater than one suggests that the sub-region has a revealed comparative advantage in the product.

The Revealed Comparative Advantage in sawnwood production in Europe lies largely in the east (see Figure 59). In Western Europe, the index has always been less than one and has not increased over the last two decades. Of course, there are some countries in Western Europe (e.g. Sweden and Finland) where the sawmilling sector is an export-oriented sector, but the majority of countries in Western Europe do not currently have a comparative advantage in sawmilling.

The most notable feature of Figure 59 is the dramatic increase that has occurred in the index of Revealed Comparative Advantage in Eastern Europe over the last decade. This sub-region clearly has a comparative advantage in the production and export of sawnwood (although, again, this may be due to the dominance of a few countries in the sub-region). The index for the CIS sub-region has declined in recent years (presumably due to the relative increase in the importance of oil and gas exports), but remains well above one.

The Revealed Comparative Advantage in wood based panel production in Europe has increased across the region over most of the last decade. If this trend continues, all three sub-regions will soon have a comparative advantage in the production of wood based panels. Currently, Eastern Europe has the greatest potential, showing a trend similar to that for sawnwood. However, it seems likely that the other two regions will also develop significant export potential in this sector in the near future.

Figure 60 shows the trends in Revealed Comparative Advantage in the pulp and paper sectors in Europe. As the earlier text has already suggested, Europe is not a significant exporter of wood pulp and does not have a comparative advantage in this product, except in the CIS sub-region. A few countries in Western Europe are able to compete successfully in global wood pulp markets, but this is not an export-oriented sector in the majority of countries.

Another point worth noting is the divergence in the Revealed Comparative Advantage indices for wood pulp between the CIS sub-region and the other two European sub-regions. This suggests that there is huge potential for exports of wood pulp from the CIS sub-region to the rest of Europe. Given the trends for paper and paperboard production (see below), it seems likely that such trade will increase in the future.

The pattern of competitiveness in the paper and paperboard sector in Europe is almost the opposite of what has been described above. In this sector, Western Europe clearly has a comparative advantage in production, suggesting that there is a very high potential for future export growth. Furthermore, the index of Revealed Comparative Advantage in Western Europe has increased over the last two decades (although only slowly). Eastern Europe and the CIS sub-region do not currently enjoy a comparative advantage in paper and paperboard production, although the increasing trends suggest that they may do so in the future. In the near-term, it seems likely that the flow of paper and paperboard exports from west to east in Europe will increase and will also increase from Western Europe to the rest of the World.

Figure 59   ***Revealed Comparative Advantage for solid wood products since 1980***

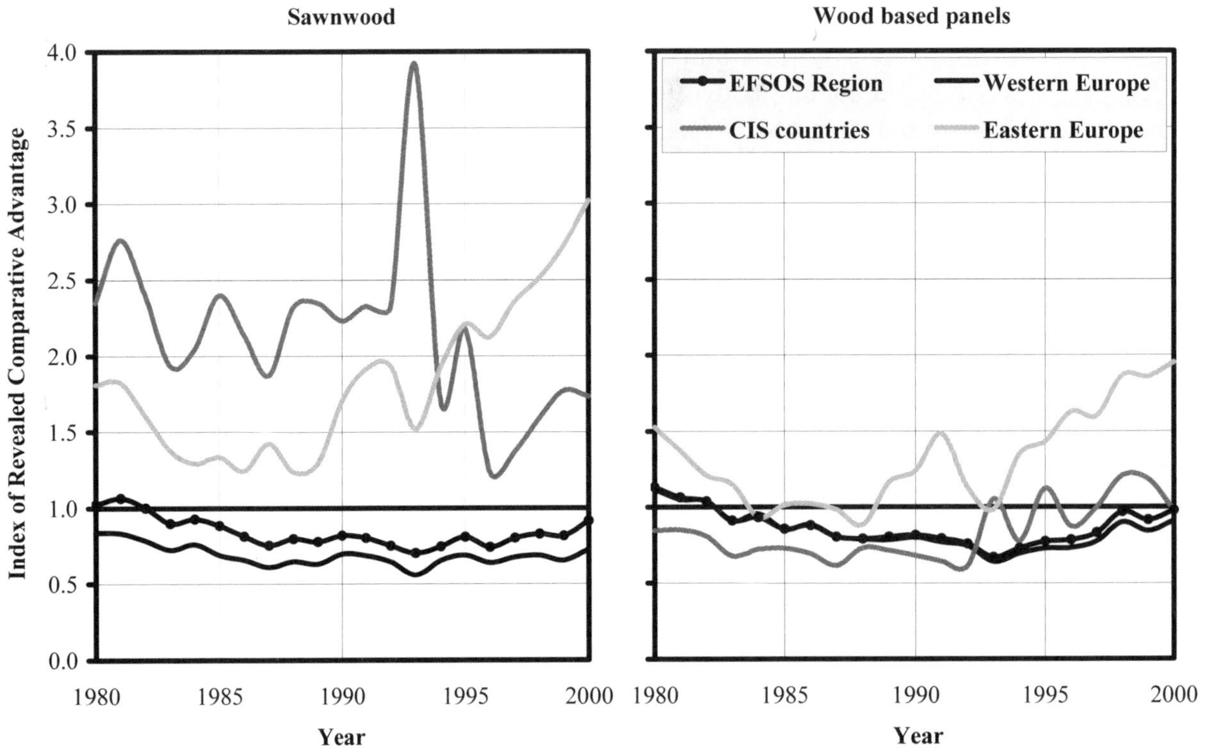

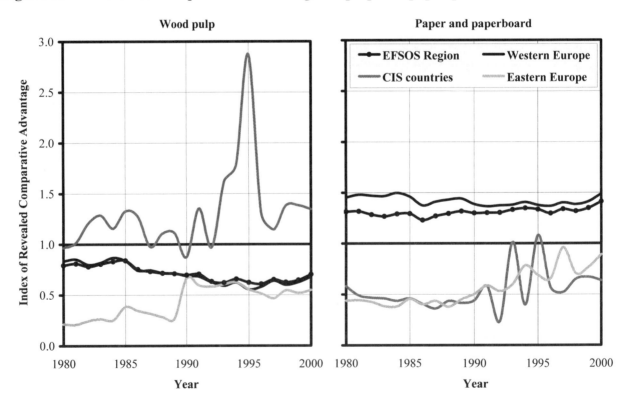

Source: derived from FAOSTAT production and trade statistics (http://faostat.external.fao.org). Note: figures for the Eastern Europe and CIS sub-regions before 1992 have been estimated from statistics for the USSR (see Section 1.4.2).

Figure 60   ***Revealed Comparative Advantage for pulp and paper products since 1980***

Source: derived from FAOSTAT production and trade statistics (http://faostat.external.fao.org). Note: figures for the Eastern Europe and CIS sub-regions before 1992 have been estimated from statistics for the USSR (see Section 1.4.2).

2.7 *Prices of wood products*

Globally, historical trends in the prices of wood products have shown a great deal of fluctuation, with periods of price increases, declines and stability. In nominal terms (i.e. unadjusted for inflation), prices increased throughout the 1960s, in many cases faster than the rate of inflation. At the start of the 1970s, prices peaked at the time of the first oil price shock (as did the prices of many other commodities). From this point until the 1990s, trends in prices have varied by product and region. For some products in some regions, prices continued to rise faster than inflation. In other cases, nominal prices rose by less, leading to constant or falling real prices (i.e. prices adjusted for inflation). During the 1990s, prices of wood products have generally remained about the same or fallen in nominal terms at the global level, leading to significant falls in real prices (see Figure 61).

Figure 61   *Global trends in export prices for the main wood product categories since 1990*

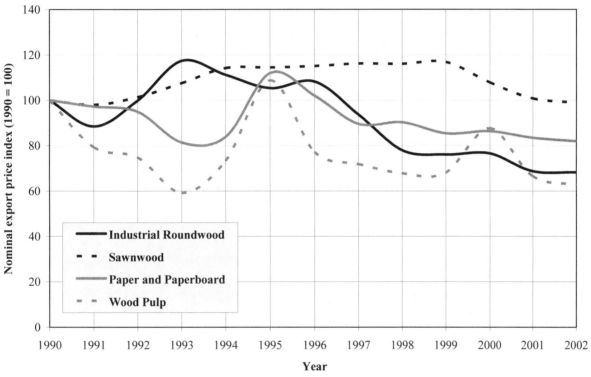

Source: derived from FAOSTAT production and trade statistics (http://faostat.external.fao.org).

The following analysis describes the historical trends in real prices for all of the main forest product categories in Europe since 1970. FAOSTAT does not contain information about domestic prices, so trends in trade prices are used here. These were calculated (for every year in each country) by adding together total import and export values, then dividing this by total import and export volumes. Western Europe has a high volume of imports and exports of wood products, so the averages of import and export prices can be considered as broadly indicative of the prevailing prices in this sub-region. For the other two sub-regions, the amounts of trade are generally much smaller (and may be flowing predominantly in one direction), so these figures should be treated with more caution.

FAOSTAT records the value of trade in current US Dollars, so these figures were converted to real prices (in Euros at 2000 prices and exchange rates). This was done by converting all of the figures to national currencies (using the prevailing exchange rate in each year), deflating them using national GDP deflators[11] and then converting them to Euros at the exchange rates of 2000. The price series for each sub-region and Europe as a whole were calculated as the weighted averages of the price series for each country, using traded volumes as the weights.

The analysis only extends back to 1970, because of the lack of information about GDP deflators for all countries in earlier years. Furthermore, because of the price and exchange controls in place in many countries outside Western Europe before 1990, the trends for Eastern Europe and the CIS sub-region should be considered as only broadly indicative of the price trends for these two sub-regions in the earlier years.

2.7.1   Real prices of solid wood products

Figure 62 shows the trends in real prices for sawnwood in Europe over the last three decades. As the figure shows, the real price of sawnwood has tended to fall in recent years, particularly in the case of coniferous sawnwood in Western Europe.

Figure 62   Trends in real sawnwood prices in Europe since 1970

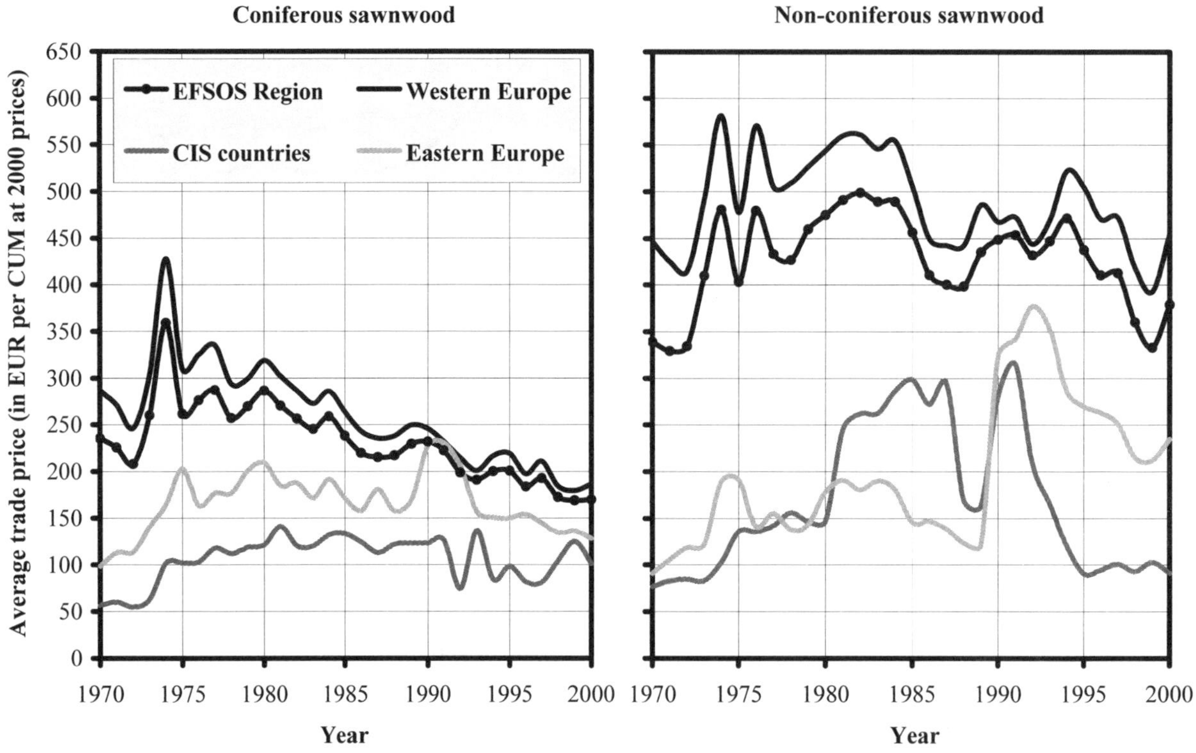

Source: derived from FAOSTAT production and trade statistics (http://faostat.external.fao.org). Note: figures for the Eastern Europe and CIS sub-regions before 1992 have been estimated from statistics for the USSR (see Section 1.4.2).

The decline in the real price of coniferous sawnwood has not been as steep as at first appears, because the price in 1974 was unusually high. A more realistic interpretation of these trends is that real prices in Western Europe were around EUR 300 per CUM throughout the late 1970s and fell by one-third to slightly less than EUR 200 per CUM by the year 2000. Real prices in Eastern Europe were between EUR 150 and EUR 200 per CUM for most of the period, but have also fallen in recent years to the lower end of this range. Prices in the CIS sub-region have remained fairly constant, at around EUR 100 per CUM. The prices for the latter two sub-regions are weighted heavily towards sawnwood exports, so domestic prices may be somewhat lower than suggested here.

---

[11]   A GDP deflator is a measure of general price inflation in a country. GDP deflators were used to convert nominal prices in each country to real prices measured against the general price level in the year 2000.

European non-coniferous sawnwood prices have also generally fallen in real terms since 1970, but not by as much as in the case of coniferous sawnwood. In Western Europe, real prices were mostly in the range of EUR 500 to EUR 550 per CUM until the mid-1980s. Since then, non-coniferous sawnwood has generally traded in the range of EUR 450 to EUR 500 per CUM. Prices in Eastern Europe rose dramatically in the early-1990s, to over EUR 300 per CUM, but have since fallen back to around EUR 200 per CUM. Trade prices with the CIS sub-region show a similar pattern, but have fallen back to a level of only EUR 100 per CUM.

At a broad level, the figure also shows two other interesting features in the real price trends for sawnwood in Europe. The first is that there has been some convergence of prices in the region, particularly in terms of the reduction in the gap between prices in Western and Eastern Europe. Secondly, the immediate increases in prices experienced in most of Eastern Europe and the CIS sub-region in the early-1990s have not been sustained, as prices there have generally declined over the last decade. While the expansion of production and exports in the east may have had some short-term impact on prices in Western Europe, it seems likely that this has been only one of many factors contributing to the general decline in prices in the region.

Historical trends in the real price of wood based panels in Europe are given in Figure 63 and Figure 64. In general, these also show declines in real prices in Europe across all product categories. However, most of the trends do not shown the same consistently falling real prices. Furthermore, the situation in Western Europe has been quite different to that of the other two European sub-regions.

The real price of fibreboard traded in Western Europe has fluctuated a lot over the last three decades, but has remained mostly in the range of EUR 350 to EUR 400 per CUM. At the end of the 1990s, the price fell below this level, but this may be only a temporary fall in the price of fibreboard. In both of the other two sub-regions, the real price of fibreboard has shown an upward trend, rising from a real price of around EUR 100 per CUM at the start of the period to EUR 200 per CUM in 2000. The apparent ability of fibreboard prices to avoid the declines in real prices shown in so many other product categories is probably due to the introduction of new products such as MDF.

In contrast, particleboard prices in Western Europe have shown a consistent downward trend in real terms over the period, from over EUR 350 per CUM in 1970 to under EUR 250 per CUM for most of the 1990s. Based on the trend shown in Figure 63, it appears that the price may now have stabilised at this level. Again, the real price of particleboard traded in Eastern Europe and the CIS sub-region has increased from under EUR 100 per CUM in 1970 to around EUR 200 per CUM in Eastern Europe and EUR 150 per CUM in the CIS sub-region.

The real price trends for plywood and veneer sheets show that prices fell significantly over the period 1970 to 1985, but appear to have stabilised since then. Currently, plywood is traded at a price of around EUR 500 per CUM in Western and Eastern Europe (or about half this amount in the CIS sub-region). Veneer sheet prices have stabilised at a price of around EUR 1,250 per CUM in Western Europe or slightly less than this in Eastern Europe. The trade prices for the CIS sub-region probably do not reflect the price trends for most of the veneer sheets produced and consumed in this sub-region, because the volumes of trade are very small.

Again, these figures show that wood based panels prices have converged between Western and Eastern Europe and, to a lesser extent, with the CIS sub-region. However, in this case, prices in Western Europe appear to have stabilised in recent years, while prices in the east have risen to meet them.

Figure 63   *Trends in real fibreboard and particleboard prices in Europe since 1970*

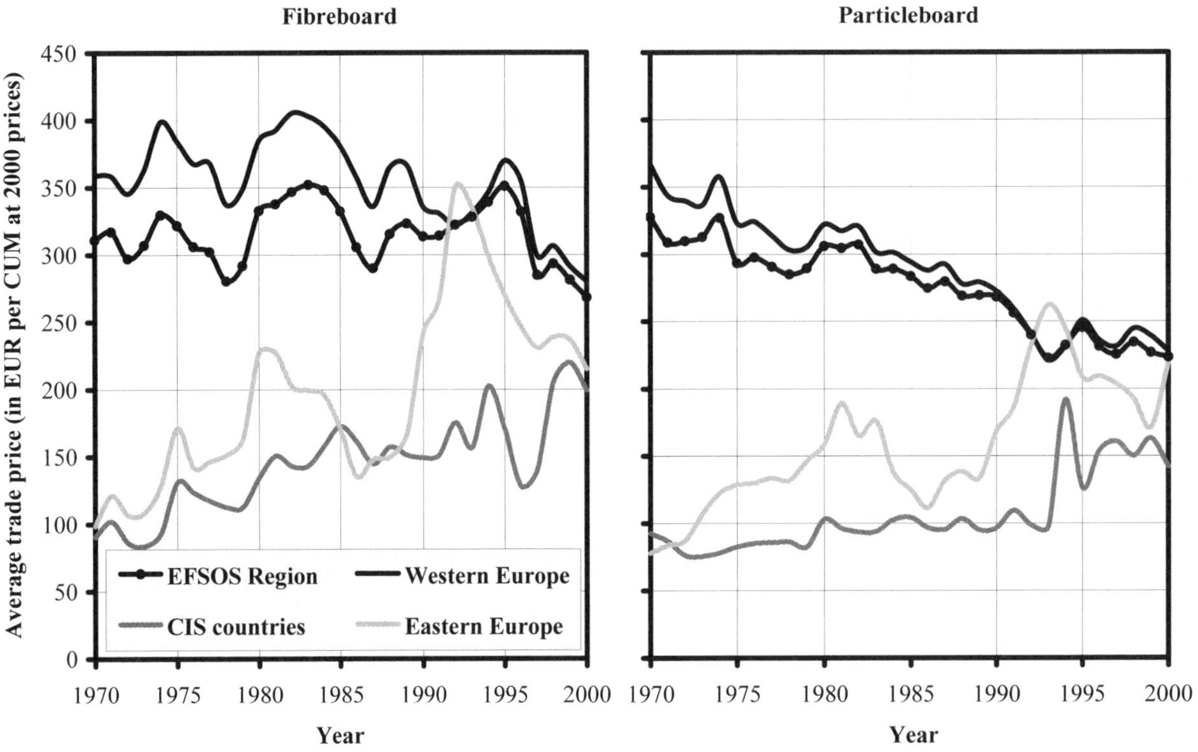

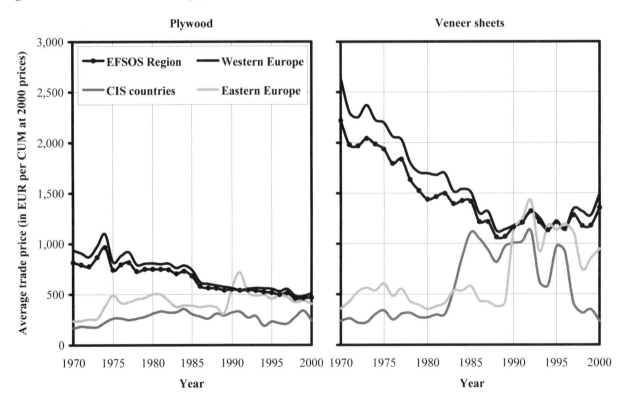

Source: derived from FAOSTAT production and trade statistics (http://faostat.external.fao.org). Note: figures for the Eastern Europe and CIS sub-regions before 1992 have been estimated from statistics for the USSR (see Section 1.4.2).

Figure 64   *Trends in real plywood and veneer sheets prices in Europe since 1970*

Source: derived from FAOSTAT production and trade statistics (http://faostat.external.fao.org). Note: figures for the Eastern Europe and CIS sub-regions before 1992 have been estimated from statistics for the USSR (see Section 1.4.2).

2.7.2   Real prices of wood pulp and paper

Real price trends for wood pulp traded in Europe are shown in Figure 65 and Figure 66. The first point worth noting is that wood pulp prices fluctuate a lot. This is due to changes in demand (related to the business cycle and strongly dependent on inventory movements) combined with the supply inflexibility due to the large investments required for pulp production, which restrict the ability of producers to alter production significantly from year to year.

Western Europe accounts for the majority of wood pulp traded in Europe and the figures show that semi-chemical and mechanical wood pulp prices have remained roughly the same over the period. The markets for semi-chemical wood pulp are relatively small and the real price of semi-chemical wood pulp has varied from about EUR 400 per MT to EUR 600 per MT over most of the period. Mechanical wood pulp has generally traded in a similar or slightly lower price range over the same period. In the last decade, real prices for both products have been somewhat lower than in the period from 1970 to 1990, but it is difficult to tell whether this represents a permanent shift to a lower price range or a temporary decline in real prices.

In the chemical wood pulp sector, (by far the most important from the trade point of view) there has been a much more pronounced fall in real prices in the last decade. From 1970 to 1990, the real price of chemical wood pulp fluctuated widely, from EUR 600 per MT to EUR 1,000 per MT with an average real price of around EUR 750 per MT. During the last decade, the real price of chemical wood pulp has fluctuated from EUR 400 per MT to EUR 700 per MT, with an average value in the middle of this range.

Chemical wood pulp is by far the most important type of wood pulp traded internationally and this product is produced in a large number of countries around the World. The lower prices in recent years are likely to reflect the entry of new low-cost producers from the Southern Hemisphere into these markets. The continued presence of these producers and the increased globalisation of trade in this product suggest that the lower price range experienced in the last decade may be a permanent feature of this market.

The availability of trade price statistics for wood pulp in the other two sub-regions is very limited, because few countries in these sub-regions have imported or exported wood pulp over the last three decades. What little evidence there is suggests that real wood pulp prices in Eastern Europe have probably remained more or less the same over much of the period, at levels that are close to or slightly below those in Western Europe. The production and trade (export) of chemical wood pulp is quite significant in the CIS sub-region and the figures suggest that real prices may have increased slightly over the period. Over the last decade, the real price of chemical wood pulp traded with the CIS sub-region has fluctuated between EUR 200 per MT and EUR 500 per MT and prices in this sub-region have followed the variation in prices displayed in Western Europe.

Historical trends in the real price of paper and paperboard products traded in Europe are shown in Figure 66 and Figure 67. International trade in paper and paperboard accounts for a relatively high share of production and consumption in all three sub-regions, so these trends are quite likely to reflect the more general trends in real prices experienced in all three sub-regions over the last thirty years.

At a broad level, the real price trends for each of the three main product categories show the same features, with a declining real price trend in Western Europe and rising prices in Eastern Europe and the CIS sub-region. Average real trade prices in Eastern Europe have converged with those in Western Europe over the last decade, while prices in the CIS sub-region remain somewhat below those in the rest of Europe.

Figure 65   *Trends in real semi-chemical and chemical pulp prices in Europe since 1970*

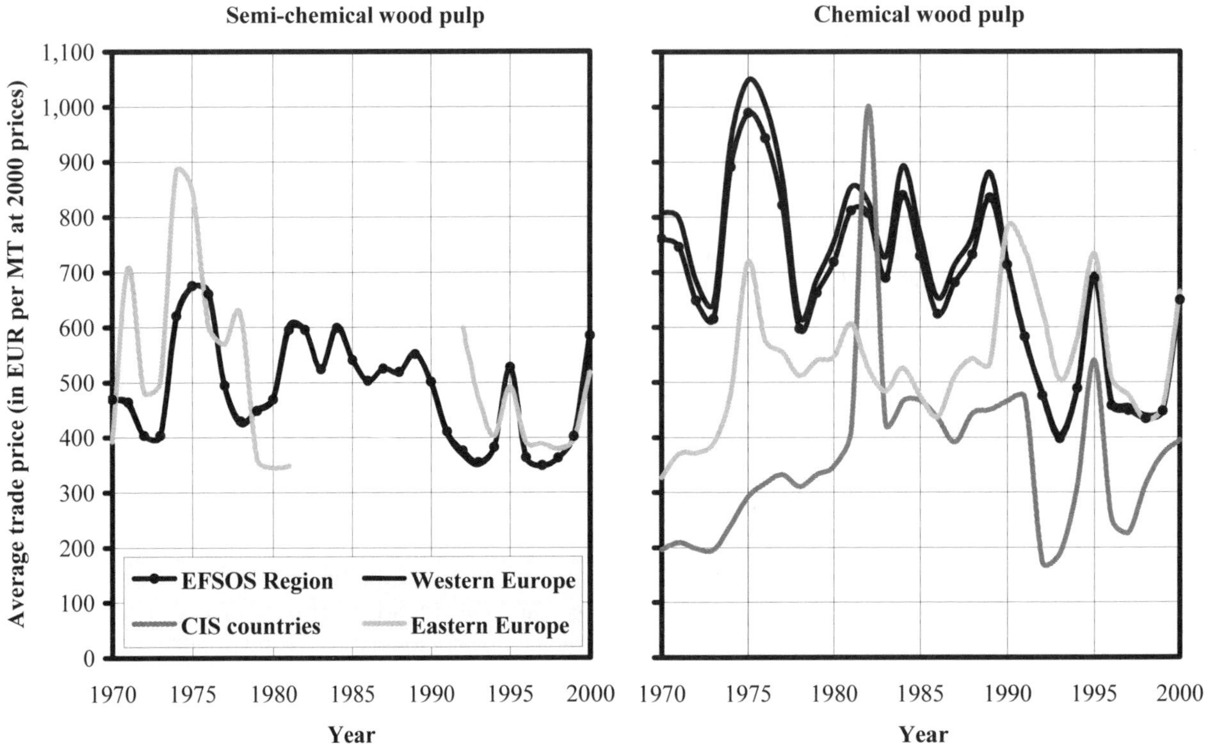

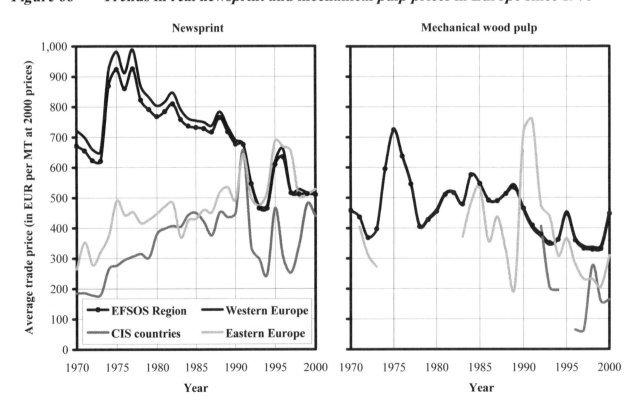

Source: derived from FAOSTAT production and trade statistics (http://faostat.external.fao.org). Note: figures for the Eastern Europe and CIS sub-regions before 1992 have been estimated from statistics for the USSR (see Section 1.4.2).

Figure 66   *Trends in real newsprint and mechanical pulp prices in Europe since 1970*

Source: derived from FAOSTAT production and trade statistics (http://faostat.external.fao.org). Note: figures for the Eastern Europe and CIS sub-regions before 1992 have been estimated from statistics for the USSR (see Section 1.4.2).

Figure 67   **Trends in the real price of printing and writing paper and other paper and paperboard in Europe since 1970**

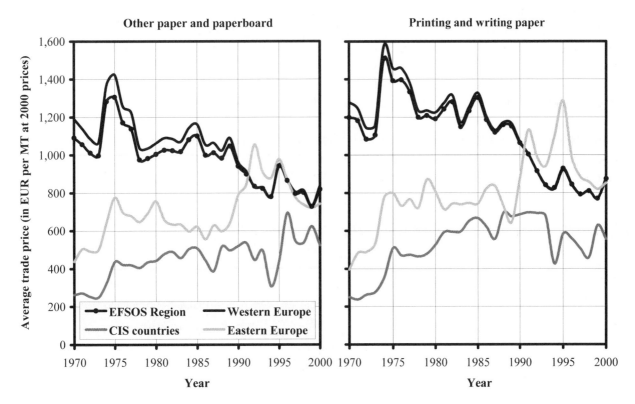

Source: derived from FAOSTAT production and trade statistics (http://faostat.external.fao.org). Note: figures for the Eastern Europe and CIS sub-regions before 1992 have been estimated from statistics for the USSR (see Section 1.4.2).

In Western Europe, the real price of newsprint has declined over the last three decades, from a range of EUR 800 per MT to EUR 1,000 per MT in the late-1970s to a range of EUR 500 per MT to EUR 700 per MT in the last decade. Prices in Eastern Europe were around EUR 300 per MT in 1970, but have converged with prices in Western Europe over the last decade. Prices in the CIS sub-region started at a lower level of EUR 200 per MT in 1970 and have also risen over the period. However, newsprint traded with the CIS sub-region (mostly exports from the sub-region) is currently priced about EUR 200 per MT lower than in the rest of the Europe.

The real prices of printing and writing paper and other paper and paperboard in Western Europe have also fallen over the last three decades. Over the period 1970 to 1990, the average real price of other paper and paperboard was around EUR 1,100 per MT, while the real price of printing and writing paper was around EUR 1,300 per MT. Over the last decade, both products have generally traded in the range of EUR 800 per MT to EUR 1,000 per MT. As in the case of newsprint, the prices of both products in Eastern Europe and the CIS sub-region have risen over the last thirty years. Prices in Eastern Europe have more or less converged with those in Western Europe, while prices in the CIS sub-region seem to have stabilised at a level that is about EUR 200 per MT lower than in the rest of the Europe.

The explanation for the trends in these markets is probably very similar to the explanation given above for chemical wood pulp. Paper and paperboard markets are increasingly globalised and a number of low-cost producers have entered the market in recent years. Thus, it seems likely that an environment of lower prices will persist in the future. The difference between prices in the CIS sub-region compared with the rest of Europe probably reflects the fact that these prices are heavily weighted towards export prices, which are measured as "free on board" (FOB) and will be slightly lower than in the rest of Europe due to transportation costs. Taking this into account, it is probably true to say that prices in the CIS sub-region have also converged with prices in the rest of Europe.

2.7.3   Real prices of standing timber (stumpage)

The price of industrial roundwood traded on international markets is not a very good indictor of general roundwood prices, because only a small proportion of industrial roundwood production and consumption is exported or imported. However, the availability of information about domestic roundwood prices is limited and is not generally available for every country in Europe. In addition to this, there is the problem that the data that is available is measured at a number of different points along the roundwood production chain (i.e. standing, at roadside or delivered).

To the forest owner or manager, the most important measure of the value of their roundwood production is the price of standing timber (or "stumpage" price). Information about the trends in stumpage prices in selected European countries were collected and converted to real prices (at 2000 price levels and exchange rates) and are presented here below.

Figure 68   Trends in real stumpage prices in Northern Europe since 1970

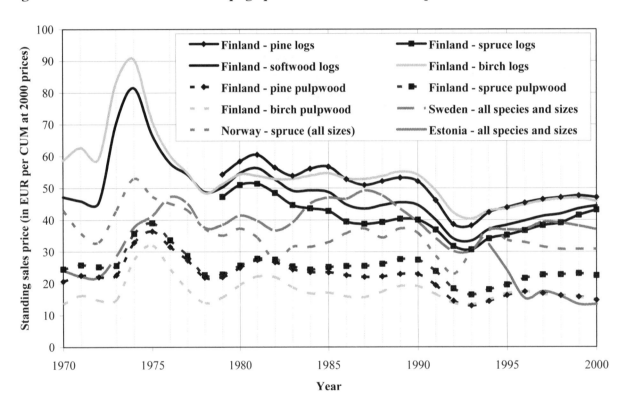

Sources: METLA (2003); Skogsstyrelsen (2004); Solberg (in prep); and RMK (2004).

Figure 68 shows the recent trends in real stumpage prices in a number of countries in Northern Europe since 1970. To a large extent, these trends are similar to those presented earlier for processed forest products and wood pulp, showing a peak in real prices in the mid-1970s, followed by a gradual decline in real prices since then.

In general, prices in Finland and Norway have declined by about EUR 10 per CUM across all types of industrial roundwood over the last three decades. Sawlogs sold standing in Finland achieved prices in the range of EUR 50 per CUM to EUR 60 per CUM during the latter half of the 1970s, but currently sell in the range of EUR 40 per CUM to EUR 50 per CUM. The price trend shown for Norway has been derived by subtracting average felling and extraction costs from average roadside sale prices. This shows a decline from around EUR 40 per CUM in the 1970s to an average price of around EUR 30 per CUM during the last decade.

In Sweden, it appears that stumpage prices have remained roughly the same over the period (in real terms) at a level of around EUR 40 per CUM. However, there is some weak evidence that prices may have also fallen slightly there in recent years. The price series for Estonia is too short to make any reliable statements about prices in that country, but it is notable that nominal prices have stayed about the same in the country since 1994, while inflation has reduced the real stumpage price by about half.

Figure 69   Trends in real stumpage prices in Belgium and the United Kingdom since 1970

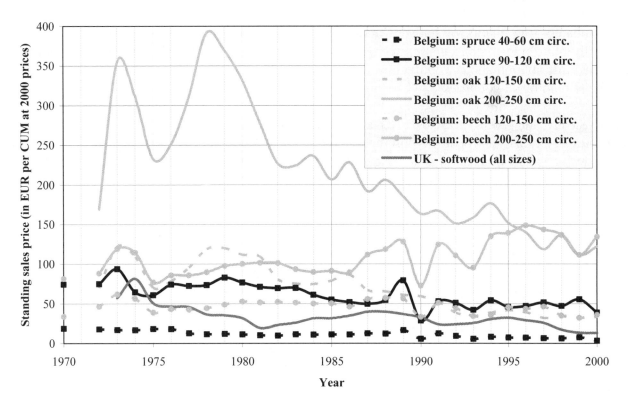

Sources: Gerkens and Gérard (2004) and FC (2002).

As a contrast to the figures for Northern Europe, Figure 69 presents trends in real stumpage prices for the Wallonne Region of Belgium and the United Kingdom. Although these figures also show a general decline in real prices, they also show that trends in real stumpage prices can be affected by a number of local variables.

For example, in the case of very large sized non-coniferous industrial roundwood in Belgium (roundwood with a circumference of 200 cm to 250 cm at breast height), the real price of oak has fallen by about half since the 1970s. In contrast, the real price of beech has risen by about 40 percent, from an average of around EUR 100 per CUM over the period 1970 to 1985, to an average price of around EUR 140 per CUM over the last five years. To some extent, this difference in price trends is due to greater interest shown in recent years in the use of beech for higher value products.

The real price trend for spruce in Belgium is very similar to the trend for Finland shown in the previous figure. However, in the United Kingdom, the trend for standing sales of all coniferous industrial roundwood shows a much more severe decline in real prices, with prices falling by almost two-thirds in the last decade. This could be due to the rapid expansion of production from maturing forest plantations there in recent years, leading to a situation where supply has been increasing more rapidly than demand.

As these figures have shown, the main factor that determines stumpage prices is the prices paid for processed forest products. Thus, in view of the trends presented in earlier sections, it follows that the trends in real stumpage prices have also generally declined in recent years. However, the trends from Belgium and the United Kingdom also show that local market conditions can affect stumpage prices. Currently, the challenge for most forest owners is to maintain the economic viability of forest management in an environment of low wood prices.

2.8   *Woodfuel*

Unfortunately, the quality of statistics about woodfuel production and consumption in Europe is generally quite poor. For example, of the 38 countries included in the EFSOS, only 27 countries provided information about woodfuel production in 2000 and FAO estimated woodfuel production for the remaining 11 countries.

Until recently, the process used by FAO to estimate missing woodfuel statistics was very simplistic. Estimates of per capita woodfuel consumption were produced in the late-1980s and these were used (along with population statistics) to produce estimates of total woodfuel production for countries where no data is available. More recently, an improved methodology was developed to estimate missing data (see Whiteman *et al*, 2002) and this has been used to revise all historical estimates of woodfuel production in Europe. Although this methodology is believed to produce better estimates than before, it should be noted that the trends presented here are based on a mixture of statistics reported by countries and FAO estimates. Furthermore there are many ambiguities concerning the reported figures: do they cover all production or only that entering commercial channels? Are branches etc. covered (they are not generally included in forest inventories of standing volume)? what about trees outside the forest or other woody vegetation, which accounts for millions of m3 of wood fuel in some cases? What about bark, wood residues and recovered wood used for energy? Are the data collected from surveys of suppliers, or by user surveys?

Figure 70   Trends in production and consumption of woodfuel from 1961 to 2000

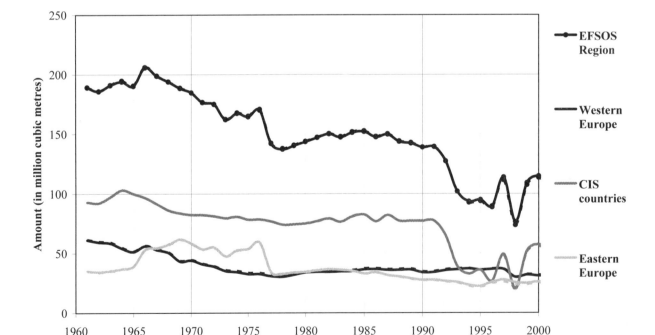

Solid lines represent production and dashed lines represent apparent consumption

Source: derived from FAOSTAT production and trade statistics (http://faostat.external.fao.org). Note: figures for the Eastern Europe and CIS sub-regions before 1992 have been estimated from statistics for the USSR (see Section 1.4.2).

Figure 70 shows the trends in woodfuel production and consumption in Europe over the last four decades, as contained in the international data bases. The first point to note is that production and consumption are more or less the same, because international trade in woodfuel is insignificant. Broadly speaking, the annual production and consumption of woodfuel reported in Europe has fallen by almost half over the last four decades, from 189 million m^3 in 1961 to 113 million m^3 in 2000.

At the sub-regional level, production and consumption of woodfuel also is reported to have fallen in all three EFSOS sub-regions. In Western Europe, consumption declined from around 60 million m^3 in 1961 to 33 million m^3 in 1975. Since 1975, annual consumption has fluctuated between 30 million m^3 and 35 million m^3, with no strong visible trend upwards or downwards.

In Eastern Europe, woodfuel consumption appears to have declined from around 35 million m^3 in 1961 to 25 million m^3 in 2000. The increase shown for the period from the mid-1960s to mid-1970s is due to Turkey, where increased production was reported for a number of years. It is not known whether this represents a true change in production over these years or is a statistical anomaly. Apart from this period, the statistics show a slight but strong downward trend until the mid-1990s, after which it appears that woodfuel production may be increasing slightly.

In the CIS sub-region, production and consumption declined gradually until the early-1990s, when both variables fell by about 50 percent. Since then, production and consumption have fluctuated a lot, but the statistics suggest that the use of woodfuel may be increasing slightly.

Traditionally, woodfuel has been mostly used in one of two forms, either directly as fuelwood or as charcoal. The definition of "woodfuel" used to compile these statistics only includes these two types of woodfuel (i.e. wood burned directly as fuelwood plus the wood used to make charcoal). More recently, there has been growth in the use of wood for a variety of different energy uses such as electricity generation, and in larger heating units, for district heating, co-generation or the energy needs of larger buildings such as schools and barracks, increasingly with modern systems for clean combustion and automatic boiler feeding. Furthermore, the use of wood chips and wood residues for energy production is quite common in the forest processing industry and has probably increased in the forest processing industry and elsewhere. It is not known whether these statistics capture some of these uses of wood for energy, so this is another reason why these trends must be treated with some caution. There may be a recovery in the use of wood energy under way at present, but the statistical data are not yet able to monitor or analyse this trend

2.9 Non-wood forest products

It is frequently stated that the production of NWFPs and forest services is just as important as wood production in Europe and that this importance is increasing. Indeed, some of the most sensitive and complex policy questions over the last decade in Europe have concerned NWFPs and forest services. In order to assess how true this might be, this section and the following section briefly summarise the trends and current status of the supply and demand for NWFPs and forest services from European forests.

2.9.1 Statistical issues

There is no recognised standard classification of NWFPs and forest services although, in consultation with countries, FAO is working towards an internationally agreed classification and set of definitions (FAO, 1999). For the purpose of this study, NWFPs and forest services have been divided into the following broad groups:

Non-wood forest products (NWFPs):

- edible plant products (e.g. fruits, nuts, mushrooms, herbs and saps);
- animal products (e.g. honey, game meat and pelts);
- medicinal plants;
- bark, foliage and vegetation (including cork and cork products);
- Christmas trees; and
- other non-food products (e.g. gums, resins and oils).

Forest services:

- recreation;
- mitigation of climate change;
- conservation of biodiversity;
- protection of soil, water and infrastructure; and
- cultural aspects

With respect to data sources, it is important to note that the quality of the statistics used in this section is significantly lower than the quality of the statistics used elsewhere in this study. For example, there is incomplete country coverage for many of the NWFPs and forest services and there are numerous problems of comparability in the statistics produced in different countries. This is particularly a problem for the estimation of production and consumption trends.

Another problem that exists is with the aggregation of production and consumption. Strictly speaking, with the wide range of measurement units used to quantify NWFPs and forest services, the only reliable way to aggregate these statistics is to use the value of production and consumption. Information about the value of these outputs is also crucial for the forest manager and policy maker, when they come to assess the relative importance of roundwood production versus the production of these outputs in their decisions. Unfortunately, however, information about the value of these outputs is even more scarce than statistics about their quantity (indeed, in some cases, there is still considerable debate about how some of these outputs can be valued). Therefore, the presentation of information about values in this section is very brief.

Despite the problems highlighted above, the availability of information about NWFPs and forest services has improved significantly over the last decade, due to the creation of datasets related to the measurement of criteria and indicators of sustainable forest management. In particular the FRA 2000 (UN, 2000) and the report on the State of Europe's Forests in 2003 (MCPFE, 2003a) have brought together the best ever dataset in this area and it is to be hoped that this improvement in statistics will be maintained in the future. The majority of the statistics presented here for recent years have been drawn from these sources, with historical information coming from a variety of earlier reports by FAO, UNECE and others.

2.9.2   Edible plant products

Edible plant products from forests comprise a wide variety of tree products (fruits, nuts and edible saps) plus other edible plants that are commonly found growing in forests (e.g. mushrooms and herbs). One of the problems with statistics for these products is identifying the amount of products that have come from forests as opposed to those that have been grown in commercial orchards or non-forest areas. In addition to this, there is also the problem that a lot of production is consumed by the collectors of these products and does not appear in forestry statistics. However, despite these problems, there are quite good statistics for some of edible plant products and these can be used to assess production and consumption trends.

Forest fruits and berries. Forest fruits and berries include fruits that come from various forest tree species, plus a number of fruits that grow on shrubs and bushes that are usually part of the forest ecosystem. Information about production, consumption and trade of forest fruits and berries is scarce, but the FRA 2000 (UN, 2000) contains some statistics for the amount and value of production during the 1990s. In addition to this, statistics for a few other countries not included in FRA 2000 have been obtained from other sources (UN, 1998; Zajac *et al*, 2004; Chobanova *et al*, 2004; Bouriaud *et al*, 2004).

Table 10   ***Production of forest fruits and berries in some European countries in the 1990s***

Sub-region	Quantity statistics			Real value statistics		
	No. of countries	No. of observations	Total annual production (in '000 MT)	No. of countries	No. of observations	Total annual value (in EUR million)
Western Europe	7	10	94	7	8	134
Eastern Europe	10	23	108	6	6	207
CIS countries	3	3	9	2	2	9
Europe	**33**	**23**	**211**	**15**	**16**	**349**

Sources: UN (1998 and 2000); Zajac et al (2004); Chobanova et al (2004); and Bouriaud et al (2004). Note: all values have been converted to Euros at 2000 prices and exchange rates.

The statistics for forest fruit and berry production are shown in Table 10. This table includes statistics from a variety of years during the 1990s and the values have all been converted to Euros at 2000 prices and exchange rates. Where there are statistics for more than one year in a country, the average over the years has been calculated and used instead of individual values. The totals show the sum of the averages and individual values for the countries where statistics exist.

The table above includes statistics for most of the European countries where forest fruit and berry production is probably significant, with the exception of Germany, Greece, Spain, Portugal, Hungary and Turkey. It shows that total annual production is about 211 thousand tonnes, with an average annual value of production of about EUR 350 million. Countries that have recorded a significant amount of forest fruit and berry production include the Scandinavian countries, Albania and the Czech Republic.

The little information that is available about trends, suggests that the majority of production in Western Europe is consumed by the collectors and that the amounts have not changed very much. However, there is some evidence that the small amounts collected commercially have declined, due to increased competition from Eastern Europe. There is slight evidence of an upward trend in production in the few Eastern European countries that have statistics for more than a single year, but there is not enough data for this to be a reliable indication of a trend.

It should also be noted that potential supply of forest fruits and berries is far higher than demand in remote and rural forest areas. For instance, it is estimated that only 10 percent of the natural yield of mushrooms and berries is currently harvested in Finland. However, natural supplies are under pressure near urban areas and especially in countries where there is a strong tradition of personal collection of edible plant products. In a few cases, restrictions have been imposed to keep the harvest at a sustainable level (e.g. harvesting limits per person, restrictions of access to certain days, etc.).

Carob. The Carob tree can be found in many Mediterranean countries and the fruit of the Carob tree is used for a variety of purposes from chocolate making to cattle feed (Ciesla, 2002). Production of this fruit is only significant in a few European countries, with approximate levels of production in the late 1990s as follows: 130,000 MT in Spain; 50,000 MT in Italy; 35,000 MT in Portugal; 20,000 MT in Greece; and 15,000 MT in Turkey. This gives a total level of production in Europe of around 250,000 MT, equal to 70 percent of the total world production of 350,000 MT.

Tree nuts. The most important tree nuts that are produced in Europe are almonds, walnuts, chestnuts and hazelnuts. Minor tree nuts include pistachios and pine nuts. Some of these nuts are collected from forests as one of a range of products, but a proportion is collected from forests and trees grown specifically for the purpose of nut production.

The FRA 2000 presents information about the amount and value of nut production for only a few countries. However, there are a lot of statistics about nut production in FAO's statistical database (FAOSTAT), so this information is presented and analysed here.

Figure 71   Trends in production and consumption of tree nuts from 1961 to 2000

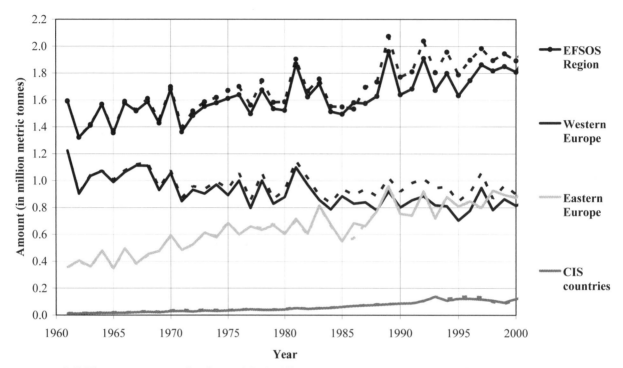

Solid lines represent production and dashed lines represent apparent consumption

Source: derived from FAOSTAT production and trade statistics (http://faostat.external.fao.org). Note: totals for the Eastern Europe and CIS sub-regions before 1992 have been estimated from statistics for the USSR (see Section 1.4.2).

Figure 71 shows the trends in European tree nut production and consumption over the last four decades. For Europe as a whole, annual production and consumption has increased slightly, from around 1.4 million MT to 1.6 million MT in the 1960s, to 1.8 million MT to 2.0 million MT in the 1990s. Furthermore, a slight gap has developed between consumption and production, with consumption exceeding production by around 100 thousand MT per year in recent years.

At the sub-regional level, production and consumption have declined slightly in Western Europe over the last four decades. In addition, net imports into Western Europe have increased, accounting for the negative trade balance in tree nuts for Europe as a whole (production and consumption are roughly equal in the other two European sub-regions). These trends could be due to the labour intensive nature of nut collection, which has resulted in increased competition over time from other countries with lower labour costs.

Production and consumption has more than doubled in Eastern Europe since 1960, but a significant proportion of this increase is attributable to one country (Turkey). Production and consumption have increased in many of the other countries in Eastern Europe, but by much less than the average for this sub-region as a whole. Production and consumption have also increased significantly in the CIS sub-region, but the current level of production and consumption - around 100 thousand MT per year - is relatively small.

Figure 72 shows the historical trends in European tree nut production by type of nut. Production of almonds has remained roughly the same over the period, accounting for about one-quarter of total production. Production of chestnuts has declined significantly, from about 400 thousand MT per year in the 1960s to less than 200 thousand MT per year at present. Walnut production has increased very slightly and currently accounts for about 400 thousand MT per year. The greatest increase in production has occurred in the production of hazelnuts, which amounted to less than 200 thousand MT in 1960, but has since increased to an annual production level of around 700 thousand MT. Almost all of this production comes from Turkey.

Figure 72   Trends in the production of different types of tree nuts from 1961 to 2000

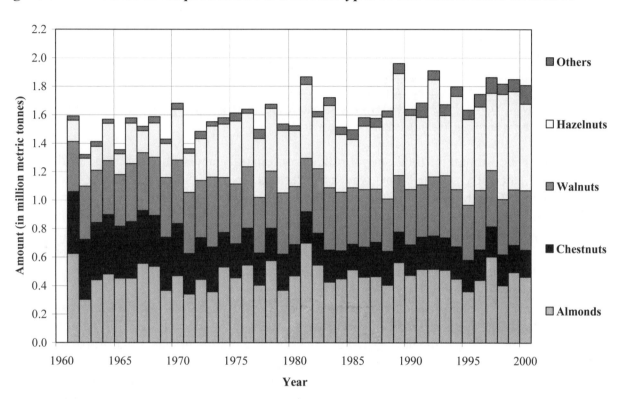

Source: derived from FAOSTAT production and trade statistics (http://faostat.external.fao.org). Note: totals for the Eastern Europe and CIS sub-regions before 1992 have been estimated from statistics for the USSR (see Section 1.4.2).

International trade in tree nuts is relatively small. About 10 percent of European production is exported and most of this trade is between European countries. Net imports of tree nuts into Europe come from a variety of countries and important imports include chestnuts, walnuts and pistachios. In addition to these, there are also imports of nuts that can not be grown in Europe (e.g. Brazil nuts).

Information about the value of tree nut production in Europe is only available for a very small number of countries (UN, 2000). However, using the European trade prices, it is possible to estimate what the value of production might be. An estimate of the value of tree nut production has been calculated using the average of import and export prices for each type of tree nut and sub-region (i.e. total value of trade divided by total amount of trade) and by multiplying the production levels in 2000 by those prices.

The result of this calculation is an estimated total value of tree nut production in Europe of EUR 2,989 million in 2000. This is divided as follows: EUR 1,626 million (54 percent) in Western Europe; EUR 1,257 million (42 percent) in Eastern Europe; and EUR 106 million (four percent) in the CIS sub-region.

Mushrooms and truffles. The importance of mushroom and truffle production varies across Europe, depending on local traditions, growing conditions and the intensity of management for mushroom and truffle production. In general, it is believed that there is strong demand for mushrooms, particularly for wild mushrooms (which come from forests in most cases). However, there is also increasingly strong competition from cultivated mushrooms and truffles.

Table 11   ***Production of mushrooms and truffles in some European countries in the 1990s***

Sub-region	Quantity statistics			Real value statistics		
	No. of countries	No. of observations	Total annual production (in '000 MT)	No. of countries	No. of observations	Total annual value (in EUR million)
Western Europe	9	12	31	8	9	177
Eastern Europe	10	23	37	5	7	67
CIS countries	2	2	10	1	1	18
Europe	**21**	**37**	**77**	**14**	**17**	**262**

Sources: UN (1998 and 2000); Zajac et al (2004); Chobanova et al (2004); and Bouriaud et al (2004). Note: all values have been converted to Euros at 2000 prices and exchange rates.

Table 11 shows an estimate of total annual production quantity and value in Europe in the 1990s. This has been calculated in the same way as described above. The totals include most of the European countries where production is probably significant, except Germany and Spain. As with forest fruits and berries, it is unknown whether these statistics include all of the mushrooms that are picked and eaten by collectors. For example, some commonly-quoted references to mushroom production in Finland only include commercial production, which is about ten percent of the estimated total production (the figures used here are an estimate of the total).

The figures show that total production may be around 77 thousand MT, with a total real value of EUR 263 million. The highest value of production occurs in Western Europe (67 percent of the total). This is almost twice the level of the value of production in Eastern Europe, where the quantity of production is higher. This is due to the collection of truffles, which have extremely high market prices. Most truffle collection in Europe takes place in France, Italy and Spain. Therefore, the absence of any statistics for Spain suggests that the total value of production in Europe could be somewhat higher than the figures presented here.

There is not sufficient information to assess trends in mushroom production. In the case of truffles though, there has been a long-term decline in production in France, which has stabilised in recent years. It is also worth noting that truffle production has probably intensified in recent years, with the establishment of truffle orchards in some places. This increase in management intensity may result in higher production in the future (in Europe and elsewhere), resulting in a fall in prices.

Other edible plant products. The production of other edible plant products is relatively minor, although individual products may be significant in specific countries (e.g. birch sap in Finland and Belarus). It is not possible to assess the volumes or values of production of these other products at the European level, due to the lack of available data.

2.9.3   Animal products

The main animal products produced in European forests are honey, game meat and pelts (furs) and statistics on the quantity and value of production are presented here below.

Honey. One of the main problems with assessing the level of honey production from forests is to identify how much honey production is dependent on the forest resource[12]. For example, FAO statistics for total honey production record a level of European production that is more than ten times higher than the amounts reported in FRA 2000.

Most of the figures presented below come from the FRA 2000 (UN, 2000). In some cases, countries provided figures for honey production that only included production that takes place on FOWL. In other cases, countries provided figures for total honey production (i.e. figures that match the statistics in FAOSTAT). Even if honey production does not take place on FOWL, it may still rely on forests as a source of nectar (and could, therefore, be counted as a NWFP), so the figures below are probably an underestimate of the true quantity and value of this production.

Table 12   Production of honey in some European countries in the 1990s

Sub-region	Quantity statistics			Real value statistics		
	No. of countries	No. of observations	Total annual production (in '000 MT)	No. of countries	No. of observations	Total annual value (in EUR million)
Western Europe	4	4	6	3	3	12
Eastern Europe	5	11	24	3	3	22
CIS countries	3	3	<1	3	3	<1
Europe	**12**	**18**	**31**	**9**	**9**	**34**

Sources: UN (1998 and 2000); Zajac et al (2004); Chobanova et al (2004); and Bouriaud et al (2004). Note: all values have been converted to Euros at 2000 prices and exchange rates.

Table 12 shows that total annual production amounts to some 31 thousand MT, with a value of about EUR 34 million. However, figures are missing for many European countries in this total. This would suggest that the total volume and value of production could be several times higher than these figures. For comparison, the total volume and value of all European honey production in 2000 was 350 thousand MT and EUR 518 million.

Information about trends in honey production from FAWS is not available. However, Figure 73 shows the historical trends in the markets for honey (from all sources). This shows that there has been a gradual increase in production and consumption in the past, although this seems to have levelled-off in recent years. It is also worth noting that Western Europe is a significant net importer of honey (and Eastern Europe is a very small net exporter). Given current changes in consumer preferences towards natural and organic products, it could be suggested that the markets for honey produced from FAWS may be increasing slightly, as consumers switch towards this natural product.

---

[12] For instance, even if the beehives are in the forest or on the forest edge, the bees will take pollen from plants inside and outside the forest. Is the resulting honey a "forest product"?

Figure 73   Trends in total production and consumption of honey from 1961 to 2000

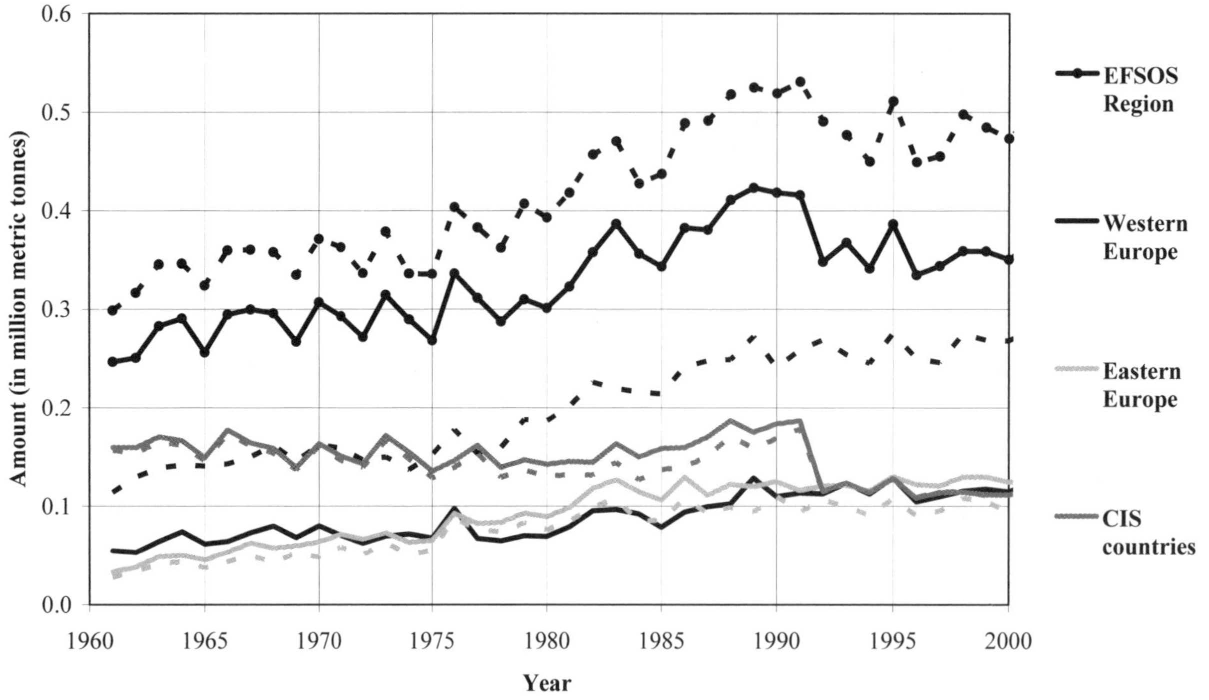

Solid lines represent production and dashed lines represent apparent consumption

Source: derived from FAOSTAT production and trade statistics (http://faostat.external.fao.org). Note: totals for the Eastern Europe and CIS sub-regions before 1992 have been estimated from statistics for the USSR (see Section 1.4.2).

Game meat and pelts. Game meat comprises the meat of all hunted birds and mammals, such as: partridge; pheasant; hare; deer; and wild pigs. Pelts refers to the skins or furs of some of these animals, which are used to produce rugs, clothing and footwear.

Table 13   Production of game meat and pelts in some European countries in the 1990s

| Sub-region | No. of countries | Quantity statistics | | | Real value statistics | |
		Game meat production (in '000 MT)	Game harvest numbers (in '000)	No. of pelts (in '000)	Annual value of meat (in EUR million)	Annual value of pelts (in EUR million)
Western Europe	8	34	3,949	243	417	24
Eastern Europe	9	22	881	14	19	<1
CIS countries	2	3	6,827	20,684	3	n.a.
Europe	**19**	**59**	**11,657**	**20,941**	**442**	**24**

Sources: UN (1998 and 2000); Aldrian et al (2004); and Cooper et al (2004). Note: all values have been converted to Euros at 2000 prices and exchange rates. It should also be noted that quantities and values are not comparable, because some countries only provided one of these figures (e.g. pelt production in the Russian Federation).

Production statistics for game meat and pelts are quite good in many countries, because licences are often required for hunting and trapping of wildlife. However, the statistics available in FRA 2000 (UN, 2000) are quite incomplete, covering only half of the countries in the Europe. Furthermore, the figures for quantity and value of production are not comparable because some countries only provided one of these figures. The most prominent example of this is the Russian Federation, which provided statistics showing a huge output of game and pelts, but could not provide any statistics for the value of this output.

Table 13 shows that average annual game production in the 1990s was about 59 thousand MT of meat, plus a further 11.6 million animals. In addition to this, annual production of pelts amounted to about 21.9 million, with the majority of production in the CIS sub-region. The total recorded value of production was EUR 466 million per year, but this is probably a large underestimation of the true value of production in these countries. For Europe as a whole, it would also seem likely that the total quantity and value of production is somewhat higher than the figures here imply.

All of the above information was supplied for only one year (or as an average of several years). Therefore, it is not possible to analyse trends in the production of game meat and pelts. However, at least one country - the Netherlands- has indicated that hunting is becoming less popular.

2.9.4   Medicinal plants

The size of markets for medicinal plants varies considerably across Europe. In some countries in Eastern Europe, production and consumption of medicinal plants has been significant for many years. In Western Europe, many countries do not have significant markets for medicinal plants. However, in the few countries with a market for these products (e.g. Germany and Italy) these markets can be huge.

Table 14   ***Production of medicinal plants in some European countries in the 1990s***

Sub-region	No. of countries	Total annual production (in '000 MT)	Total annual value (in EUR million)
Western Europe	3	15	72
Eastern Europe	7	27	46
CIS countries	3	1	<1
Europe	**13**	**43**	**118**

Sources: UN (1998 and 2000); Chobanova et al (2004); and Collier et al (2004). Note: all values have been converted to Euros at 2000 prices and exchange rates. It should also be noted that quantities and values are not comparable.

Table 14 shows the total quantity and value of medicinal plant production in a few European countries. These figures have been calculated in the same way as described above, from FRA 2000 statistics, plus statistics from additional sources. These statistics are probably a large underestimation of the total quantity and value of production and consumption at the regional and sub-regional level, because many countries are not included in the totals. Italy is one of the main consumer markets that is missing from these figures. In addition, the value statistics only include the value of exports from Germany and Bulgaria. At least in the case of Germany, the total size of the market is likely to be much larger than the figures included here.

There is little information available about the trends in this market, although Collier *et al* (2004) report that there is some evidence that production is declining in a few countries in Western Europe, due to greater competition from Eastern European countries.

2.9.5   Bark, foliage and vegetation (including cork and cork products)

Cork and cork products. Cork is used for a variety of purposes, including: bottle stoppers; floor covering; insulation; shoe soles; construction materials; and even car parts (Iqbal, 1993). Of these, bottle stoppers are by far the most valuable product manufactured from cork. In addition to the production of cork, the value of cork oak forests for conservation and amenity has also been recognised in recent years.

Natural cork is produced in only a few Mediterranean countries (France, Italy, Portugal and Spain, plus a few other countries in Southern Europe and North Africa). Portugal is the most important producer and exporter of cork, accounting for around half of total world production and exports. Furthermore, a significant cork production and processing industry has developed in Portugal, which now processes raw cork imported from other countries as well as domestic production. The management of Cork oak forests in Portugal is also very well developed, with regulations for harvesting and processing and strict quality control standards.

The FRA 2000 (UN, 2000) presents information about cork production in four countries in the 1990s. This was used to produce the figures shown in Table 15, along with additional information from the Italian State Forest Service (1990), Carvalho Mendes (2004) and Wine Business Monthly (2001).

Table 15 **Recent trends in the production of natural cork in Europe**

Country	Average annual production (in '000 MT)				Annual real value in the mid-1990s (in EUR million)
	1970s	mid-1980s	mid-1990s	Current	
France	slightly higher	5	4	5	1
Italy	similar	10	10	18	6
Portugal	similar	170	135	185	130
Spain	slightly higher	90	85	88	65
Albania	n.a.	n.a.	18	n.a.	6
Europe	**slightly higher**	**275**	**252**	**296**	**209**

Sources: UN (2000); Italian State Forest Service (1990); Wine Business Monthly (2001); and Carvalho Mendes (2004).
Note: all values have been converted to Euros at 2000 prices and exchange rates.

Currently, annual production of cork is around 296 thousand MT, with a total value of production of around EUR 209 million (at 2000 prices and exchange rates). The trends indicate that production of cork has declined in France over the last few decades and, to a lesser extent, in Spain. In Italy and Portugal, production has been very variable, but has possibly increased slightly in recent years. In particular, production in Portugal was showing a declining trend until recently, but appears to have benefited from efforts to ensure high quality control standards in the industry (see Box 2).

Box 2 **Increased competition from non-wood substitutes: the case of the Portuguese wine cork industry**

A recent development in the market for bottle stoppers has been increased competition from the use of artificial (plastic) corks. These have been particularly popular amongst wine producers in some of the new wine producing countries. This trend has been partly driven by price, as plastic corks are generally cheaper than natural corks. However, a more significant concern has been the problem of "corked" wine, with some sources estimating that as much as five percent of wine production is affected by this problem.

In response to this problem, the European associations representing the cork industry investigated the problem of wine contamination in the early-1990s (the Quercus Project). One of the recommendations of this research was that a guide of good practice in cork manufacturing should be produced. This led to the production of the *"International code of cork stopper manufacturing practices"* and accreditation of cork producers from 2000. The code is designed to ensure that high quality control standards are implemented throughout the cork production process, from the forest to the vineyard. Accreditation also guarantees to wine producers and bottlers that they have a product that should be free from contamination and has followed these rigorous procedures.

Research has shown that the problem of contamination has been a far more important issue for cork users than price. It has also shown that there is a slight preference towards the natural cork product (although the results in this area have been mixed). It seems likely, therefore, that these improvements in quality should result in a more secure outlook for this industry in the future.

Sources: Cork Information Bureau (2002), plus various news items.

Better information is available about trends in international trade in cork and cork products and trends in exports are shown in Figure 74. These trends appear similar to the trends in production described above. In particular, it is notable that exports have increased since the early-1980s. The total value of cork exports in 2000 was EUR 1,334 million, of which EUR 216 million was exports of raw cork and waste and EUR 1,118 million was exports of products manufactured from cork.

Figure 74   Trends in European exports of cork and cork products since 1960

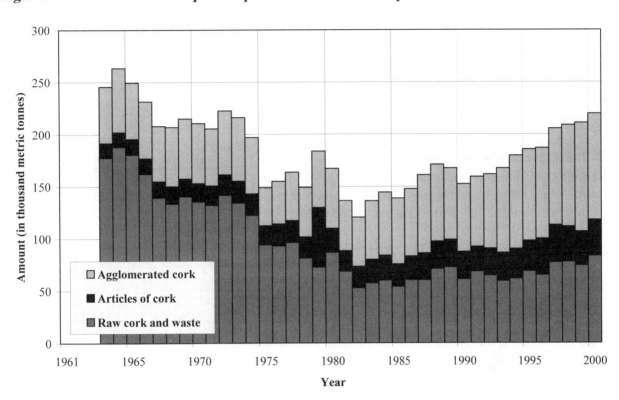

Source: derived from the UN COMTRADE database, available at: http://unstats.un.org/unsd/comtrade/default.aspx. Note: the figure includes statistics for France, Italy, Spain and Portugal, which account for almost all European exports.

Decorative foliage. Information about the quantity and value of foliage production in Europe is scarce, but the figures obtained from some recent sources are presented in Table 16. These figures are probably quite unreliable, as statistics are not available for many European countries. Based on these figures, it is estimated that the total annual amount of production could be at least 45 thousand MT, with a value of about EUR 49 million.

Table 16   Production of decorative foliage in some European countries in the 1990s

Sub-region	No. of countries	Total annual production (in '000 MT)	Total annual value (in EUR million)
Western Europe	6	36	47
Eastern Europe	2	9	2
CIS countries	1	<1	n.a.
Europe	**10**	**45**	**49**

Sources: UN (2000); Chobanova et al (2004); Cooper et al (2004); and Collier et al (2004). Note: all values have been converted to Euros at 2000 prices and exchange rates. It should also be noted that quantities and values are not comparable and that the high figures for Albania reported in FRA 2000 are not included here (see: UN, 2000).

Other plant products. Other major plant products include bark (used to make compost and mulch), fodder and forage. The amount and value of production is unknown and probably varies significantly between countries. In FRA 2000 (UN, 2000), most countries reported that the use of forests for grazing (i.e. fodder and forage) is declining. For the five European countries that provided estimates of the value of fodder and forage production, the total annual value of production in the mid 1990s was about EUR 36 million (at 2000 prices and exchange rates).

2.9.6 Christmas trees

Christmas trees are a major seasonal crop and exports of Christmas trees are significant in some countries (e.g. Denmark). The production of Christmas trees is a major activity in some locations, although it is not clear to what extent the trees come from forests as opposed to specialised horticultural plantations. For example, many Christmas trees are of a species that is not usually found in European forests (e.g. *Abies nordmannia*).

Slightly better information is available about the production of Christmas trees in Europe. Table 17 presents the information collected in FRA 2000 (UN, 2000) and shows that the average annual production in Europe in the mid-1990s was at least 43 million trees, with a total value of EUR 444 million (at 2000 prices and exchange rates).

Table 17   Production of Christmas trees in some European countries in the 1990s

Sub-region	No. of countries	Total annual production (in millions)	Total annual value (in EUR million)
Western Europe	12	41	418
Eastern Europe	5	1	27
CIS countries	0	n.a.	n.a.
Europe	**18**	**43**	**444**

Sources: UN (1998 and 2000). Note: all values have been converted to Euros at 2000 prices and exchange rates. It should also be noted that quantities and values are not comparable.

Information about trends in production is not available, although a few countries have increased production in recent years as part of deliberate efforts to increase this part of the sector (e.g. Ireland).

2.9.7 Other non-food products

Other non-food products include beeswax and various gums, resins and essential oils produced from wood, bark and leaves. Most of these products have relatively small and specialised markets, although the value of production can be quite high. The only significant production in Europe is production of resins (mostly in Portugal, France and the Russian Federation) and Eucalyptus oil (mostly in Portugal). Resin production has declined, due to the labour costs of resin collection and competition from low-cost suppliers (China and, more recently, Brazil). There are good markets for Eucalyptus oil, but these markets are dominated by production from Australia and Europe's share of this market is insignificant.

2.9.8 Value of NWFP production compared to wood production

Table 18 summarises all of the information presented above about the value of NWFP production and compares this with the estimated total annual value of wood production in Europe in the mid-1990s from FRA 2000 (FAO, 2000). It is clear that the relative importance of NWFPs depends upon how much of the value of tree nut production should be considered as an activity that can be legitimately included as part of the forest sector (the same is true of honey production - the figures here only include the very low values reported in FRA 2000).

If the production of tree nuts is included, the production of NWFPs accounts for slightly less than one-quarter of the total value of all forest products produced in Europe. In Eastern Europe, the importance is much higher, but this is largely due to the high quantity and value of tree nuts produced in Turkey. Excluding Turkey, the contribution of NWFPs (including tree nuts) to the total value of forest product production in Eastern Europe would be about 15 percent. If tree nuts are excluded from the equation altogether, the relative importance of NWFPs falls to just slightly more than 10 percent. This is a relatively small share but, at an amount of EUR 1.9 billion, it is still quite a large amount of money.

Table 18   ***The total average annual value of NWFP production in Europe in the mid-1990s (in EUR million at 2000 prices and exchange rates)***

Component	Europe	Sub-regions		
		Western Europe	Eastern Europe	CIS
Fruits and berries	349	134	207	9
Tree nuts	2,989	1,626	1,257	106
Mushrooms and truffles	262	177	67	18
Honey	34	12	22	<1
Game meat and pelts	466	441	20	6
Medicinal plants	118	72	46	<1
Cork	209	203	6	0
Foliage	49	47	2	n.a.
Christmas trees	444	418	27	n.a.
All NWFPs	4,921	3,128	1,654	139
All NWFPs excluding nuts	1,932	1,502	397	33
Wood	15,963	9,886	2,859	3,217
Importance of NWFPs	24%	24%	37%	4%
Importance of NWFPs excluding nuts	11%	13%	12%	1%

Note: the figures for the importance of NWFPs are the shares of NWFPs in the total value of production.

2.10 Forest services

2.10.1 Recreation

European forests are used for a wide variety of recreation activities. The most popular is simply walking in the forest, but forest recreation also includes specialised activities, such as: hunting (see Box 3); orienteering; horseback riding; mountain biking; and war games (e.g. "Paintball").

There have been many efforts to quantify visits to forests in European countries, but these have often highlighted some of the methodological difficulties with measuring the recreational use of forests. First, there is the problem of how to collect this information. Site surveys can give reliable indications of the use of specific locations, but they often fail to capture large numbers of visitors that do not go to formal recreation sites (Schmithüsen and Wild-Eck, 2000). In contrast, household surveys usually produce much larger estimates of visitor numbers, but it is difficult to assess how many of these numbers really refer to forest visits as opposed to visits to other areas where some trees can be found.

It is also difficult to interpret forest visitor numbers, without a standard measurement unit for a visit. For example, frequent forest visitors often account for a large proportion of visits, but their visits probably tend to be much shorter in duration than those of the visitors who go less frequently. As a result of this, the most common unit used to measure visitor numbers - the number of visits per year - may not be comparable across different locations or between years.

Box 3   ***The importance of hunting as a source of income for forest owners***

A previous section described the quantity and value of game and pelts produced from hunting in European forests. In addition to this, the value of hunting licences and trophies is also a major source of income in some areas. For example, in FRA 2000, nine countries provided figures for the value of licence fees, hunting leases and trophies amounting to about USD 75 million per year (Belgium, Denmark, Hungary, Lithuania, Netherlands, Poland, Portugal, Slovakia and Slovenia. This is likely to be a significant under-estimate of the total value of such charges in Europe, as it does not include some countries with a strong tradition of hunting (e.g. France, Germany, Italy and Spain).

Revenue from hunting is often particularly important for small private forest owners and, in such cases, the revenue from hunting may outweigh the income from roundwood production. Hunting in Eastern Europe is also a significant invisible export, producing a lot of income (and foreign currency) from foreign hunters.

Hunting is becoming less popular in some countries (e.g. Netherlands and the United Kingdom), due to social trends. Another concern is that the high stocking level of some game animals, notably deer, may threaten the regeneration capacity of the forest. However, it seems likely that hunting will remain popular in many countries (particularly those with a strong tradition of hunting) and will continue to be an important source of income for forest owners in the future.

Source: UN (2000).

In the FRA 2000, both Poland and the Russian Federation indicated that visiting the forest is the country's main leisure activity (but neither country provided estimates of total forest visitor numbers). Denmark indicated that 90 percent of adult Danes visited the forest at least once a year and Sweden reported that 47 percent of Swedes visited the forest between 1 and 20 days a year (with 40 percent visiting more than 20 days a year).

The FRA 2000 also included information about the total use of forests for recreation in a number of countries. These were all reported in terms of the number of visits or visitors to forests. In addition to this, information on visitor numbers was obtained from a variety of other sources and all of these statistics are summarised in Table 19.

Table 19   ***Summary of forest visitor number estimates for a number of European countries in the mid-1990s***

Country	Year	Annual number of visits (in million)	Annual number of visits per capita	Source	Comments
Austria	1998	103.7	12.8	Aldrian et al, 2004	Very approximate estimate, based on average frequency of visits per person.
Denmark	n.a.	50.0	9.4	Helles and Thorsen, 2004	
Finland	2000	1.0	0.2	Erkkonen and Sievänen, 2003	Visits on state land only.
Ireland	1998	8.9	2.3	Clinch, 1999	
Italy	n.a.	230.1	4.0	Pettenella et al, 2004	Average of four visits per year.
Netherlands	n.a.	205.0	12.9	UN,2000	Average of 180-230 million visits per year.
Portugal	n.a.	2.3	0.2	Carvalho Mendes, 2004	Expert opinion, based on limited available data.
Sweden	n.a.	153.4	17.3	UN,2000	420,000 visitors per day.
Switzerland	n.a.	177.7	24.8	Baruffol et al, 2003	Derived from average frequency of visits per person (minimum).
United Kingdom	n.a.	240.0	4.1	UN,2000	55 million day visits to state owned lands and 185 million day visits to other public lands.
Total/average		**1,172.0**	**6.5**		
Czech Republic	n.a.	210.4	20.5	UN,1998	Derived from average frequency of visits per person.
Lithuania	1996	7.0	2.0	UN,2000	A fall from 17.8 million visitors recorded for 1990.
Serbia and Montenegro	n.a.	0.5	<0.1	UN,2000	500,000 visitors per year to state forests.
Turkey	n.a.	10.0	0.1	UN,2000	
Total/average		**227.9**	**2.5**		

This table indicates that, for all of the countries shown here, the total annual number of visits to forests could be around 1.4 billion. This is equivalent to an average of 6.5 visits per person per year in Western Europe or 2.5 visits per person per year in Eastern Europe. However, the variety reported in the figures also suggests that there may be some significant differences in the methodologies and measurement techniques used to arrive at these estimates. For example, the differences in the annual number of forest visits per person are huge and there are even significant differences between countries that might be expected to have similar figures (e.g. Switzerland and Austria or Finland and Sweden).

Little information was provided on trends in visitor numbers, although Lithuania reported that visitor numbers had declined significantly between 1990 and 1996. A similar indication was reported in another report from Bulgaria (Bouriaud *et al*, 2004), but this also reported that visitor numbers have started to increase again. This could be explained by the dramatic fall in incomes in these countries in the early-1990s, which suggests that this may have been a common trend across all of Eastern Europe.

Although nearly all forests support some recreation activities, the most intense visitor pressure is in forests near large population centres or holiday centres. For instance, Denmark reported that 20 percent of visits occurred on two percent of the forest area while in the Netherlands, one 5,600 ha forest receives 5 million visits per year (i.e. nearly 900 visits per hectare per year) and another of 2,000 ha receives 2 million visits per year (1,000 visits per hectare per year).

In forests used intensively for recreation, there are many consequences for the forest manager, notably:

- Management should take into account aesthetic, practical and safety considerations, with measures such as: keeping older trees; providing more open spaces; reducing possible risks to forest users; and avoiding clearfelling.

- The need to provide equipment such as: benches; shelters; car parks; and notice boards.

- The need to communicate with the different user communities and the local authorities, to ascertain their needs and, sometimes, to resolve conflicts between users

These measures will tend to raise the costs of forest management (compared to management for roundwood production) and may lower income (if roundwood sales are reduced). To compensate for this, it is sometimes possible to charge specialised user groups (e.g. motor rallies, war gamers) for their use of the forest but, in general, charging may not be economically feasible because of the high cost of collecting charges. A further difficulty with charging is that there is a legal or customary right of free access to forests (especially pubic forests) in most European countries.

In some countries, an intensively used forest may receive help in some way from the forestry authorities (e.g. grants and subsidies to cover the cost of providing recreational facilities). In addition, the recreation services provided by public forests are often used to justify management regimes that are not financially viable. However, as the financial viability of forest management comes under increasing pressure and public budgets are also under stricter control, it will be necessary to make a more direct comparison between the public support given to forest managers and the benefits of forest recreation. At the very least it will be necessary to improve the estimation of visitor numbers in order to justify continued public support, if it is not possible to estimate the value of forest recreation (see Box 4). Thus, it can be expected that the recreational use of the forests will be more closely monitored and quantified in the future.

Box 4   ***How important is forest recreation compared to roundwood production in Europe?***

Valuation of forest recreation is a subject that is even more difficult and complicated that the issue of how to count and measure visitor numbers. Numerous studies from many different countries have produced a wide range of estimates of the value of a forest visit, depending on the valuation technique used, forest characteristics and socio-economic variables (see: Wibe (1994), for a comprehensive review of the literature in Europe). Given these difficulties, countries were not asked to provide value figures in FRA 2000. However, with estimates of the number of forest visits, it is possible to ask the question: how important is forest recreation at various levels of value per visit?

The table above suggested an average frequency of visits to forests of 6.5 per person per year in Western Europe. Multiplying this by total population, it would suggest that around 2.6 billion visits are made to forests each year in the whole of Western Europe. Assuming an average value per visit of EUR 1.00, this would amount to an annual value of EUR 2.6 billion, compared with a total annual value of wood production of EUR 9.9 billion. Thus, under this assumption, the value of forest recreation would be about one-quarter of the value of wood production. Of course, there would be huge variations between countries, with small densely-populated countries with low forest cover (e.g. Netherlands and the United Kingdom) having a much higher value of forest recreation compared to wood production. Other countries, such as Sweden and Finland, would be in the opposite position.

In Eastern Europe and the CIS sub-region, the estimated frequency of visits is lower (assuming that this is the same in the CIS sub-region as in Eastern Europe) and it could be assumed that the value of a visit would be lower (due to lower incomes). Assuming an average value per visit of EUR 0.25, the annual value of forest recreation in Eastern Europe would be EUR 120 million (compared with the figure of EUR 2,859 for wood) and in the CIS sub-region it would be EUR 130 million (compared with the figure of EUR 3,217 for wood). These estimates of recreation value would both be less than five percent of the value of wood production.

Of course, the above figures are highly speculative. However, they probably indicate the magnitude of the difference between the value of forest recreation and the value of wood production. They also give an indication of the differences in the relative importance of forest recreation between sub-regions (and countries).

2.10.2 Mitigation of climate change

The FRA 2000 (UN, 2000) contains a considerable amount of information about the levels and changes in carbon stocks in Europe's forests. Therefore, the text below describes only some of the most important features of recent developments in this area. It is currently not possible to estimate the relative importance of this forest service, although a value for carbon storage in forests may emerge in the near future.

Trends in carbon storage in forests. Changes in the global carbon cycle are believed to be the cause of ongoing change in the global climate. Forests are one of the major elements in the carbon cycle, being the largest terrestrial biotic carbon store and a significant source and sink of carbon flows. Deforestation, mostly in the topics, is one of the major sources of carbon entering the atmosphere (equal to about a fifth of the carbon emissions from combustion of fossil fuels). On the other hand, growing trees sequester carbon from the atmosphere, so if a forest is managed for sustained yield (i.e. where the growing stock does not diminish over time) it does not increase atmospheric carbon. Furthermore, if the growing stock increases, then the forest actually takes carbon from the atmosphere.

Because of continuing deforestation, the forests in tropical areas are, overall, a source of carbon. However, forests in Europe are large carbon sinks. Information collected in FRA 2000 suggested that the carbon stored in European forests (woody biomass only, not counting soils or other vegetation) amounts to 47 billion MT, of which 37 billion MT (80 percent) is in the Russian Federation. Furthermore, because European forests are expanding in area and removals are currently less than increment, the carbon in woody biomass in Europe is estimated to be expanding at present at a rate of 556 million MT per year (of which 440 MT per year occurs in the Russian Federation).

The above figures should be treated with some caution, however, because there is a large area of uncertainty about the carbon content of forest soils, which are one of the largest carbon stocks. The volume of carbon in different types of forest soil is not well known and it appears that certain silvicultural practices, such as ploughing or draining peat soils, may release large amounts of carbon. This has important implications for the benefits of carbon storage in forests under different forest management regimes.

Other carbon benefits from the forest sector. In addition to issues linked strictly to the forest ecosystem's role in carbon cycles, there are also other considerations. For example, carbon is stored in forest products, sometimes for a long time (e.g. in houses and books). Forest products may also reduce carbon emissions by replacing products that result in more carbon emissions during their production, distribution, use and recycling. In addition, wood products produced from a sustainably managed forest are carbon neutral, which will also tend to further reduce total carbon emissions. All of these considerations are highly dependent on how wood products are produced and used, so life cycle analysis of the carbon "footprint" of different products must be carefully analysed before policy decisions are taken.

Box 5　　　*Is a market emerging for carbon storage in forests?*

The Kyoto Protocol to the UN Framework Convention on Climate Change was signed in 1997 and signatories have committed themselves to reducing greenhouse gas emissions, notably from fossil fuels, with quantitative commitments for the developed countries. Within certain strict limits, they are also allowed to offset their carbon emissions by "human induced" measures to increase carbon sequestration.

Afforestation and reforestation projects can be counted against the commitments for limiting greenhouse gas emissions in the industrialised countries. Therefore, capturing and maintaining carbon in forest ecosystems may be set against carbon emissions, provided that these measures are monitored by a third party and are not considered normal silviculture.

The Protocol also allows emitters of carbon to pay others to sequester carbon on their behalf (and to claim the credit for doing so though, for example, a system of tradeable permits). Thus, a market in carbon emissions permits is likely to develop in the future.

2.10.3 Conservation of biodiversity

Various studies on the role of forests show that the preservation of the natural environment and biodiversity, as well as the protective functions of forests, are widely recognised and highly valued by the European public (Rametsteiner and Kraxner, 2003). Over the last two decades, the biodiversity functions of forests have also been highly visible in policy debates and European governments have made many public commitments to maintain and preserve forest biodiversity.

Measurement of the output and value of this forest service is extremely difficult. For example, biological diversity should be maintained at the ecosystem, species and genetic level. However, the natural biodiversity of ecosystems varies widely, so it is not sufficient to count species. Instead, it is more important to monitor trends in biodiversity. This is also difficult, but progress in this area is being achieved by monitoring a number of different indicators, such as the following:

- direct indicators (e.g. number of species or ecosystems, degree of genetic variation, etc.);

- features that and known to have a clear relationship with biodiversity (e.g. the presence of dead wood and of certain indicator species);

- measures taken to protect biodiversity (e.g. the establishment of protected forest areas);

- the species composition of the forests; and

- the degree of human intervention (e.g. the presence or absence of introduced species).

The desirable values of each of these indicators will, of course, vary according to the ecosystem in question. However, taken together, it is now possible to provide some indications of the current status of biodiversity in European forests. The following presents a summary of some of the main features of forest biodiversity in Europe from the State of Europe's Forests in 2003 (MCPFE, 2003a).

- Vast forests undisturbed by man exist in the Russian Federation (260 million ha or 32 percent of the country's forest resources), along with significant areas in the Nordic countries (about 8 million ha). A few other countries (e.g. Bulgaria, Romania, Albania, Slovenia) have large undisturbed forests, but elsewhere in Europe there are only small and scattered remnants of undisturbed forest.

- More than two-thirds of Europe's forests are "semi-natural", but this definition includes a wide range of ecosystems from nearly undisturbed to quite intensively managed forests. The common feature of these forests is that their ecological dynamics have been influenced by human intervention, but they have kept their natural characteristics to some extent.

- About 40 percent of Europe's forests are "mixed".[13] Predominantly coniferous forests occur mostly in the boreal zone (Russian Federation and the Nordic countries), as well as in Central Europe (Austria, Germany and Poland) and Turkey. In the Nordic countries, there is evidence that the share of predominantly coniferous forests has reduced, due to an increase in mixed and predominantly broadleaved forests. It is thought that this may have occurred as a reaction to the widely expressed belief that there is more biodiversity in mixed forests.

- Many plant and animal species in European forests are threatened, but the data are not yet fully validated or comparable, so it is difficult to assess the seriousness of the situation.

- The regeneration method used will strongly influence the biodiversity of the forest: natural regeneration will conserve genetic diversity and tend to maintain species composition. Among reporting countries, two-thirds of regeneration in recent years has been natural regeneration, with natural regeneration accounting for over half of all regeneration in: Albania; Austria; Croatia; Russian Federation; Slovenia; and Switzerland. This does not include areas under continuous cover systems, which will also tend to maintain genetic diversity.

- Introduced tree species are often used in Europe, although there are no reliable data about the extent to which they have replaced domestic species. In total, about 200,000 ha of introduced species are planted annually (about 20 percent of the area afforested).

- Based on data from 34 European countries, 127 million ha (or 12 percent of the FOWL area in those countries) is protected for biodiversity or for landscape. Of this 127 million ha, three percent of the area has no active intervention and another three percent has minimum intervention, 79 percent is actively managed for conservation management and 15 percent is in landscape protection areas. In addition, in the EU, the Natura 2000 programme has set-aside large areas for biodiversity conservation.

It is necessary to point out, once again, the extraordinary variation in European forests with respect to biodiversity. They range from forests in densely populated regions that have been intensively managed for roundwood production and recreation over hundreds of years, to vast expanses of completely natural forest with undiminished biodiversity. This should be taken into account when considering the relative importance of biodiversity as measured though indicators such as those above.

---

[13] Where neither coniferous or broadleaved species account for more than 75 percent of crown cover.

2.10.4 Protection of soil, water and infrastructure

Most forests perform some protective functions related to regulating water flow or preventing erosion, not to mention micro-climatic functions, such as shelter from wind, sun, noise or dust. In many regions, these protective functions are of marginal importance compared to wood production, recreational services or biodiversity conservation (see Figure 12). However, in some areas (notably mountains), protective functions are extremely valuable.

Without the presence of a stable forest ecosystem in mountains, erosion would occur, leading to a loss of soil and soil fertility and destruction of settlements, transport infrastructure and other parts of the forest. Ultimately, without forests, mountain areas would become uninhabitable and the long-term consequences (e.g. in the form of uncontrolled flooding, siltation, etc.) could extend far downstream.

Recognition of the value of the protective functions of forests played a vital role in reversing the deforestation trend in Europe in the nineteenth century. At that time, many forests in mountain areas had been over-exploited and were losing their integrity. As a consequence, local and downstream communities suffered the negative consequences of erosion, dangerous floods and landslides. The realisation of these dangers caused European countries to enact strict forest laws and to institute long-term public programmes to protect and re-establish forest cover in sensitive areas. For example, the French programme *"Restoration des terrains de montagne"* was started in the mid-nineteenth century and continues today in what is probably the longest ever reforestation programme. Thus, in mountain regions, the protective functions of forests play an important and symbolic role and are important in defining the general public's view of forest issues.

It is very difficult to quantify the importance of the protection functions of forests, because most forests (even in fragile mountain ecosystems) produce multiple outputs. Sometimes the necessity to maintain protective functions is a compulsory management objective. Elsewhere, protective functions are produced as a by-product of forest management.

In 2003, the approved the *"Assessment guidelines for protected and protective forest and other wooded land in Europe"*, which has a separate category for FOWL where the main management objective is the maintenance of protective functions (MCPFE, 2003b). To be included in this category implies the following: the existence of a legal basis for the management objective, a long term commitment (minimum 20 years) and explicit designation of the functions in question. For Class 3 (protective functions), the main objectives and management restrictions are that forest management should be clearly directed to protect soil and its properties or water quality and quantity or to protect infrastructure and managed natural resources against natural hazards. In addition, forest management must ensure that any operation negatively affecting these functions is prevented.

According to the first survey of protected and protective forests following these guidelines, there are 125 million ha of designated protective forest (i.e. MCPFE Class 3) in Europe, of which 100 million ha is in the Russian Federation. More than 1 million ha are classified as protective forest in Germany, Norway, Poland, Sweden, Turkey and the Ukraine. In Austria, 24 percent of FOWL is in this category and in Switzerland the amount is over 60 percent.

Recent severe and exceptional floods (e.g. in Central Europe in 2002 or Southern France in 2003) have attracted public attention to the question of the management of mountain watersheds, especially as the exceptional rainfall that caused the floods was attributed by some to climate change. Although there is no suggestion that poor forest management or lack of forest cover was even a contributory factor in these floods, they have drawn the public's attention to the necessity of maintaining stable forest ecosystems in mountain regions. This may be used to justify public support (i.e. funding) for forest management in these regions, where costs are significantly higher than in other locations.

2.10.5 Cultural and spiritual aspects

European forests have enormous cultural importance, from their role in legends and fairy tales to their place in the symbolism of Romantic poets. They also include historical and archaeological sites and are used as places for contemplation or ceremony. Many countries have historical sites and monuments related to forests, giant or unusual trees and sites for special ceremonies and customs. A number of countries have special legislation or other programmes to protect cultural and spiritual values, as well as inventories of such sites.

By their very nature, the cultural and spiritual values of forests are often subjective, localised and abstract in nature. As such they can not be easily quantified and aggregated in the same way that many other figures have been in this study. Furthermore, it is even less likely that they can be evaluated in monetary terms or analysed.

There is at present no quantitative information on this forest service, but there is an increasing awareness of the importance of cultural and spiritual aspects of forests, which directly appeal to public opinion. In view of this, countries will start to record information about the number of sites within FOWL that are designated as having cultural or spiritual values (for reporting to the MCPFE).

2.11 Forestry policies

As already noted in Section 1.3.1, government policies have a significant impact on the forest sector, both in terms of their direct impact on the way that forests are managed and their indirect impact on the sector through alterations to the markets for forest products and services. It would be beyond the scope of the EFSOS to produce a comprehensive analysis of recent trends in forestry policies (let alone an analysis of trends in all government policies). Furthermore, as with some aspects of forest management, it would be very difficult to measure trends or changes in forestry policies in the past. However, it is possible to mention some of the main features of forestry policies in Europe and describe how they have changed in recent years.

The following text focuses mainly on forestry policies and is divided into two parts. The first describes some general aspects of forestry policies in European countries that have probably not changed by very much in the past, while the second describes a few areas where there have been some quite significant changes in recent years.

2.11.1 Aspects of forestry policy that have remained quite stable

Information on forestry polices in Europe over the last two decades is available in publications such as FAO (1988), Peck and Descargues (1997), Schmithüsen (2000), Bauer *et al* (2004) and UN (2001a), as well as the FRA 1990 and FRA 2000 (UN, 1993 and 2000). A review of these publications reveals that there are some aspects of European forestry policy that have remained remarkably stable in the past.

Non-declining forest area. One of the main pillars of forestry policy in most European countries is the principle that the forest area should not decline. For example, a recent review of forest legislation in Europe (Bauer *et al*, 2004) shows that many European countries have specific legal measures that support this objective by ensuring that forests are replanted after harvesting. The review also shows that most other countries have rules or regulations to control forest management and harvesting that tend to serve the same purpose. In addition, the deliberate conversion of forest to other land uses is generally quite difficult in most European countries.

Evidence of the success of these policies is given by the forest area statistics from the FRA 2000 and previous forest resource assessments, which show that the forest area in Europe has consistently increased in almost all countries in Europe in the recent past (see, for example, Section 2.1). Furthermore, the results of national forest inventories from the last 50 years suggests that this objective of forestry policy in Europe has been in place (and has been achieved) over a much longer historical time period (see Section 2.1.2). Given the current interest in taking land out of agriculture (especially in Western Europe), it seems likely that forestry policy in Europe will continue to emphasise and achieve this objective.

Multi-purpose forest management. A second aspect of forestry policy in many European countries is the principle that forests should be managed to produce a wide range of benefits to society. Again, there is a long tradition of multi-purpose forest management or "multi-functionality" in many European countries, supported by policies that encourage public access to forests, legal protection of a number of important forest functions or services and measures to support increased production of specific non-market benefits from forests. Evidence of the importance of multi-functionality is given by the statistics in earlier sections of this report, which show that European forests are managed for a number of different objectives and that the production of non-wood forest products and services remains significant in many countries.

Support for afforestation and forest management. A third feature of forestry policies in Europe is the level of public support given to the sector. A number of European countries have offered some form of incentives for forestry for many years (for example, see FAO (1988) for details of forestry incentive schemes in a number of European countries in the late 1980s). Forestry incentives have included: favourable tax treatment of the income from forest operations; subsidies to cover part of the costs of afforestation, forest management or specific forestry activities; and, more recently, compensation payments to cover the loss of income from afforestation of agricultural land.

The level of incentives for forestry in Europe is quite high, as is shown in Figure 75. This shows the total level of forestry incentives paid from 1990 to 1999 to eleven European countries (Belgium; Finland; France; Germany; Netherlands; Portugal; Switzerland; Czech Republic; Estonia; Poland; and Slovenia). It includes national grant schemes, the costs of favourable tax treatment, other national subsidies and some, but not all, EC support to the sector. The average annual total level of incentives for the sector is about EUR 6 billion (at 2000 prices and exchange rates). For comparison, the total value of wood production in these eleven countries in the mid-1990s was about EUR 7 billion (at 2000 prices and exchange rates).

Figure 75   Incentives for forestry in eleven European countries from 1990 to 1999

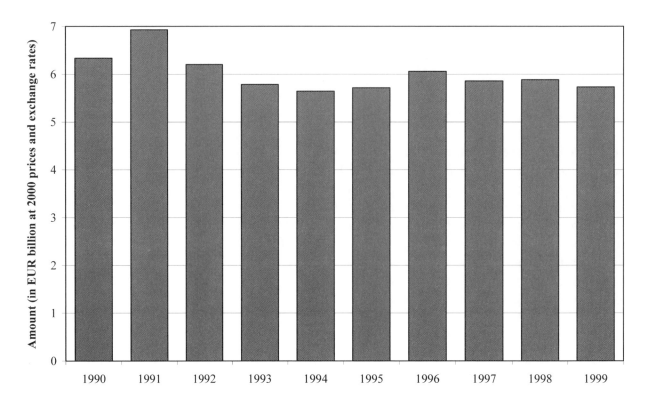

Source: EFFE (2003). Note: the eleven countries included in these figures are: Belgium; Finland; France; Germany; Netherlands; Portugal; Switzerland; Czech Republic; Estonia; Poland; and Slovenia.

These levels of support look a lot higher than the figures quoted in FAO (1988). In addition to this, the EU has also started to offer significant amounts of forestry incentives since the early-1990s. Up until 1992, the EC provided support for specific forestry activities in only a few locations but, with the implementation of Council Regulation (EEC) No. 2080/92 in 1992, the EC increased the geographical scope and level of financial support significantly (Lawson *et al*, 1998).

The objective of EC support for forestry has been to promote afforestation as an alternative use of agricultural land. It has included: payments to cover part of the costs of afforestation and forest management; payments to compensate for the loss of income from converting agricultural land to forests; and payments to cover part of the costs of specific investments in woodland improvement.

Total EC support under Regulation 2080/92 is estimated at EUR 1,519 million over the period 1993 to 1999 or about EUR 217 million per year (Seoane, 2002). Further support is planned under Council Regulation (EC) No. 1257/99 for the period 2000 to 2006. The total planned EC contribution over this period is estimated at EUR 4,738 million or about EUR 677 million per year. It should be noted that these amounts are only the contribution from the EC to national forestry incentive schemes. In most countries, forestry incentive schemes also include significant additional amounts of funding from domestic government resources in addition to the funds available from the EC (e.g. national funding sources account for about 93 percent of the total shown in Figure 75).

It should also be noted that public financial support for forestry is not restricted to countries in the EU. For example, in a review of state forest enterprises in 11 countries in Eastern Europe, Simula (2003) shows that four countries spend more than they earn from forestry, four make a very modest profit and only three have a level of income that is more than 10 percent higher than their level of expenditure. Many of these countries have introduced reforms to increase the efficiency of state forest enterprises, but these figures show that they still have some way to go to create economically viable forest enterprises.

2.11.2 Recent changes in forestry policy

In contrast to the stability of the three major aspects of forestry policy described above, there have also been a number of recent changes to forestry policy in European countries. In particular, the following two policy changes appear to have occurred in many if not most countries and are starting to have an impact on the sector.

Public participation. A trend towards greater public involvement in policy-making has been noted all over the World in many different areas of government policy. This trend is described succinctly by Fraser (2004), who states that: *"there is a tendency to think of policy as a matter for governments, but it is now more widely appreciated that all shareholders in the forest sector have a legitimate interest in both the policy objectives and the means that will be used to implement it"*. This trend in the forest sector is part of a broader trend in governance that has appeared in many countries with measures such as the decentralisation of government policy making and policy implementation and devolution of power to regional, state and local public bodies.

A recent review of forestry policies in Europe (UN, 2001a) states that public participation in forestry policy is increasing in most European countries and provides a number of examples of changes in policies and legislation to support this statement. Another study (ILO, 2000) provides further examples of how these policies are being implemented on the ground in a variety of different ways. Based on reports such as these, it seems likely that there has been a trend towards greater public participation in the sector and that this trend will continue into the future. An important advantage of public participation is not only that it helps find acceptable solutions to values-based conflicts on forestry issues, but helps to build bridges to "non-forest" issues and values. National forest programmes, which are increasingly seen as one of the main policy tools, in Europe as elsewhere, are essentially mechanisms for structured public participation with a particular emphasis on the cross-sectoral dimension

Public ownership and management of forests. The FRA 2000 and FRA 1990 present information about the distribution of FOWL between public and private ownership. Unfortunately, it is not possible to produce reliable numerical estimates of these changes, due to differences in measurement and the wide range of reference periods used to compile these statistics. However, it is possible to assess broad changes over the last two decades from the changes reported by countries.

Over the last two decades in Western Europe, the proportion of FOWL in public ownership has declined in 10 of the 18 countries, remained about the same in four countries and increased in four countries. The four countries where the proportion of public ownership appears to have increased are relatively small (e.g. Luxembourg and The Netherlands) and in at least one case - the United Kingdom - it is likely that the change is due to differences in the measurement of total FOWL area between the two reference periods, rather than a real change in the structure of forest ownership.

This trend towards gradually more private ownership of forests in Western Europe has been driven by two forces. In a few countries (notably Sweden and the United Kingdom) some of the public forest estate has been privatised over the last 20 years. However, the contribution of this to the total change at the sub-regional level is quite small. A much more important factor has been the significant increase in the privately owned FOWL area in recent years due to afforestation of bare land. This has increased in nearly all countries in Western Europe over the last two decades, at a very approximate rate of around 1 million ha per year.

The structure of forest ownership in Eastern Europe has also changed over the last decade, with nine out of the 16 countries reporting a fall in the proportion of FOWL in public ownership, four reporting no change and three reporting an increase. The three countries where public ownership appears to have increased are all countries of the former Yugoslavia, where the comparison has been made between the level of public ownership reported in FRA 2000 and the level of public ownership reported for Yugoslavia in FRA 1990. In reality, public ownership may not have actually increased in these countries.

In Eastern Europe, the change in public ownership has been largely driven by the restitution of public forests to their former private forest owners. The Baltic States, Hungary, Czech Republic and Slovakia all show increases in the private forest estate that are matched by a fall in the area of FOWL in public ownership. This has resulted in the creation of a large number of private forest owners, many of whom now own relatively small areas of forest. In addition to this, in a few countries, the private forest area has actually increased beyond the areas transferred as part of the restitution process. This is presumably due to natural regeneration on abandoned agricultural land and, in a few cases, the deliberate afforestation of bare land.

The CIS sub-region is the one part of Europe that has not followed this trend towards reduced public ownership of FOWL. In this sub-region, 100 percent of the FOWL area remains in public ownership.

Changing role of state forest organisations In addition to the trends in public ownership reported above, there is also evidence of a change in policy in several countries with respect to the management of forests that remain in public ownership. For example, many European countries, including, to different degrees, and against differing legal and social backgrounds, Austria, Finland, Sweden, Ireland, Poland, Latvia, have reorganised their state forest management organisations[14], to function as quasi-private companies, with clearly defined commercial objectives and much more operational freedom than the previous structure which was more administrative in spirit. These state owned companies have become more efficient (leading in particular to reduced employment), with a more entrepreneurial spirit (e.g. operating abroad as management consulting companies), and have insisted on a clearer definition of which public goods and services they should supply and on what terms, as it is no longer possible simply to absorb the provision of public services within an enterprise whose main income comes from wood sales. In many cases, these management roles have been clearly separated from the supervisory and policy functions of public forest administrations.

---

[14] In some countries, such as France and UK, a similar arrangement has been in place for some time.

2.12 The contribution of the forest sector to national economies

One measure of the contribution of the forest sector to society is the contribution of the sector to GDP and exports. This is also an indicator of the economic dimension of sustainable forest management. In addition to this, employment in the forest sector is an indicator of the social dimension of sustainable forest management.

One of the studies prepared as part of the EFSOS examined trends in forest sector employment (Blombäck *et al*, 2003). A more recent study by FAO (Lebedys, in prep) expanded on this to include an analysis of trends in value-added and exports from the sector. The main findings of these two reports are presented here below.

2.12.1 Forest sector employment

Figure 76 shows the trends in forest sector employment in Europe over the last decade. The height of each bar represents the total number of people employed (in full-time equivalents[15]), measured against the axis on the left-hand side of the figure. The bars also indicate the level of employment in each of the three main components of the forest sector. These are defined according to the International Standard Industrial Classification (ISIC), where forestry includes forest management and harvesting, and woodworking includes the production of sawnwood and wood based panels.[16] The line shows the total contribution to employment, measured as the number of people employed in the forest sector divided by the total workforce (i.e. economically active population).

The figure shows that total employment in the sector has declined slightly in Europe over the last decade, from a figure of 4.3 million in 1990 to 3.9 million in 2000. Similarly, the contribution to employment has also declined slightly from around 1.1 percent to 1.0 percent over the same period.

This decline has occurred for two reasons. Firstly, improvements in labour productivity have resulted in a reduction in the demand for labour, particularly in the two forest processing sectors. The second reason for this decline has been the reduction in production over the last decade in Eastern Europe and the CIS sub-region.

Another interesting feature of this figure is the distribution of employment between the different components of the sector. Broadly speaking, employment was divided almost equally between the three components of the sector in 1990, with a slightly higher proportion of people employed in the woodworking industries. By 2000, employment in forestry and manufacturing of paper and paperboard had both shrunk, while employment in the woodworking industries had remained about the same. Thus, the woodworking industry now accounts for a much greater share of total employment in the forest sector.

At the sub-regional level, all three sub-regions show some subtle differences in the trends and structure of employment in the forest sector and these are shown in Figure 77 to Figure 79 and discussed in the text below.

---

[15] So, for instance, two people working half time count as one "full time equivalent"

[16]   Note: the ISIC definitions of the three main components of the forest sector are slightly different to the definitions used in the rest of this report, as they include some processing activities under "woodworking" and "paper and paperboard" that go beyond manufacturing products included here (e.g. production of cardboard boxes). However, these additional activities are negligible.

Figure 76   Trends in employment in the European forest sector from 1990 to 2000

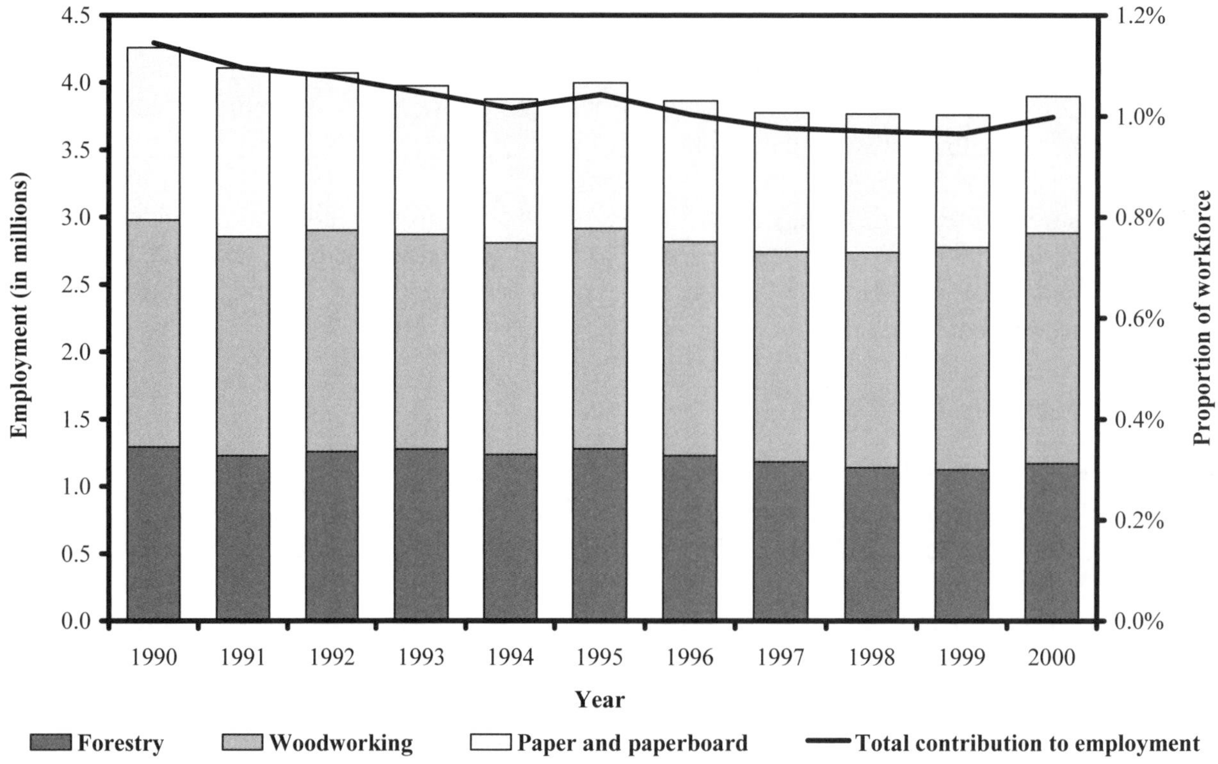

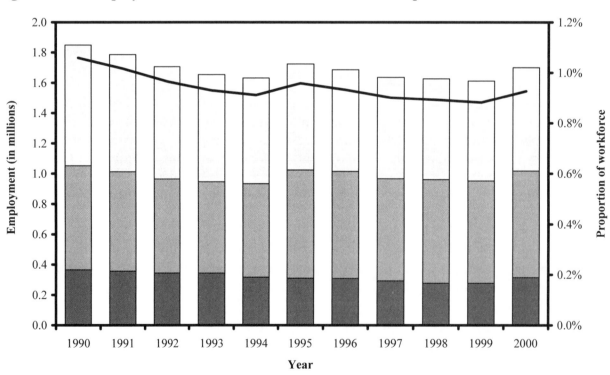

Source: Lebedys (in prep).

Figure 77   Employment in the forest sector in Western Europe from 1990 to 2000

Source: Lebedys (in prep).

Figure 77 shows the trends in forest sector employment in Western Europe over the last decade. Western Europe accounts for slightly less than half of total European employment in the sector. Employment has declined from slightly over 1.8 million in 1990 to 1.7 million in 2000. The contribution of the sector to total employment is also much lower than in the rest of Europe and has fallen more dramatically. In 2000, only about 0.9 percent of the workforce was employed in forestry, compared with a figure of almost 1.1 percent in 1990.

Much of this decline has occurred in paper and paperboard manufacturing, where productivity gains have reduced the demand for labour. A slight decrease in forestry employment has also occurred. It is also notable that employment in forestry accounts for a relatively small share of total employment in the sector.

Figure 78 presents the same information for Eastern Europe. Eastern Europe accounts for about one-quarter of forest sector employment in Europe and total employment has fallen significantly, from over 1.2 million in 1990 to under 1.0 million in 2000. The contribution of the sector to total employment is higher than elsewhere, but has fallen dramatically from over 1.4 percent in 1990 to under 1.1 percent in 2000.

Employment has fallen across all three components of the sector, broadly in line with the reduction in output. The exception to this is employment in forestry, which has declined at the same time that production has increased. This suggests that labour productivity has increased over the last decade, but there are many differences in these trends at the country level. It is also notable that employment in forestry accounts for a much greater share of the total than elsewhere. This is due to one country - Turkey - where employment has been increasing and now accounts for over half of all forestry employment in Eastern Europe.

Figure 79 shows the trends in forest sector employment in the CIS sub-region over the last ten years. The CIS sub-region also accounts for about 25 percent of total European employment in the forest sector. In this sub-region, employment has varied over the last decade, but has not increased or decreased overall. The average level of employment has been slightly less than 1.2 million, or just under 1.1 percent of the total workforce. In the CIS sub-region, the woodworking industries account for around 50 percent to 60 percent of total employment in the sector.

A final point worth noting about the differences in employment between the sub-regions is the vast differences in labour productivity that exist. For example, Western Europe produces about twice as much industrial roundwood as each of the other two sub-regions, but employs fewer people in forestry. In the processing sectors, the differences are even greater, with labour productivity in Western Europe between two and four times higher than in the other two sub-regions. This is an indication of the differences in the structure of production costs in the different sub-regions. It also suggests that producers in Eastern Europe and the CIS sub-region will face some interesting challenges as incomes increase in these countries in the future.

Figure 78   **Employment in the forest sector in Eastern Europe from 1990 to 2000**

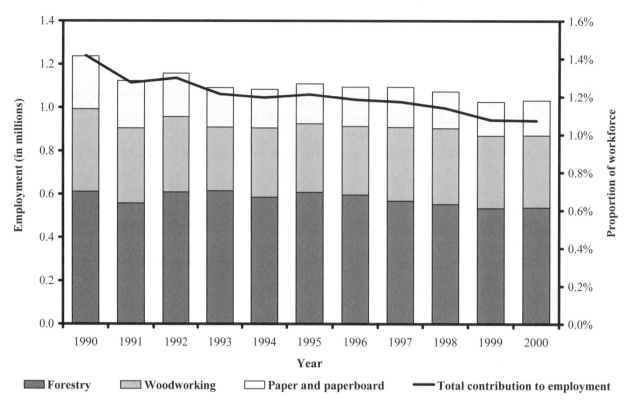

Source: Lebedys (in prep).

Figure 79   **Employment in the forest sector in the CIS sub-region from 1990 to 2000**

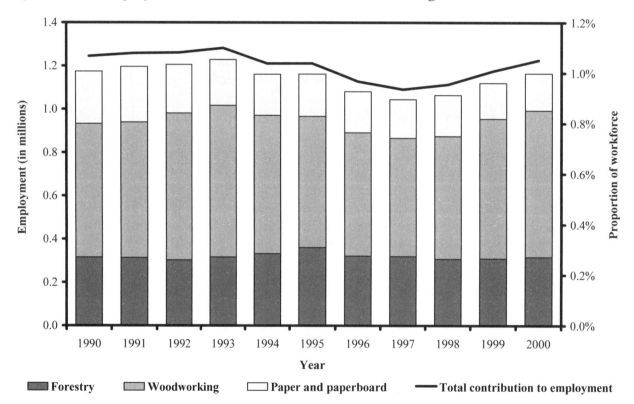

Source: Lebedys (in prep).

2.12.2 Value-added in the forest sector

Value-added is the total value of all goods and services produced by the sector less the costs of all purchases from other sectors in the economy. Value-added is the surplus value from production that is distributed to investors and employees in the form of rents, profits and wages. The total value-added by all sectors in the economy is also the total value of all output or GDP.

Figure 80 shows the real (i.e. inflation adjusted) trends in value-added in the European forest sector over the last decade. This shows that total value-added has declined in real terms from around EUR 115 billion in 1990 to EUR 100 billion in 2000. Furthermore, the contribution of the sector to GDP has declined from 1.5 percent to 1.1 percent over the same period.

Figure 80   Trends in value-added in the European forest sector from 1990 to 2000

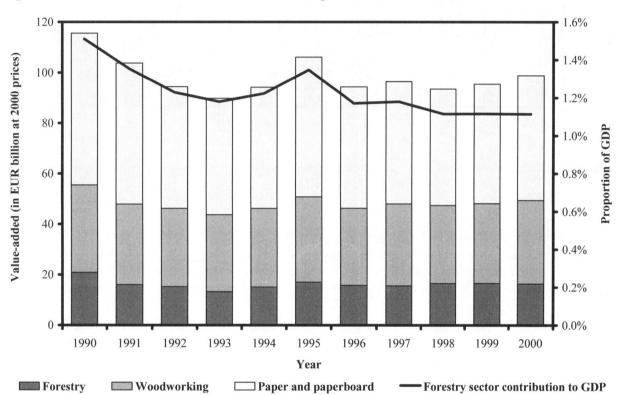

Source: Lebedys (in prep).

Paper and paperboard manufacturing accounts for the greatest share of value-added in the forest sector and the decline in value-added in this sector accounts for most of the decline for the sector as a whole. Value-added in this sector has also varied a lot over the last decade. This is due to the cyclical nature of the pulp and paper industry. Increased global competition in the markets for pulp and paper is likely to continue to put downward pressure on value-added in this sector in the future.

Value-added in forestry has also declined over the last decade, but the figure for 1990 is unusual in that it reflects the high level of roundwood production in that year. Excluding this year, the level of value-added in forestry has not changed by very much over the last decade. Similarly, the value-added in the woodworking industries is the same in 2000 as it was in 1990.

Again, there is considerable variation between the three European sub-regions and this is discussed below.

Figure 81 **Value-added in the forest sector in Western Europe from 1990 to 2000**

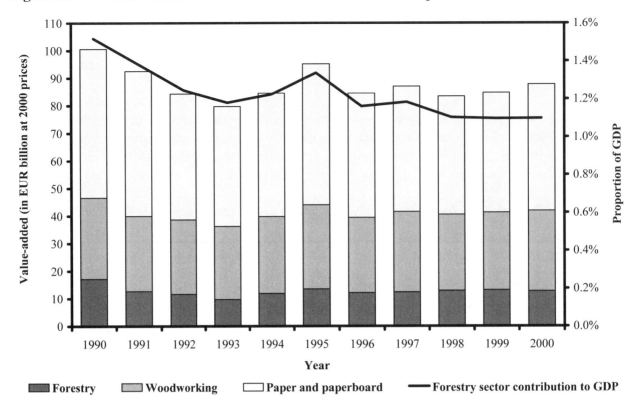

Source: Lebedys (in prep).

Figure 81 shows the trends in forest sector value-added in Western Europe over the last decade. Western Europe accounts for a huge proportion (around 90 percent) of the value-added in the sector in Europe, so the trends here are very similar to those presented above. Total value-added has declined from around EUR 100 billion in 1990 to slightly less than EUR 90 billion in 1990.

In Western Europe, value-added in the woodworking industries has remained unchanged over the period at around EUR 30 billion. Excluding 1990, value-added in forestry has also remained about the same, at a level of EUR 12 billion to EUR 13 billion. Value-added in paper and paperboard manufacturing has declined slightly from EUR 54 billion in 1990 to EUR 46 billion in 2000. This distribution of value-added across the three component of the forest sector (with a ratio of 4:2:1 between paper and paperboard, woodworking and forestry) is typical of the forest sector in most developed countries.

In Eastern Europe, value-added in the forest sector is relatively more important to national economies and has not fallen by as much as in other part of Europe (see Figure 82). The figure shows a decline in 1990 to 1991, which is probably due to the fall in production in these countries in the early 1990s. After this, it appears that value-added has increased slightly over the rest of this decade.

The figure also shows that the distribution of value-added is almost equal between the three components of the forest sector, with slightly less in paper and paperboard manufacturing. This is an indication of the sectors that may be most competitive in Eastern Europe, which are forestry and woodworking rather than paper and paperboard manufacturing.

Figure 82   Value-added in the forest sector in Eastern Europe from 1990 to 2000

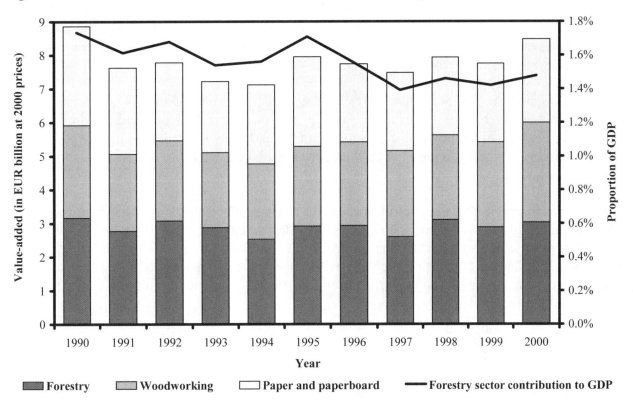

Source: Lebedys (in prep).

Figure 83   Value-added in the forest sector in the CIS sub-region from 1990 to 2000

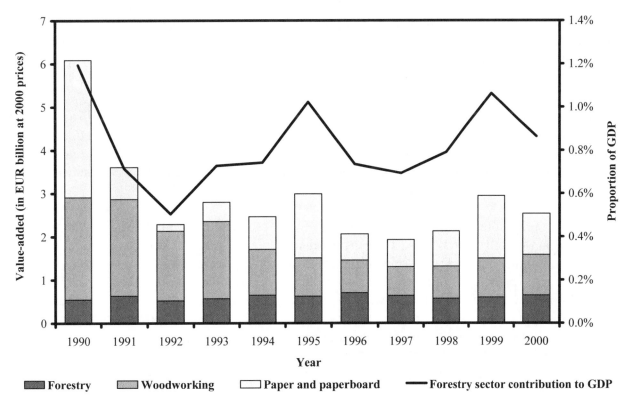

Source: Lebedys (in prep).

Figure 83 presents the same information about value-added for CIS sub-region. The trends show the significant decline across all components of the forest sector after the economic shocks of the early 1990s. However, in the case of the CIS sub-region, the effect of these shocks was much greater and the sector has taken a lot longer to recover. There is some indication of an increase in value-added after 1996, but the upward trend is not strong.

In the CIS sub-region, forestry appears to be the one component of the forest sector that has suffered the least over the last decade and has, in fact, increased the value-added from activities. Value-added in both of the processing sectors fell in the early-1990s, gradually in the woodworking industries and very sharply in paper and paperboard manufacturing. These sectors now appear to be recovering slowly.

It is also worth noting that the contribution of the forest sector to GDP is lower here than in the other two sub-regions. This is surprising, given the importance of production in the CIS sub-region at the European level and the traditional image of the scale and importance of the forest sector in this sub-region. However, this is likely to reflect the increased importance of other extractive industries in this sub-region (particularly oil and gas) and the greater contribution that they have made to GDP in recent year.

Comparing the trends between the three sub-regions, these figures show an even more startling difference in the levels of productivity. Value-added per employee and value-added per unit of output are an order of magnitude lower in Eastern Europe and the CIS sub-region compared with Western Europe. At the moment, this makes these countries very cost competitive in the production of basic forestry products. The challenge for these countries will be to develop the skills and attract the investment necessary to increase value-added in the forest sector in the future.

2.12.3 Forest products trade

Section 2.6 described many of the features of the historical trends in forest products trade in Europe over the last few decades. This section describes the importance of forest products trade to economies in terms of the contribution of forest products exports to total exports of goods (i.e. merchandise exports).

Figure 84 shows the historical trend in the contribution of forest products to merchandise exports in Europe since 1980. In contrast to the figures for employment and value-added, this figure shows that forest products are quite important exports for European economies. Over the last two decades, forest products have accounted for between 2.5 percent and 3.0 percent of all merchandise exports (by value) and this trend has not moved upwards or downwards.

Western Europe accounts for the vast majority of forest products trade in Europe, so the trends in this sub-region closely match those for Europe as a whole. In Eastern Europe, there is a notable upward trend in the importance of forest products exports. This occurred during the early 1990s and appears to have levelled-off in recent years at about 3.3 percent. The importance of forest products exports from the CIS sub-region has always been higher than the average in Europe, accounting for about 3.5 percent of the value of all merchandise exports. This figure has varied widely over the last two decades, but shows a trend that is neither increasing nor decreasing.

These figures suggest that the forest sector is important in many countries as a source of export income and that this importance has been relatively stable in the past. It has already been noted that forest products trade is increasing, so it seems likely that the importance of forest products to trade balances will also continue into the future.

Figure 84   ***Trends in the importance of forest products exports in Europe from 1990 to 2000***

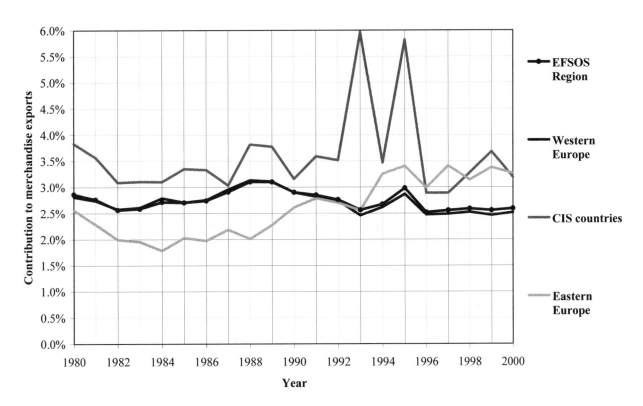

Source: Lebedys (in prep).

3   DRIVING FORCES IN THE FOREST SECTOR

This chapter describes some of the main driving forces that have affected the forest sector in the past and are likely to affect the sector in the future. Many of these driving forces are complex and inter-related. For example, changes in income can lead to changes in demand that are then amplified by changes in government policies. Therefore, the presentation of this information under different headings below is somewhat arbitrary.

The chapter follows the methodological framework described in Section 1.3.1 and is divided into four main sections. The first two sections examine driving forces in exogenous factors and demands of society. This is followed by a section that examines the policy and market frameworks together. Following this, the final section describes the alternative scenarios developed for the outlook analysis.

3.1   *Exogenous factors*

The main exogenous factors affecting the forest sector are socio-economic developments (e.g. changes in population and income) and changes in environmental factors. Traditionally, most analyses of trends and outlook for the forest sector have tended to focus almost exclusively on economic variables (particularly income and forest product prices) and, to some extent, this approach has been repeated in this study. However, changes in other variables can also have a more subtle effect on the sector, so some of these are also described here below.

3.1.1   Population

Changes in population affect the forest sector in several ways. On the demand-side, population growth results in expanding markets for forest products and services. Changes in the population age structure can also have an important effect on markets, by altering patterns of demand and income levels. On the supply-side, an increasing population results in greater competition for land (for a variety of alternative uses), but it also leads to an increasing workforce for the forest sector.

The population of Europe has increased consistently over the last 50 years, rising from around 568 million in 1950 to 795 million in 2000 (an increase of 40 percent). At the sub-regional level, population has increased in Western Europe from 303 million in 1950 to 389 million in 2000 (an increase of 28 percent) and in Eastern Europe it has increased from 115 million in 1950 to 197 million (an increase of 71 percent). In the CIS sub-region, population has increased from 150 million in 1950 to 210 million in 2000 (also an increase of 40 percent). However, in recent years, the population growth rate has slowed down in Europe and has actually reversed in the CIS sub-region and a number of other countries in Europe.

Figure 85 shows the trends in population density in Europe from 1950 to 2000 and long-term projections to 2050 (derived from the UN medium-fertility scenario for population growth). This figure shows the broad trends in total population in the different European sub-regions and, by converting this to population density (persons per square-kilometre) it shows how the different sub-regions compare in terms of population pressure on the land.

Figure 85*   *Trends and projections for population density in Europe from 1950 to 2050

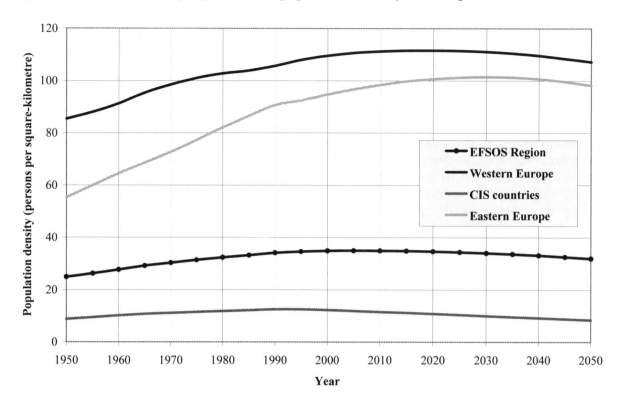

Source: derived from UN (2000 and 2002).

The figure shows that, over the period 2000 to 2020, population density in Western Europe will not increase by very much from the current level of 110 persons per square-kilometre. In Eastern Europe, over the next 20 years, population density will increase slightly, from 95 persons per square-kilometre to slightly over 100 persons per square-kilometre in 2020. In the CIS sub-region, population density will decline slightly from the current level of about 12 persons per square-kilometre. Of course, these sub-regional averages mask a lot of differences in population density at the country level (e.g. between Sweden and Belgium), but they clearly show that population pressure on the land is generally quite high in Western Europe and extremely low in the CIS sub- region.

In addition to total population, another factor that influences the demand for land is the location of where people choose to work and live. Figure 86 shows the trends in urbanisation in Europe since 1950 and projections to 2030. This figure shows that urbanisation has increased consistently in Europe and across all three sub-regions since 1950. Furthermore, it is expected to continue to increase in the future, particularly in Eastern Europe.

Combining the information about total population and urbanisation, the net effect of these two projections will be that the rural population in Europe will decrease significantly over the next 20 years. In Western Europe it will fall by 16 percent (14 million), in Eastern Europe it will fall by 13 percent (10 million) and in the CIS sub-region it will fall by 20 percent (12 million).

Figure 86   Trends and projections for urbanisation in Europe from 1950 to 2050

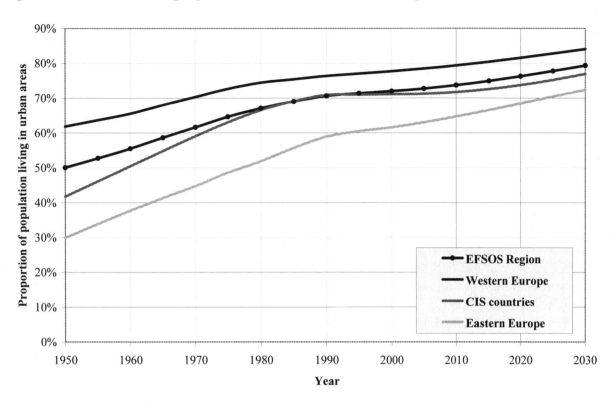

Source: derived from UN (2001b and 2002).

Figure 87   Trends and projections for the population of working-age in Europe from 1950 to 2050

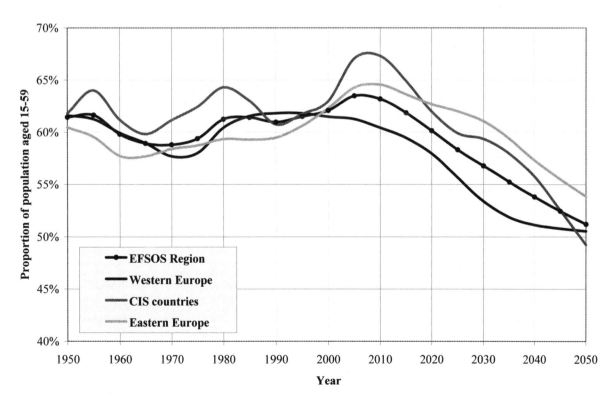

Source: derived from UN (2002).

Another important population variable that affects the forest sector is the age-structure of the population and trends and projections for this are shown in Figure 87. The population age-structure affects the demand for forest products and services, because income levels and consumer preferences change as people get older. However, a more important effect of the changing population age-structure is likely to be the effect that this will have on the workforce.

Figure 93 shows that, over the last 50 years, the proportion of the population that is of working age (defined here as 15 to 59 years old) has stayed roughly constant at about 60 percent. The long-term projection shows that this will fall in all of the three European sub-regions, to levels of between 50 percent and 55 percent in 2050. However, over the next 20 years, there are some marked differences between the three sub-regions.

In Western Europe, many countries have already started to experience a decline in the working-age population and, for the sub-region as a whole, the working-age population is expected to decline over the next 20 years by about five percentage points. The current age-structure of the population in Eastern Europe and the CIS sub-region will result in an increase in the working-age population over the next 10 years, but a gradual decline after this. In total, by the year 2020, the working-age population in Western Europe will fall by four percent (10 million), it will increase by seven percent (8 million) in Eastern Europe and fall by 14 percent (18 million) in the CIS sub-region.

In combination, these projections will affect the forest sector in many different ways. First and foremost, all three of these projections are going to reduce the rural workforce and reinforce the difficulties that are already experienced in some countries in attracting people to work in forestry (Blombäck *et al*, 2003). This may result in some upward pressure on labour costs, but it is also likely to lead to a further increase in the mechanisation of forest operations. This, in turn, will increase the need for investment in machinery and training.

These pressures will also be felt in the forest processing sector, although probably not as much. Indeed, in the near-term, there may be an increase in the availability of labour in Eastern Europe and the CIS sub-region. This could result in some migration of workers from east to west, particularly in the enlarged EU.

In terms of land-use, increased urbanisation is likely to lead to less demand for agricultural land (and this trend will no doubt be amplified by government policies with a similar aim - see below). This will be replaced by more demand for land for housing and infrastructure, but the net effect will probably be to increase the availability of land for forestry.

Larger urban populations are also likely to demand more access to land near urban areas and to demand environmental improvement in and around urban areas. Afforestation and changes in the management of existing forests are likely to be a preferred option for meeting some of these demands.

A more subtle effect of increased urbanisation, along with an ageing population (particularly in rural areas), is going to be a changing perception of the role of forests in modern life. Numerous studies have shown that there is a wide difference between rural people (who tend to see the countryside as a productive resource), compared with urban people (who tend to place more importance on the non-market benefits that rural areas can provide). Therefore, these trends will tend to increase society's demands for non-wood forest products and services relative to forest products.

3.1.2   Income

Economic growth is probably the most important factor that influences the outlook for the forest sector. Prolonged and rapid economic growth will lead to increased trade, investment and personal incomes, resulting in stronger growth in demand for all forest products and services. However, it may also have a detrimental effect on forest resources if demands exceed the biological capacity of forests to meet those demands or if rapid economic growth results in other factors that harm forests (e.g. increased air pollution).

The importance of economic growth is reflected in the models used in the EFSOS to produce the forest product market projections for the next 20 years. The level of GDP is one of the main variables used in these models, so forecasts of economic growth are required for the period 2000 to 2020 in order to produce the market projections. Unfortunately, however, most official forecasts of economic growth only cover the next five to ten years.

To overcome the limitations of official forecasts, a special study was implemented to produce forecasts of economic growth to 2020 for all of the countries included in the EFSOS (NOBE, 2002). In particular, this study focused on the prospects for economic growth in the countries in transition (i.e. the countries in Eastern Europe and the CIS sub-region). The study examined historical trends in economic growth and the main factors that have influenced economic growth in the past. On the basis of this analysis, it then produced three scenarios for future economic growth in each country. The following text summarises the main findings of the analysis and describes some of the main features of the three growth scenarios.

Historical analysis. The factors underlying long term economic growth are the subject of considerable theoretical discussion, which it is not appropriate to summarise here (for further details, refer to: NOBE, 2002). However there is a general consensus that the main driving forces for economic growth are: population; investment; and total factor productivity. Furthermore, the latter is influenced by the level of education in a country and the ability of a country to adopt new technology. Currently in Europe, there are considerable differences between Western Europe and the other two sub-regions in terms of these driving forces.

Historically in Western Europe, economic growth has been driven by a combination of the factors listed above. In particular, the availability of factors of production (labour and capital) has consistently increased and this has been a major driving force for economic growth. In the future, however, Western Europe will no longer be able to rely on increased factor availability. For example, as already noted above, the workforce will decline over the next 20 years. Furthermore, labour scarcity will increase capital intensity above current levels that are already very high. This will tend to reduce the productivity of capital (due to falling marginal productivity). Therefore, in the future, a crucial factor for economic growth in Western Europe will be the ability of countries to continue to enhance the quality of capital and human resources. This will most likely be achieved by technological advancement and knowledge-based growth.

In the case of Eastern Europe and the CIS sub-region, there is currently a wide gap (compared with Western Europe) in terms of productivity and income levels. In addition, these two sub-regions are also far behind Western Europe in the levels of technology employed in the economy. Therefore, these sub-regions have two forces that they can use to drive economic growth in the future. The first is that they could attract significant investment (due to their higher marginal productivity of capital). The second is that they could increase factor productivity by importing technology from more developed countries (in Europe and elsewhere). In both cases, the prospects for future growth in Eastern Europe and the CIS sub-region will depend on the extent to which these countries exploit the opportunities for convergence with Western Europe, through increased trade and investment.

Scenario description. The forecasts of economic growth for each country have been based on an analysis of past trends in growth and assumptions about how the driving forces (described above) will develop in the future. Broadly speaking, some of the main features of the economic growth projections are as follows:

- GDP will continue to grow in all countries and subregions;

- in Western Europe, economic growth will be generally be slower than in the past and slower than in the rest of Europe;

- in Eastern Europe and the CIS sub-region, economic growth will not change markedly from current levels, but will gradually slow down as levels of GDP per capita start to converge with those in Western Europe; and

- in general, educational levels and the employment of technology will gradually converge all over Europe.

In addition to the above, it is also worth noting that the analysis suggests that economic growth rates in several other regions (notably Asia and South America) will continue to be higher than in Europe for the foreseeable future. The consequences of this will be that forest products markets in other regions may expand more rapidly than in Europe. However, global competition in the sector will also continue to increase as other countries outside Europe increase their investment and levels of productivity in the sector.

A summary of the economic growth projections produced in the analysis is given in Table 20 and projections for real per capita GDP (under the baseline scenario) are shown in Table 21. Further description of the three scenarios is given in the text below.

Table 20 ***Projections of average annual economic growth in Europe from 2000 to 2020 under three different growth scenarios***

Region/sub-region	Economic growth scenario		
	Low	**Baseline**	**High**
Western Europe	1.1%	1.3%	2.6%
Eastern Europe	2.6%	4.2%	5.3%
CIS sub-region	2.4%	4.0%	5.3%
Europe	1.5%	2.2%	3.5%

Source: NOBE (2002).

Table 21 ***Trends and projections in real per capita GDP in Europe from 1990 to 2020 under the baseline scenario (at 2000 prices and exchange rates)***

Region/sub-region	Year			
	1990	**2000**	**2010**	**2020**
Western Europe	16,256	18,982	21,236	24,094
Eastern Europe	2,515	2,697	3,903	5,759
CIS sub-region	2,187	1,292	2,029	3,204
Europe	9,065	10,300	12,037	14,359

Source: derived from UN (2002), World Bank (2004) and NOBE (2002).

Low growth scenario. The low growth scenario assumes that total population will follow a low fertility projection in the future (UN, 2002), leading to a significant decrease in population levels and a rapid ageing of the population across all of Europe.

In Western Europe, it assumes that policies to accelerate technological progress and enhance human capital will be relatively weak (leading to almost no progress beyond the current situation). Given the very high capital intensity and low marginal productivity of capital, this leads to a very low economic growth rate.

In Eastern Europe and the CIS sub-region, it assumes that there is very slow progress in political, social and economic stabilisation, a lack of policies to enhance domestic saving and investment, low adoption of new technology and little investment in the human capital. This economic and social outlook is very unfavourable for convergence and, combined with the slow economic growth projection for Western Europe, leads to relatively low economic growth rates.

Baseline scenario. The baseline scenario assumes that total population will follow the medium fertility projection in the future (see Section 3.1.1). It assumes that education will improve across the region, along with the adoption of new technology. It also assumes that real per capita GDP will start to converge in Europe.

In Western Europe, it assumes that there will be steady improvement in the implementation of policies aimed at accelerating knowledge-based growth. This leads to an economic growth rate only slightly lower than in the past.

In Eastern Europe and the CIS sub-region, it assumes that there will be steady improvement in the implementation of policies aimed at accelerating convergence. It also assumes that new technology will be widely adopted, leading to efficiency gains and a steady reduction in the technological gap between these sub-regions and Western Europe. This results in a continuation of current economic growth rates.

High growth scenario. The high growth scenario assumes that total population will follow a high fertility projection in the future, leading to much less of a decrease in total population levels.

In Western Europe, it assumes that policies to accelerate technological progress and strengthen human capital are implemented aggressively, with measures such as significantly increased investments in education, research and development. This results in an economic growth rate slightly higher than in recent years.

In Eastern Europe and the CIS sub-region, it assumes that the process of economic, social and political stabilisation will be accelerated, with a rapid expansion of EU enlargement to cover Turkey and the Balkan states. It also assumes that policies will be implemented to enhance domestic saving and investment, rapidly improve human capital and encourage the adoption of new technology. This leads to much more rapid convergence with Western Europe that, combined with the high projected growth rate there, leads to relatively high economic growth.

3.1.3 Accessibility of forests

The accessibility of forests is another factor that has increased in the past and is likely to continue to increase in the future. Section 2.2.2 has already described how people have legal rights of access to much of the forest area in Europe (see Figure 13). In addition to this, socio-economic trends have also increased the ability of people to access forests for a variety of purposes.

This increase has occurred due to a combination of factors, such as:

- increased leisure time (e.g. shorter working hours and longer holidays);

- improved rural infrastructure (e.g. improved road networks, accommodation, etc.);

- an increase in the income available for non-essential purchases (see Section 3.2.1); and

- increased car ownership.

For example, Figure 88 shows trends in vehicle ownership since 1960. This is measured as the number of vehicles per 1,000 people (of which about 80 percent to 90 percent are cars). The figure shows a strong upward trend in all three European sub-regions, with approximately one vehicle for every two people in Western Europe in 2000. The level of vehicle ownership in Eastern Europe is currently about half of this and the level in the CIS sub-region is about one-third of this level. However, if current trends continue, the level of vehicle ownership in Eastern Europe will equal one for every two people by 2020 and the level of vehicle ownership in the CIS sub-region will be only slightly less than this.

Figure 88 **Trends in vehicle ownership in Europe from 1960 to 2000**

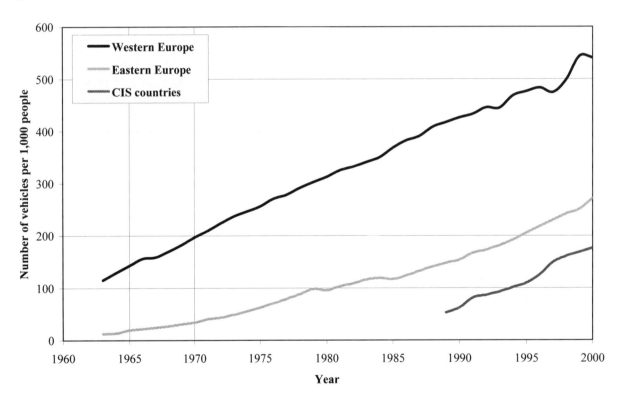

Source: derived from World Bank (2004) and IRF (1990). Note: the above figure excludes Turkey where, on the basis of the little data available, vehicle ownership is about half of the average for other Eastern European countries

The most obvious effect of these trends will be an increase in the use of forests for leisure and recreation in the future. However, these trends may also result in other changes, such as an increase in the numbers of people working in urban areas but choosing to live in the countryside where the environment is better. This will reinforce the gradual shift towards greater demand for non-wood forest products and services relative to forest products. It is also likely to increase public interest in forestry issues.

3.1.4   Environmental factors

Environmental factors encompass a number of climatic, biological and geographical factors that affect forests. The impact and importance of these factors varies between sub-regions and countries. Furthermore, changes in some of these factors are short-term and occur infrequently and erratically. For example, short-term variations in climate can lead to sudden changes in damage to forests from fires, storms and outbreaks of pests and diseases.

In the case of these short-term environmental factors, it is very difficult to analyse trends or to produce projections of how they might affect forests in the future. For example, the analysis of historical trends in forest fires and defoliation (see Section 2.2.1) suggested that these problems may have increased slightly in the past, but may not be increasing very much at the moment. However, the historical trends show a great deal of variation from year to year and the underlying causes of these problems are complex and can not be projected into the future.

What can be said about some of these short-term environmental factors is that they could potentially persist in the future. Thus, the precautionary principle would suggest that individuals in the forest sector should continue to monitor their effects and investigate options for reducing their impact on forest resources in the future.

In addition to the short-term environmental factors discussed above, there are also some environmental factors that have changed more gradually and are likely to have more of a long-term impact on forest resources. Two of the most prominent of these are global climate change and changes in the age-structure and growth rates of forest resources.

Outside of North America (Sedjo and Sohngen, 1998), there has been little research into the effects of climate change on forest products markets. However, there has been some research into the possible effects of climate change on forest resources in Europe (see Box 6). This has suggested that climate change will affect forest growth rates and alter the optimal locations for growing different tree species. In addition, there is some evidence that a warmer climate will also be a more unpredictable and erratic climate, which will possibly lead to an increase in some of the problems already described above.

Box 6   ***Possible consequences of climate change on European forests***

According to the scientific community working through the Intergovernmental Panel on Climate Change, it is generally expected that climate change will lead to temperate climatic conditions moving northward. Thus, the southern extremity of the boreal zone (e.g. southern Finland and Sweden, Baltic states and huge areas of the Russian Federation) will become warmer, with a longer growing season and perhaps more precipitation. The vegetation limits in mountain areas will move higher up and parts of southern Europe will become hotter and dryer, with extended desertification in some regions in the south of the Iberian Peninsula. In addition, more extreme climatic events (e.g. high winds, heavy rainfall, long droughts, etc.) are also expected with a warmer European climate.

If these climate projections are realised, all of these changes would alter the species composition and productivity of Europe's forests over many decades. This would benefit some regions, but harm others. For example, some more fragile forest ecosystems (notably of species at the edge of their climatic range) could collapse, but others would take their place (in most cases).

These changes would only become visible on a significant scale after many decades. However, it is clear that managers of the more fragile forest ecosystems should already be considering the possible consequences of the climate changes that are projected.

The extent and likely impact of future climate change is still a subject of intense scientific debate. However, the changes that may occur are likely to be very gradual and appear over several decades. Therefore, it does not seem likely that global climate change will have a significant impact on the European forest sector within the next two decades.

A much more potent and visible change in environmental factors, at least in the medium term, has been the historical increase in growing stock and growth rates of forest resources in Europe. For example, Section 2.1 showed that both growing stock and NAI have increased significantly in Europe over the last 50 years.

These changes have occurred due to historical levels of harvesting over the last five decades, which have always been less than the annual increment. They have also probably occurred as a result of increases in forest yield, due to advances in silviculture, increased intensity of forest management, better selection of species for different forest sites and improvements in tree breeding and forest establishment.

The effect of these changes has been that the potential supply of roundwood from European forests has increased gradually over the last 50 years, to a level that is now much higher than the current level of harvesting. In the same way that this abundance of potential roundwood supply has accumulated very gradually in the past, it will probably persist for many years in the future.

This increase in potential roundwood supply could have both positive and negative effects on the forest sector in the future. On the negative side, it will continue to exert downward pressure on standing roundwood prices (particularly if potential supply continues to increase faster than the level of harvesting). For example, it has probably contributed already to some of the historical long-term decline in roundwood prices noted in Section 2.7.3. On the positive side, it also presents an opportunity to use large areas of forest for purposes other than industrial roundwood production and to enhance some of the environmental aspects of production forest management (e.g. by lowering the use of chemicals and other intensive forest management techniques).

It should also be noted that these effects have a different impact on each of the stakeholders in the sector. For example, low roundwood prices harm forest owners, but they benefit the forest processing sector. Each of the stakeholders will also be in a different position to take advantage of the opportunities that are presented. The challenge for the sector will be to take these effects into account as part of the future development of the forest sector.

3.2 *Demands of society*

At present, the demand for forest products is probably still the most important demand placed on forests in many countries and it is certainly the most important demand in terms of income for the forest owner. Historical changes in this demand have been examined in the statistical analysis of market trends and, based on this analysis, future projections for forest products markets have been produced.

However, this analysis does not examine some of the more subtle changes in demand that may occur in the future, such as changes in the demand for NWFPs and services. Nor will it capture any recent structural changes in the demand for wood products, because they will not have affected the historical statistics.

There are two important changes in demand that may not be fully captured by the statistical analysis of forest products markets presented earlier and these are briefly discussed below.

3.2.1 Changes in human needs

Human needs can be arranged into a hierarchy (Ernst, 1978), starting with basic needs such as food, shelter and security, followed by other activities that are less of a "need" and more of a personal pleasure. The latter include the accumulation of material possessions and personal development, followed by the acquisition of knowledge and self-awareness.

As personal incomes increase, individuals tends to spend a higher proportion of their income on activities that are higher up in this hierarchy and less on satisfying their basic needs. Thus, for example, in most developed countries only a small proportion of personal income is currently spent on food, while in developing countries this can account for a significant proportion (if not the majority) of personal expenditure.

The relationship between personal income and the hierarchy of human needs is shown in Figure 89. From the information on per capita GDP given above, it is clear that most countries in Western Europe are somewhere towards the right-hand side of this figure, leading to patterns of demand that are skewed towards meeting higher-order needs. Most countries in Eastern Europe are probably closer to the middle of the figure, with the CIS sub-region slightly behind. Thus, in these countries, it would be expected that consumer demand will be focused on a broader range of goods and services.

Figure 89   The relationship between human needs and the level of personal income

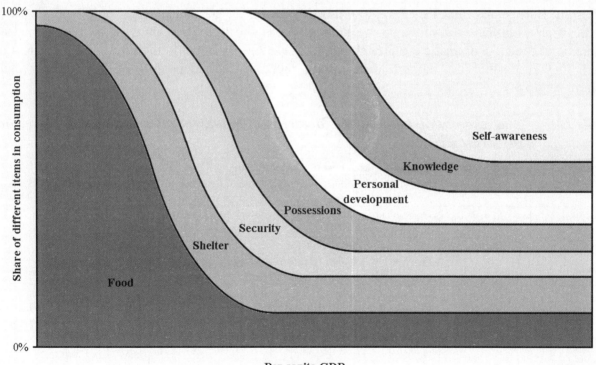

Source: Rennel (1984).

To some extent, the relationship shown in Figure 89 is reflected in the statistical analysis of forest products markets. For example, the income elasticities of demand[17] for printing and writing paper are generally higher than those for sawnwood. This partly reflects of the fact that printing and

---

[17]   The amount by which consumption changes with a given change in income (e.g. an elasticity of 1.4 would indicate that a 1.0 percent increase in income would lead to a 1.4 percent increase in consumption).

writing paper is devoted to fulfilling the need for personal development and knowledge, whereas sawnwood is used mainly to provide shelter and manufacture personal possessions. These differences are also reflected in the differences in elasticities between the sub-regions, with generally lower elasticities for Western Europe where incomes are higher and consumption is less sensitive to changes in income. However, the statistical analysis probably does not capture all of the implications of rising incomes on the demands placed on the forest sector.

Table 22 attempts to go beyond the statistical analysis of forest products markets, to show how increasing incomes may lead to other more subtle changes in the demands placed on the forest sector. As incomes rise, countries will move up the hierarchy towards a pattern of demand that will focus more on higher needs. Thus, for example, there will be more demand for fashionable, well-designed forest products with a greater range of choice and consumers will focus less on price in their purchasing decisions. Wealthier societies will also place greater emphasis on forest services (such as conservation and recreation) relative to the production of forest products and, in product markets, consumers will have a greater interest in the environmental credentials of those products. At the highest levels, there will also be more interest in organised and educational recreational activities and individuals are more likely to take an active interest in forestry affairs.

As already noted, consumption patterns in many of the countries in Western Europe are already focused on the higher needs. However, there are some countries that will still be moving up the hierarchy over the next 20 years. In addition, some of the projected changes (e.g. greater preference for quality over price) will probably occur to some extent in nearly all countries in the future.

In Eastern Europe and the CIS sub-region, most countries are starting in a position lower down in this hierarchy, but they will move up the hierarchy over the next 20 years. It is in these countries that some of the more dramatic changes shown in Table 22 may occur in the future and the extent to which they reach the very highest levels of the hierarchy will depend upon how rapidly their economies grow,

Table 22   ***The relationship between the hierarchy of human needs and demands placed on the forest sector***

Order	Human need	Demands placed on the forest sector
Basic	Food	Harvesting of food (plants and animals) from the forest out of necessity. Unlikely to currently be important in most European countries.
Basic	Shelter	Demand for basic construction materials (sawnwood and wood based panels). Still very important in all European countries.
Basic	Security	Not very relevant for the forest sector.
Low	Possessions	Demand for wooden furniture, packaging materials and other articles. Still very important in all European countries.
Medium	Personal development	Demand for improved health and leisure. Important in richer European countries. Expressed as higher demand for forest recreation (including hunting and NWFP collection as a leisure activity). Greater interest in protecting the environment (for health reasons).
High	Knowledge	Demand for paper, especially for books, magazines and newspaper. Interest in learning about the forest environment (e.g. through organised recreation activities). Important in a few of the richer European countries.
Very high	Self-awareness	Demand for high quality forest products with a greater focus on fashion and design. Greater interest in active participation in forestry affairs. Demand for environmental improvement for altruistic reasons. Important in some of the richer European countries.

3.2.2 Changes in industrial demand for forest products

The second important change that will occur in the future concerns the impact of the ageing workforce on the demand for forest products in end-use industries. As the population age-structure changes and the workforce declines, labour costs will rise and industries will be looking for ways to increase labour productivity. Thus, industrial users of wood products will compare the labour required to utilise those products compared with non-wood alternatives and, to remain competitive, the forest processing sector will have to provide them with products that reduce their total production costs in an environment of rising labour costs.

For the forest processing sector, the most important changes in the future may occur in the construction sector. Construction currently accounts for a significant share of sawnwood consumption (over 50 percent in most countries) and construction has traditionally been a labour intensive industry. The shrinking workforce will have more of an impact on construction than in many other sectors. Furthermore, with the expected social trends towards a better educated workforce and knowledge-based economies, the attraction of working as skilled or unskilled manual labour in the construction sector is likely to decline in the future.

The trends described above will lead to pressures to substitute technology in the forest processing facility for labour at the construction site. Thus, the demand for engineered wood products and products such as pre-cut lumber is likely to increase. An increase in modular or panelised construction is also likely, with the added advantage that these types of building systems reduce construction waste and reduce the costs of handling and recycling waste (Schuler, 2002). This trend favours forest products as a whole which are generally more suited for factory assembly and pre-manufacture than other building techniques (e.g. bricks and mortar).

An example of what might happen is given by recent trends in Japan, where the construction sector has already suffered from the effects of an ageing population for a number of years (see Box 7). Already some European countries are starting to feel these effects and are moving in the same direction (e.g. Germany and the United Kingdom) and it can be expected that more will do so in the future.

Figure 90   ***Recent trends in the use of pre-cut lumber in Japan***

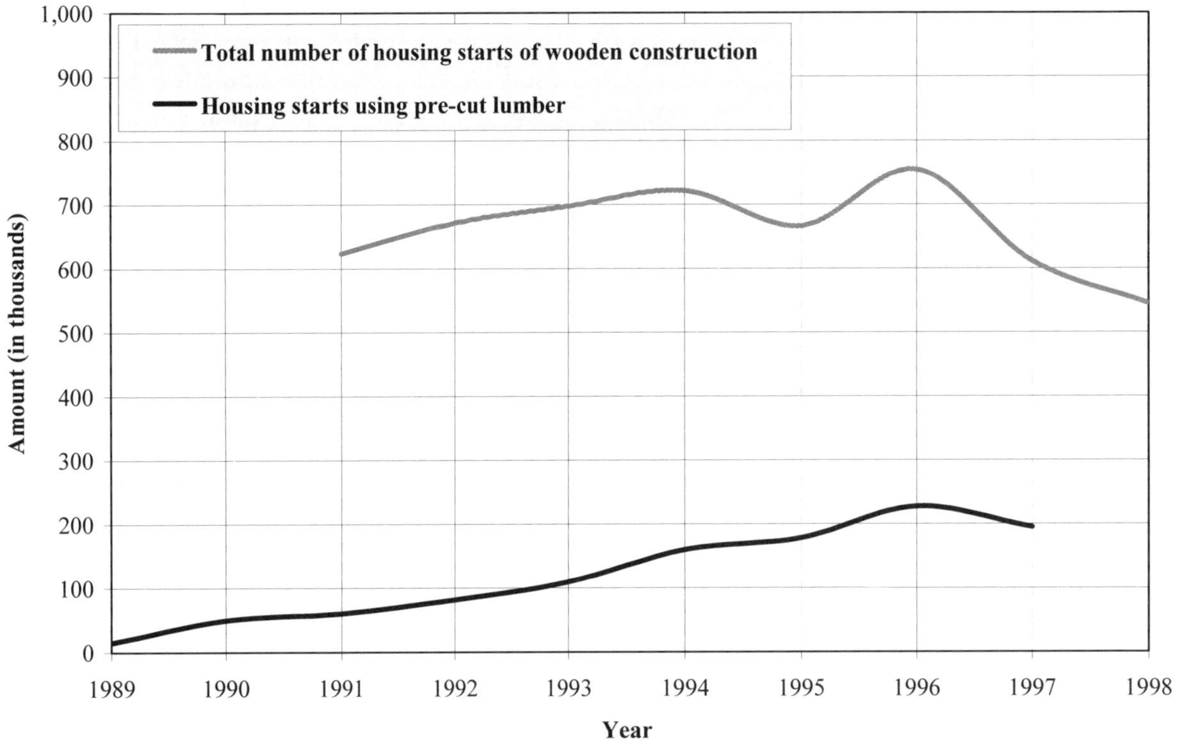

Source: Roos (2000).

Box 7   ***Technological change in Japan's residential construction market***

The 1990s have brought dramatic technological change to Japan's residential construction market. Changes in building techniques and new legislation have combined to create a dynamic residential construction market that, up until the 1990s, had been dominated by Japan's traditional post and beam construction methods.

There have been a number of driving forces behind these changes. Firstly, the cost of imported sawnwood from North America increased in the early-1990s and there was growing concern about the quality of the (mostly green) sawnwood used in construction. Secondly, traditional construction methods were labour intensive, expensive and led to a quality of buildings that was far behind what could be achieved with modern technology (e.g. better resistance to earthquakes, higher insulation). Thirdly, with an ageing population, labour costs were rising and it was becoming increasingly difficult to attract young people into the construction sector. In addition, in response to these forces, policies were introduced to modernise Japanese building techniques and standards

Some of the main changes that occurred were the development of modernised post and beam construction and a great increase in the use of pre-cut lumber in order to reduce labour costs (see figure). By 1997, the use of pre-cut lumber had risen from almost nothing to account for around one-third of all housing starts of wooden construction. The production of pre-cut lumber requires kiln dried sawnwood, which is expensive to produce in Japan due to high energy costs. European suppliers rapidly moved to meet this demand, taking advantage of their economies of scale in kiln dried sawnwood production. For example, exports of spruce and fir sawnwood from Europe to Japan increase from almost nothing in 1992 to 600 thousand m^3 in 1998. Another European success story was the rapid increase in exports of laminated lumber to Japan, which occurred for similar reasons to those described above.

Source: Roos (2000). The trends identified by Roos have continued in the recent years, as evidenced by various issues of the UNECE/FAO Forest Products Annual Market Review

3.3   Policy and market frameworks

3.3.1   Background

So far, the discussion in this section has concentrated on the underlying forces that have affected the sector in the past and will do so in the future. In addition to these, developments in the forest sector are also very strongly affected by changes in government policies and market frameworks (and these are often inter-related). These changes can amplify the underlying forces or, in some cases, try to work against them.

The policies that affect the forest sector are not only the policies specifically designed for the sector (i.e. forestry policies), but also policies in other sectors, such as: energy; environment; trade; and agriculture. Often these "external" policies have cross-sectoral impacts (i.e. they lead to unintended or unexpected consequences outside the sectors where they have been implemented) and there is growing recognition that these cross-sectoral impacts are a major driving force in the forest sector (Dubé and Schmithüsen, 2003). This is hardly surprising given the relatively small size of the forest sector in most countries compared with some of the huge policy initiatives in other sectors (e.g. the Kyoto Protocol or the EU Common Agricultural Policy).

The interactions between different policies are often complex and difficult to understand. This is because different policies often have different (and possibly conflicting) objectives. Furthermore, they may cover different geographical locations and they may be implemented with little co-ordination. They may also have unexpected or unintended impacts on markets. These complexities make it difficult to analyse the full range of policies that could have an effect on the forest sector. However, it is important to attempt to understand some of these forces, as they present both challenges and opportunities for the forest sector in the future.

3.3.2   Methodology

The analysis presented here was developed out of the earlier work on this subject by Peck and Descargues (1997). Their work was based on in-depth discussions with a small sample of policy experts from a variety of sectors, which led to a description of some of the main trends in policies (and other areas) that will affect the forest sector in the future.

In this more recent analysis, the results of their work were taken a step further and were used as the basis for discussions with a wider group of policy experts. This discussion progressed through a number of iterations that, at each stage, attempted to focus and clarify the scope, scale and impact of future trends on the sector. In particular, the discussions and surveys of expert opinion examined the following questions:

- Which policies influence the forest sector and in what way?

- What are the most likely future developments in those policies?

- What might be the consequences of those future policy developments for the forest sector?

It is very important to note that some of the issues that were uncovered as part of this investigation are not policy issues, but are other more general trends that the experts considered might be important in the future. These have been included in this section, because they were grouped together with expected future policy directions, to form a number of broad scenarios that could move the forest sector in different directions. Thus, there is something of a mixture of policy trends, other trends and causes and effects presented here.

It also should be noted that the analysis of policies and development of future scenarios is not an exact science, but requires some judgement to assess the expert opinions and other qualitative information that was collected. This was done in an open and transparent way by, for example, frequently communicating with the network of policy experts. In addition, the information collected was assessed objectively, as far as that is possible.

The results presented below are based on the responses of this group of selected policy experts. While these experts are highly respected for their knowledge about the sector, any expert review may be biased somewhat towards a "technical" view of the sector or suffer from common mis-conceptions. It should also be noted that most of this work was implemented in 2001, so some parts may now be out of date. It is highly recommended, therefore, that these results should be disseminated and discussed amongst a wider European audience, both to get a better idea of current policy issues and developments and to promote a deeper understanding about some of these issues within and outside the sector.

A complete description of the analysis is given in Thoroe _et al_ (2004), which also describes the above process in greater detail. The remainder of this section describes the results obtained from the analysis, grouped into five main scenarios. For each scenario, the text presents some background information, a description of the expected future trends (including the probability that they will occur) and a description of the possible impacts on the forest sector (compared against a baseline of a continuation of current trends and policies).

3.3.3   Greater emphasis on biodiversity and nature conservation

The importance of biodiversity and nature conservation in Europe's forests has already been described in Section 2.10.3. In order to sustain and enhance these values, most governments have implemented a variety of biodiversity and nature conservation policies over the last few decades. In particular, governments have made specific commitments to enhance biodiversity and nature conservation in several international policy processes, such as the Convention on Biological Diversity, the MCPFE and the pan-European Ministerial Process "Environment for Europe".

While there is probably general agreement about the objectives of these policies, some conflicts have arisen about their implementation. In particular, concerns have been expressed in some parts of the forest sector about the economic consequences of such policies, which tend to reduce roundwood supply and increase costs. There has also been debate about the process used to designate protected areas, the strength of protection given to protected areas, the management regimes that should be used in these areas and the possibility (or not) of compensating forest owners for economic losses due to these policies.

Based on the assessment of current trends in this area, the analysis identified three possible future directions, each of which would probably be supported by a variety of activities and policy measures. The directions are shown below (in bold), followed by a description of the expected changes.

More emphasis on nature conservation and the promotion of biological diversity of forest ecosystems. This trend would include increases in the area of forest protected for nature conservation and a reduction of harvesting in such areas. Ecological networks (e.g. core areas, corridors, buffer areas and restoration areas) would be expanded and forest fire protection would be increased. Diversification of species composition and structure of ecological communities in forests would also occur.

More emphasis on nature-oriented forest management. This trend would include eliminating or reducing clear-cutting, replacing this with more selective harvesting. It would also include planting endemic and indigenous species, increasing mixtures of coniferous and broadleaved species in forests and increasing rotation lengths. Forest operations could also be affected by, for example, the abandonment or reduction of drainage systems and reducing the use of chemicals in forests.

Increasing demand for certification of forest management and wood products. This would include increased certification of forest management, forest products and the wood processing industry.

Table 23   ***Conclusions of the scenario analysis about the likely probability and impact of greater emphasis on biodiversity and nature conservation in the future***

Sub-region	Probability (%)	Impact compared to the baseline				
		Area FAWS	**Removals**	**Production**	**Trade**	**Consumption**
More emphasis on nature conservation and promotion of biodiversity in forest ecosystems						
Western Europe	>90	Lower	Lower	Lower	Baseline	Baseline
Eastern Europe	50-70	Lower	Lower	Baseline	Baseline	Baseline
CIS countries	50-70	Baseline	Baseline	Baseline	Baseline	Baseline
More emphasis on nature oriented forest management						
Western Europe	North >90, South 50-70	Baseline	Baseline	Lower	Baseline	Baseline
Eastern Europe	50-70	Baseline	Baseline	Baseline	Baseline	Baseline
CIS countries	50-70	Baseline	Baseline	Baseline	Baseline	Baseline
Increasing demand for certification of forest management and wood products						
Western Europe	~50	Lower	Baseline	Baseline	Higher	Higher
Eastern Europe	20-30	Lower	Baseline	Baseline	Baseline	Baseline
CIS countries	20-30	Lower	Baseline	Baseline	Baseline	Baseline

Source: based on Thoroe et al (2004).

Table 23 presents a summary of the expert opinion about the probability of these trends occurring and their effects on the forest sector. This shows that it is considered to be quite likely that these trends will occur in the future, especially in Western Europe. It is also highly likely that they would reduce the FAWS area. In most sub-regions, it is expected that removals, consumption, production and trade would not be affected by these trends. However, it is expected that an increase in nature conservation would reduce removals in Western and Eastern Europe (presumably due to an expansion of protected areas). It is also expected that an increase in certification might increase trade and consumption in Western Europe, due to an improvement in the image of forest products.

3.3.4   Agricultural, rural and regional development policies

Several earlier parts of this report have already described how agriculture and land-use change have been strongly influenced by government policies for many years. In the past, agricultural policies have largely been implemented in isolation, leading to various cross-sectoral impacts. However, these have sometimes had a positive effect on the forest sector (e.g. support to intensify agriculture has reduced the demand for less fertile areas and has been one of the main driving forces behind forest expansion in Europe).

It is now increasingly clear that policy makers wish to consider forestry and agriculture together within the broader context of rural development. The main objective of rural development policy in Europe is to protect the rural population, economy, ecology and landscape from the multiple threats posed by an increasingly urban society that has a minimal understanding of (and sympathy for) rural concerns.

In Europe, there is also now a strong political will to modify agriculture policies, most notably the EU Common Agricultural Policy (CAP). The aim is to move away from measures that have stimulated agricultural production (e.g. market measures), which have sometimes had unintended results in the past. In the future, policy will aim towards broader rural development, which will be more balanced and focused on the general goals of society and, above all, less expensive.

The process of agricultural policy reform will be implemented by "decoupling" rural development from the level of agricultural production. This will be done, for instance, by replacing production support with direct payments for the provision of ecological, landscape protection or recreational services. However, this transformation will not be easy (as the recent protracted negotiations on the CAP have shown) and the final outcome is still far from certain.

Linked to these rural development policies is the move to initiate policies to provide economic incentives for the production of social and environmental benefits from forest sector activities. Such policies may include measures to encourage the protection of forests, the production of recreational services, nature-oriented forest management and the conversion of forests used for wood production to nature conservation forests. However, it has proved difficult in practice to design policies that will provide such incentives in a way that is efficient and focused. In particular, it has been difficult to identify priorities, because these outputs have been provided free of charge in the past, as by-products of wood production.

Under this heading, the analysis identified the following two future policy directions and possible supporting measures.

Incentives for social and environmental benefits from forestry and wood products use. This would include economic incentives for forest protection and the production of forest recreation, incentives for nature oriented management of forests and incentives to convert forests used for wood production to nature conservation forests.

Changes in agricultural, rural and regional development policies. This would include changes in the subsidies for agricultural production and exports, extension of CAP payments to cover forestry activities (e.g. the afforestation of agricultural land), new forestry measures in agriculture (e.g. to support biomass production) and promotion of the forest sector as an integral part of rural development.

Table 24   Conclusions of the scenario analysis about the likely probability and impact of changes in agriculture and rural development policies in the future

Sub-region	Probability (%)	Impact compared to the baseline				
		Area FAWS	Removals	Production	Trade	Consumption
Incentives for social and environmental benefits from forestry and wood products use						
Western Europe	65	Baseline	Baseline	Baseline	Baseline	Baseline
Eastern Europe	60	Baseline	Baseline	Baseline	Baseline	Baseline
CIS countries	50	Baseline	Higher	Higher	Higher	Higher
Changes in agricultural, rural and regional development policies						
Western Europe	80	Higher	Baseline	Baseline	Baseline	Baseline
Eastern Europe	80	Higher	Higher	Higher	Higher	Higher
CIS countries	40	Baseline	Baseline	Baseline	Baseline	Baseline

Source: based on Thoroe et al (2004).

The conclusions of this part of the analysis are summarised in Table 24. This shows that, in Western and Eastern Europe, it is considered quite likely that economic incentives will be established for the production of social and environmental services from forests. However, it is also believed that these will be unlikely to influence the main market forces. For the CIS countries, these economic incentives are considered slightly less likely to occur, but they would be expected to increase production and consumption of forest products.

Changes in agriculture and rural development policies are considered very likely in Western and Eastern Europe, leading to an expansion of FAWS area. In Western Europe, these policy changes are not expected to change market forces, but they are expected to increase removals, production, trade and consumption of forest products in Eastern Europe. For the CIS countries, changes in agriculture and rural development policies are considered rather unlikely and, if implemented, would not be expected to change market forces.

3.3.5 Consequences of the transition process

The process of transition from centrally-planned to market economies has been the most profound social and economic structural change in Europe in the 1990s. Conditions now vary enormously between these countries, in particular between those closer to Western Europe and the others. For example, eight countries have progressed so rapidly that they joined the EU in 2004, having implemented numerous policy reforms across all sectors over less than a decade. Others have made much less progress and remain in the transition process or even at the beginning of it, with levels of GDP still below the those of the early 1990s.

The economic scenarios described in Section are based on specific assumptions about the progress of these countries through the transition process and how this will influence their long-term economic growth. In addition to this, it is also worthwhile considering the direct influence of the transition process on the forest sector. Important variables that could have a major impact on the forest sector might include: changes in forest ownership through privatisation or restitution; the weakening of forest sector institutions during the transition (e.g. reducing their ability to enforce forest law); the privatisation of forest industries; and changes to state subsidies (e.g. as shown by the significant impact of increased railway freight charges on the Russian forest sector).

Under this heading, the analysis identified two future directions, with the following associated changes.

Strengthened policies to develop the market framework in countries in transition. This would include the recovery of the forest sector in these countries and changes in forest land ownership.

Progress in EU enlargement. This would result in accelerated enlargement of the EU to include all European countries (i.e. current candidate countries and then the others).

Table 25   *Conclusions of the scenario analysis about the likely probability and impact of changes to the transition process in the future*

Sub-region	Probability (%)	Impact compared to the baseline				
		Area FAWS	**Removals**	**Production**	**Trade**	**Consumption**
Strengthening policies to develop market framework in countries with economies in transition						
Western Europe	75	Baseline	Baseline	Lower	Much higher	Higher
Eastern Europe	90	Higher	Higher	Much higher	Much higher	Higher
CIS countries	80	Higher	Much higher	Much higher	Much higher	Much higher
Progress in EU enlargement						
Western Europe	80	Baseline	Baseline	Lower	Higher	Higher
Eastern Europe	100	Higher	Higher	Much higher	Higher	Higher
CIS countries	50	Baseline	Higher	Much higher	Higher	Higher

Source: based on Thoroe et al (2004).

The results of this analysis are shown in Table 25. These indicate that both the strengthening of the market framework and the enlargement of the EU are considered very likely (except for expansion of the EU to include CIS countries). These two developments are expected to result in higher or much higher production, consumption and trade in both Eastern Europe and CIS countries. In Western Europe, consumption and trade (i.e. imports) of forest products are expected to be higher if these developments were to occur. However, removals and the FAWS area would be unchanged, while production would be lower (i.e. imports from the east would be expected to increase their share of Western European markets).

Some caution is required in interpreting these results in quantitative terms, as there is overlap between the opinions about the transition process set out above and those already included in the economic growth scenarios.

3.3.6 Globalisation, innovation and market structures

Globalisation has been a major driving force in recent years and has been supported by policies that have reduced barriers to the movement of goods, capital and technology across national boundaries. For the forest sector, the main effect of globalisation has been the reduction in transport costs that has led to increased exports of forest products (see Figure 54 and Figure 55) and the creation of a truly global market for forest products.

Globalisation has also resulted in the emergence of 10 to 20 major global forest products companies. These companies can restructure their operations all over the world in the response to changing market conditions. They are also in a stronger position to invest in research and development, innovation and marketing, which makes it easier to develop new products and markets and increase the competitiveness of the sector.

Another major effect of globalisation has been that it has reduced the dependence of the forest processing sector on local supplies of raw materials. For example, companies can now utilise materials from different sources and locate manufacturing facilities in different locations all along the production chain from the forest to the consumer. Thus, the location and development of the forest processing sector is now influenced less by the availability of forest resources and more by the prevailing investment climate and general economic conditions in a country (see Brown (2000) for a discussion of this transition from an environment of "natural advantage" to one of "competitive advantage" in the forest sector).

While globalisation has undoubtedly brought widespread benefits (e.g. to consumers who have benefited from better access to good quality, well priced goods and services), it may have also led to some negative effects. For instance, increased competition may have resulted in pressures to lower environmental and labour standards in some countries. These advantages and disadvantages of globalisation have been hotly debated at all levels of society.

Under this heading, the policy study identified the following two future trends and effects.

Impact of globalisation on the competitiveness of the European forest sector. This would include increased international flows of capital, cross-border mergers and relocation of companies across national boundaries.

Intensified innovations and changes in competitiveness of wood products. This would include innovations in: harvesting techniques and facilities; wood processing technologies; and information technologies. It would also include development of new products (e.g. engineered wood products), new non-wood forest products and new fields of application for existing products. It would also include improvements in transport and logistics.

Table 26   ***Conclusions of the analysis about the likely probability and impact of trends towards globalisation, innovation and changing market structures in the future***

Sub-region	Probability (%)	Impact compared to the baseline				
		Area FAWS	Removals	Production	Trade	Consumption
Impact of globalisation on the competitiveness of the European forest sector						
Western Europe	50	Baseline	Higher	Higher	Higher	Higher
Eastern Europe	60	Higher	Higher	Higher	Higher	Higher
CIS countries	70	Baseline	Higher	Higher	Much higher	Higher
Intensified innovations and changes in competitiveness of wood products						
Western Europe	60	Baseline	Higher	Higher	Higher	Higher
Eastern Europe	70	Baseline	Higher	Higher	Higher	Higher
CIS countries	75	Baseline	Much higher	Much higher	Higher	Higher

Source: based on Thoroe et al (2004).

The expectations about the future of globalisation, innovation and changing market structures are summarised in Table 26. This shows that an increase in globalisation and innovation (above the current baseline trend) is considered rather likely (with a probability of 50 percent to 75 percent). This is expected to have little effect on the FAWS area, but would result in much higher levels of removals, production, trade and consumption.

It is also interesting to note that globalisation and innovation are perceived as having a stimulating effect not only in Eastern Europe and the CIS sub-region, but also in Western Europe. This is despite the threat to Western Europe of increased competition from these low-cost countries. Possible reasons for this perception could be a belief in the ability of a highly competitive global economic environment to stimulate all countries to increase dynamism and efficiency. It could also reflect confidence in the ability of European multi-national forestry companies to develop their skills and efficiency so that they do not lose (and may even gain) market share in the future (see, for example, Figure 56).

3.3.7   Energy and environment

At present, some of the most difficult policy issues concern the increased demand for energy and environmental improvement and the linkages between these two issues. For example, there is great interest in identifying future sources of energy that are sustainable, economically feasible, safe and renewable. Policymakers are considering how energy prices should be modified to take into account the externalities of production (e.g. environmental damage from air pollution) and the need to care for the interests of future generations. They are also looking at how patterns of energy use can be modified to minimise and eventually reverse anthropogenic climate change without imposing an intolerable burden on today's energy users. The policies chosen to deal with these problems will affect every inhabitant of the world for many years to come.

Future developments in this area will affect all countries at the broadest level (i.e. leading to changes in economic, social and environmental trends) and will influence the outlook for all sectors. However, there are some aspects these developments that will have a direct impact on the forest sector. For example, wood is a source of renewable energy and may be promoted in future renewable energy strategies. This may then have an effect on the future wood raw material balance. In addition, forest products can substitute for products that require a greater use of energy in manufacturing and they also store carbon (as do forests). Therefore, greater use of forest products may be promoted as part of policies to reduce climate change.

Important issues that will have to be examined include: the relative importance (and cost) of forestry's contribution to these policies; the reconciliation of these new demands with existing demands for wood materials; and the changes in forest management techniques that might be required to support such policies. Given the potential economic costs of such polices, it also remains in doubt whether governments will have the political will to implement some of these policies.

In addition to the above, there is also a wide range of other environmental issues that may affect the forest sector in the future. These include demands to reduce pollution and waste (e.g. through improved manufacturing processes and increased recycling). Changes in these areas could also alter costs and prices in the forest sector and change the supply and demand relationships between wood raw materials and processed forest products (see Box 8).

Under this heading, the analysis identified the following three future trends.

Promotion of renewable energy sources. This would include a greater emphasis on the use of wood biomass as a source of energy in the future, increased taxes on fossil fuel production and utilisation, the abandonment of nuclear power stations and promotion of energy saving technologies.

Improvement of waste management and emission control. This would include increased recycling of waste paper and waste wood, implementation of best practices in the forest processing industry (e.g. cleaner production and waste minimising technologies), implementation or extension of integrated pollution control, rationalisation in the use of wood products and reductions in harvesting and transport losses in the forest sector.

Climate change. Climate change may affect forest growth in the future (e.g. higher temperatures may lead to higher precipitation and more frequent (and stronger) storms). There may also be greater acceptance to include changes in forests as part of strategies to comply with emission reduction targets and acceptance of to include the carbon stored in harvested wood products.

Box 8   Landfill taxes - a new driving force in the forest sector?

With increasing concerns about waste and the environment, many countries are continuing to introduce measures to reduce waste and encourage recycling. In particular, the EU has passed several Regulations and Directives on this subject since the early 1990s. The overall EU policy on reducing waste establishes a hierarchy of waste management, which prioritises: prevention of waste; followed by its re-use and recycling; and finally, its disposal through energy recovery.

Policy instruments that have been used by countries include: stricter laws governing how and where waste can be disposed; compulsory packaging return programmes; subsidised waste recovery and sorting schemes; compulsory domestic waste separation requirements; and landfill taxes. These measures have been in place for many years now in some countries but one in particular - landfill taxes - has been very effective at encouraging recycling.

Landfill taxes provide a very strong incentive to recycle, as they impose a direct cost on industry that varies in relation to how much waste is produced and has to go to landfill. Furthermore, landfill taxes can be continually updated and increased to constantly raise performance in the area of waste control and waste management. Some sources have estimated that waste disposal costs could amount to between 5 percent and 10 percent of turnover in major timber using sectors.

The total potential volume of available waste wood (as opposed to wood residues) is unknown, but one estimate puts the figure as high as 40 million MT to 80 million MT per year in nine EU countries (Austria, Denmark, Finland, Germany, Greece, Italy, Netherlands, Norway and Sweden). For comparison, these same nine countries produced 184 million MT of industrial roundwood in 2000.

Already, landfill taxes and other waste control policies appear to be having a significant impact on fibre supply. Germany has reported the use of waste wood rising from almost nothing in 1990 to 1,800 thousand MT in 1997 and estimated use of wood waste in the United Kingdom in 2001 was 770 thousand MT. Although these figures are only equal to about 5 percent to 10 percent of industrial roundwood production in these countries, they could rise to ten times as much in the future.

Source: based on Dengg et al (2000), Remade Scotland (2004), EC (2002) and Bromhead (2000).

Table 27   ***Conclusions of the analysis about the likely probability and impact of trends in energy and environment in the future***

Sub-region	Probability (%)	Impact compared to the baseline				
		Area FAWS	Removals	Production	Trade	Consumption
Promotion of renewable energy sources						
Western Europe	100	Baseline	Higher	Higher	Higher	Higher
Eastern Europe	100	Higher	Higher	Higher	Higher	Higher
CIS countries	100	Baseline	Higher	Higher	Higher	Baseline
Improvement of waste management and emission control						
Western Europe	100	Baseline	Baseline	Baseline	Baseline	Baseline
Eastern Europe	100	Baseline	Baseline	Baseline	Higher	Baseline
CIS countries	100	Baseline	Baseline	Baseline	Baseline	Baseline
Climate change						
Western Europe	100	Higher	Higher	Higher	Higher	Baseline
Eastern Europe	100	Baseline	Higher	Higher	Baseline	Baseline
CIS countries	100	Baseline	Higher	Higher	Baseline	Baseline

Source: based on Thoroe et al (2004).

The summary of this part of the analysis is shown in Table 27. This shows that all of the trends energy and environment described above are considered highly likely to occur. The trends in waste management and emission control are not expected to have a significant impact on FAWS area or markets. The trends in renewable energy and climate change are not expected to influence the FAWS area, except in Western and Eastern Europe. In the case of Western Europe, trends in climate change are expected to increase FAWS area, perhaps with the establishment of new forests as carbon sinks. In Eastern Europe, trends in renewable energy are expected to have this effect. This could reflect an expectation that new forests may be planted to produce woodfuel.

The trends in renewable energy and climate change are expected to raise the level of removals, production and trade in almost all subregions. Trends in renewable energy are also expected to raise consumption in Western and Eastern Europe, but it is not clear whether this expectation refers to consumption of all forest products or only woodfuel. However, higher consumption of forest products might be expected with this trend if forest products were to replace products requiring a higher use of energy during the manufacturing process (e.g. if renewable energy policies resulted in an increase in energy prices).

3.4 Three future scenarios for the forest sector

Scenarios are used to bring together a package of future trends and choices that will tend to move the sector in a certain direction. For example, trends towards a greater emphasis on the environment could be amplified by policy changes in support of environmental objectives. They may also result in changes in the market, such as changes to forest product prices and investment in alternative technologies. It is very important to understand that scenarios include both exogenous factors (e.g. trends in the underlying forces pushing the sector in one direction or another) and policy choices that can work for or against these developments. Therefore, they include a mixture of elements that can be made to happen in the future, plus other elements that would probably occur anyway.

Three alternative scenarios were developed for the forest sector outlook, based on the analysis of driving forces presented in the rest of this chapter. The first is a baseline scenario, which basically assumes that there will be a continuation of historical trends in all of the main variables affecting the sector. This is largely based on the historical analysis of trends in exogenous factors and forest products markets. The other two scenarios assume that driving forces will be altered in the future (particularly in the case of government policies) and will tend to move the sector in a slightly different direction (compared with the baseline). A brief description of these three alternative scenarios is given below.

3.4.1   Baseline scenario

The baseline scenario assumes that the long-term historical relationships in forest products markets (i.e. elasticities of supply and demand with respect to GDP and prices) will remain the same in the future. It assumes that population and economic growth will follow the baseline projections described in Section 3.1 and that the real prices of forest products will not change in the future (see Table 28). It also assumes that the historical trends in the supply and demand of NWFPs and forest services will continue unchanged into the future.

In terms of forest resources, it assumes that future developments in the bio-physical characteristics of Europe's forests (e.g. growing stock and increment) will be largely determined by the existing status of forest resources. However, it does assume that the historical trends towards a gradually expanding FAWS area will continue into the future.

3.4.2   Conservation scenario

The conservation scenario assumes that there will be an accelerated shift towards environmental enhancement and conservation of forest resources in the future. This will be driven by an increase in public awareness of and demand for environmental benefits and will be supported by policies that will move society in this direction. Specifically, in the forest sector, it assumes that the trends in nature conservation and biodiversity (described in Section 3.3.3 above) and energy and environment (Section 3.3.7) will occur in the future. It also assumes that some of the changes in agriculture described above may occur in the future (e.g. a redirection of support from crop production towards the production of environmental benefits in the countryside, including support for forestry activities).

Unfortunately, the models used to produce the market projections are not sophisticated enough to take into account all of the effects of these trends on forest products markets. These models are largely driven by projections of economic growth and forest product prices. Thus, it has been assumed that, under this scenario, forest products prices may increase slightly (e.g. due to higher costs as a result of a greater emphasis on nature conservation in forest operations). It has also been assumed that economic growth will be slightly slower in the future (see Table 28). This is not to suggest that a greater emphasis on nature conservation will reduce economic growth, but that the impact of economic growth on future markets will be less (e.g. economic growth would lead to less of an increase in roundwood removals (compared to the baseline scenario) with more emphasis on nature conservation).

For NWFPs and forest services, the lack of data and analytical tools prevents a thorough investigation of the impacts of this scenario on the future supply and demand of these outputs. However, it can be expected that production and consumption of some of these outputs will increase. For forest resources, this scenario makes the same assumptions as in the baseline scenario

3.4.3   Integration scenario

This scenario assumes that there will be more rapid economic integration and market liberalisation across all of Europe. This will result in higher economic growth, so the higher economic growth projections (described in Section 3.1) have been used to produce the forest product market projections under this scenario. It also assumes that integration will encompass some of the trends in globalisation, innovation and market structures described in Section 3.3.6. These will tend to exert downward pressure on forest prices, so an assumption of a small decline in forest product prices has used to produce the market projections (see Table 28).

Again, it has not been possible to investigate the impacts of this scenario on the outlook for NWFPs and forest services. However, in the case of forest resources, it has been assumed that there may be a slight increase in the FAWS area (above that assumed in the baseline scenario), due to the increased establishment of forest plantations and increased investment in forest infrastructure (e.g. forest roads) that would open up some new forest areas for harvesting.

Table 28   ***Assumptions used to produce the forest product market projections under the three alternative scenarios***

Scenario	Average annual rate of economic growth in Europe (in percent)	Average annual change in the real prices of forest products (in percent)
Baseline	2.2	0.0
Conservation	1.5	+ 0.5
Integration	3.5	- 0.5

Note: the economic growth figures presented above are an average for Europe. The figures actually used in the projections differed by country (see: Kangas and Baudin, 2003).

The three alternative scenarios are conceptually quite distinct and reflect different assumptions about both the forces acting on the sector in the future and the deliberate actions (e.g. policies) that may be taken to move in different directions. Some elements are likely to occur under all three scenarios (e.g. changes in agricultural policy), but others may arise as a matter of choice. Together, they present three very different pictures of what the future might look like that can be used as a basis for future discussions on forestry policy in Europe.

4   THE OUTLOOK FOR THE FOREST SECTOR

The outlook for the forest sector comprises two main parts. Firstly, there are the projections of future developments that are largely driven by external forces. Secondly, there are elements of the outlook that are based on the choices that are taken by individuals currently working in the sector. This chapter of the report focuses on the first part of the outlook, while the choices for future action are discussed in the next and final chapter of the report.

The chapter is divided into seven main sections. The first three sections present the outlook for industrial forestry. This starts with the outlook for processed products, then the outlook for raw materials (excluding industrial roundwood). The third section presents the outlook for the raw material balance and, derived from this, the outlook for industrial roundwood.

Sections 4.4 and 4.5 present the outlook for woodfuel and non-wood forest products and services. Following this, the outlook for forest products markets under the three alternative scenarios are compared and discussed. Finally, the outlook for forest resources is presented, along with a discussion of the outlook for forest management.

4.1   *Production and consumption of processed wood products*

The majority of the projections presented here are based on the work of Kangas and Baudin (2003), who produced projections of production, imports, exports and consumption to the year 2030 for the eight most important processed forest product categories under all three scenarios. For completeness, additional projections were produced for the few products not covered in their analysis and the assumptions used in this process are explained in the text of this and following sections.[18]

4.1.1   Sawnwood production and consumption

Figure 91 shows the projected production and consumption of coniferous sawnwood to 2020 under the assumptions in the baseline scenario. The most notable feature of this figure is the expected increase in production and consumption to the year 2020, which will continue the trend experienced in the latter half of the 1990s. Overall, production in 2020 will surpass the level reached in 1990, due to continued growth in Western and Eastern Europe and a recovery in production in the CIS sub-region. However, consumption outside Western Europe will continue to fall behind the expansion in production, leading to an increase in net exports from the region as a whole.

For Europe as a whole, production and consumption of coniferous sawnwood are expected to grow at an average annual rate of 2.3 percent and 1.8 percent respectively. Annual production and consumption at the end of the 1990s were around 111 million m^3 and 101 million m^3 respectively. Production will rise to 176 million m^3 in 2020, while consumption is projected to increase to 144 million m^3, leading to an increase in net exports from 10 million m^3 per year to 32 million m^3 per year. It is expected that the bulk of this increase in net exports will be exported to newly industrialising countries in Asia.

In Western Europe, growth in production and consumption is expected to slow slightly compared with the last decade, to resume the rate of growth experienced in earlier decades. In addition, the sector will probably revert back towards processing more roundwood grown in the sub-region (i.e. with relatively less use of imported industrial roundwood) as countries in the East develop their own sawmilling industry.

---

[18]   In addition, due to the limitations of data, Kangas and Baudin (2003) did not include Bosnia and Herzegovina in their analysis. It has been assumed here that the markets in this country will expand at the same rate as the average for the other countries in the former Yugoslavia.

Figure 91   *Trends and projections for the production and consumption of coniferous sawnwood under the baseline scenario*

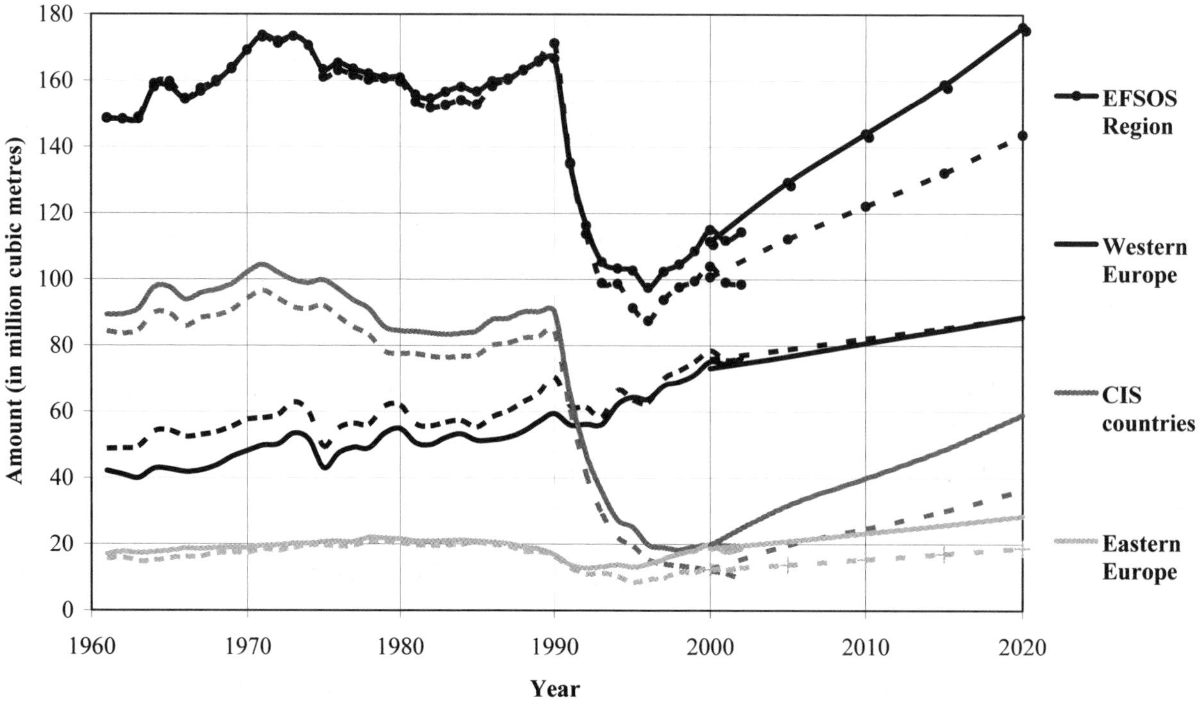

Solid lines represent production and dashed lines represent apparent consumption

Source: trends derived from FAOSTAT production and trade statistics and projections from Kangas and Baudin (2003).

Production and consumption of coniferous sawnwood are expected to grow at an average annual rate of 1.0 percent and 0.8 percent respectively. At the end of the 1990s, annual production in Western Europe amounted to 73 million m^3, while annual consumption amounted to 76 million m^3. By 2020, production and consumption are both expected to reach 89 million m^3 and Western Europe will no longer be a net importer of coniferous sawnwood.

In Eastern Europe, the outlook for coniferous sawnwood is similar to that expected in the West. Growth will slow down compared to the last decade and resume a trend similar to earlier decades. Although the availability of forest resources is not a variable in these projections, a slightly slower rate of growth would also be consistent with the likely supply of industrial roundwood, as the recent benefit of increased supply from the restitution of forests starts to come to an end.

However, net exports from Eastern Europe are likely to persist and will even increase slightly. In addition, production and consumption will expand twice as fast as in the West, with an average annual growth rate of 2.1 percent. Annual production and consumption of 19 million m^3 and 12 million m^3 respectively at the end of the 1990s will increase to 28 million m^3 and 19 million m^3 respectively by 2020, leading to a very small increase in net exports from this sub-region.

The fastest expansion of coniferous sawnwood production and consumption in the future is expected in the CIS sub-region, where average annual growth of 5.6 percent is expected for both production and consumption. This rate of growth is more than twice the rate of growth expected in Eastern Europe or five times higher than the projections for Western Europe and will lead to a three-fold increase in production and consumption by 2020.

This rapid expansion is due to the high rate of economic growth expected in the CIS sub-region over the next two decades. However, the projected increase in production will be feasible, due to the abundance of forest resources in this sub-region. For example, the projected levels of production and consumption in 2020 will still be well below the levels achieved in the past.

Production is expected to increase from 20 million m³ per year to 59 million m³ per year by 2020, while consumption will increase from 12 million m³ per year to 36 million m³ per year. Consequently, net exports will increase from 8 million m³ per year to 23 million m³ per year, accounting for most of the expected increase in net exports from Europe as a whole. Given that the Russian Federation will account for most of this increase, it is expected that much of these exports will be sold in the Asian market rather than the European market.

The very marked differences in expansion of coniferous sawnwood production and consumption across Europe will lead to realignment in terms of the relative importance of the three main sub-regions. Although Eastern Europe and the CIS sub-region are currently starting from relatively low levels of production and consumption, the very high rates of growth expected there will lead to a gradual decline in the dominance of production from Western Europe from around 66 percent of the European total now to only 50 percent of the total in 2020. Given that Europe as a whole is also likely to become an even larger net exporter of coniferous sawnwood (and Western Europe will no longer be a net importer by 2020), it seems likely that the competitiveness (or lack of it) of the European sawmilling sector in international markets will become increasingly important in determining levels of production and consumption.

Figure 92   ***Trends and projections for the production and consumption of non-coniferous sawnwood under the baseline scenario***

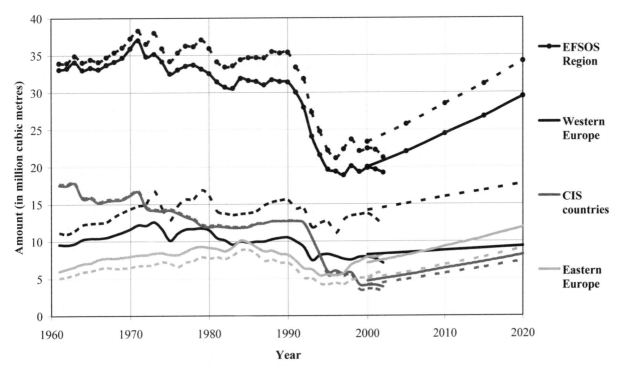

Solid lines represent production and dashed lines represent apparent consumption

Source: trends derived from FAOSTAT production and trade statistics and projections from Kangas and Baudin (2003).

Figure 92 shows the projection for the production and consumption of non-coniferous sawnwood to 2020 under the baseline scenario. For the region as a whole, production and consumption in 2020 are expected to return to levels just slightly below those of 1990, with an expected average annual increase in production and consumption of 2.0 percent and 1.9 percent respectively over the next two decades.

These expected increases are in the opposite direction of recent trends in this market, where production and consumption of non-coniferous sawnwood have generally declined in the past. Most of the growth in this market is expected in Eastern Europe and the CIS sub-region. However, consumption in Western Europe is also expected to grow quite strongly over the next two decades, largely due to increased imports from Eastern Europe.

In Western Europe, production of non-coniferous sawnwood is expected to grow only slightly at an average annual rate of 0.7 percent, from 8.2 million m^3 in 2000 to 9.4 million m^3 in 2020. Consumption will increase at a faster rate of 1.1 percent per year, from 14.2 million m^3 in 2000 to 17.8 million m^3 in 2020. The level of net imports is likely to expand from 6.0 million m^3 per year to 8.4 million m^3 per year over the same period. As in the past, imports of tropical sawnwood and non-coniferous sawnwood from North America will account for a large share of these net imports, although the recent increase in imports from Eastern Europe is also expected to continue.

Production and consumption of non-coniferous sawnwood in Eastern Europe are expected to grow significantly in the future, continuing the recovery in this sector that started in the mid-1990s. Production and consumption are expected to grow at an average annual rate of 2.6 percent and 3.0 percent respectively over the period and Eastern Europe will account for the greatest share of European non-coniferous sawnwood production by around 2005.

Eastern Europe is a significant net exporter of non-coniferous sawnwood and this is not expected to change. Production will increase from 7.1 million m^3 in 2000 to 11.9 million m^3 in 2020, while consumption will increase from 5.0 million m^3 per year to 9.1 million m^3 per year over the same period. Therefore, the level of net exports will expand slightly from 2.1 million m^3 per year to 2.8 million m^3 per year.

In contrast to the coniferous sawnwood sector, the CIS sub-region accounts for the smallest share of the European market for non-coniferous sawnwood and the sector is expected to grow only modestly. The sector will expand at about the same rate as in Eastern Europe, with average growth in production and consumption of 2.8 percent per year and 2.9 percent per year respectively. By 2020, production in the CIS sub-region will approach the same level of production projected for Western Europe, but will still be far below the levels reached in earlier decades. Production will increase from 4.7 million m^3 in 2000 to 8.2 million m^3 in 2020 and consumption will increase from 4.2 million m^3 per year to 7.4 million m^3 per year, leading to a slight increase in net exports from 0.5 million m^3 per year to 0.8 million m^3 per year.

As in the coniferous sawnwood sector, the expected changes in the markets for non-coniferous sawnwood will lead to a shift in the balance of production and consumption from west to east over the next 20 years. However, in this case, Eastern Europe will become the dominant producing region, with a 40 percent share of all European production, while the remaining 60 percent of production will be divided almost equally between Western Europe and the CIS sub-region. Western Europe will remain the main consumer of non-coniferous sawnwood and it can be expected that the trade of non-coniferous sawnwood from Eastern Europe to Western Europe will expand.

4.1.2   Wood based panel production and consumption

Strong growth in all parts of the wood based panels sector is expected in the future, reflecting the continued expansion across this sector in Western Europe and the continued recovery of the sector in Eastern Europe and the CIS sub-region.

The outlook for fibreboard production and consumption to 2020 is shown in Figure 93. For Europe as a whole, production and consumption are expected to increase at an average annual rate of 3.1 percent and 2.9 percent respectively. This rate of expansion will be somewhat slower than in the last decade, but still well above the long-term trend in this sector. As already noted in Section 2.3.2, it is expected that this increase will be partly driven by expansion of the markets for MDF.

Production and consumption of fibreboard will almost double over the next 20 years, with production increasing from around 12.7 million m^3 in 2000 to 23.5 million m^3 in 2020 and consumption increasing from 12.4 million m^3 per year to 22.2 million m^3 per year over the same period. Europe's position as a net exporter of fibreboard is also expected to increase significantly, from 0.3 million m^3 per year to 1.3 million m^3 per year, due to an expected increase in net exports from the CIS sub-region.

Western Europe is the largest market for fibreboard in Europe and will continue to dominate this sector. Average annual growth in production and consumption is expected to amount to 2.4 percent and 2.1 percent respectively over the next two decades. This will result in a total increase in the size of the market from around 9 million m^3 in 2000 to 15 million m^3 in 2020 (or an increase of slightly more than 50 percent). The levels of production and consumption in Western Europe are quite similar, so net trade is insignificant. However, it is expected that Western Europe will change from a small net importer of fibreboard to a small net exporter over the period.

In Eastern Europe, the market for fibreboard is expected to grow rapidly, with an average annual increase in production of 4.1 percent and growth in consumption of 4.7 percent. Production will expand from around 2.4 million m^3 in 2000 to 5.4 million m^3 in 2020, while consumption will expand from 2.1 million m^3 per year to 5.3 million m^3 per year over the period. As in Western Europe, production and consumption are roughly in balance, although the small amount of net exports from Eastern Europe is expected to decline by 2020.

The highest growth in the fibreboard sector is expected in the CIS sub-region, where production and consumption are projected to increase by 6.0 percent per year and 6.3 percent per year respectively. Although the sector will not reach the levels of production and consumption of 1990, production and consumption will both increase by more than 200 percent in total. Production will expand from around 1.0 million m^3 in 2000 to 3.4 million m^3 in 2020 and consumption will expand from 0.7 million m^3 per year to 2.4 million m^3 per year over the period, leading to a significant increase in net exports amounting to 1.0 million m^3 in 2020.

Figure 93   Trends and projections for the production and consumption of fibreboard under the baseline scenario

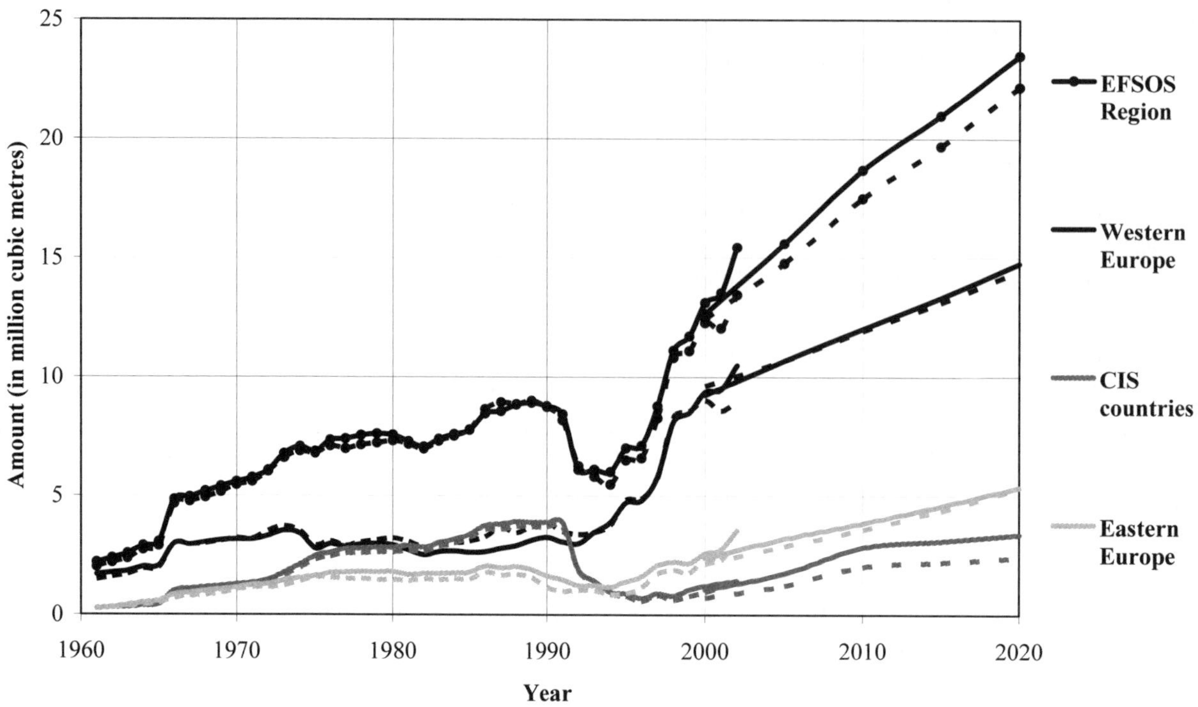

Solid lines represent production and dashed lines represent apparent consumption

Source: trends derived from FAOSTAT production and trade statistics and projections from Kangas and Baudin (2003).

The rapid expansion of the fibreboard sector in Eastern Europe and the CIS sub-region will also lead to an increase in the importance of these two sub-regions in total European production and consumption. However, Western Europe will remain the main market for this product, accounting for around 65 percent of European production and consumption in 2020. It is also notable that all three sub-regions will become net exporters of this product by 2020, suggesting that producers will have to continue to look for markets outside Europe to sell this product.

The outlook for the particleboard sector is very similar to the outlook described above for fibreboard. In general, the markets for this product will expand rapidly (compared with the markets for sawnwood) and the highest rates of growth are expected in the east. However, Western Europe will remain the major market for this product in Europe.

Figure 94 shows the outlook for particleboard production and consumption in Europe to 2020 under the baseline scenario. The projections of production and consumption follow the long-term trend in Western Europe and the more recent trends of recovery in the sector in the other two sub-regions. Overall, production and consumption are both expected to increase at an average annual rate of 2.6 percent, with an increase in production from 40 million m^3 in 2000 to 67 million m^3 in 2020 and a corresponding increase in consumption from 38 million m^3 to 64 million m^3.

Production and consumption in Western Europe are projected to increase by 1.9 percent and 1.8 percent respectively each year, leading to an increase in net exports. Production will expand from around 30.5 million m^3 in 2000 to 44.2 million m^3 in 2020 and consumption will expand from 28.7 million m^3 per year to 40.7 million m^3 per year over the period. Consequently, net exports will increase from 1.8 million m^3 per year to 3.5 million m^3 per year by 2020.

Figure 94   **Trends and projections for the production and consumption of particleboard under the baseline scenario**

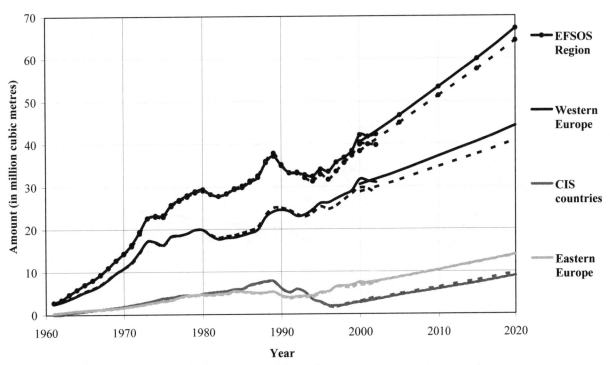

Solid lines represent production and dashed lines represent apparent consumption

Source: trends derived from FAOSTAT production and trade statistics and projections from Kangas and Baudin (2003).

In Eastern Europe, production and consumption of particleboard are expected to grow at an average annual rate of 3.4 percent and 3.7 percent respectively (or double over the next 20 years). Production will increase from 7.1 million m^3 per year to 13.9 million m^3 per year and consumption will increase from 6.7 million m^3 per year to 13.8 million m^3 per year over the period. Eastern Europe is a very small net exporter of particleboard and net exports are expected to decline to almost zero by 2020.

As in other sectors, the highest rate of growth in the future is expected in the CIS sub-region, although this will start from a very low level in 2000. Production will more than treble, from 2.7 million m^3 in 2000 to 9.0 million m^3 in 2020 (an average increase of 6.2 percent per year). Consumption will increase slightly faster than this, from 2.9 million m^3 in 2000 to 9.7 million m^3 in 2020 (an average increase of 6.3 percent per year). Thus, net imports into the CIS sub-region will increase, but remain quite insignificant.

As in the fibreboard sector, the importance of the different sub-regions will change slightly as production and consumption expands more rapidly in the east. However, Western Europe will remain the major market for this product, with only a modest fall in the share of total European production and consumption from around 75 percent in 2000 to 65 percent in 2020.

Figure 95   **Trends and projections for the production and consumption of plywood and veneer sheets under the baseline scenario**

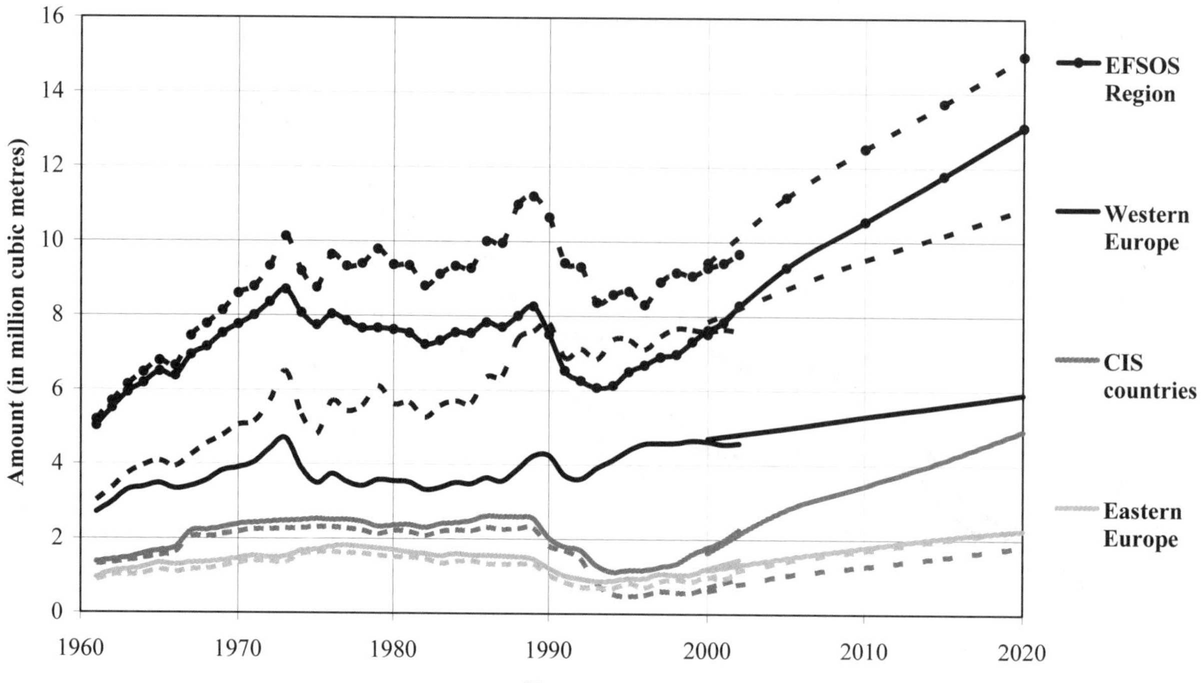

Solid lines represent production and dashed lines represent apparent consumption

Source: trends derived from FAOSTAT production and trade statistics and projections from Kangas and Baudin (2003).

The analysis by Kangas and Baudin (2003) only examined the markets for plywood in Europe and did not cover veneer sheets. As noted in Section 2.3.2, the share of veneer sheet production and consumption in total production and consumption of veneer sheets and plywood has remained roughly constant in the past. Therefore, it has been assumed here that the markets for veneer sheets will follow the same pattern as the projections for plywood.

The outlook for the production and consumption of plywood and veneer sheets under the baseline scenario is shown in Figure 95. For Europe as a whole, a relatively high rate of growth in production and consumption is projected, with average annual increases of 2.8 percent and 2.3 percent respectively. Production will increase from 7.5 million m^3 per year to 13.1 million m^3 per year, while consumption will increase from 9.4 million m^3 per year to 15.0 million m^3 per year. To a large extent, this growth in Europe as a whole will be driven by expected increases in production in the CIS sub-region.

Western Europe is currently the largest producer and consumer of plywood and veneer sheets in Europe and this is expected to continue, although Western Europe's dominance of production is expected to decline. Average annual growth in production and consumption is expected to amount to 2.4 percent and 2.1 percent respectively over the next two decades. Production will increase from 4.7 million m^3 per year to 5.9 million m^3 per year and consumption will increase from 7.9 million m^3 per year to 10.9 million m^3 per year, leading to an increase in net imports into Western Europe from 3.2 million m^3 per year to 5.0 million m^3 per year. Tropical plywood accounts for a significant proportion of plywood and veneer sheet imports into Western Europe, but it is expected that imports from the CIS sub-region will increase in importance in the future.

Eastern Europe is the least important of the three European sub-regions in terms of the production of plywood and veneer sheets, although consumption there is higher than in the CIS sub-region. Production and consumption in Eastern Europe will grow quite rapidly, at an average annual rate of 3.3 percent and 4.4 percent respectively, but the amount of production will remain far behind the other two sub-regions. Production is expected to increase from 1.2 million m³ in 2000 to 2.3 million m³ in 2020 and consumption will increase from 1.0 million m³ per year to 2.3 million m³ per year over the same period. Net exports of plywood and veneer sheets from Eastern Europe are insignificant and are expected to decline to zero by 2020.

The most interesting feature of the outlook for the plywood and veneer sheets sector is the rapid expansion of production and consumption expected in the CIS sub-region over the next 20 years, where both production and consumption are expected to increase by about 5.7 percent per year on average. Production will increase from 1.6 million m³ in 2000 to 4.9 million m³ in 2020, while consumption will increase from 0.6 million m³ per year to 1.8 million m³ per year over the same period. This will lead to a dramatic increase in net exports from 1.0 million m³ in 2000 to 3.1 million m³ in 2020. Much of this increase in exports will probably be sold to Western Europe.

4.1.3 Paper and paperboard production and consumption

Broadly speaking, the outlook for the paper and paperboard sector in Europe will follow the historical trends in this sector. However, at the sub-regional level there will be some interesting developments with respect to changes in the shares of production and consumption of the different paper and paperboard products among the three European sub-regions.

Figure 96 shows the outlook for the production and consumption of newsprint in Europe to 2020 under the baseline scenario. For Europe as a whole, production and consumption are expected to expand at roughly the same rate as in the past (or maybe slightly higher), with expected annual growth rates of 2.6 percent and 2.4 percent respectively. Production will increase from 12.7 million MT in 2000 to 21.3 million MT in 2020, while consumption will increase from 12.0 million MT per year to 19.5 million MT per year over the same period. Consequently, the level of net exports will expand slightly from 0.7 million MT per year to 1.8 million MT per year.

Western Europe is currently the largest producer and consumer of newsprint in Europe and this is expected to continue, although Western Europe's dominance of production is expected to decline. Average annual growth in production and consumption is expected to amount to 1.3 percent and 1.8 percent respectively over the next two decades. Production will increase from 10.4 million MT per year to 13.5 million MT per year and consumption will increase from 10.3 million MT per year to 14.7 million MT per year. This will lead to net imports of 1.2 million MT per year by 2020, compared with the current situation of approximately equal production and consumption of newsprint in Western Europe.

In Eastern Europe, production and consumption of newsprint will grow quite rapidly, at an average annual rate of 4.3 percent and 4.1 percent respectively, but this sub-region will remain relatively insignificant compared with the other two sub-regions. Production will increase from 0.6 million MT per year to 1.3 million MT per year and consumption will increase from 1.0 million MT per year to 2.3 million MT per year, leading to an increase in net imports from 0.4 million MT per year to 1.0 million MT per year over the next two decades.

Again, the most significant change in the future is expected in the CIS sub-region, where both production and consumption of newsprint are expected to increase at about 7 percent per year. Production will increase from 1.7 million MT per year to 6.5 million MT per year, while consumption is expected to increase from 0.7 million MT per year to 2.5 million MT per year.

The CIS sub-region is already a net exporter of newsprint of about 0.7 million MT per year, but this is expected to increase significantly to 4.0 million MT per year. This increase in net exports is expected to flow to the rest of Europe and Asia.

Figure 96   ***Trends and projections for the production and consumption of newsprint under the baseline scenario***

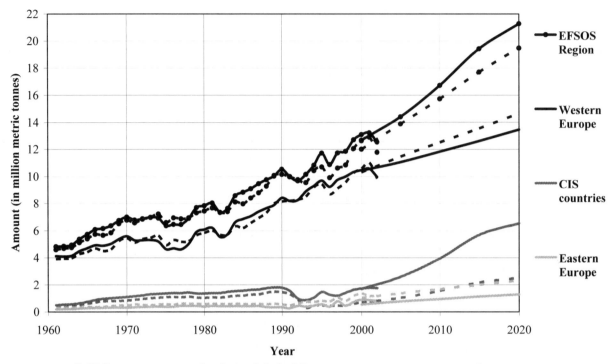

Solid lines represent production and dashed lines represent apparent consumption

Source: trends derived from FAOSTAT production and trade statistics and projections from Kangas and Baudin (2003).

The outlook for the production and consumption of other paper and paperboard in Europe is shown in Figure 97. Similar to the outlook for newsprint, production and consumption are expected to expand at roughly the same rate as in the last decade, with an average annual growth rate of 2.5 percent and 2.6 percent respectively. In this sector, Western Europe is by far the largest market and the relative importance of Western Europe will not decline by very much.

Production of other paper and paperboard in Europe as a whole will increase from 51.0 million MT in 2000 to 83.7 million MT in 2020 and consumption will increase from 47.7 million MT per year to 79.8 million MT per year. This will lead to a very small increase in the level of net exports from 3.3 million MT in 2000 to 3.9 million MT in 2020.

In Western Europe, production and consumption will both increase at about 2.0 percent per year on average. Production amounted to about 42.9 million MT in 2000 and is expected to increase to 63.3 million MT in 2020. Consumption will increase from 39.8 million MT per year to 59.3 million MT per year over the same period. Net exports of around 3 million MT per year will remain unchanged.

The market for other paper and paperboard in Eastern Europe is expected to increase by about 150 percent over the next two decades and this sub-region is expected to remain in second place after Western Europe (but still a long way behind). Production is projected to increase at 4.5 percent per year on average, from 4.7 million MT in 2000 to 11.3 million MT in 2020. Consumption is projected to increase at 4.7 percent per year on average, from 5.2 million MT in 2000 to 12.8 million MT in 2020. Net imports to Eastern Europe are relatively small, but are expected to increase slightly.

Figure 97   ***Trends and projections for the production and consumption of other paper and paperboard under the baseline scenario***

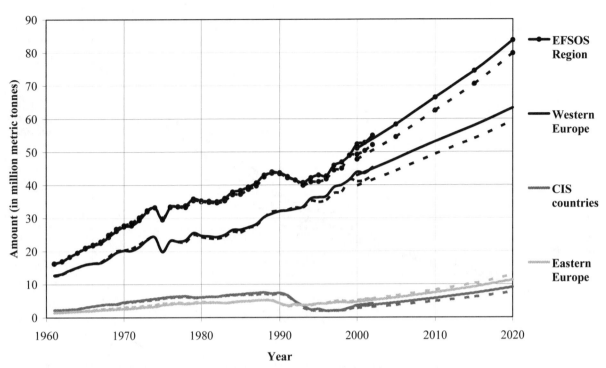

Solid lines represent production and dashed lines represent apparent consumption

Source: trends derived from FAOSTAT production and trade statistics and projections from Kangas and Baudin (2003).

In the CIS sub-region, average annual growth in production will be slightly higher than in Eastern Europe, at 5.1 percent and 5.2 percent respectively, but the size of the market in this sub-region will remain relatively small. Production will increase from 3.4 million MT in 2000 to 9.2 million MT in 2020 and consumption will increase from 2.8 million MT per year to 7.7 million MT per year. Net exports will increase slightly, from 0.6 million MT in 2000 to 1.4 million MT in 2020.

The outlook for the production and consumption of printing and writing paper in Europe is shown in Figure 98. The interesting feature of these projections is the expected reversal of Europe's position as a net exporter of printing and writing paper (5.0 million MT in 2000) to a net importer of 1.4 million MT in 2020. This is largely due to the high growth in consumption expected in Eastern Europe and a reduction of growth in production expected in Western Europe. For Europe as a whole, production is expected to increase from 35.8 million MT in 2000 to 60.4 million MT in 2020, while consumption will double from 30.8 million MT per year to 61.8 million MT per year over the same period.

Figure 98   ***Trends and projections for the production and consumption of printing and writing paper under the baseline scenario***

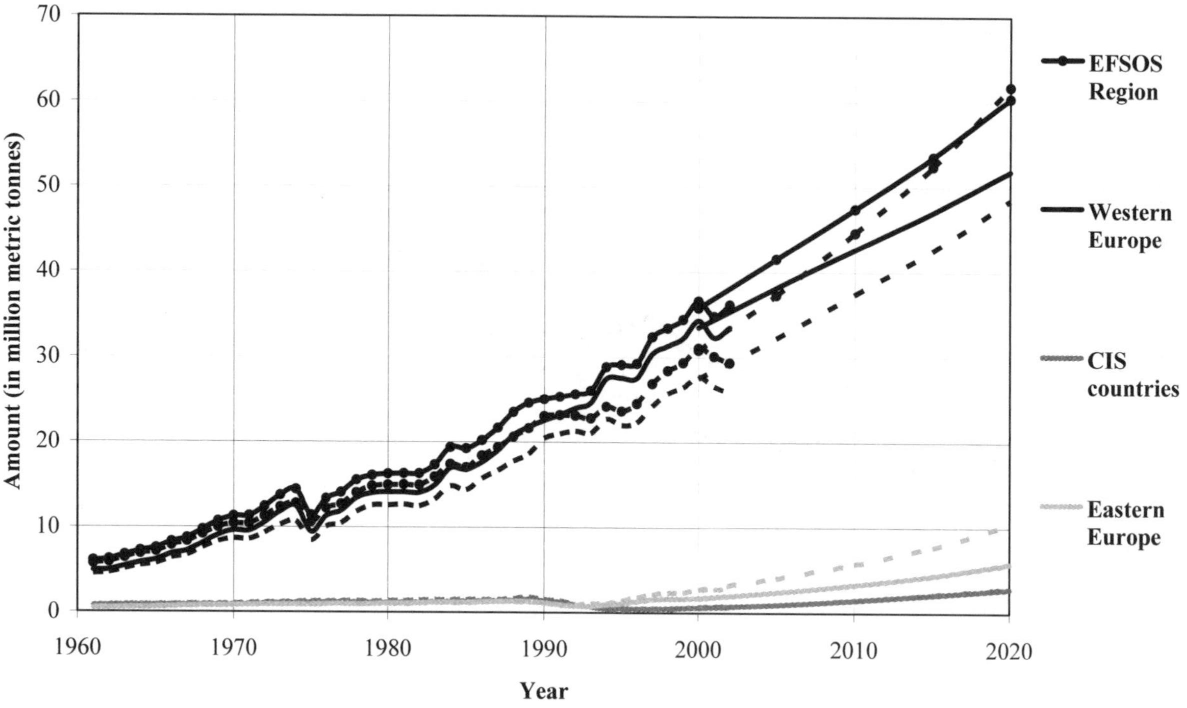

Solid lines represent production and dashed lines represent apparent consumption

Source: trends derived from FAOSTAT production and trade statistics and projections from Kangas and Baudin (2003).

In Western Europe, growth in production is expected to slow slightly compared with the past, to an average annual rate of 2.2 percent. Production of around 33.5 million MT in 2000 will increase to 51.9 million MT in 2020. Consumption will continue to grow strongly, at an average annual rate of 2.9 percent, increasing from 27.5 million MT in 2000 to 48.5 million MT in 2020. Consequently, the level of net exports from Western Europe will decline from 6.0 million MT per year to 3.4 million MT per year over the period.

The greatest change in the printing and writing paper sector is expected in Eastern Europe, where consumption is expected to rise rapidly due to economic development in the sub-region. Production and consumption will increase at an average annual growth rate of 6.4 percent and 6.9 percent respectively, leading to an increased level of net imports into the sub-region. Production will increase from around 1.7 million MT in 2000 to 5.8 million MT in 2020, while consumption will increase from 2.7 million MT per year to 10.4 million MT per year over the same period. Net imports will expand from 1.0 million MT per year to 4.6 million MT.

In the CIS sub-region, growth in the market for printing and writing paper will be higher than in the other two sub-regions, but starting from a very low level. Production will increase by 7.9 per year on average, from 0.6 million MT in 2000 to 2.8 million MT in 2020. Consumption will increase by 8.2 per year on average, from 0.6 million MT in 2000 to 2.9 million MT in 2020. The level of net trade with the CIS sub-region will remain insignificant.

4.1.4   Structural changes in the markets for processed wood products

Overall, the structural changes in markets described in Section 2.3.4 are expected to continue in the future, but at different rates in each of the three European sub-regions. For example, for Europe as a whole, consumption of reconstituted panels is expected to continue to account for a greater share of consumption of solid wood products in the future, due to higher growth in fibreboard and particleboard consumption compared to the expected growth in sawnwood consumption.

Figure 99   *Trends and projections for the consumption of sawnwood and wood based panels in Europe under the baseline scenario*

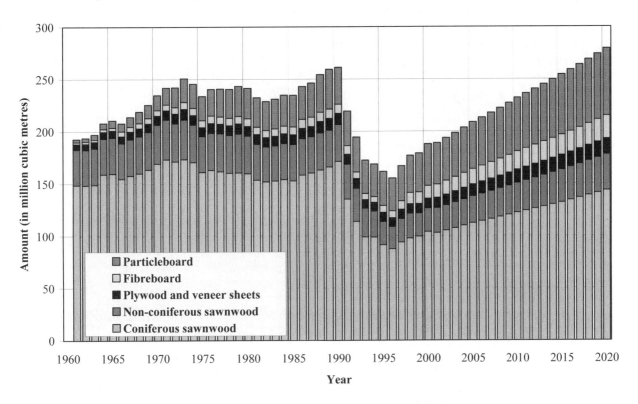

Source: trends (to 2000) derived from FAOSTAT production and trade statistics and projections (2001- 2020) from Kangas and Baudin (2003).

Figure 99 shows the outlook for the consumption of solid wood products in Europe under the baseline scenario. Overall, the share of reconstituted panels in total solid wood product consumption is likely to continue to increase slightly from 28 percent in 2000 to 31 percent in 2020. However, this shift towards reconstituted panels will be much stronger in Western and Eastern Europe than in the CIS sub-region (see Figure 100).

In the CIS sub-region, consumption of sawnwood will continue to dominate the domestic market (see

Figure 101). Furthermore, given the huge increase in net exports of coniferous sawnwood expected in the CIS sub-region, the share of sawnwood in total production of solid wood products will be much larger and will increase in the future. Thus, the demand for sawlogs and veneer logs in this sub-region will remain high and increase significantly in the future.

Figure 100   ***Trends and projections for the importance of reconstituted panels under the baseline scenario***

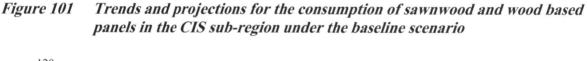

Source: trends derived from FAOSTAT production and trade statistics and projections from Kangas and Baudin (2003).

Figure 101   ***Trends and projections for the consumption of sawnwood and wood based panels in the CIS sub-region under the baseline scenario***

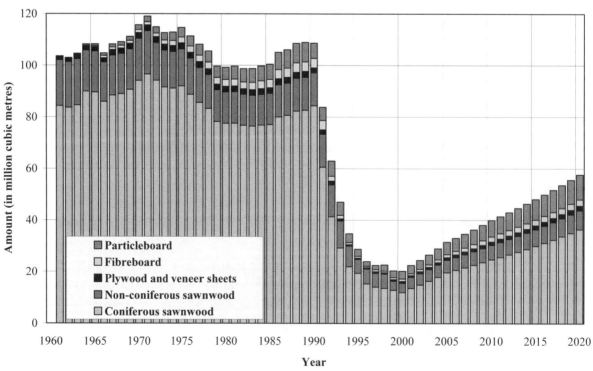

Source: trends (to 2000) derived from FAOSTAT production and trade statistics and projections (2001- 2020) from Kangas and Baudin (2003).

In the markets for paper and paperboard, the shift towards relatively more consumption of printing and writing paper is also expected to continue in the future, with the total market share of this product category increasing from 35 percent in 2000 to 40 percent in 2020 (see Figure 102). Conversely, the shares of newsprint and other paper and paperboard in total paper and paperboard consumption will both decline by a small amount.

Figure 102   ***Trends and projections for the consumption of paper and paperboard in Europe under the baseline scenario***

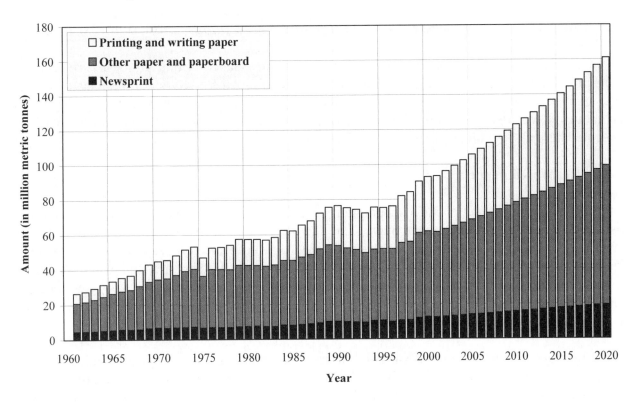

Source: trends (to 2000) derived from FAOSTAT production and trade statistics and projections (2001- 2020) from Kangas and Baudin (2003).

Again, this shift will be largely driven by the outlook for Western Europe, although printing and writing paper consumption is expected to increase more rapidly than other types of paper and paperboard in both of the other two sub-regions. In addition, a significant increase in the production of newsprint is expected to occur in the CIS sub-region, leading to a major shift there towards the production of this product.

From a broad perspective, the expected changes in forest products markets in each of the three European sub-regions reflect the different patterns of consumer demand and competitiveness in the different sub-regions. Thus, for example, consumption will grow most rapidly in the east, where economies are expected to grow faster than in the west. However, the pattern of consumption between the different sub-regions will be subtly different, with the west focusing on products that meet the demands of a richer society (e.g. printing and writing paper), while the east will focus more on products that meet the more basic needs of housing and industrial development (e.g. sawnwood).

An even clearer distinction between the three sub-regions exists in the projections of production. The CIS sub-region will increase in importance for the production of products such as coniferous sawnwood, plywood, fibreboard and newsprint, where the abundance of forest resources will offer this region a distinct advantage and the availability of skills, capital and technology is suited to these types of forest product.

In contrast, Western Europe will focus more on the production of products that are less demanding on the raw material supply and require a higher level of development in production and marketing skills and technology (e.g. particleboard and printing and writing paper). In general, Eastern Europe will be in a curious position, somewhere between these two extremes. Consumer markets there will probably develop along similar lines to Western Europe, while the production of forest products will probably develop in a way that is more similar to the CIS sub-region. Thus, these changes in emphasis in the future in all three sub-regions will continue to influence the trade flows of forest products between the three sub-regions and between Europe and the rest of the World.

4.2 Production and consumption of pulp, recovered paper and wood residues

In order to produce projections for the wood raw material balance in the future, it is necessary to make projections about the production and consumption of raw materials and intermediate products. The analysis by Kangas and Baudin (2003) did not examine these products, so a variety of techniques were used to complete the analysis. The methodologies and assumptions used are presented here along with the main results of this part of the analysis.

4.2.1   Recovered paper

Projections for the production and consumption of recovered paper were based on an analysis of the historical trends in wastepaper recovery and the utilisation of recovered paper in paper and paperboard production. The policy analysis showed that both of these variables are expected to continue to follow past trends and increase in the future. However, there are technical limits to both of these variables; for example, some types of paper are very difficult to recover (e.g. household and tissue paper) and, as already noted, some types of paper are difficult to manufacture from recycled paper.

The projections for both of these variables were based on a simple extrapolation of past trends, subject to the limitations described above. For countries where these figures were already high, it was assumed that they would not increase. For countries that have experienced some growth in the past, the trends in wastepaper recovery were continued up to a limit of 50 - 60 percent, depending on the level of urbanisation in the country (recovery rates are generally higher in more urbanised countries). Trends in the use of recovered paper were also extrapolated (up to a limit of 70 percent in the few countries with high historical rates of recovered paper utilisation). For countries where the historical trends showed low rates of wastepaper recovery and utilisation, it was assumed that both variables would grow modestly by about 10 - 15 percentage points in total over the next two decades.

The results of this analysis are shown in Figure 103 and

Figure 104 and, based on this, the projections for recovered paper production and consumption are shown in Figure 105.

Figure 103   Trends and projections for wastepaper recovery

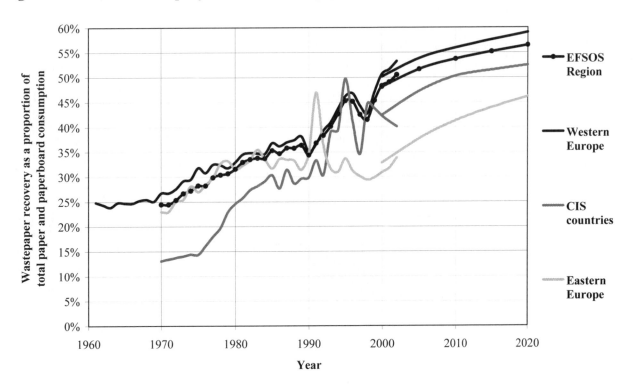

Source: trends derived from FAOSTAT production and trade statistics; for projections - see Section 4.2.1.

Figure 104   Trends and projections for the importance of recovered paper as a source of raw material supply for the pulp and paper industry

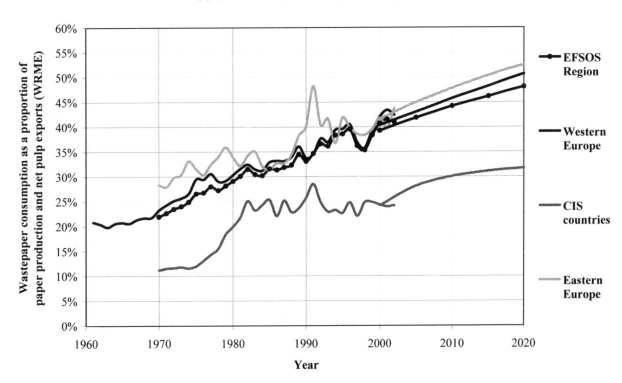

Source: trends derived from FAOSTAT production and trade statistics; for projections - see Section 4.2.1.

Figure 105   Trends and projections for the production and consumption of recovered paper under the baseline scenario

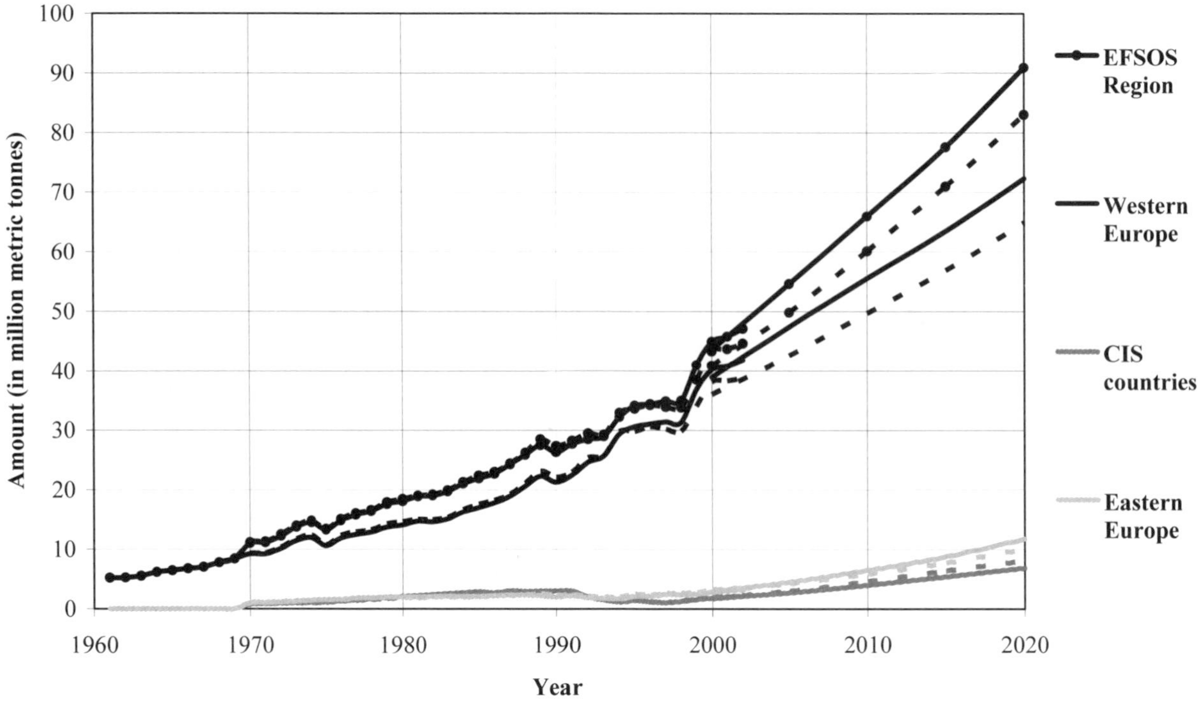

Solid lines represent production and dashed lines represent apparent consumption

Source: trends derived from FAOSTAT production and trade statistics; for projections - see Section 4.2.1.

Figure 105 shows that production and consumption of recovered paper in Europe is expected to double over the next 20 years, with production increasing from around 44 million MT in 2000 to 91 million MT in 2020 and consumption increasing from 41 million MT to 83 million MT over the same period. Consequently, net exports of recovered paper are expected to increase from about 3 million MT to 8 million MT.

Western Europe will continue to account for the largest share of European recovered paper production and consumption and will experience the largest increase in production and consumption. This is due to the high levels of paper and paperboard production and consumption there. However, production and consumption in the other two sub-regions is likely to grow faster (in percentage terms) than in Western Europe, due to faster growth in the markets for paper and larger expected increases in the recovery and utilisation rates for wastepaper.

In Western Europe, recovered paper production and consumption will increase at about the same rate as in the past, at an average annual rate of 3.1 percent and 3.0 percent respectively over the next two decades. Production will increase from around 39 million MT in 2000 to 72 million MT in 2020, while consumption will increase from 36 million MT to 65 million MT over the same period.

In Eastern Europe, recovered paper production and consumption will increase much more quickly than in the past. This will be partly driven by the implementation of EU recycling policies in many countries. This will lead to average annual growth in production and consumption of 7.2 percent and 6.3 percent respectively. Production will increase from around 2.9 million MT in 2000 to 11.7 million MT in 2020, while consumption will increase from 3.0 million MT to 10.1 million MT over the same period. It is expected that the increase in production (driven by recycling policies) will increase slightly faster than the capacity of the industry to absorb these materials, leading to a small amount of net exports.

Recovered paper production and consumption will also increase much more quickly than in the past in the CIS sub-region. In this case, this will be driven by the expansion of the paper industry as well as recycling policies. Here, production and consumption will grow at rates of 7.1 percent per year and 7.7 percent per year respectively, equal to an increase in production from 1.7 million MT in 2000 to 6.9 million MT in 2020 and an increase in consumption from 1.8 million MT to 8.1 million MT. Net imports of recovered paper will increase to around 1.2 million MT in 2020, with much of these imports probably coming from Eastern Europe.

4.2.2   Wood pulp

Projections for the production and consumption of wood pulp were also not covered in the detailed analysis by Kangas and Baudin (2003). However, a crucial variable in the wood raw material balance is the net trade in wood pulp between Europe and the rest of the world (see Section 2.5.3). The main objective of the analysis presented here was to make projections of future net trade in wood pulp, but the results may also be useful to some users of the study.

Projections of the consumption of wood pulp by the paper and paperboard sector[19] were calculated by subtracting the projections for consumption of recovered paper (converted to WRME) from the projections for paper and paperboard production (in WRME). By definition, after converting all of these figures to WRME, the remaining fibre requirement must be equal to pulp consumption by the paper and paperboard industry in WRME. The historical trends in pulp consumption (in WRME) were calculated in the same way and the resulting trends and projections were converted to year-on-year changes (in percent). The growth rates for the projections were then used to extrapolate the historical trends in consumption of wood pulp by the paper and paperboard sector to give projections for wood pulp consumption to the year 2020.

For projections of wood pulp production, the historical statistics for total wood pulp production were converted to multipliers of the level of consumption (e.g. if a country produced 20 percent more wood pulp than it consumed in a year, the multiplier would be 120 percent). These multipliers were then examined to see if they displayed any trends upwards or downwards.

For countries that are net importers of wood pulp (i.e. with a multiplier of less than 100 percent) the trends in recent years were mostly stable, suggesting that wood pulp production closely follows consumption. This is what might be expected in such countries, where most pulp production is in integrated pulp and paper production facilities and is used for the production of paper rather than for sale. The exception was Germany, where wood pulp production has declined slightly in relation to consumption in recent years.

For most of the countries that are net exporters of wood pulp, the trends were also stable. However, in a few cases, there were some slight declines in the multipliers. Presumably, this reflects a shift towards further processing of wood pulp into paper and paperboard for export in these countries.

The trends in the multipliers described above were extrapolated forwards and applied to the projections for wood pulp consumption, to give projections for wood pulp production to the year 2020. The two main exceptions to this were the Russian Federation and Portugal. In the Russian Federation, an expansion in pulp production (for export) was projected. This was based on the results of the outlook study for the Russian Federation, specially prepared for the EFSOS (OAO NIPIEIlesprom, 2003). In the case of Portugal, wood pulp production currently exceeds

---

[19]   The analysis in these two paragraphs only applies to wood pulp used for paper production - i.e. mechanical, semi-chemical and chemical wood pulp. Production and consumption of dissolving pulp is insignificant and was simply assumed to continue at the same level in the future as in the past. Other fibre pulp is also negligible and was excluded from the analysis.

consumption by a large amount. However, production of paper and paperboard in Portugal is projected to increase significantly over the next 20 years. Given the availability of forest resources (i.e. potential pulpwood supply) in Portugal, a continued high level of net pulp exports can not be supported and a greater proportion of pulp production will probably be used domestically in the future. This adjustment to the outlook for wood pulp production was included in the projections.

Figure 106   Trends and projections for the production and consumption of total wood pulp under the baseline scenario

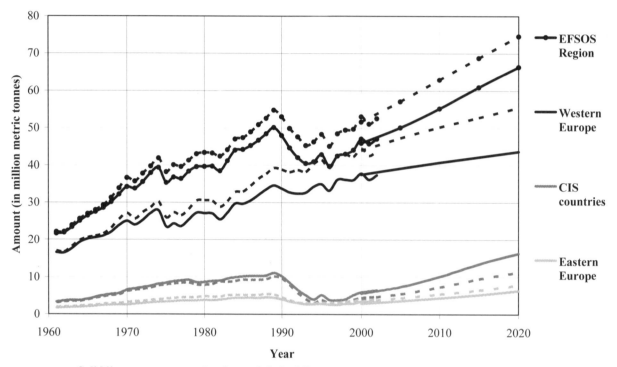

Solid lines represent production and dashed lines represent apparent consumption

Source: trends derived from FAOSTAT production and trade statistics; for projections - see Section 4.2.2.

Figure 106 shows the trends and projections for the production and consumption of wood pulp in Europe under the baseline scenario. (It was assumed that production and consumption of dissolving pulp would remain the same in the future and these figures include dissolving pulp in the total). As the figure shows, the projected growth in production and consumption will return to the long-term historical trend experienced before the 1990s and Europe as a whole will remain a major net importer of wood pulp.

Production is projected to increase from 46 million MT in 2000 to 66 million MT in 2020, while consumption is projected to increase from 52 million MT to 75 million MT over the same period. These increases are both equal to average annual growth of about 1.9 percent. Net imports will expand slightly from 6 million MT to 9 million MT over the period.

Growth in Western Europe will be subdued by the continued substitution of recovered paper for wood pulp in paper making and a reduction in the growth of wood pulp production for export. Production and consumption are projected to grow at an average annual rate of 0.8 percent and 1.2 percent respectively. This is equal to an increase in production from 38 million MT in 2000 to 44 million MT in 2020 and an increase in consumption from 44 million MT to 55 million MT. Net imports into Western Europe will increase significantly from 6 million MT to 11 million MT over the same period.

In Eastern Europe, wood pulp production and consumption will both double, growing at an average annual rate of 4.0 percent and 4.1 percent respectively. Production will increase from 2.9 million MT to 6.3 million MT over the next 20 years, while consumption will increase from 3.5 million MT to 7.8 million MT. Eastern Europe will remain a small net importer of wood pulp.

The greatest change in the wood pulp sector is expected in the CIS sub-region, where average growth in production and consumption is expected to reach 5.5 percent per year and 5.1 percent per year respectively. The projected three-fold increase in production will far exceed the expected increase in consumption, leading to an increase in net exports. A significant proportion of these exports will probably be destined for European markets, although an increase in trade with Asia can not be ruled-out. Production will increase from 5.6 million MT in 2000 to 16.4 million MT in 2020 and consumption will increase from 4.2 million MT to 11.3 million MT. Thus, net exports will increase from 1.4 million MT in 2000 to 5.1 million MT in 2020.

4.2.3   Wood residues

In the historical part of this analysis, wood chips and particles and wood residues[20] were treated as an unquantified source of wood raw materials. Estimates of the utilisation and consumption of these materials were produced by subtracting the consumption of all known sources of wood and fibre from total wood and fibre demand. In the outlook, the historical trends in this source of wood raw materials have been analysed and have been used to make projections for the future. These projections can then be used to produce the derived demand for industrial roundwood.

This analysis comprised two main parts: an analysis of international trade in wood residues and an analysis of the residue utilisation rate.

For the analysis of international trade, it was noted that net exporters of wood residues tend to be countries where sawmilling accounts for a relatively large proportion of the whole forest sector. Conversely, net importers tend to have relatively small sawmilling sectors. This is as expected, as it broadly reflects the supply and demand for wood residues in each country. Therefore, countries were divided into two groups: net exporters and net importers.

For net exporters, net exports of wood residues were projected to increase in proportion to the projected increases in sawnwood, plywood and veneer sheet production (i.e. the rates of growth in production in these sectors - converted to WRME - were used to extrapolate the historical time-series of net exports of wood residues). For net importers, the same process was applied, but using the projected increases in reconstituted panel production and paper production (after adjusting for the use of recovered paper). These calculations gave plausible projections for net trade in wood residues (see Figure 107), showing that increased flows of wood residues from east to west might be expected in the future.

To produce projections of the consumption of wood residues in the future, the historical trends in the residue utilisation rate were examined. Residue utilisation is the amount of residues consumed by the forest processing industry plus exports and minus imports and the utilisation rate is this amount divided by total residue availability (calculated from the sawnwood, plywood and veneer sheet conversion factors).

---

[20]   In international trade, these materials are divided into two categories: "wood chips and particles" and "wood residues". For brevity, the term "wood residues" is used here to imply both types of material.

Figure 107   Trends and projections for net trade in wood chips, particles and residues

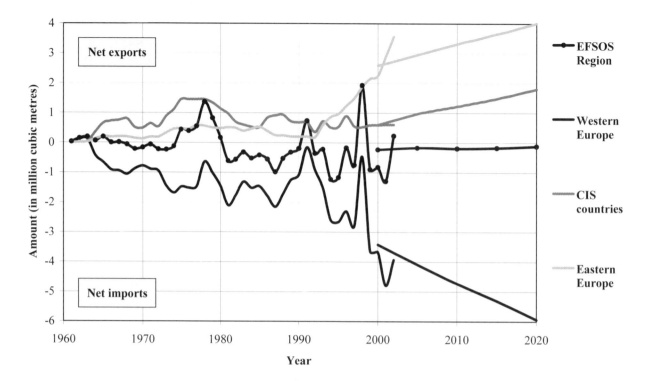

Source: trends from FAOSTAT trade statistics; for projections - see Section 4.2.3.

As already noted, Western Europe already has a utilisation rate of over 100 percent, due to the consumption of other unrecorded or unknown sources of wood and fibre, probably recovered wood, which is known to be important in some countries including Germany. Thus, for the majority of countries in this region the projected utilisation rate was held constant. For the few countries in Western Europe with currently low residue utilisation rates, a modest increase in the residue utilisation rate was included in the projections. For countries in Eastern Europe and the CIS sub-region, it was assumed that residue utilisation would return to the levels experienced up until the 1990s. These projections of residue utilisation (see Figure 108) were then applied to the projected total availability of wood residues (see Figure 109) to produce figures for projected residue consumption.

Although the presence of utilisation rates of over 100 percent is a weakness in the analysis and reflects problems of consistency in the forest products statistics, it is reasonable to assume that residue utilisation will increase in the east as the forest processing industry in these countries develops in the future. Furthermore, it can also be assumed that whatever is causing this problem (e.g. consumption of recovered wood products) will continue in the future. Based on the projections of increased utilisation of wood residues (and changes in trade), it is projected that residue consumption will increase by 30 million m^3 in Western Europe, 25 million m^3 in the CIS sub-region and 10 million m^3 in Eastern Europe. In addition, the final projected level of residue consumption in the latter two regions would return to levels similar to those achieved in the late 1980s.

Figure 108   Trends and projections for the utilisation of wood residues

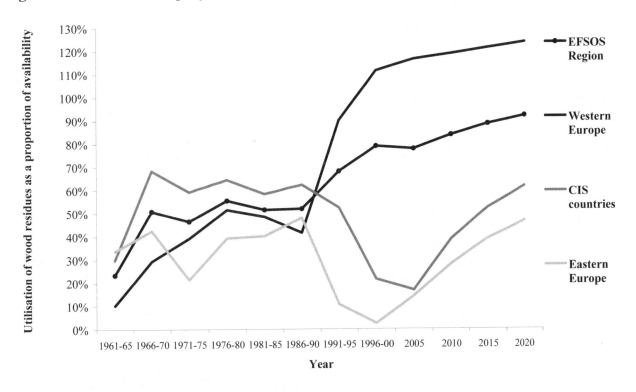

Source: trends derived from FAOSTAT production and trade statistics; for projections - see Section 4.2.3.

Figure 109   Trends and projections for the potential availability of wood residues

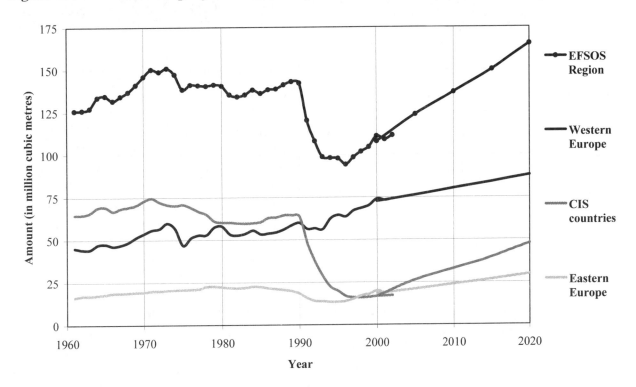

Source: trends derived from FAOSTAT production and trade statistics; for projections - see Section 4.2.3.

4.3   The raw material balance and the outlook for industrial roundwood

4.3.1   Wood raw material demand by sector

Projections for the future levels of wood raw material demand were produced in the same way as explained in Section 2.5.2 and it was assumed that the conversion factors (amount of wood required to produce one unit of forest product) would not change in the future. Based on the projections for the production of forest products, the projections shown in Figure 110 to Figure 113 were produced.

Figure 110   Trends and projections for wood raw material demand in Europe

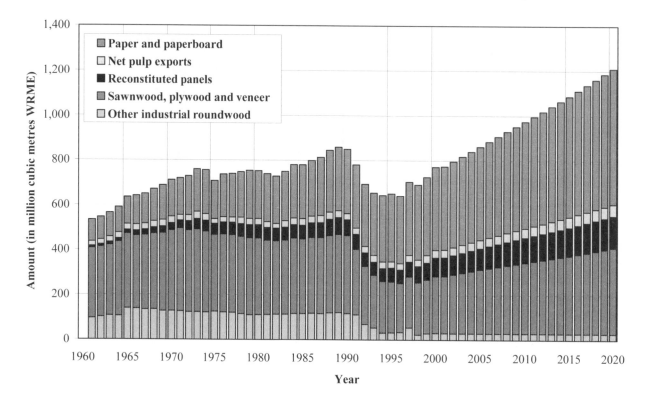

Source: trends derived from FAOSTAT production and trade statistics; projections based on the outlook study analysis.

Figure 110 shows the projections for total wood raw material demand in the whole of Europe to 2020. This figure shows increases in the demand for wood and fibre across all major product categories except other industrial roundwood.[21] Total demand is projected to increase by about 2.4 percent per year on average, from 771 million m³ WRME in 2000 to 1,210 million m³ WRME in 2020. Demand for wood and fibre for the reconstituted panel and paper and paperboard sectors will increase faster than average (2.9 percent and 2.6 percent respectively), while demand for sawnwood, plywood and veneer sheet production and net pulp exports will increase more gradually (2.2 percent and 2.0 percent respectively). As already noted, the projections for the different sub-regions of Europe will vary dramatically from the projection shown in Figure 110.

The projection for total wood raw material demand in Western Europe is shown in Figure 111. In Western Europe, total demand will increase by only 1.6 percent per year on average, from 573 million m³ WRME in 2000 to 771 million m³ WRME in 2020. In this sub-region, the demand for reconstituted panel production and paper and paperboard production will both increase by 2.0 percent per year, while demand for sawnwood, plywood and veneer sheet production will only grow at half this rate. A slight decrease in net pulp exports is anticipated, due to the reasons described in Section 4.2.2.

---

[21]   For other industrial roundwood, projections of future production were based simply on an extrapolation of historical trends. In most countries, this resulted in a slight decline in production over the next two decades.

Figure 111   Trends and projections for wood raw material demand in Western Europe

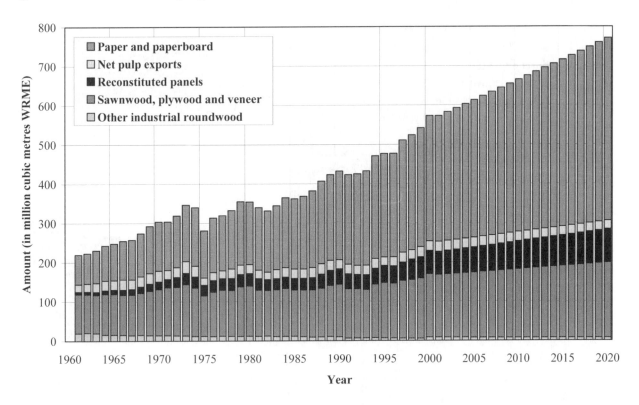

Source: trends derived from FAOSTAT production and trade statistics; projections based on the outlook study analysis.

In the CIS sub-region, wood raw material demand is expected to increase by 5.3 percent per year on average, or a total increase of over 150 percent over the next two decades (see Figure 112). In 2000, total demand was around 93 million m^3 WRME and this is expected to increase to 252 million m^3 WRME in 2020. A projected increase in the consumption of sawlogs and veneer logs will account for the majority of the increase in total demand, with a projected three-fold increase in consumption from 43 million m^3 WRME in 2000 to 120 million m^3 WRME in 2020. The consumption of wood and fibre for the other three processing sectors (pulp, paper and reconstituted panels) will actually grow faster than the consumption of sawlogs and veneer logs (at over 6.0 percent per year), but the structure of industrial roundwood demand will remain heavily focused on sawlogs and veneer logs.

The projected growth in wood raw material demand in Eastern Europe will be equally dramatic, but will occur more broadly across all parts of the forest sector. Total demand will increase by 3.2 percent per year on average, from around 105 million m^3 WRME in 2000 to 187 million m^3 WRME in 2020 (see Figure 113). Growth in demand from the paper and paperboard sector will be highest, increasing at an annual average growth rate of 5.1 percent or from 26 million m^3 WRME to 70 million m^3 WRME over the period. Demand from the reconstituted panels sector will increase by 3.6 percent per year while demand from the sawmilling and plywood sectors will increase by 2.3 percent per year.

Figure 112   Trends and projections for wood raw material demand in the CIS sub-region

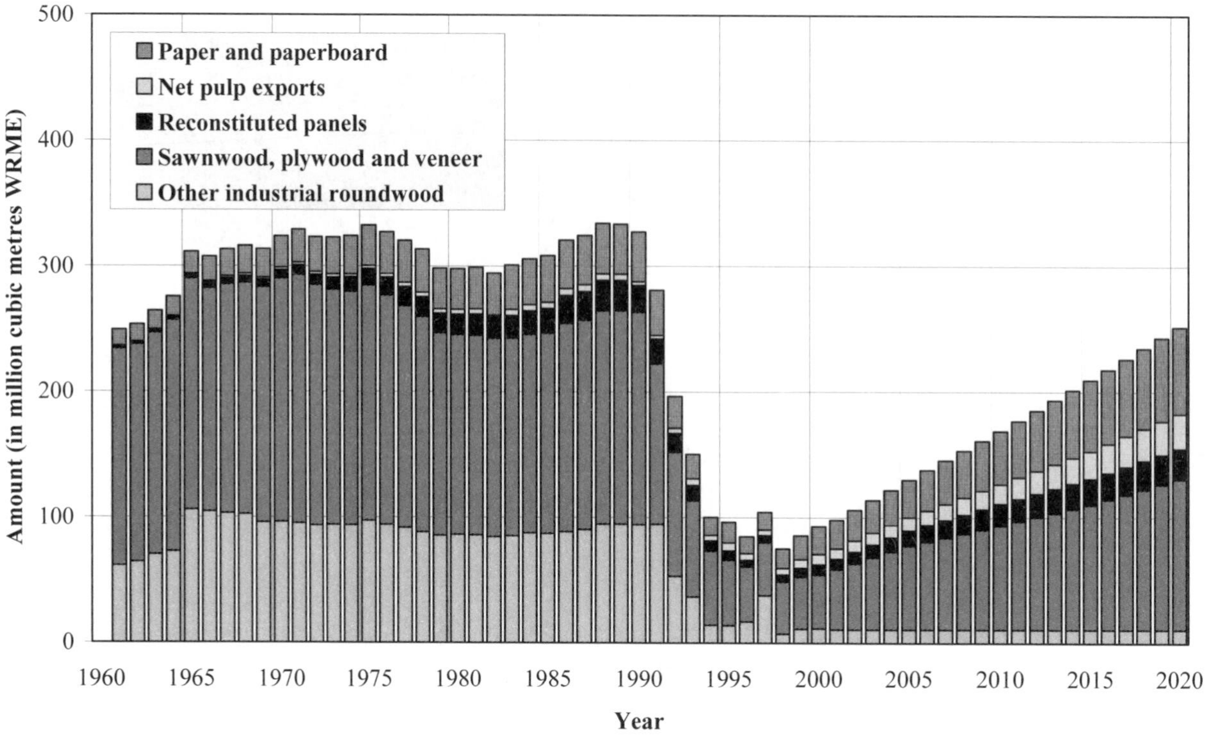

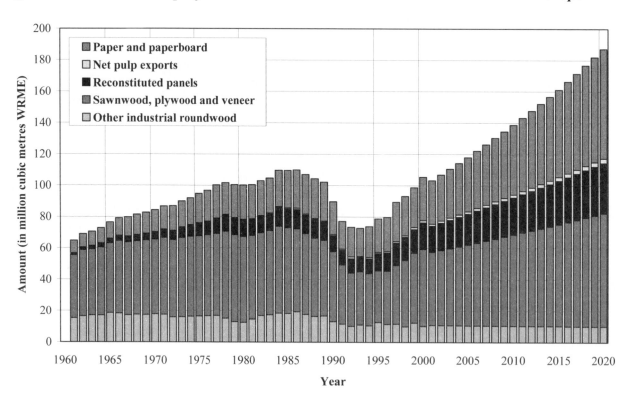

Source: trends derived from FAOSTAT production and trade statistics; projections based on the outlook study analysis.

Figure 113   Trends and projections for wood raw material demand in Eastern Europe

Source: trends derived from FAOSTAT production and trade statistics; projections based on the outlook study analysis.

4.3.2   Wood raw material supply by source

As noted in Section 4.2.3, the methodology used to identify the sources of wood raw material supply in the outlook projections was slightly different to the methodology used in the analysis of historical trends. In this case, the projections for consumption of recovered paper, wood residues and net pulp imports were subtracted from the projections of total wood raw material demand to produce projections of the consumption of industrial roundwood (or the derived demand for industrial roundwood). The results of this analysis are shown in Figure 114 to Figure 117. As before, the gap between the line and the total height of each bar represents the consumption of wood residues by the forest processing industry.

Figure 114   Trends and projections for wood raw material consumption in Europe

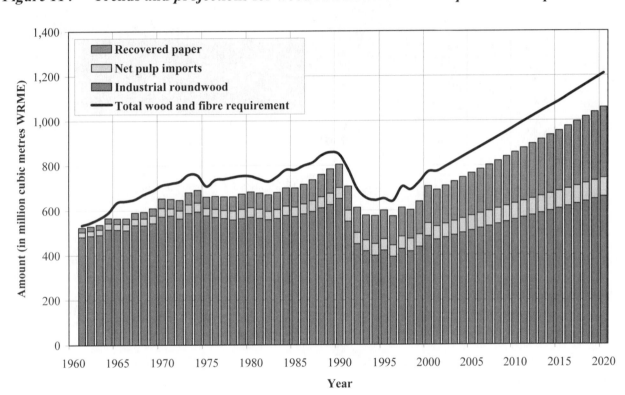

Source: trends derived from FAOSTAT production and trade statistics; projections based on the outlook study analysis.

Figure 114 shows the projections for consumption of each of the main sources of wood and fibre supply in Europe to 2020. Consumption of industrial roundwood and net pulp imports are both projected to increase at an average annual rate of 1.8 percent. Recovered paper consumption will increase by 3.6 percent per year on average and consumption of wood residues is projected to increase by 3.2 percent per year.

In Western Europe, consumption of industrial roundwood will increase by 0.8 percent per year on average, while consumption of recovered paper will increase by 3.0 percent per year (see Figure 115). Consumption of wood residues will increase by 1.4 percent per year on average. This rate of growth is relatively low, due to the low rate of growth projected for the sawmilling and plywood sectors. In addition, some of this growth in residue consumption will be due to the projected increase in net imports of wood residues into Western Europe. Net pulp imports will increase at an average annual growth rate of about 1.5 percent.

Figure 115   Trends and projections for wood raw material consumption in Western Europe

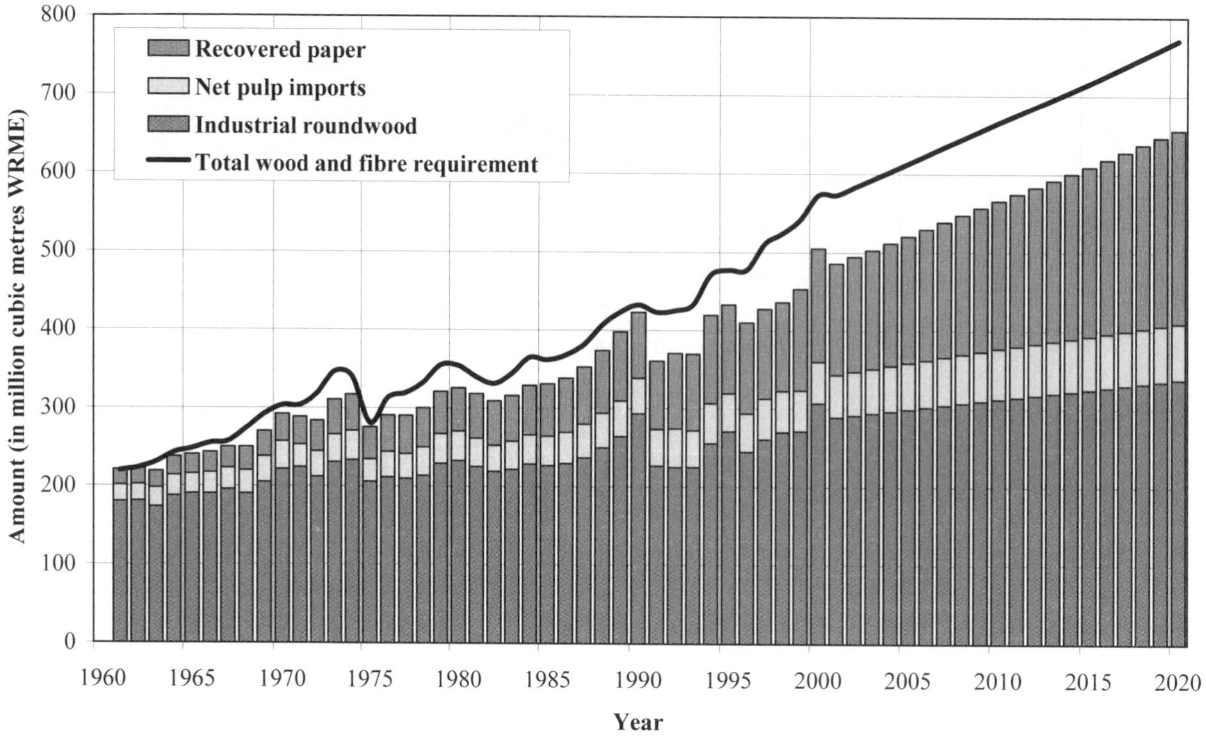

Source: trends derived from FAOSTAT production and trade statistics; projections based on the outlook study analysis.

Figure 116 shows the projected consumption of wood raw materials in the CIS sub-region. In this sub-region, industrial roundwood will remain by far the most important source of wood and fibre for the forest processing sector. However, consumption of recovered paper will grow more rapidly, at an average annual rate of 7.7 percent compared with a rate of growth of 4.2 percent for industrial roundwood. Similarly, consumption of residues is likely to expand rapidly over the next 20 years.

The pattern of projected wood raw material consumption in Eastern Europe will fall somewhere between the other two sub-regions (see Figure 117). Consumption of recovered paper will grow quite rapidly, at 6.3 percent per year on average. In contrast, consumption of industrial roundwood will increase at an average annual rate of only 2.0 percent. Given that recovered paper is already quite important in this sub-region, the dominance of industrial roundwood in the wood raw material supply is likely to be eroded significantly. Furthermore, net pulp imports are quite important in this sub-region and will grow at an average annual rate of 4.4 percent.

Figure 116   Trends and projections for wood raw material consumption in the CIS sub-region

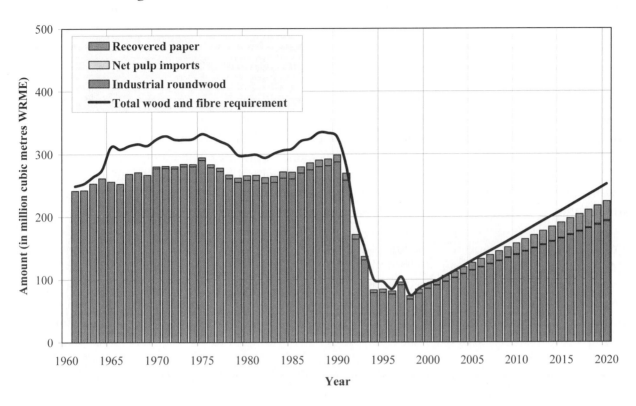

Source: trends derived from FAOSTAT production and trade statistics; projections based on the outlook study analysis.

Figure 117   Trends and projections for wood raw material consumption in Eastern Europe

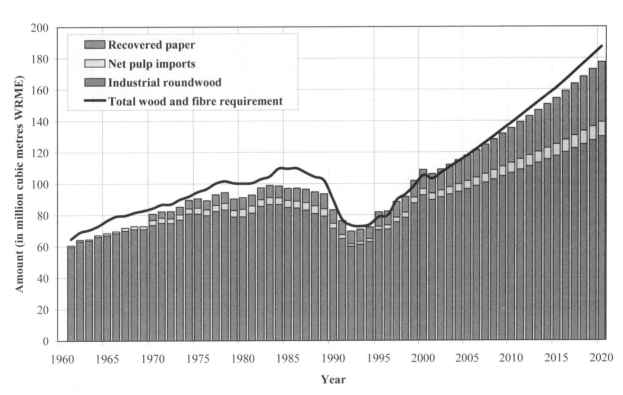

Source: trends derived from FAOSTAT production and trade statistics; projections based on the outlook study analysis.

4.3.3 Industrial roundwood

One of the limitations of the current outlook study is that it was not possible to obtain projections for roundwood supply in Europe. Roundwood supply projections were produced for ETTS V (Pajuoja, 1995), based on information supplied by national experts. However, based on past experience and the advice of the national experts, it was decided not to attempt this part of the analysis in the EFSOS.

Projections of roundwood production and consumption are a very important component of any outlook study, as this information can be used to assess the impact of future forest harvesting on the forest resource. Projections of roundwood production are also, of course, of major interest to forest owners and managers. Therefore, an attempt was made to produce some tentative projections about the future level of industrial roundwood production. It should be noted that these are not officially endorsed statements of future production, but projections of the level of production that might occur in the future, based on market forces and other currently available information.

Projections of future industrial roundwood consumption were derived from the projections of wood raw material demand and supply of non-forest wood and fibre sources (as described above). The staring point for the projections of future industrial roundwood production was to assume that production would increase in the future at the same rate as consumption. These preliminary projections were then examined country by country and adjusted to take into account other published information such as:

- the previous projections of roundwood production used in ETTS V (Pajuoja, 1995);

- published national forecasts of future roundwood production, such as those from the United Kingdom Forestry Commission (2002);

- the outlook study for the Russian Federation (OAO NIPIEIlesprom, 2003); and

- information about future production from forest plantations (Brown, 2000).

In addition, information about the ratio of fellings to increment in each country was used to adjust the projections. Broadly speaking, the projections of future industrial roundwood production were adjusted upwards by a slight amount in countries with a high proportion of forest plantations, while production was reduced (or limited to no growth at all) in the few countries where the felling to increment ratio is already very high.

A further assumption that was incorporated into these projections was that the trade flows of industrial roundwood between the three sub-regions and between Europe and the rest of the world would remain roughly the same over the next two decades. Broadly speaking, industrial roundwood trade accounts for only a very small proportion of forest products trade and the quantities traded do not generally change by very much. However, Europe has experienced some major shifts in trade over the last decade, particularly in terms of increased exports of industrial roundwood from east to west. There are signs that this trade is stabilising, so it seemed reasonable to assume that trading patterns would not change significantly in the foreseeable future.

Figure 118 shows the projections for the production and consumption of industrial roundwood that were produced as a result of this part of the analysis. They show that production in Europe may expand by slightly less than consumption in the future, altering net trade from the current situation of net exports of 3 million m^3 per year to net imports of 2 million m^3 in 2020. Production in Western Europe is expected to increase by slightly more than consumption, due to increased production from forest plantations in some countries (Ireland, Spain, Portugal and the United Kingdom).

In addition, growth in production may revert to the rates experienced in the 1980s in some of the traditional large producers (Sweden, Finland, Germany and France). In Eastern Europe, it is expected that net exports (currently 12 million m^3 per year) will decline to zero, because production will not keep up with consumption. The ratio of harvesting to increment in a few of these countries is already very high (e.g. Latvia and Estonia) and it was assumed that production in such countries would not increase over the next two decades. In the CIS sub-region, it is expected that net exports may increase very slightly to replace some of the losses in net exports expected from Eastern Europe.

Figure 118   Trends and projections for the production and consumption of industrial roundwood under the baseline scenario

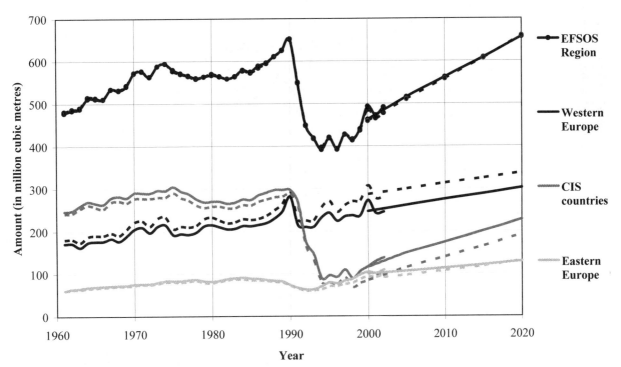

Solid lines represent production and dashed lines represent apparent consumption

Source: trends derived from FAOSTAT production and trade statistics; projections based on the outlook study analysis.

Based on the projected growth in consumption of industrial roundwood and the growth in demand from the sawmilling and plywood sector, consumption of sawlogs and veneer logs may grow slightly faster than consumption of pulpwood in Eastern Europe and the CIS sub-region, but growth for both types of industrial roundwood is expected to be about the same in Western Europe.

As in the past, the rate of growth in industrial roundwood production and consumption will fall behind the rates of growth in product markets due to the continued substitution of other types of wood and fibre for industrial roundwood. The importance of industrial roundwood as a source of wood raw material supply will fall slightly in Western Europe, as the scope for increased substitution of other types of wood and fibre is limited by technical factors. However, in Eastern Europe and the CIS sub-region, it is expected that the opposite will occur, as environmental policies are strengthened and changes in the structure of the processing sector open-up new opportunities to use recycled fibre and wood residues (see Figure 119).

Figure 119 **Trends and projections for the importance of industrial roundwood as a source of wood raw material supply**

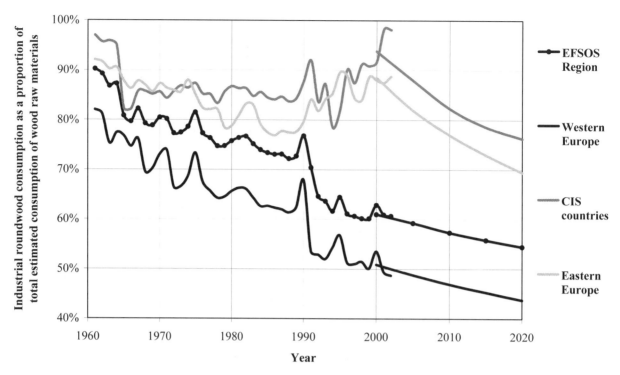

Source: trends derived from FAOSTAT production and trade statistics; projections based on the outlook study analysis.

Table 29 **The European wood raw material balance in 2020**

Component	Europe	Sub-regions		
		Western Europe	Eastern Europe	CIS
Derived demand for wood raw materials				
Other industrial roundwood	27.7	6.9	10.1	10.7
Sawnwood, plywood and veneer sheets	383.9	191.8	72.1	119.9
Reconstituted panels	141.8	85.2	32.1	24.4
Net pulp exports	52.1	21.5	3.0	27.7
Paper and paperboard	604.1	465.1	69.9	69.1
Total derived demand	**1,209.7**	**770.6**	**187.2**	**251.8**
Consumption of wood raw materials				
Industrial roundwood	659.4	337.4	130.0	192.0
Recovered paper	315.4	246.5	38.3	30.7
Net pulp imports	83.1	72.3	9.2	1.6
Other	151.8	114.5	9.8	27.6
- net imports of chips, particles and residues	*0.1*	*5.9*	*-4.0*	*-1.8*
- utilisation of wood residues	*151.7*	*108.5*	*13.8*	*29.4*
Total consumption	**1,209.7**	**770.6**	**187.2**	**251.8**

Note: the above figures are expressed in million m³ WRME. For trade in chips, particles and residues, imports are shown as a positive number and exports are shown as negative numbers.

4.3.4   The wood raw material balance

Table 29 shows the projected wood raw material balance for the whole of Europe and the three sub-regions in 2020. Compared with Table 7, this shows that the structure of the forest sector in Eastern Europe and the CIS sub-region will start to diversify and look slightly more similar to Western Europe in 2020. However, the dominance of industrial roundwood and sawnwood production is likely to remain a feature of these two sub-regions for many years to come.

4.4   Woodfuel

The EFSOS analysis of forest products markets did not examine trends in woodfuel production and consumption or produce an outlook for this component of the forest products sector. However, an earlier FAO study (Broadhead *et al*, in prep) examined global trends in the use of woodfuel and produced projections for every country in the World.

These projections were based on a statistical analysis of cross-sectional and time series data from countries, including official statistics at the national level (recorded in FAOSTAT) plus additional field-level information from a variety of sources. The study only examined trends in the consumption of woodfuel, which was modelled at the national, sub-regional and regional level, depending on the availability of data.

A number of statistical models were used to estimate trends in woodfuel consumption and produce projections to the year 2030. All consumption statistics were converted to consumption per capita and the models used the following explanatory variables: GDP; level of urbanisation (proportion of population living in urban areas); forest cover; temperature; level of oil production; total land area; and country-specific dummy variables. All of these variables were found to have a significant effect on the levels of per capita woodfuel consumption in countries and the variables had the expected signs (e.g. woodfuel consumption is generally higher in colder countries and countries with a higher level of forest cover, but lower in countries that have a higher GDP and higher level of urbanisation). The projections produced in this analysis are shown in Figure 120 below.

Overall, annual consumption of woodfuel in Europe is expected to decline from the current level of around 116 million m^3 to 90 million m^3 in 2020. Consumption in Eastern Europe and the CIS sub-region is expected to continue the declining trends in consumption recorded over the last four decades. In Eastern Europe, annual consumption of woodfuel is projected to decline from around 26 million m^3 in 2000 to 17 million m^3 in 2020. In the CIS sub-region, the projections show a decline from 57 million m^3 in 2000 to 43 million m^3 in 2020.

In Western Europe, the projections show almost no decline in future woodfuel consumption. The level of annual consumption recorded in 2000 - 33 million m^3 - is expected to fall slightly to 31 million m^3 in 2005, but remain at this level until 2020. This projection is due to some countries in Western Europe showing a declining trend in woodfuel consumption, while others show an increasing trend.

It should be noted that these projections follow a baseline or "business as usual" scenario. They assume that consumption is driven by socio-economic factors such as income growth and growth in urbanisation, which all tend to reduce woodfuel consumption over time. They do not take into account the possibility of new policy measures to increase the use of woodfuel as part of strategies to increase the use of renewable energy. Furthermore the data on which the projections are based are unfortunately unreliable and incomplete, and the resulting projections are significantly different from the upward trend desired by policy, such as the EU White Paper on renewable energy, and with trends observed in the early 2000s. Thus, they should be treated with a great deal of caution (see Section 4.6.6 for further discussion of an alternative scenario for the woodfuel sector).

Figure 120   Trends and projections for the consumption of woodfuel in Europe

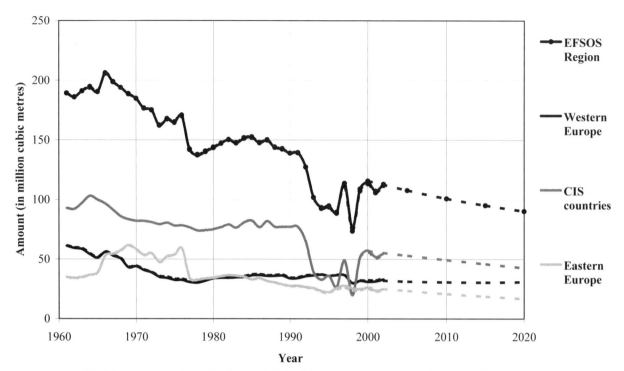

Solid lines represent production and dashed lines represent apparent consumption

Source: Broadhead et al (in prep). Note the caveats about data quality and methods set out in the text

4.5   Other forestry benefits

The statistics available for NWFPs and forest services are quite weak, so it has not been possible to undertake a detailed and quantitative analysis of the trends in these forest outputs or construct models and produce projections for the outlook. However, based on the information that is available, it is possible to present a qualitative assessment of what the future might look like for these outputs and this is done below. Following this, a short section also examines the outlook for employment in the forest sector.

4.5.1   Non-wood forest products

In general, the outlook for NWFPs will vary by product and by sub-region, depending on future trends in the main socio-economic driving forces. Broadly speaking, the following market developments might be expected in the future:

Collection of NWFPs as a recreation activity. Already, the collection of NWFPs is more of a recreational activity than a commercial activity or necessity in most of Western Europe. Thus, it can be expected that the production of some NWFPs might increase in future in line with an expected increase in forest recreation. In particular, an increase in production of fruits and berries, mushrooms and (possibly) medicinal plants might occur in the future.

Commercial collection of NWFPs. In Western Europe, commercial collection of NWFPs is likely to continue to decline, due to the labour intensive nature of these activities and the relatively high labour costs in Western Europe. This is most likely to affect the production of those NWFPs already listed above. The existing trend towards more intensive management should work in the opposite direction in the case of truffles and cork, leading to increased production in the future. In addition, it is possible that active management of medicinal plant and foliage production might occur (e.g. with deliberate planting of desired plants) if increased market demand makes this a financially viable proposition. This would lead to growth in production, but this is far from certain.

In Eastern Europe and the CIS sub-regions, relatively low labour costs will continue to give these sub-regions a comparative advantage in commercial NWFP production. However, there is a risk that some sectors will decline in the face of competition from countries outside Europe with better growing conditions and even lower labour costs (e.g. China).

Demand for edible NWFPs. In Western Europe, it is possible that demand for many edible NWFPs will increase in the future as social trends continue to stimulate interest in natural and organic foods. In particular, this may affect some of the higher value products such as mushrooms and honey. The outlook for these products in the other two sub-regions is far from certain. On the one hand, these could be viewed as inferior goods, in which case rising incomes would tend to reduce demand. On the other hand, they could experience trends that are similar to those expected in Western Europe. On balance, a safe assumption would be that demand will not change by very much in these countries in the future.

Demand for medicinal plants. Based on the socio-economic projections for Western Europe, an increase in demand for medicinal plants might be expected in this sub-region in the future. However, if such an increase were to arise, it would probably be only a gradual increase. In the other two sub-regions, the problem noted above (for edible NWFPs) would also apply to this market, making it very difficult to suggest what the future market might look like.

Markets for cork. Stable and moderate growth appears to have returned to the market for cork bottle stoppers and it seems unlikely that producers of high quality wines will switch to alternative materials, so long as the product remains price competitive and reliable. Low-cost competition from other producers (e.g. in North Africa) reduced demand in the 1980s, but this problem also seems to have been overcome, Therefore, there is little reason to suggest that cork production and consumption will not continue to increase modestly, in line with recent historical trends.

Decorative foliage and Christmas trees. Both of these NWFPs are luxury items, so there is always a possibility to raise prices in Western Europe, with innovative marketing and advertising. Studies of the wider market for floral products have suggested that future growth will be very strong (especially in Western Europe), so the prospects for increased demand for decorative foliage seem quite good. In the case of Christmas trees, it seems reasonable to assume that demand will largely be driven by population numbers. Therefore, only very slight growth in the demand quantity might be expected in the future (although, as noted above, growth in the value of this market could be higher).

Tree nuts. The historical statistics for tree nut production and consumption show quite strong trends, indicating level consumption with declining production in Western Europe and increasing consumption and production in the other two sub-regions. It would be reasonable to assume that these trends will continue.

Hunting (game meat and pelts). It is not possible to make projections for this activity without more in-depth information about the economic and social driving forces that underlie this activity.

4.5.2   Forest services

Protection of soil, water and infrastructure. Historical statistics have shown that demand for this forest function is quite small overall, but very high in specific locations. It has also shown that supply and demand have not changed very much in the past (see Figure 12). It seems likely that the importance of this function will remain unchanged in the future.

Recreation demand. Demand for forest recreation is already probably very high in Western Europe, so high growth in visitor numbers seems unlikely given the expected changes in population. Furthermore, high growth would probably lead to more problems of overcrowding in some countries, which would also tend to have a self-regulating effect on the growth in numbers. In the future, it seems most likely that demand will increase for a higher quality of forest recreations experience (e.g. more organised and specialised recreation activities and a higher expectation of visitor facilities). In contrast, high growth in forest recreation can be expected in the other two sub-regions, as these countries rapidly develop in the future.

Demand for biodiversity conservation. Demand for biodiversity conservation will probably increase in all countries, due to the projected changes in socio-economic forces. Again, the largest increases in demand might occur in the future in Eastern Europe and the CIS sub-region, where economic growth will be most rapid.

Recreation and biodiversity supply. The supply of these forest services in the future will very much depend upon government policies. Some forest owners will probably develop commercial forest recreation businesses, but even this will be determined in part by government policies (e.g. planning regulations). Apart from this, supplying forest recreation services will remain a loss-making activity (in a financial sense) for the majority of forest owners and managers, as will biodiversity conservation. The future supply of these services will depend upon future public support for these activities, so this is an area where individuals in the sector can have an influence on the future course of events and it would be inappropriate to speculate about this here.

Mitigation of climate change. On the supply-side, Europe's forests are almost certainly going to continue to increase in volume over the next 20 years, so increased "supply" of carbon storage in the future is virtually guaranteed. On the demand-side, much will depend on future policies and the incentive mechanisms that are developed to encourage reductions in net carbon emissions.

There remains considerable uncertainty about the exact mechanisms for controlling carbon emissions that will be chosen by countries. However, it seems likely that climate change will be taken info account in the formulation of policies for the forest sector in the future. These might include measures such as the following:

- measures to maintain carbon stock in forest ecosystems, by keeping losses of woody biomass below increment and by avoiding silvicultural practices leading to carbon loss from forest soil;

- incentives for wood energy use (from existing forests and trees outside the forest, new plantations, industry residues or recovered wood products) as part of the general promotion of renewable energy;

- measures to encourage the use of forest products instead of less "carbon-friendly" materials, based on sophisticated and detailed life cycle analysis (it should be noted that life cycle analysis will not always endorse the use of forests products, but may be expected to be a positive influence overall); and

- incentives to encourage the establishment of new fast-growing plantations, some for the supply of wood energy and some for carbon sequestration: in Western and Central Europe, the extent of these plantations is likely to be limited by competing land uses, but in the rest of Europe, there is considerable development potential.

4.5.3   Forestry employment

At present, employment in the European forest sector is about 3.9 million full-time equivalents (FTE). Over the last few decades, labour productivity has been rising faster than the volume of production, so total employment in the sector has been falling steadily. It is expected that this trend will continue, so that total employment in 2010 would be just over 3.5 million FTE.

Regarding employment quality, wage levels in the pulp and paper sector compare favourably with those in the other two forestry sub-sectors and with average manufacturing wages, but wages in forestry and the wood industries are typically lower than average. Furthermore, the wages paid to females continue to be significantly lower than those paid to male employees.

The health and safety situation has improved in the forest processing industry but continues to be a major problem in forestry in many countries. In some regions and for some groups, the situation has actually deteriorated significantly over the past decade, most notably for the self-employed and private forest owners in Eastern Europe.

4.6   Alternative scenarios for production and consumption

Projections of future wood product production and consumption have been produced for all three of the alternative scenarios described in Section 3.4. Overall, the projections are quite sensitive to the choice of alternative scenarios, with the conservation scenario reducing market growth (compared to the baseline scenario) by between 30 percent and 60 percent (depending on the product) and the integration scenario increasing growth by similar amounts in the opposite direction. However, there are significant differences between sub-regions and products. In general, the CIS sub-region is most affected by the choice of scenario, followed by Eastern Europe, while market expansion in Western Europe is generally less sensitive to the choice of scenario. The following text describes some of the main differences between these projections by sub-region and product.

4.6.1   Sawnwood production and consumption

Figure 121 shows the projections for coniferous sawnwood production and consumption under the three alternative scenarios. This shows that, at the European level, total growth in the production and consumption of coniferous sawnwood would be reduced by about 50 percent (compared to the baseline) under the conservation scenario or increased by about 50 percent under the integration scenario.

Comparing the three alternative scenarios, the figure shows that the relatively small changes anticipated under each of the scenarios would have a significant impact on the growth of coniferous sawnwood markets in Europe. For example, under the conservation scenario, total production is projected to increase by around 28 percent, while under the integration scenario it would increase by 88 percent. For consumption, the corresponding increases would be 21 percent and 65 percent.

However, at the sub-regional level, there are significant differences between the alternative projections in each of the three sub-regions. In Western and Eastern Europe, the differences between the three alternatives scenarios are quite small. Compared with the baseline scenario, total growth in coniferous sawnwood markets in Western Europe would be reduced by 40 percent under the conservation scenario or increased by 40 percent under the integration scenario. In Eastern Europe, the projections show a variation in total growth of +/- 35 percent under the two alternative scenarios.

The figure shows that the CIS sub-region is the location that is most sensitive to the alternative socio-economic scenarios. Under the conservation scenario, total production and consumption would both increase by about 80 percent by 2020 (compared with the baseline scenario of total growth of around 200 percent in both cases). However, under the integration scenario, production is projected to increase by 316 percent by 2020, with a projected increase in total consumption of 309 percent over the same period. This variation between the different scenarios in the CIS sub-region accounts for the majority of the variation between scenarios at the European level. It also accounts for nearly all of the difference in net exports from Europe under the different scenarios.

Figure 121 **Projections for the production and consumption of coniferous sawnwood in 2020 under the three alternative scenarios**

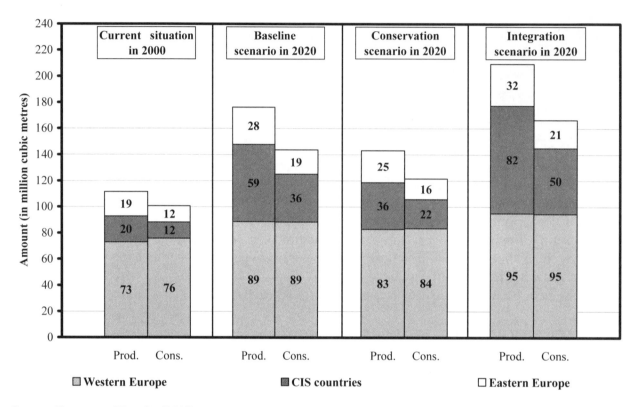

Source: Kangas and Baudin (2003).

Figure 122 presents the same information for non-coniferous sawnwood markets. In this case, the sensitivity of the projections to the alternative scenarios is about the same, with total growth reduced by about 50 percent under the conservation scenario or increased by about 50 percent under the integration scenario. Furthermore, the projections in all three sub-regions change significantly between the different scenarios. The only exception to this is non-coniferous sawnwood production in Western Europe, which is not affected very much by the different underlying scenarios.

Figure 122 **Projections for the production and consumption of non- coniferous sawnwood in 2020 under the three alternative scenarios**

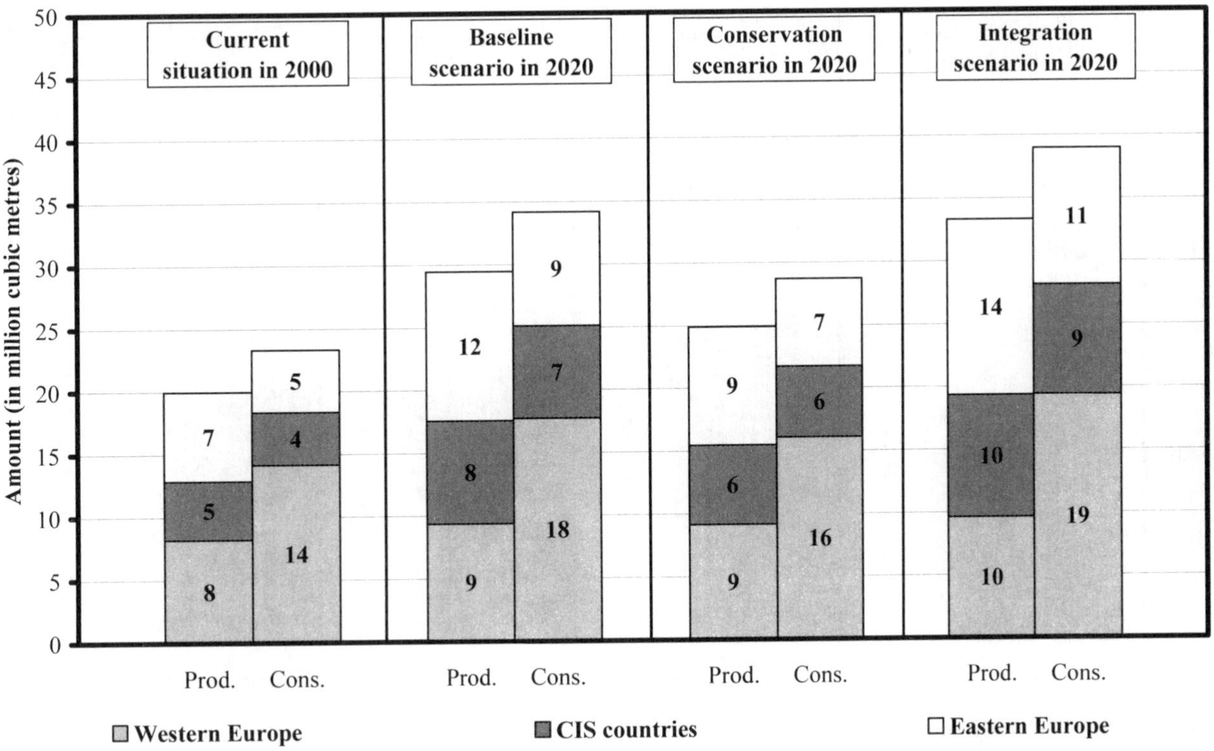

Source: Kangas and Baudin (2003).

4.6.2   Wood based panel production and consumption

Figure 123 presents the outlook for European fibreboard markets under the three different scenarios. Again this shows that the alternative scenarios have a significant impact on total growth in European production and consumption, with changes of +/- 50 percent in total growth under the integration and conservation scenarios.

Markets in Western Europe are least sensitive to the alternative scenarios. Production and consumption are projected to increase by 60 percent and 50 percent respectively under the baseline scenario. Under the conservation scenario, the corresponding figures would be 38 percent and 28 percent while, under the integration scenario, they would be 81 percent and 73 percent. Thus, total growth would be approximately one-third higher under the integration scenario or one-third lower under the conservation scenario.

Eastern Europe is the second largest fibreboard market in Europe and is very sensitive to the alternative scenarios. Under the baseline scenario, production and consumption are projected to grow by 125 percent and 150 percent respectively by 2020. Under the conservation scenario, this growth would be cut by more than half, resulting in increased production of only 56 percent and an increase in consumption of only 64 percent. Under the integration scenario, total growth in production and consumption would be 193 percent and 237 percent. The projections for the CIS sub-region show a similarly high sensitivity to the alternative scenarios, with an increase or reduction in total growth of more than 50 percent under the integration and conservations scenarios.

Figure 123 **Projections for the production and consumption of fibreboard in 2020 under the three alternative scenarios**

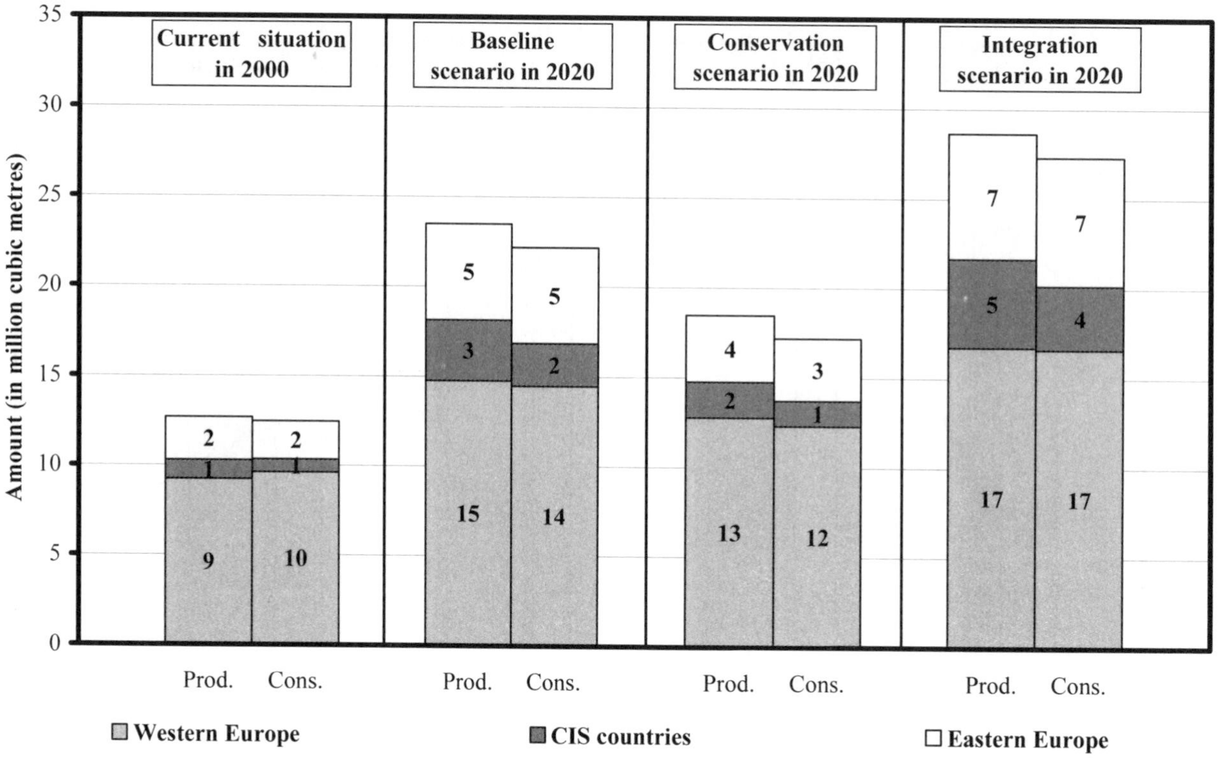

Source: Kangas and Baudin (2003).

Figure 124 shows the projections for production and consumption of particleboard under the three different scenarios. In this case, the outlook is much less sensitive to the alternative scenarios, with a baseline projection of production and consumption growth of 66 percent and 68 percent respectively, projections of growth in production and consumption of 40 percent and 36 percent under the conservation scenario and projections of 93 percent growth and 100 percent growth in production and consumption under the integration scenario.

The reduced impact of the alternative scenarios on production and consumption is due to the dominance of Western Europe in this market and the low sensitivity in this sub-region to the underlying differences between the alternative scenarios. For example, total growth in production and consumption would only change by about one-third under the conservation and integration scenarios (compared with the baseline scenario).

The projections for Eastern Europe are also not greatly affected by the choice of scenario, with a variation in total growth of about +/- 40 percent under the integration and conservation scenarios. The CIS sub-region has the largest projected growth of all three sub-regions (230 percent growth in production and 238 percent growth in consumption under the baseline scenario), but is the most sensitive to the alternative scenarios. Total growth would be reduced by more than half under the conservation scenario or increased by more than half under the integration scenario. Although these results are very different under the three alternative scenarios, these differences have less of an impact at the European level because the CIS sub-region accounts for only a small share of the total European market.

Figure 124   ***Projections for the production and consumption of particleboard in 2020 under the three alternative scenarios***

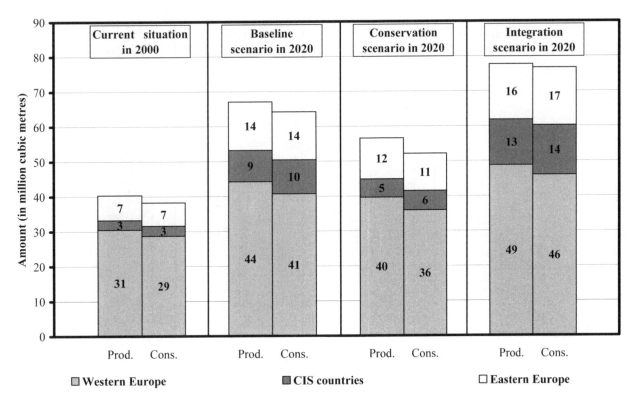

Source: Kangas and Baudin (2003).

One other point worth noting is that the projections of consumption are affected much more than the projections of production by the choice of future scenario. Thus, under the baseline and conservation scenarios, the level of net exports from Europe is projected to increase compared to the current situation while, under the integration scenario, the level of net exports would diminish.

Figure 125 shows the projections for plywood and veneer sheet production and consumption under the three alternative scenarios. The markets for these products are the most sensitive to the choice of alternative scenario, showing a decline in total growth of production and consumption of over 50 percent under the conservation scenario or an increase in growth of more than 50 percent under the integration scenario. This sensitivity of the projections to the choice of scenario is almost the same across all three sub-regions.

Figure 125 **Projections for the production and consumption of plywood and veneer sheets in 2020 under the three alternative scenarios**

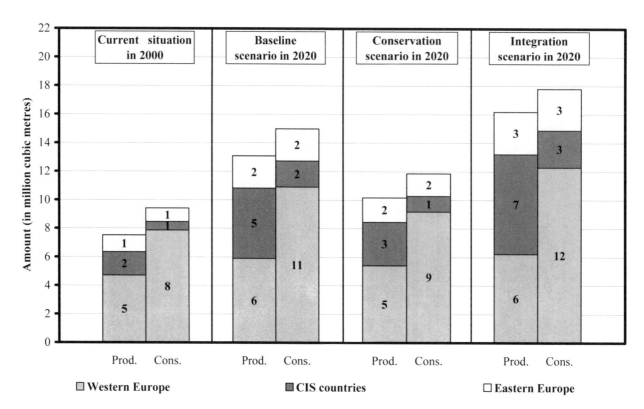

Source: Kangas and Baudin (2003).

4.6.3 Paper and paperboard production and consumption

Figure 126 shows the newsprint production and consumption projections under the three alternative scenarios. At the European level, the projections are very sensitive to the choice of scenario. The baseline scenario shows a total increase in production of 68 percent by 2020 and an increase in consumption of 62 percent. Under the conservation scenario, these figures would fall to 31 percent and 35 percent respectively while, under the integration scenario, they would increase to 106 percent and 90 percent. Thus, the difference in total production growth between the baseline scenario and the two alternative scenarios is +/- 50 percent (and slightly less than this in the case of growth in consumption).

The CIS sub-region accounts for most of the difference between the projections under each of the three alternative scenarios. Under the baseline scenario, production in the CIS sub-region is projected to increase by 288 percent by 2020. Under the conservation scenario, the projected increase is cut to 104 percent while, under the integration scenario, it is raised to 467 percent. These differences are huge and would result in a very different balance of production across Europe as a whole. For example, under the conservation scenario, the relative importance of the CIS sub-region will remain about the same as it is now, accounting for slightly less than 20 percent of all European production. However, under the Integration scenario, the CIS sub-region would account for almost 40 percent of total European newsprint production.

The differences between the alternative scenarios in the CIS sub-region also account for the differences in European net trade under the alternative scenarios. Under the conservation scenario, net exports from Europe will diminish slightly but, under the integration scenario, Europe would become a major net exporter of newsprint, largely from the CIS sub-region.

Figure 126   **Projections for the production and consumption of newsprint in 2020 under the three alternative scenarios**

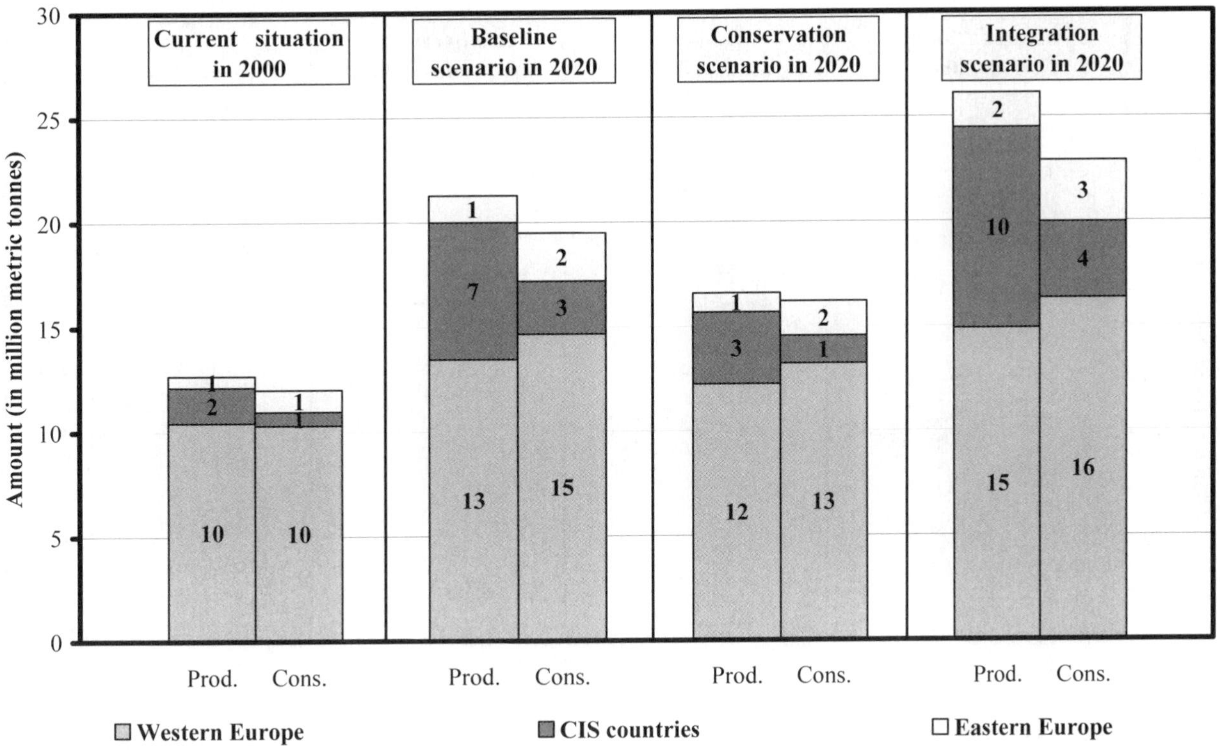

Source: *Kangas and Baudin (2003).*

Projections for production and consumption of other paper and paperboard under the three alternative scenarios are given in Figure 127. This figure shows that the expansion of this market is not affected as much by the choice of alternative scenario. The baseline scenario shows total growth in production and consumption of 64 percent and 67 percent respectively. Under the conservation scenario, these figures would both be 37 percent while, under the integration scenario, they would increase to 90 percent and 96 percent respectively.

The sensitivity of this market to the choice of scenario is quite low because of the dominance of Western Europe in this market. Market expansion in both Western Europe and Eastern Europe would fall by less than 50 percent under the conservation scenario (or increase by less than 50 percent under the integration scenario).

The CIS sub-region is more sensitive to the choice of scenario. For example, the conservation scenario shows a projected increase in production and consumption of 72 percent, compared with a baseline projection of a 170 percent increase in production and a 173 percent increase in consumption. However, the CIS sub-region accounts for only a small share of the total European market, so these results have little effect at the European level.

Figure 127 *Projections for the production and consumption of other paper and paperboard in 2020 under the three alternative scenarios*

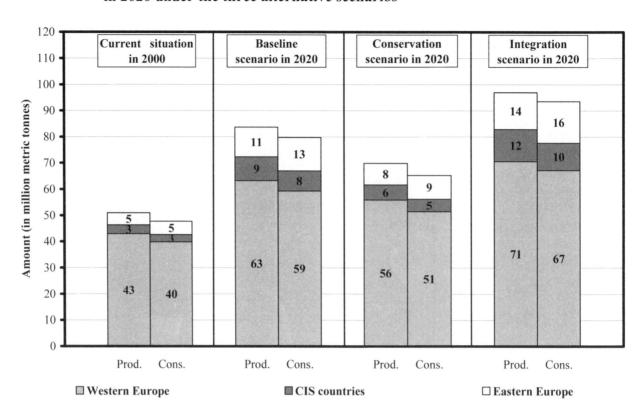

Source: Kangas and Baudin (2003).

Figure 128 shows the difference between the projections for production and consumption of printing and writing paper under the three alternative scenarios. This also shows that the expansion of these markets is not strongly affected by the choice of scenario, although projected net trade from Europe is quite different under the alternative scenarios.

Again, this market is dominated by Western Europe, where market expansion is not greatly affected by the choice of scenario. The baseline projection for Western Europe shows growth in production and consumption of 55 percent and 76 percent by 2020. Under the conservation scenario, total growth would only amount to 39 percent and 50 percent for production and consumption respectively. Under the integration scenario, the corresponding figures would be 70 percent and 104 percent. The much greater sensitivity of consumption to the choice of scenario also affects the net trade position for Western Europe (and Europe as a whole), with a significant level of net exports in 2020 under the conservation scenario and a much lower level of net exports under the integration scenario.

In Eastern Europe, projected total growth in production and consumption is 246 percent and 282 percent respectively under the baseline scenario. The corresponding figures under the conservation scenario are 124 percent and 127 percent, or around half of the expected increase under the baseline scenario. The integration scenario shows a similar change in market expansion in the opposite direction, with an increase in the growth in production and consumption by more than 50 percent. The different levels of growth in East European consumption also contribute significantly to the differences in net trade in Europe under the alternative scenarios.

The CIS sub-region shows a similar amount of sensitivity to the choice of scenario, but the effect on European markets as a whole is relatively small, because this sub-region accounts for only a small share of the total European market for printing and writing paper.

Figure 128 ***Projections for the production and consumption of printing and writing paper in 2020 under the three alternative scenarios***

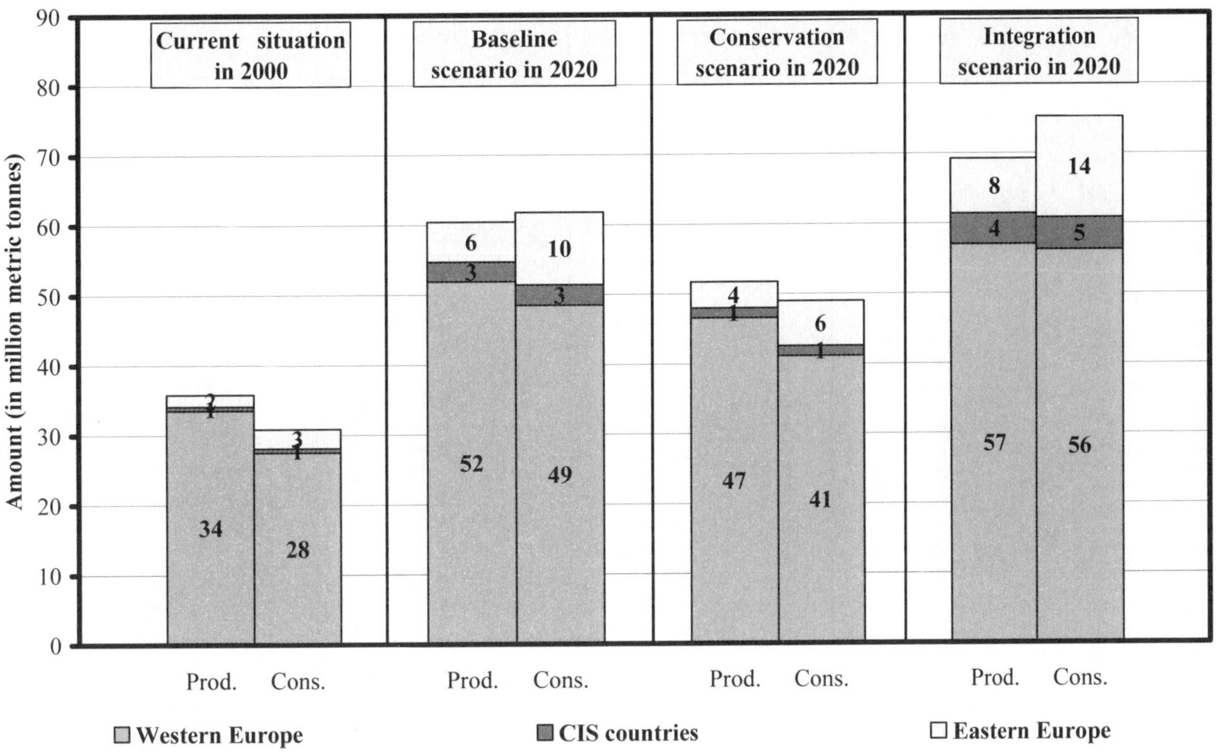

Source: Kangas and Baudin (2003).

4.6.4 Wood pulp

Projections for the future production and consumption of wood pulp in Europe were constructed as previously described (in Section 4.2.2), by calculating wood pulp consumption from the wood and fibre required to produce the projected levels of paper production, after subtracting the projected consumption of recovered paper (all in WRME). Also as before, production of wood pulp was estimated from the trends in the historical relationship between wood pulp production and consumption in individual countries. The assumptions about future levels of wastepaper recovery and use were not changed in the alternative scenarios (although it might be expected that higher levels of wastepaper recovery could be reached in some countries under the conservation scenario).

Figure 129 shows the projections for wood pulp production and consumption in 2020 under the three alternative scenarios. These show that the projections are very sensitive to the choice of future scenario. Under the baseline scenario, production and consumption of wood pulp are both projected to increase by 44 percent by 2020. Under the conservation scenario, these increases are cut by almost two-thirds, with a projected increase in production of only 15 percent and a projected increase in consumption of 19 percent. Under the integration scenario, the corresponding increases are 74 percent and 70 percent. The relatively large differences between the alternative scenarios are due to the different effects that each scenario has on the production and consumption of paper and paperboard (and, as a result of this, the changes to wastepaper recovery).

Figure 129 **Projections for the production and consumption of wood pulp in 2020 under the three alternative scenarios**

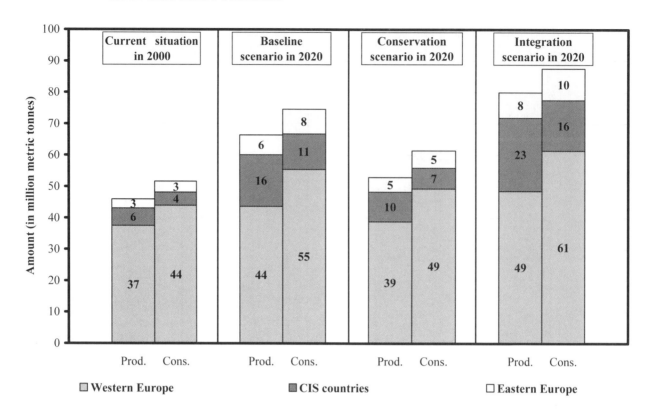

Source: based on the outlook study analysis (see Section 4.2.2).

Western Europe accounts for the largest proportion of European wood pulp production and consumption and accounts for most of the differences between the alternative scenarios. For example, under the conservation scenario, wood pulp production would increase by only three percent by 2020 compared with a total increase of 16 percent under the baseline scenario and an increase of 30 percent under the integration scenario.

The other sub-region that is greatly affected by the choice of scenario is the CIS sub-region, but this sub-region is a net exporter of wood pulp and the differences between the alternative scenarios are not that great and tend to act in the opposite direction. For example, under the conservation scenario, production still increases by 70 percent by 2020, compared with the baseline scenario increase of 192 percent. Although this is less than half of the projected increase under the baseline scenario, the cut in expansion is nowhere near as dramatic as that for Western Europe.

The net effect of these sub-regional differences is that the level of net imports of wood pulp into Europe is not significantly affected by the choice of scenario as differences in net trade with Western Europe are balanced by changes in the opposite direction in the CIS sub-region.

4.6.5   Industrial roundwood

Projections of industrial roundwood production and consumption have also been produced for each of the three alternative scenarios. As before, the projections of consumption have been based on the derived demand for industrial roundwood, while the projections of production have been based on the demand projections and modifications to take into additional available information about roundwood supply and the condition of Europe's forest resources (see Section 4.3.3).

The projections for production and consumption of industrial roundwood under each of the three alternative scenarios are shown in Figure 130. At the European level, the choice of scenario has a significant impact on the total growth in industrial roundwood production and consumption. For example, under the baseline scenario, production is projected to increase by 42 percent, while consumption is projected to increase by 44 percent by 2020. Under the conservation scenario, both figures would be cut to 16 percent. Under the integration scenario, production would increase by 70 percent, while consumption would increase by 72 percent.

Figure 130 *Projections for the production and consumption of industrial roundwood in 2020 under the three alternative scenarios*

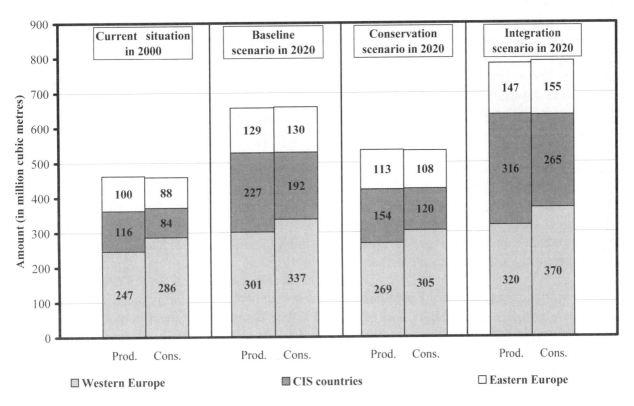

Source: based on the outlook study analysis (see Section 4.3.3).

On the demand side, the differences between the consumption projections under the three different scenarios are largely driven by the differences in the projections for products markets (described above). Furthermore, as already noted for wood pulp above, some of these differences are magnified by the different effects that each scenario has on the production and consumption of processed products and the availability of alternative non-forest sources of wood and fibre. Thus, for example, growth in the consumption of industrial roundwood in Western Europe would be cut by more than half under the conservation scenario compared with the baseline scenario.

On the supply side, the same constraints already described in Section 4.3.3 have been applied to the alternative scenarios, notably that some countries would be limited in their ability to increase wood supply significantly to meet increasing demands. However, as also noted above, some countries with forest plantation resources are not constrained so much and others have an abundance of potential supply.

The conservation scenario implies a very modest increase in the production and consumption of industrial roundwood in all three sub-regions, which can easily be achieved with the available forest resource. However, under the integration scenario, some countries in Western and Eastern Europe would find it difficult to meet additional demands from domestic forest resources.

The CIS sub-region does not face these constraints and it has been assumed that future demand for industrial roundwood could be easily met by increased production and exports from this sub-region and a very small increase in net imports from outside Europe. It should also be noted that, under this scenario, the projected level of industrial roundwood in the CIS sub-region would, by 2020, approach the levels achieved before the 1990s. Thus, although the almost three-fold increase in production may seem remarkable, it would not go beyond the level of production that has been achieved before in the past.

4.6.6 Other factors that may affect the projections

The previous five sections of this study have described what might happen to European forest products markets under a baseline or "business as usual" scenario and two alternative scenarios, focusing on greater emphasis on conservation in Europe's forests or a more rapid drive towards economic growth and integration between the different European sub-regions. For reasons of focus and clarity, the analysis does not explore in detail some of the other possible changes that might occur in the future, such as those described in Thoroe *et al* (2004). However, there are two significant issues that should be mentioned as likely to have an effect on forest products markets in the future.

Technological change. Changes in technology have already had a significant impact on European forest products markets and are likely to do so in the future. The analysis presented here is based on statistical relationships estimated from past trends in historical data. Thus, to the extent that technological changes have already occurred in the market place, they should reflect some of the current trends in technology. However, this methodology can not identify or examine the impact of new and emerging technologies on markets.

Two major changes in technology are currently developing and are not likely to be reflected in these projections. The first of these is the growth of office automation, the internet and electronic communication. Changes in the way that information is stored, reproduced and communicated could have a profound impact on the future markets for paper and paperboard. On the one hand, increased use of computers has not led to the "paperless office", but has probably tended to increase the consumption of printing and writing paper. To a large extent, this shift in technology is probably captured quite well in these projections. On the other hand, changes in the way that people communicate (e.g. e-mails, websites, etc.) could lead to lower demand for printing and writing paper and newsprint. Widespread use of the internet is only a recent phenomenon, which has increased significantly in Western Europe and, to a lesser extent in Eastern Europe. The extent to which this will reduce the demand for paper is unknown and the effect of this change in technology is still too recent to influence the statistical models that are based on historical supply and demand.

Another recent technological innovation is the development of new solid wood products and the greater acceptance of these products in the marketplace. Relatively new products such as OSB and MDF have been used for a while now in Europe and the projections probably capture most of the shift towards using these products. However, a whole new range of engineered wood products are gradually gaining acceptance in the market place (e.g. high-density fibreboard, laminated veneer lumber, I-joists, pre-cut lumber, etc.). Greater use of these products in the future is expected, but there is currently insufficient information to estimate exactly what effect they might have on forest products markets in the future. They will certainly result in some substitution between wood products as they are used in stead of older, traditional (and usually more expensive) products such as plywood and sawnwood. However, the development of these products may also expand the markets for wood products more generally.

The overall effects of these technological changes could be slightly less paper production and consumption than presented in these projections and slightly more of a shift from sawnwood and plywood towards wood based panels.

Wood energy. The other major issue that is currently highly relevant to the outlook is the future use of woodfuel as part of strategies to increase the production of renewable energy in Europe. As already noted, a baseline scenario for woodfuel consumption suggests that this will continue to decrease in the future, in line with historical trends. However, if policies are put in place to deliberately encourage the use of woodfuel in the future, the consumption of woodfuel could increase significantly.

The impact of renewable energy policies on the outlook for woodfuel will depend upon how much encouragement (e.g. subsidy) is given to promoting the use of woodfuel and the focus of such support. Broadly speaking, the lowest cost sources of wood for energy production are likely to be residues from the wood processing sector. These are already concentrated at specific sites (i.e. wood processing facilities), many of which are in urban areas (where demand for energy is highest). The next most cost-effective sources of woodfuel are likely to be forest residues and thinnings, followed by tree crops grown specifically for woodfuel production (energy crops).

Demand-side policies that encourage renewable energy production at the lowest possible cost (e.g. subsidies per unit of energy produced) are likely to result in the diversion of wood processing residues to energy production. However, supply-side policies that encourage the utilisation of forests or the establishment of new energy crops are likely to favour alternative sources of woodfuel supply. The latter may be chosen in order to meet broader objectives of rural development and the reduction of agricultural production, as well as the objective of increasing renewable energy supply.

Given the very different effects of these policies on forest products markets, this would suggest that the outlook for woodfuel production is currently very uncertain and could have both positive and negative effects on the rest of the forest sector. In view of the outlook presented above, this is a potentially interesting area for further discussion and analysis.

4.7 Forest resources and forest management

The projections of roundwood production presented above suggest that a significant increase in roundwood production will occur in Europe over the next 20 years. In order to examine the impact of these changes on the development of forest resources in Europe, the EFISCEN model was used to show how the projected level of fellings might affect forest resource parameters such as growing stock volume and NAI.

The EFISCEN model was used to examine two of the alternative scenarios described above, namely the baseline scenario and the integration scenario. These two scenarios result in the highest levels of projected fellings in Europe, so they are the two scenarios where the sustainability of future roundwood production might be constrained by the productive capacity of European forest resources. The conservation scenario results in a much lower level of projected fellings, which is very unlikely to exceed the potential availability of wood supplies.

Full details of the methodology used in the EFISCEN model are given in Schelhaas *et al* (in prep) and will not be repeated here. The following text presents the main findings of the forest resource analysis,[22] followed by some comments about possible future developments that might occur in the management of forests.

---

[22]   It should be noted that the projections of fellings used in the EFISCEN analysis were preliminary estimates and differed from those presented here. However, the differences between those projections and the final projections are relatively small at the sub-regional level, so the major conclusions of the EFISCEN analysis would not be affected significantly by these changes. It should also be noted that Schelhaas *et al* (in prep) only refer to the European part of the Russian Federation, whereas the results presented here include the whole of the Russian Federation (and are derived from the EFISCEN results).

4.7.1 Area of forest available for wood supply

Under the baseline scenario, trends in the FAWS area were extrapolated into the future. In most countries, this resulted in a slight expansion of FAWS area, presumably because the growth in total forest area will be larger than the area of forest transferred from avaialbale to unavailable for wood supply. For the Russian Federation it was assumed that the recent reported decline in FAWS area (see Section 2.1.2), which may be a classification problem, rather than a trend, would not continue into the future. For the integration scenario, the work of Thoroe *et al* (2004) suggested that a modest expansion in FAWS might be expected in the future (over and above the baseline scenario) and this increase was included in the projections. These projections of FAWS were checked with national correspondents and were, where necessary, adjusted on the basis of their expectations about the future. In most of the few cases where adjustments were suggested, this resulted in a slight reduction of FAWS in the future compared with the original assumptions.

Figure 131   Outlook for the area of forest available for wood supply (FAWS) under the baseline and integration scenarios

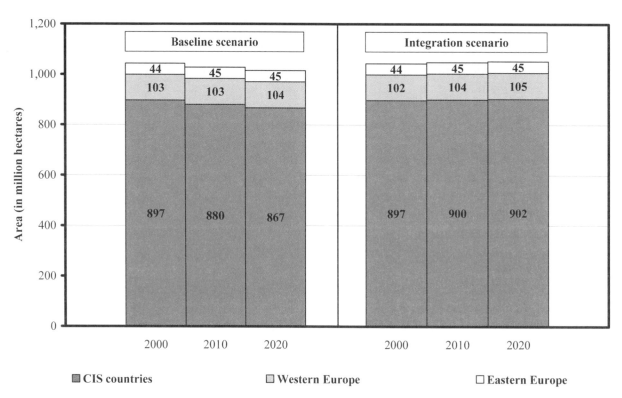

Source: derived from Schelhaas et al (in prep). Note: all of the countries included in the EFSOS are included in these figures except Bosnia and Herzegovina, where no statistics were available.

Figure 131 shows the outlook for FAWS area under the two alternative scenarios. Under the baseline scenario, it is expected that the total FAWS area in Europe will decline by about 28 million hectares. However, this decline is all due to the projected decrease of 30 million ha in the FAWS area in the CIS sub-region. In contrast to this, a very slight increase in the FAWS area is expected in the future in Western and Eastern Europe (and in the majority of countries included in these two sub-regions).

4.7.2 Growing stock of forest available for wood supply

The EFISCEN model produced projections for the volume of growing stock on FAWS under each of the scenarios and these are shown in Figure 132 below. Under the baseline scenario, growing stock volume is projected to increase significantly, from 109 billion m³ o.b. in 2000 to 129 billion m³ o.b. in 2020. However, the majority of this increase will occur in the CIS sub-region (despite the expected decline in FAWS area). In Western and Eastern Europe, growing stock volume is expected to increase in both sub-regions throughout the period, but at a much lower rate of growth.

Figure 132   Outlook for the volume of growing stock on FAWS under the baseline and integration scenarios

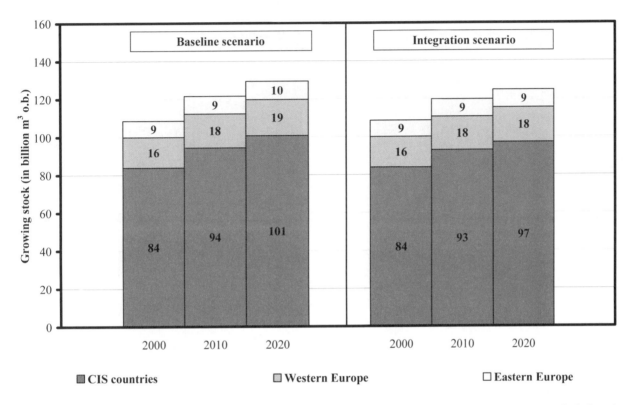

Source: derived from Schelhaas et al (in prep). Note: all of the countries included in the EFSOS are included in these figures except Bosnia and Herzegovina, where no statistics were available.

The volume of growing stock is also expected to increase under the integration scenario, but by about 15 percent less than under the baseline scenario. Under this scenario, the European growing stock volume is projected to increase to 125 billion m³ o.b. by 2020. Again, the CIS sub-region accounts for the majority of this increase. In Western Europe, growing stock volume is expected to increase slightly at first, but remain about the same over the period 2010 to 2020. In Eastern Europe, very little increase in the growing stock volume is projected for the whole period 2000 to 2020 under this scenario. This reduction in the projected increase in growing stock volume is due to the fact that the level of fellings will approach the level of increment in these two sub-regions under this scenario (see below).

Figure 133   Outlook for the volume of growing stock per hectare on FAWS under the baseline and integration scenarios

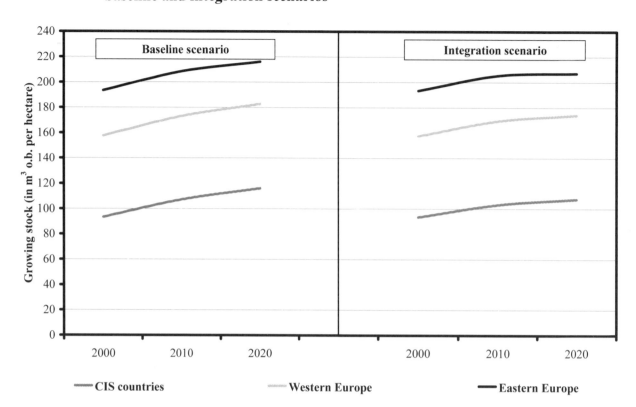

Source: derived from Schelhaas et al (in prep). Note: all of the countries included in the EFSOS are included in these figures except Bosnia and Herzegovina, where no statistics were available.

Figure 133 presents this information in a slightly different way, showing the projected level of growing stock per hectare in each of the three sub-regions under the two alternative scenarios. This shows that growing stock volume per hectare will continue to increase under the baseline scenario. Under the integration scenario, the increase in growing stock per hectare will slow down over the next 20 years. In particular, in Eastern Europe, it will level-off by 2020 at a level of around 210 m³ per hectare.

4.7.3   Annual increment of forest available for wood supply

The outlook for total annual increment (i.e. NAI) of FAWS is shown in Figure 134 and the corresponding figures for NAI per hectare are shown in

Figure 135. These show that total annual increment is expected to fall over the ten years 2000 to 2010, then remain about the same under the baseline scenario or increase slightly under the integration scenario. Again, almost all of the projected changes occur in the CIS sub-region, which accounts for the majority of increment in European forests due to the size of the forest resource there. In Western and Eastern Europe, the projected levels of fellings will have little impact on total annual increment, although the historical trend towards an increase in annual increment in these sub-regions (particularly in Western Europe - see Figure 7 on page 19) will be halted.

The projections of annual increment per hectare present a slightly different picture, with a slight decline in annual increment projected for Western and Eastern Europe and very little change projected for the CIS sub-region. Furthermore, there is very little difference between the two alternative scenarios. The reasons behind these changes are complex and are related to the age-class structure of European forests.

Figure 134   **Outlook for NAI on FAWS under the baseline and integration scenarios**

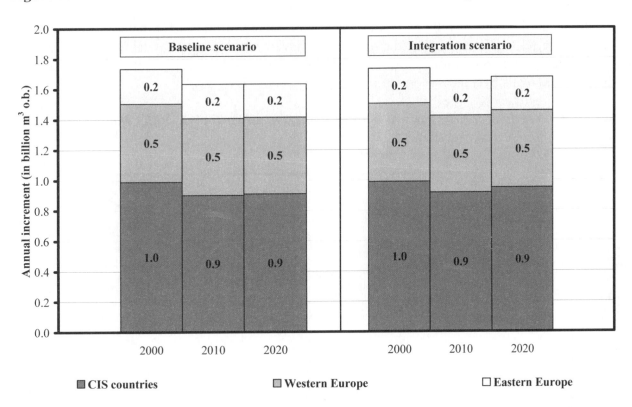

Source: derived from Schelhaas et al (in prep). Note: all of the countries included in the EFSOS are included in these figures except Bosnia and Herzegovina, where no statistics were available.

Figure 135   **Outlook for NAI per ha on FAWS under the baseline and integration scenarios**

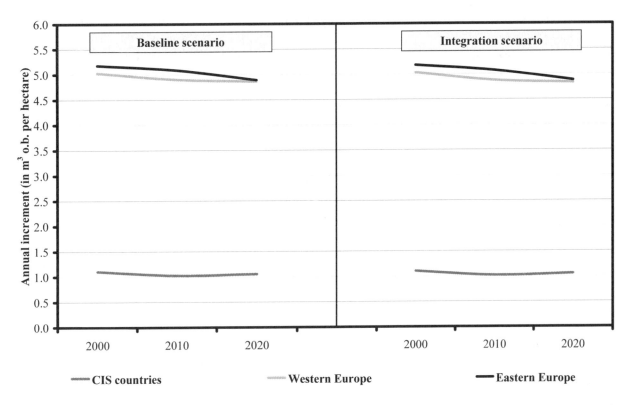

Source: derived from Schelhaas et al (in prep). Note: all of the countries included in the EFSOS are included in these figures except Bosnia and Herzegovina, where no statistics were available.

4.7.4 Comparison of removals and increment

The outlook for the ratio of fellings to increment is presented in Figure 136 below. As before, the projections for fellings used to construct this figure have been calculated by taking the projections for industrial roundwood production and woodfuel consumption and multiplying these total roundwood removals by a factor derived from the FRA 2000 (UN, 2000).

Figure 136   ***Outlook for the ratio of fellings to increment on FAWS under the baseline and integration scenarios***

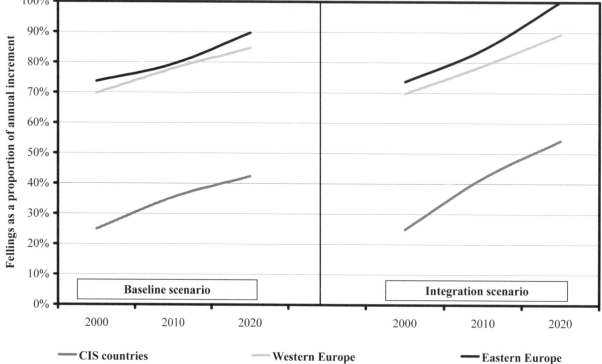

Source: derived from Schelhaas et al (in prep). Note: all of the countries included in the EFSOS are included in these figures except Bosnia and Herzegovina, where no statistics were available.

The figure shows that the ratio of fellings to increment is expected to increase significantly over the next 20 years in all sub-regions and under both scenarios. This would represent a reverse in the historical trends in this variable, which has tended to decline over most of the last 40 years in Europe.

Under the baseline scenario, the ratio remains under 100 percent in all three subregions and in most European countries. Under the integration scenario, the higher projected level of fellings pushes the ratio to 100 percent in Eastern Europe by 2020. The countries where the ratio is higher than 100 percent are mostly the same in both scenarios and the industrial roundwood supply projections assume that fellings will not increase in the future in these countries. Thus, the higher ratio for Eastern Europe under the integration scenario is largely due to a number of other countries approaching a fellings to increment ratio of 100 percent by 2020.

At first sight, the projections in Figure 136 suggest that a number of countries in Eastern Europe may be harvesting at a level that is above the sustained yield (or will do so in the near future). However, these projections must be interpreted with some caution. Firstly, the projections of fellings include woodfuel consumption, which may be harvested from a variety of sources outside FAWS and would probably include non-stem biomass that is not included in the annual increment figures. Furthermore, it may be incorrect to apply the removals to fellings conversion figures to this component of roundwood production. Secondly, the annual increment figure is only for FAWS and it is possible that some industrial roundwood is harvested from other areas not included in the calculations of projected annual increment. Finally, as noted above, annual increment depends on a range of complex factors related to the age-class structure of forests, site productivity and the felling regimes used in countries. Thus, it is possible for increment to start to increase again after a period of harvesting at a level above the annual increment (the "allowable cut effect", where old slow-growing forests are harvested and replaced by younger more vigorous stands). The currently available tools and statistics are not adequate for a detailed investigation of the complex dynamics of forest growth at the European level, but these results suggest that this is an area where further research might be useful, particularly in some countries in Eastern Europe.

4.7.5   Forest management

Forest management is one area where individuals working in the sector have a lot of control or influence over the future and a discussion of the merits of different courses of action will be presented in the conclusions to this study. However, there are certain aspects of forest management that are determined largely by events outside the sector and these will be discussed here below.

Expansion of forest management objectives. The first trend that is likely to continue into the future is that the demands placed on forests will continue to expand in scope. In response to this, it is also likely that the objectives of forest management will continue to change and expand.

It is now quite well understood by the public that forests produce a wide range of market and non-market products and services. As accessibility to the countryside increases with expanding incomes and leisure time, it can be expected that the public will place ever greater demands on forests for the production of non-market services such as recreation, landscape and conservation.

This projection that the demand for goods and services will expand in scope can not be quantified, nor can it be projected with any degree of accuracy. However, there is a significant amount of partial and anecdotal evidence at the country level that this trend will continue into the future.

Public support for forest management. In support of the above trend, there is also likely to be continued public support for the forest sector, based on the genally positive views the public has of forests and foresters, and with higher priority given to non-wood functions and objectives, widely believed to be forests' main contribution to the general welfare (Rametsteiner and Kraxner, 2003). However, given the continual desire to increase the efficiency of government an unavoidable limits on public spending, it can be expected that these incentives will be increasingly targeted to meet specific objectives or to produce specific outputs. It already seems quite likely that incentives are increasing in importance relative to the demands of the forest processing sector. In the future it can be expected that forest management may be driven more by the requirements necessary to obtain such subsidies and less by the need to produce roundwood for the industry.

Continued strong public interest of the sector. It was already noted in Section 2.2.2 that public participation in forestry policy making is increasing. This is due to a number of factors such as greater accessibility to the countryside (noted above), changing social values and the greater ease of communication between stakeholders and government (e.g. by e-mail and the internet). It is also a natural response to the increase in public support for the sector noted above, as well as realisation that conflicts concerning forest use are of political/value nature, not purely technical.

This trend is likely to lead to increased public scrutiny of the sector and may also lead to expectations of higher standards in the quality of forest management. In addition, it increases the risk that the reputation of the sector can be harmed by the actions of a few or by the misdirection of public opinion. The result of this could be increased public pressure to manage forests in a certain way, which may not always be technically valid or economically feasible. Increasingly, it will be the role of forest sector professionals to structure these public discussions about priorities, and to inform participants of the technical and economic consequences of the various options, rather than being the ultimate decision makers.

Management capability. Forest privatisation and restitution has led to a huge increase in the number of small forest owners across much of Europe in recent years. In addition to this, public subsidies have encouraged many farmers to plant forests and this trend is likely to continue in the near-term. The capacity of these new forest owners to manage their forests is unknown. However, it would seem likely that a large proportion of them are probably lacking in financial and technical capability, particularly in light of the new demands being placed on the sector. The same applies to the millions of "old" private forest owners in western Europe who are increasingly unable to manage their forests in a rational way and to handle the complex and public dilemmas associated with forest management in the twenty-first century. Many countries have maintained or reinforced systems of extension services, cooperatives etc. to provide support and guidance to these owners, without encroaching on their property rights. These problems are more urgent and severe in the countries which have recently restituted significant forest areas.

The projections for forest management described above do not apply to all forest managers in all countries. However, they do give an indication of some of the challenges for forest management in the future that probably apply to many different forest owners. The business of forest management is becoming more complicated and will probably require a wider range of skills in the future. At the same time, many more people are now forest managers. How the sector responds to these challenges will influence public opinion and could affect the outlook for forest products markets.

5   CONCLUSIONS AND RECOMMENDATIONS

This study is the result of a major cooperative effort involving nearly a hundred experts on the team of specialists and as national correspondents, within a formally agreed thematic structure discussed at the intergovernmental level.   The aim has been to analyse the past situation and trends and to project those trends in to the future identifying scenarios and options, as a basis for decision making by actors primarily in the forest sector: governments of course, but also industries, forest owners and social and environmental NGOs.   The study is certainly not intended to provide a single, authoritative view of the future and what should be done: to attempt to create such a single "correct conclusion" would be counterproductive as EFSOS is intended to generate productive debate, between actors who do not necessarily have the same values or interests, rather than to pre-empt it.

These conclusions and recommendations therefore are the views of the UNECE and FAO secretariats alone, although they have benefited greatly from discussion at numerous fora, notably the team of specialists meetings and at the Joint FAO/UNECE Working Party on Forest Economics and Statistics and the joint session of the UNECE Timber Committee and the FAO European Forestry Commission in October 2004

5.1   Background

Most of Europe is densely populated and rather prosperous compared to other parts of the world. As a result of this, the contribution of the forest sector to European society has changed somewhat over the last few decades.

Starting with the negative trends, the economic importance of the sector is declining in most countries, as it has not grown as fast as other parts of the economy. Indeed, in most European countries, the forest sector now accounts for less than one-half percent of GDP. Currently, about 4 million Europeans work in the forest sector, but this has also declined in the past and is likely to continue to do so in the future.

In addition to these macroeconomic trends, forest products are also no longer indispensable elements of life in Europe. For example, in most cases, they can easily be substituted by other non-wood products. Forest products can only maintain their position in the marketplace by continued investment in skills and technology, development of new markets, competitive pricing, improved performance and a better understanding of customers needs.

On a more positive note, there have also been many successes in the forest sector and some elements of the outlook present great opportunities for the sector. For example, forests cover about one-third of the land area in Europe and have been expanding for 50 years or more. Furthermore, urbanisation is reducing the population pressure on the land, opening up new opportunities for forests to expand. Forest products are also more sustainable than ever before, with a high recycled content, low energy requirements for production and low inputs of roundwood per unit of output.

In addition to these trends, Europe's forests remain very important for many Europeans, but in a broader social and environmental context. For example, forests are recognised as important parts of the landscape and are valued for the important services that they provide, such as protection and biodiversity conservation and as a setting for recreation. There is also growing recognition of the role that they could play in mitigating climate change.

The importance of forests in Europe is also recognised by governments. Evidence of this is the strong European support given to national and international policy processes related to forests. In addition, there has often been a rapid and strong response to perceived threats to forests, such as the concern over "forest death" in the 1980s or concerns regularly expressed about forest fires.

For many Europeans, particularly in Western Europe, the non-wood benefits of forests are probably now more important than those connected with the supply of wood. This presents some challenges for the sector, because it is still the production of forest products that creates most of the income for forest owners. Many of these other benefits may be valued highly, but this value can not be easily translated to income in the marketplace. The challenge for the sector will be to mobilise the public and political support behind European forestry to ensure that Europe's strong traditions of high quality forest management can be sustained in the future.

The trends described above reflect the gradual transition in Europe towards a post-industrial society. This is a natural consequence of the historical trends in income, population, urbanisation and economic development. It is against this background that the future role of the forest sector in society needs to be assessed.

5.2   *Summary of the main conclusions*

The analysis presented in this report has described in great detail the trends in the forest sector over the last few decades and the outlook to 2020. Despite this immense amount of detail, there are four major conclusions that can be drawn from this analysis. They are presented here below, before the remainder of this chapter goes on to describe the conclusions and recommendations of the study in more detail.

Wood production will shift to the East. The forest sector in Europe will continue to develop along different paths, depending on the trends in socio-economic development in the different sub-regions. In Eastern Europe and the CIS sub-region, the rapid and dramatic changes that have occurred over the last decade have placed these countries in a very competitive position in terms of wood supply and production costs. Production of forest products in these two sub-regions is expected to increase dramatically in the future. In contrast, the forest sector in Western Europe is likely to continue to expand to meet a broader set of objectives that will meet the changing needs of society in these countries. The industry in Western Europe will have a competitive advantage in the production of high value-added products and is likely to continue to focus on technology and marketing as part of knowledge-based growth in the future.

Policy developments will continue to have a major impact on all parts of the forest sector. The analysis has shown how historical policy developments have resulted in significant shifts in the sector, in terms of costs, prices, technology and raw material supplies. In particular, it has shown that cross-sectoral policy impacts have a strong influence on the sector. The challenge for the future will be for the forest sector to adapt and evolve to remain competitive in the changing policy environment.

Forests have a huge potential to contribute to sustainable development. To some extent, the forest sector in Europe has been a victim of its own success. Improvements in processing technology, silviculture and recycling have led to a sector that is now more sustainable than ever before. High quality products can now be produced from much lower inputs of wood raw materials and this trend is likely to continue in the future. Forests in Europe are also growing faster than ever before and faster than they are being cut. This presents an opportunity to further broaden the scope of management objectives if the difficulties of financing can be resolved.

Economic conditions are likely to remain challenging in the future. The current trends towards globalisation, competition from low-cost suppliers and greater demands placed on the sector are likely to continue in the future. However, it is expected that the sector will adapt and rise to meet these challenges, as it has done in the past.

5.3   General market outlook

Over the next 20 years, GDP growth rates will decrease in Western Europe in line with historical trends. For example, the baseline projection suggests that annual GDP growth in Western Europe will decrease from 2.4 percent to 1.2 percent over the next 20 years. In the other two sub-regions, GDP growth is expected to increase over the next two decades, due to convergence between these countries and Western Europe. The main risk to this growth is related to whether these countries will continue to progress towards democracy and a market economy as fast as they have in the past.

Based on these economic growth rates, consumption and production of forest products is expected to show stable growth in Western Europe, with growth gradually declining in the later part of the period. Paper consumption will increase most rapidly in the future, while sawnwood will become relatively less important due to a low growth rate of consumption. During the next 20 years, average annual growth in consumption is expected to amount to 2.0 percent for paper and paperboard, 1.9 percent for wood-based panels and 0.9 percent for sawnwood.

Growth rates will be considerably higher in Eastern Europe and the CIS sub-region as per capita consumption levels in these two sub-regions rise towards the level in Western Europe. This is partly due to the relatively high income elasticity of consumption in these countries and the high economic growth expected in the future. A summary of the projected growth rates for all of the sub-regions is given in Table 30

Table 30   *Average annual projected growth rates in production and consumption of forest products from 2000 to 2020 under the baseline scenario*

Product	Europe	EFSOS sub-regions		
		Western Europe	Eastern Europe	CIS
Production				
Sawnwood	2.3%	0.9%	2.3%	5.2%
Wood based panels	2.7%	1.9%	3.6%	6.0%
Paper and paperboard	2.6%	2.0%	5.0%	6.1%
Consumption				
Sawnwood	1.8%	0.8%	2.4%	5.0%
Wood based panels	2.6%	1.8%	4.0%	6.2%
Paper and paperboard	2.9%	2.3%	5.4%	6.0%

The forecasts of production show that the balance of production in the European forest products sector will shift firmly towards the east. For example, annual growth in production in Eastern Europe will be about twice the level of growth in Western Europe across all product categories and growth in the CIS sub-region will be as much as three times higher. Nevertheless, Western Europe will remain the largest producer of all forest products in Europe, accounting for 78 percent of paper production, 63 percent of wood based panel production and 48 percent of sawnwood production in the year 2020.

Likewise, trade patterns will change, with a significant absolute and relative increase in exports from the east. This will occur as the Russian Federation and other countries succeed in redeveloping their forest sectors to supply the world's expanding markets in Asia as well as the traditional European markets.

5.4 Shifting balance in wood production

The most profound and rapid changes in the forest sector over the next 20 years will take place in the Eastern Europe and CIS sub-regions. The complex process of transition to market economies started in these countries in the early 1990s, but the nature and pace of transition has varied widely. Some "advanced reform" countries have nearly completed the transition process and have entered the EU, while others have only just started to put in place the necessary framework for reforms.

While this process is important for all sectors, the forest sector will be called upon to play a special role in many of these countries for a variety of reasons, such as the following:

- several of the countries have large forest resources with a significant economic potential;

- the forest sector requires relatively little investment to obtain significant revenues from exports of wood raw materials and primary processed products;

- labour forms an important part of the cost structure for harvesting and primary processing and many of these countries have a strong comparative advantage in labour costs;

- per capita consumption levels of forest products are low in many of these countries, chiefly because of the low levels of the housing stock and the historical preference for other materials, so forest products will play a large role in the reconstruction of these countries.

Finally, because of the sheer size of the forest resource in the Russian Federation and the potential to increase exports significantly, developments in that country will strongly influence the global supply and demand balance for forest products. For example, the CIS sub-region's share of total European production of all forest products (measured in WRME) will increase from 10 percent at present to 20 percent by 2020.

Table 31   **Sub-regional shares of total European production and consumption of forest products in 2000 and 2020**

Product	Western Europe		Eastern Europe		CIS	
	2000	2020	2000	2020	2000	2020
Production						
Sawnwood	62%	48%	20%	20%	19%	33%
Wood based panels	73%	63%	18%	21%	9%	17%
Paper and paperboard	87%	78%	7%	11%	6%	11%
Consumption						
Sawnwood	73%	60%	14%	16%	13%	25%
Wood based panels	77%	65%	16%	21%	7%	14%
Paper and paperboard	86%	76%	10%	16%	4%	8%

Table 32   **Net trade by European sub-region in 2000 and 2020 (in millions)**

Product	Western Europe		Eastern Europe		CIS	
	2000	2020	2000	2000	2020	2000
Sawnwood (in CUM)	-8.8	-8.2	+8.4	+12.5	+7.9	+23.5
Wood based panels (in CUM)	-1.7	-1.2	+0.9	+0.2	+1.2	+3.3
Paper and paperboard (in MT)	+9.3	+6.1	-1.9	-7.1	+1.6	+5.3

Note: positive values are net exports and negative values are net imports.

Over the next 20 years, it is also expected that production and consumption will increase rapidly in Eastern Europe and even faster in the CIS sub-region, shifting the balance of European forest product production and consumption to the east (see Table 31). Domestic forest products markets will be transformed, with per capita consumption figures in Eastern Europe and the CIS sub-region approaching, but not overtaking, those of Western Europe.

Trade patterns will also change as net exports increase strongly, in particular from the CIS sub-region. Net exports from Eastern Europe will increase less rapidly and even decline in some cases, because the domestic market will grow as fast as or faster than domestic production. The main developments in European net exports in the future will come from the Russian Federation (see Table 32).

According to the trade analysis and econometric projections, the comparative advantage in the Russian Federation will be in sawnwood rather than in the other products. However, exports of all forest products are expected to expand (as in recent years), but not as quickly as sawnwood.

This expansion of production, consumption and trade is, of course, dependent on higher levels of fellings in all countries in Eastern Europe and the CIS sub-region. The ratio of fellings to net annual increment, which is a crude indicator of the sustainability of wood supply, is expected to rise in all of these countries, but it is not expected to exceed 100 percent.

5.5   Cross-sectoral policy impacts

The historical analysis of markets and policy developments has shown how policies outside the forest sector can have a major impact on forest products markets and other developments in the sector. In the future, it is expected that environmental policies will continue to be particularly important in two areas: a greater emphasis on recycling; and development of renewable energy programmes and policies.

5.5.1   Recycling and residue use will continue to expand

In environmental terms, forest products have a distinct advantage in that they can generally be recycled relatively easily. At present, less than half of the wood and fibre used to manufacture forest products in Western Europe comes from trees (the figure for all of Europe is about 60 percent) and the remainder comes from recycled wood and fibre. This trend towards greater use of recycled material has been partly driven by market forces, but a much more pervasive force has been environmental legislation that has encouraged consumers to recycle waste and required producers to use recycled materials. A more recent development has been the imposition of stricter waste controls and landfill taxes that have further increased the incentives to recycle products.

In all future scenarios, it is projected that wood and wood products will be used in an efficient way, resulting in minimum waste and high use of recycled and recovered sources of wood and fibre. This will include wood residues and recovered paper, but it may also include the greater use of recovered solid wood products in the future. Furthermore, there may be a trend towards some exports of residues from the CIS sub-region (with many sawmills) to other countries.

By 2020, it is expected that recovered paper will account for 48 percent of the fibre used to manufacture paper and paperboard in Europe. Furthermore, about 57 percent of the paper and paperboard consumed each year will be recovered. In Western Europe, the collection and use of recovered paper will even be slightly higher than this and will be close to the maximum that is currently technically feasible. In broader terms, the importance of industrial roundwood in the total consumption of wood and fibre will fall slightly to 45 percent in Western Europe (55 percent in Europe as a whole) by 2020.

Furthermore, much of the recycled wood and fibre that can not be used as a raw material for the forest processing sector will probably be used to generate energy. This will make a further contribution to the sustainability of the European economy as whole and reduce the burden of waste disposal.

5.5.2 Renewable energy policies will increase the demand for wood

Over the next 20 years, it is considered very likely that policies will be put in place to promote the production and use of renewable energy. According to the policy analysis, it is expected that renewable energy policies will affect the FOWL area slightly, by encouraging the establishment of short-rotation forest plantations for woodfuel production. Furthermore, the promotion of renewable energy and policies to mitigate climate change are also expected to raise levels of removals, production and trade of forest products in almost all subregions. It is believed that this will occur partly because wood is a renewable energy source, but also because the manufacturing of forest products requires a relatively low level of energy use.

The analysis has not been able to explore the outlook for woodfuel in any depth, due to problems with the statistics for this forest product. However, it is expected that one of the likely consequences of renewable energy promotion could be the creation of a major new market for small-sized roundwood. This could also encourage more active forest management and possibly the reintroduction of coppicing systems, which are well suited to the rapid production of small-sized roundwood.

Concern has been expressed by existing consumers of small-sized roundwood about the effect of higher woodfuel demand on the availability and price of their raw material. Undoubtedly, an increase in demand will tend to lead to an increase in prices. However, this will benefit forest owners, many of whom are facing the lowest roundwood prices they have seen for decades. Furthermore, as shown above, in all three of the future scenarios there is a considerable "biological" margin (at least at the sub-regional level) between future roundwood demand and the potential roundwood supply. This would be increased further if special measures were used to increase the supply of small-sized roundwood for woodfuel production (e.g. short-rotation forest plantations). Thus, it is quite possible that very modest increases in demand could bring forth large increases in supply.

The creation of a dynamic woodfuel market probably will increase prices by creating competition for small-sized roundwood where before there had been little or none. Given the likelihood of these policies being introduced and the complex consequences and interactions that may occur, there is an urgent need to explore this issue further in a rigorous and transparent way, so that appropriate policies can be designed and implemented in the future.

5.6 Contribution to sustainable development

An innovation in this iteration of the outlook for Europe has been a deeper investigation of the outlook for some of the other non-market aspects of European forestry. The following section briefly reviews some of the conclusions about the contribution of the forest sector to sustainable development.

5.6.1 Europe's expanding forest resource

The total forest area in Europe is expected to increase by around five percent between 2000 and 2020. This will occur due to a mixture of afforestation and natural processes and will occur both on former agricultural land as well as along the tree margin in mountain and boreal areas.

The increase in Western Europe is expected to be higher than the European average, due to policies in agriculture, rural development and land-use shifting slightly in favour of forestry. However, the FAWS area might decrease, due to increasing demands to set-aside forests for other functions, such as: biodiversity conservation; recreation; and protective functions.

Due to the existing age-class structure of European forests, average increment will continue to increase over the next two decades, but this increase will slow down markedly by 2020 (and may reverse thereafter). There are also studies that indicate that the productivity of European forest sites is increasing. While experts link this phenomenon to climate change or nutrient deposition, there is not yet sufficient evidence to support this hypothesis, so it has not been taken into consideration in the outlook for forest resources.

5.6.2 Fellings and annual increment in Europe

At the moment, about 60 percent of the annual increment on FOWL is harvested in Europe. Together with the future development of increment, this will cause the growing stock volume to increase significantly over the next two decades. This expected difference between fellings and increment presents a range of opportunities to increase fellings and/or set-aside forest areas for purposes other than roundwood production. In general, forest damage does not appear to be increasing at the European level, but constant vigilance will be required to ensure that potential risks to the sustainable development of forest resources are kept under control (see Box 9).

Box 9 **Forest fires threaten long-term sustainable forest management in some areas**

Every year in southern Europe, 500 thousand ha of forest are burned, along with up to 2 million ha in the Russian Federation. These fires cause losses of life and natural resources and result in significant environmental costs. The continuing high cost of forest fires, whether in the Mediterranean forests of Southern Europe or the remote boreal forests of the Russian Federation, is preventing the affected areas from supplying the functions that they should. Even though fires are inevitable in most forest ecosystems and may even be natural and beneficial in some circumstances (e.g. assisting with regeneration of some species), the levels of fire damage experienced very recently are not sustainable.

The causes of forest fires are complex, but relatively well known to experts. They result from the interaction of the following: natural causes (e.g. lightning) or, more frequently in Europe, human negligence or arson; hot and dry weather conditions; forests with high "fuel" content; and insufficient speed and technical means for rapid and effective fire suppression. The broad lines of a fire control strategy involve attacking all of the causes simultaneously (e.g. through social/police/educational measures to reduce the human element in fire outbreaks; silvicultural measures like clearing of brush to reduce the fuel load; and rapid and effective fire response). However, to implement these measures requires significant resources and political will sustained over long periods.

In recent years, especially in 2003, the cost of not taking these measures has become clear to all – loss of life and property, charred landscapes that have lost their amenity value, economic potential and soil retention capacity, as well as enormous emissions of carbon to the atmosphere. If the forecasts of the global climate change models prove correct, this danger will increase significantly in the long-run due to the increased frequency of hot dry summers.

The roundwood supply potential in the CIS sub-region is much higher than in Western and Eastern Europe. Currently in the CIS sub-region, only 25 percent of annual increment is removed during felling. However, based on various literature sources, unrecorded and unregulated felling may be as much as 15 percent to 30 percent of recorded fellings in some places. This poses a threat to sustainable development in some areas and in for some tree species.

The projected increases in production of wood products in Europe can be covered by the potential roundwood supply, without threatening the sustainability of forest resources. However, increasing supply efficiently will depend on future costs and prices and the behaviour of forest owners. For example, there is tremendous scope for the utilisation of new, highly efficient harvesting technologies. In some countries the use of these technologies might increase, if the problems associated with small-scale forest ownership could be overcome (see Box 10). Further migration from rural to urban areas, as well as restitution or privatisation of forests in countries in transition, will also pose new challenges in many countries.

In all of the alternative scenarios examined in the analysis, the level of fellings required to meet derived raw material raw demands are lower than the potential roundwood supply at the European level, although the levels of felling and potential supply will become close to each other in some countries (especially in Eastern Europe). The ratio of fellings to net annual increment, which is a crude but robust indicator of the sustainability of wood supply, is currently around 45 percent for Europe as a whole. In the baseline scenario this ratio would rise by 2020 to 60 percent and in the "integration" scenario, which assumes the highest level of demand for forest products, it would rise to 70 percent.

5.6.3 Biodiversity and nature conservation

There is widespread consensus that significant areas of forest and other wooded land should be managed for the conservation of biodiversity and that other forest areas, to varying degrees, should also be managed for this objective. At the Ministerial Conference in Helsinki in 1993, the ministers for forestry committed themselves to conserving and maintaining biodiversity, including the establishment *"at national or regional levels (of) a coherent ecological network of climax, primary and other special forests aimed at maintaining or re-establishing ecosystems that are representative or threatened"*. However, concern has been expressed, notably by forest owners and forest industries, that these measures would constrain potential wood supply in Europe and increase the costs of silviculture to levels that are not economically viable.

The contribution of the EFSOS to this debate can only be limited, because operational decisions on conservation and the maintenance of biodiversity must be local and specific in nature (although they should also be established within in a broader framework). Forests have different biodiversity values and different financial values. For example, in many cases, forests with high biodiversity values are remote or stocked with tree species that are commercially unattractive, so the financial costs of devoting these forests to biodiversity conservation are small. However, this is not always the case. For example, it has recently been noted that the most threatened natural forest ecosystems in Europe are those on fertile land and near potential markets, precisely because these forests have high potential to generate income from the harvesting of forest products.

The smallest geographical unit examined in the EFSOS analysis is a country, so the EFSOS cannot be used to answer these detailed operational questions of whether a particular forest should or should not be managed for conservation, roundwood production or a combination of objectives. However, the EFSOS can indicate, in a very general way, what might be the possible consequences of a conservation oriented policy for the production and consumption of forest products in the future.

The conservation scenario developed in the EFSOS was used to produce projections of future forest product production and consumption, under an assumption that more emphasis would be placed on the management of forests for conservation. Unfortunately, the tools available to model forest products supply and demand are driven by projections of economic growth and forest product prices, so they are not able to account for all of the subtle developments that might occur under a scenario of more forest conservation in the future. However, the results can be used to give some indications about what might happen if more conservation were to lead to a reduction in FAWS area and roundwood fellings in the future.

Table 33 shows the projections for production of forest products in the three European sub-regions under the baseline and conservation scenarios, along with the GDP and price projections used to produce these results.

For Western Europe, the results indicate that, compared with the baseline projection for 2020, the conservation scenario would show an 11 percent decrease in industrial roundwood supply with a six percent decrease in sawnwood production, an 11 percent decrease in wood based panel and paper and paperboard production and 11 percent increase in forest product prices. The effect of a reduction in supply on sawnwood production is much less than the other products, because of the use of imported industrial roundwood for sawnwood production in Europe.

For Eastern Europe, the results are quite similar, although the effect on sawnwood production would be much greater. However, in the CIS sub-region, the conservation scenario results in much lower production of industrial roundwood (about 32 percent) and even greater falls in production of the other processed forest products (38 percent to 42 percent).

Table 33   Comparison of baseline and conservation scenarios (production in millions)

Sub-region and product category	Baseline scenario			Conservation scenario			
	2000	2020	annual change	2000	2020	annual change	Change from baseline in 2020
Western Europe							
Industrial roundwood (in CUM)	247	301	+1.0%	247	269	+0.4%	-10.8%
Sawnwood (in CUM)	81	98	+0.9%	81	92	+0.6%	-6.1%
Wood based panels (in CUM)	44	65	+1.9%	44	58	+1.3%	-10.9%
Paper and paperboard (in MT)	87	129	+2.0%	87	115	+1.4%	-10.8%
GDP			+1.3%			+1.1%	
Prices			0.0%			+0.5%	+10.5%
Eastern Europe							
Industrial roundwood (in CUM)	100	129	+1.3%	100	113	+0.6%	-12.2%
Sawnwood (in CUM)	26	40	+2.3%	26	34	+1.4%	-15.5%
Wood based panels (in CUM)	11	22	+3.6%	11	17	+2.4%	-20.3%
Paper and paperboard (in MT)	7	18	+5.0%	7	13	+3.1%	-30.1%
GDP			+4.2%			+2.6%	
Prices			0.0%			+0.5%	+10.5%
CIS sub-region							
Industrial roundwood (in CUM)	116	227	+3.4%	116	154	+1.4%	-32.3%
Sawnwood (in CUM)	24	67	+5.2%	24	42	+2.7%	-37.7%
Wood based panels (in CUM)	5	17	+6.0%	5	10	+3.3%	-40.4%
Paper and paperboard (in MT)	6	18	+6.1%	6	11	+3.2%	-42.4%
GDP			+4.0%			+2.4%	
Prices			0.0%			+0.5%	+10.5%

5.7   Future economic conditions in the forest sector

5.7.1   Forest products trade

Trade flows are projected to change significantly, continuing recent European trends in this area. In particular, intensified trade is expected between Western Europe and the other two sub-regions. This changing trade pattern is expected to have a significant impact on removals in Western and Eastern Europe and possibly also on production of lower value forest products, which might be relocated to Eastern Europe due to lower production costs there.

Trade, both within Europe and between Europe and the rest of the world, is expected to increase. Some countries in Western Europe will remain major world exporters, although the sub-region will remain a net importer of many forest products. The level of net imports of industrial roundwood into Western Europe is expected to remain about the same in the future, as are net exports from the CIS sub-region net. However, net exports from Eastern Europe are expected to decline. This is because production of products such as sawnwood or panels in Eastern Europe is projected to grow faster than production. of industrial roundwood

In line with historical trends, the European forest sector is also expected to face increasing competition from producers outside the region. In this respect, the main competition is likely to come from the expansion of the forest sectors in countries with extensive areas of fast-growing forest plantations (mostly in the Southern Hemisphere). On the other hand, foreign export markets will also increase dramatically in some countries (e.g. China, India and Southeast Asia). These markets will present opportunities for export growth that are likely to be exploited by some of the European countries with large forest sectors (e.g. high value-added products from Nordic countries, wood based panels from Western Europe and a broad range of forest products from the Russian Federation).

5.7.2   Economic viability of forest management

Over the last few years there has been increasing concern expressed about the economic viability of forest management in Europe. Recent downward trends in prices and the generally low harvesting intensities in much of Europe all indicate that the income from forest operations is declining at the same time that costs may be rising (e.g. upward pressure on costs may come from rising labour costs, new developments such as forest certification and requirements to pursue non-wood management objectives).

As income from the sale of wood is, in most areas, the only significant revenue for forest owners, their ability to manage their forest for all of the multiple functions expected by society is constrained. The analysis suggests that the outlook for forest products prices is stable (i.e. there is little expectation that prices will rise in the future) and the options for reducing the costs of forest management seem limited. In fact, even this may be an optimistic view of the future. The competitive conditions in the global markets for most forest products (e.g. the availability of extremely productive and cheap sources of wood fibre outside Europe) indicate that there may be downward pressure on prices in the future. Furthermore, the outlook for population and employment in the sector suggests that the real level of wages in the sector may also rise.

There are possibilities to reduce costs by increasing efficiency in the sector (e.g. following the example of the Nordic countries, which have expensive labour and raw material costs, but remain competitive through system optimisation), but these are limited. There is also the potential to develop markets for previously non-marketed goods and services (protection, water supply, some forms of recreation etc.), or to develop systems whereby the state substitutes for the market by paying the costs of supplying certain public goods. Therefore, it appears that, without appropriate policy intervention to correct the situation, the economic viability of European forest management will remain threatened.

5.7.3   Forest sector institutions will continue to evolve rapidly

Forest sector institutions and legal frameworks have adapted to changing circumstances, notably increases in the number of stakeholders and the complexity of forestry issues, financial pressures arising from reduced profitability of forest management and the need to control government expenditure, emerging new ownership patterns in the transition countries (see Box 10) and, in some countries, decentralisation of decision making.

Management of public forests has often been separated institutionally from administration of the forest law and laws have changed to allow more freedom of choice to owners. Extension campaigns have been carried out to influence forest owners' behaviour instead of setting up legal requirements to be enforced by administrative means. National forest programmes have been drawn up in a participatory and holistic framework to achieve consensus from all stakeholders as to broad goals and frameworks.

The continuing increase in the demand for forest services, the likely developments for energy, climate change, trade and environmental policy, as well as the reduced economic viability of forest management, will continue to place a strain on forest sector institutions and policies. This will force them to adapt to ever-changing circumstances, as well as opening the decision processes to many specialists who are not conventionally trained foresters (e.g. ecologists, sociologists, communicators, etc.).

Box 10   ***Development of a private forestry co-operative network in Lithuania - benefits to forest owners from better market organisation***

The forest restitution process in Lithuania created more than 200,000 private forest owners, each with a very small forest holding (average of 5 ha). Due to these small areas, forest management is complicated and relatively expensive. Furthermore, this problem is magnified because most forest owners have limited or no knowledge about forest management and usually live far from their property.

In 1998, the first forest owners' co-operative started activities. In a very short time, several co-operatives developed, as the industrial demand for roundwood and the demand for forestry services (from owners) rapidly increased. By 2004, a network of small companies and forestry co-operatives was established under the Forest Owners Association of Lithuania. The volume of roundwood marketed through this network increased from only 30,000 m^3 in 2001, to 500,000 m^3 by 2004. This is equal to a 20 percent share of the roundwood supply from private forests or 10 percent of total Lithuanian roundwood supply.

Currently, the network comprises more than 20 small companies and co-operatives, employing 100 skilled foresters that offer a full range of forestry services to more than 4,000 forest owners. The network operates on two levels. In the field, co-operatives advise local forest owners and consolidate production volumes. These are then marketed through a roundwood trading company that specialises in supplying the largest buyers.

Forest owners can participate in the network in a number of different ways. They can be a full member of a co-operative, they can sign a long-term forest management agreement, they can sell standing timber (or a whole forest) through the network or they can simply buy forestry services. The network has become the largest roundwood supplier in Lithuania, because it achieves sales prices that are about 10 percent higher than the market average (due to better bargaining power at the large scale). These benefits are then passed back to the forest owner. For comparison, before the co-operative movement took off, roundwood from private forests sold for 20 percent less than the market average.

The outlook for the network is very positive. The network has credibility with the largest buyers in the market. The network is also looking at future alliances, co-operation and vertical integration to lead to further benefits that can be passed on to the small-scale forest owners who are members of the co-operatives.

Source: Forest Owners Association of Lithuania.

5.8   Are European forests sustainable in the long term?

Ultimately the major question which EFSOS, like its predecessors, is designed to answer is: *"what are the threats to the long-term sustainable development of European forests and what can be done to reduce them?"* What is the required contribution of forest management to sustainable development of forest resources in Europe and how should Europe be linked to global requirements for sustainable development of forest resources?

The scenarios set out above, although focussed on the use of wood, and thus under-emphasising the non-wood aspects, do describe a number of alternative futures, all of which appear to be sustainable, at least during the next 20 years and from the perspective of roundwood supply. However, this should not lead to complacency: there are some developments that, if unchecked, could threaten sustainable forest management at the European level. These are the aspects that need to be monitored and to be the focus of concern over the forthcoming years.

A preliminary list of threats to sustainable forest management in Europe would include (sorted by the three pillars of sustainable development):

Economic pillar

- Increasing problems with economic viability of forest management, due to rising costs and stagnant prices for roundwood.

- Loss of end-use market shares to other regions' forest products and to competing materials, through reduced competitiveness and weak marketing and product development, threatening the European forest industry and forest owners.

- Constraints on public budgets, reducing governments' ability to counteract the problems of economic viability mentioned above.

- In CIS sub-region, the weakness of many institutions and the resulting governance problems that could prevent these countries achieving their full economic potential.

Social pillar

- The labour force may become too old, insufficiently skilled, too numerous to carry out the necessary tasks effectively and efficiently. There is a need to reduce numbers and train and recruit younger staff.

- Foresters and forest administrations lack skills for new participatory forest management: this could lead to policies and decisions that do not properly take into account some aspects of forestry development.

- Occupational safety and health of forest workers are still inadequate in many countries.

- Because of economic problems and declining forest sector employment, forests may not contribute properly to rural development.

- Need for improved forest law enforcement and governance where "illegal logging" is a serious problem, leading to erosion of state authority, loss of revenue and unfair competition.

- Inability to prevent forest fires (this threat concerns all 3 pillars).

Environmental pillar

- Network of protected and protective forests not yet complete. Remaining uncertainty about how much is and should be "protected" and in what way.

- Need to protect endangered forest types (including those in fertile, used areas).

- Need to improve protection of biodiversity in managed forests.

- Local damages from pollution, pests and game etc.

5.9 Policy recommendations

This section presents, on the responsibility of the secretariat, some recommendations for policy, based on the EFSOS analysis as well as other relevant documents, such as reports by the Timber Committee the European Forestry Commission and the MCPFE. Each conclusion indicates clearly to whom it is addressed (in brackets after the title). It is suggested that these should be discussed by all stakeholders at the European level as a follow-up action to this study.

5.9.1 Need for policies to stimulate the sound use of wood (governments, forest industries, forest owners)

Wood is an ecologically friendly and renewable raw material. Governments and EU institutions should develop a policy and legislative framework to support and promote the sound use of wood as an integral part of overall sustainable development considering long-term sustainable development of forest resources. All major forest sector stakeholders should identify and implement new financial mechanisms to support these actions.

This is particularly necessary in those countries where the "wood culture" is weak, which is the case in many countries in Eastern Europe at present (where changes to historical traditions in wooden house construction and the use of wood for energy generation could significantly contribute to this issue).

Policies and resources should be devoted to stimulating and facilitating the creation of multi-stakeholder partnerships to promote the sound use of wood. Wood procurement policies that encourage the sustainable management of forests, without creating barriers to trade, should be developed. Governments should provide information on, and promote the use of, environmentally friendly consumer products, energy supplies, and building construction products and systems derived from forest resources and encourage research into the sound and innovative use of wood (e.g. life cycle inventory and analysis) and take this information into account when formulating policy.

5.9.2 Urgent need to address threats to sustainability in south-east Europe and the CIS sub-region (governments, donors)

While there are few urgent problems threatening the sustainability of forest management in most countries of western, central and northern Europe, this is not the case in some of the countries of the Balkan region, the western CIS, the Caucasus and central Asia. Although the situation in these countries is not well understood by the international community (indeed some of them are not covered in a quantitative way in the present study, because of lack of data), it is clear that poverty, civil disturbance or war, with weak institutions, have put these countries in an unsustainable situation with excessive forest fires, increasing wood demand, notably for fuel wood, overgrazing, illegal logging leading to forest depletion, shortages of forest products, erosion and deforestation, even desertification. A special problem concerns the management of forests contaminated by radioactivity, notably, but not exclusively, as a result of the Chernobyl catastrophe.

In addition to these pressing threats to the forest, some of the countries (e.g. those with significant forest resources) are not using the potential of the forest sector to contribute to their development. Experience in the Baltic countries and others in Eastern Europe has shown to what extent the sector can contribute to economic development.

The countries themselves should give sufficient political priority to forest issues in their development programmes and the international community should help them. A first step would be to understand the issues better and bring these countries into closer contact with the international community so that feasible national forest programmes are developed and then implemented. The FAO and UNECE structures could play a major role in this effort.

5.9.3 Need to devote policy attention to the consequences of the dynamic developments in Eastern Europe and the CIS sub-region (governments)

The likely developments outlined above for Eastern Europe and the CIS sub-region will have a significant impact on forest products trade and production in Western Europe and Asian markets. The depth and duration of these developments will depend on the level of investment in the forest sector. Further policy analysis is needed of the consequences of these trends, and the dialogue between East and West should be intensified in order to assist with the sustainable development of the forest sector and to avoid any undesirable outcomes. Governments and other stakeholders in Eastern Europe and the CIS sub-region need be adequately involved in the international and global policy dialogue. Mutual economic opportunities and challenges should be analysed more consistently, in order to provide a basis for reliable strategic decision making.

5.9.4 Improve the economic viability of forest management in Europe (governments, forest industries, research community)

The EFSOS analysis confirms the perception that there is a significant structural threat to the economic viability of forest management, arising from falling revenues from wood sales, constantly rising management costs and the inability to transform the multiple services and non-wood goods provided by the forest into secure revenue streams. This is now widely recognised and at the Vienna Ministerial conference the ministers committed to implement a series of measures, including to:

- support sound enabling conditions for sustainable forest management that encourage investment and economic activity in the forest sector;

- promote the use of wood from sustainably managed forests;

- work towards common approaches to the practical application of the valuation of the full range of goods and services provided by forests;

- enhance the competitiveness of the forest sector by promoting innovation and entrepreneurship among all relevant stakeholders;

- support research as well as mechanisms for the dissemination of generated knowledge, enhance the quality of education, training, extension and skills;

- strengthen the support of institutions concerned with workforce safety and education as well as related research;

- enhance inter-sectoral co-ordination and collaboration, promote the incorporation of sustainable forest management into rural development policies and strategies;

- promote the use of innovative economic instruments for achieving forest related goals and targets, encourage the voluntary co-operation of forest owners in particular of small-scale forest holdings; and

- promote the development of and encourage the participation in associations of forest owners, of the forest workforce and of forest entrepreneurs, in particular in central and eastern European countries.

Governments should attach sufficient political priority to implementing the commitments made in Vienna.

5.9.5 Balanced implementation of wood energy policies (governments)

Given the likely policies to promote renewable energies and the desirability of developing new markets for roundwood, governments should promote wood energy production and use notably by acting to raise prices for fossil energies, considering a broader context of overall sustainable development. Governments should fund research and development into wood energies and create the necessary infrastructure for a modern and competitive wood energy sector (technical and economic measures, such as standards, transparent market information, standard contracts, demonstration plants).

In these circumstances, pulpwood using industries and their suppliers would probably see an increase in their raw material costs, but would also have a major commercial opportunity, to transform themselves into wood energy suppliers (in addition to their traditional activities). These policies should be developed through widespread consultation of all stakeholders to maximise wood energy's contribution to the energy economy while minimising damage to existing industries or biodiversity (e.g. through energy plantations). Energy issues should be given high importance in developing forest sector strategies and policies and the possible interactions examined in depth.

5.9.6 Forestry, wood and climate change (governments, research institutions)

Given the complexities of the climate change policy debate, and the potential for significant change in the sector, forest sector institutions should be proactive in analysing the consequences of climate change policy decisions for the sector, and urgently take measures to reconcile provisions of climate and energy policies, strategies and commitments with national forest programmes and other forest sector planning documents. These should cover not only the Kyoto Protocol provisions for land use land use change and forestry and the possibility for offsetting carbon emissions by measures in this field, but also the role of wood products as a carbon store as well as the possibility for mitigating consequences for European forest ecosystems of climate change, such as higher average temperatures, less precipitation, more "extreme events" (e.g. storms, floods) as forecast by global climate change models.

5.9.7 Forest law enforcement and governance (governments, all stakeholders)

Bad law enforcement and governance pose a threat to forests. It has a negative impact on economic development, as taxes are not provided to the public budgets. Governments should work together, first to ensure that domestic forest law enforcement and governance are at an acceptable level, and then to help other countries, inside and outside the region, to improve the situation in this respect. Another goal here is not to lose competitiveness on environmentally oriented wood markets. It should be stressed that sustainable forest management in all countries is threatened by bad governance in a few, because of the damage done to the image of wood and forest products (which may be only partially corrected by certification measures), as well as the downward pressure on prices and reduced economic viability resulting from competition from illegally logged timber and its products, on markets all over the world.

5.9.8   Institutional change in countries in transition (governments, international institutions)

There have been profound and rapid changes in the forest sector institutions of many of the advanced reform countries in Eastern Europe, which have left them much better equipped than in the past to face the challenges of the future. Examples of the areas where there have been profound changes are: restitution and privatisation of forests; help to new private forest owners; and effective law enforcement. Yet many countries are only just starting on the complex processes, and could benefit from the experience accumulated up to now. There is also considerable interest in monitoring progress in these policy and institutional developments, as witnessed by the participation in the FAO-UNECE team of specialists working in this area. A network focused on transition issues might be created to exchange opinion and experience on forest sector institutions in Europe and monitor changes, possibly based on previous FAO-UNECE work.

5.9.9   Monitoring environmental and social benefits from forests and forestry (governments, international organisations, research institutions)

Although the importance of environmental and social benefits of the forest in Europe is widely recognised, there are still rather few reliable quantitative and policy relevant data available to policy makers. The situation in this respect has improved notably over recent years, especially since the putting in place of criteria and indicators of sustainable forest management at the national and international levels, but is still not satisfactory.

If trends are to be monitored and the correct decisions taken, there is a need for a continuing monitoring network for these aspects, of comparable quality to that for wood and forest products, integrated with that for other related sectors, and preferably generating internationally comparable information, all at an acceptable cost.

Many organisations are working on these issues, but there is a need for political will and resources, over an adequate period, to provide a satisfactory instrument for well informed policy discussions, and for careful coordination of efforts and good communication between all actors.   An intermediate goal in the field of monitoring should be improved reporting to the Warsaw Ministerial Conference in 2007, compared to the report to the Vienna Conference in 2003, itself a significant improvement on earlier reports.

5.9.10 Necessity of a cross-sectoral approach (governments, all stakeholders)

Forest sector stakeholders should intensify the policy dialogue, proactively drawing the attention of other policy areas such as agriculture, trade, environment and energy to the social and environmental benefits of sustainable forest management, as one component of the overall sustainable development of society. The Timber Committee, the European Forestry Commission, MCPFE and other national and international forest sector policy bodies, active in the region, can facilitate this dialogue substantially. The goal is to strengthen the position of the forest sector on the national and international policy scene and to increase its policy weight and influence.

The policy dialogue between the forest sector and other parts of society should be strengthened by organising various forums (e.g. "Round tables") with representatives of all stakeholder groups, whose impact is related to the development of the European forest sector. The UNECE, with its unique sectoral structure, is an appropriate forum for this work, provided that the cooperation of the other UNECE Principal Subsidiary Bodies can be obtained and the necessary resources are made available.

If there is to be a rational discussion of policy issues affecting forests, institutions, inside and outside the forest sector, must be modified so that the cross sectoral approach is incorporated from the beginning, and that the results are transmitted to other policy processes. There has been considerable progress in this direction, noted by the Vienna resolution, but much remains to be done as regards concrete measures, such as institutional adaptations, and change in the mentalities of policy makers and the experts who advise them.

5.9.11 Need to control forest fires, and to intensify international cooperation in this area (governments, forest owners)

The highest political authorities of southern Europe and the Russian Federation should attach sufficient priority to controlling forest fires and to creating the necessary mechanisms and institutions, with sufficient resources, to achieve the desired goals.

There is a deep reservoir of knowledge and experience that can be accessed through international co-operation (e.g. FAO, UNECE, Global Fire Monitoring Centre and others), as well as the potential to share expensive resources (water bombers, highly trained fire crews) between countries. Thus, national strategies for forest fire control should also address international co-operation.

5.9.12 Employment and the work force (governments, employers, unions)

The continued decline in employment in the sector will further reduce the visibility of the sector and partly its direct benefits to society. Rural livelihoods will be most affected as the losses are concentrated in forestry and in small firms in the other sub-sectors. If the forest industry is to make a contribution to rural development in Europe, growth patterns need to be reviewed and altered. Small enterprise development, including of forestry contractors, pursuing a strategy of quality and higher value added in addition to the provision and marketing of non-traditional goods and services will be important elements of any strategy to mitigate the withdrawal of the forest sector from rural areas and the continued shift to capital intensive modes of production. Key players in the forest sector (in particular from Nordic countries) are acting more and more globally, shifting capacities toward eastern Europe because of lower production costs and expected increases in the demand of forest products. This process depends on further stabilization in the policy framework as well as on the economic growth in these countries. This will have an additional impact on employment in the traditional producer countries.

In spite of the decline in employment volumes, the sector is likely to be faced with difficulties in finding adequate employees with relevant qualifications in the future, not least because of demographic trends in Europe. These shortages may only concern the inability to attract new entrants with good qualifications and potential, or could translate into absolute shortages. In some major producer countries, these are expected to limit the potential for growth in output. This issue would appear to merit closer scrutiny at the national and local level. Improvements in employment quality such as wages, training and career prospects, as well as working environment and safety, will be critical to maintain adequate levels of new workers, in particular women.

5.9.13 Developing the region's comparative advantages (forest industries, governments)

In the increasingly competitive global markets, often dominated by extremely efficient low cost, large scale producers, the European industry and its raw material suppliers, the forest owners of Europe, have been put on the defensive in many areas, partly through a high cost structure and partly through inflexibility and inability to take the radical measures necessary to maintain and improve a competitive edge. There is a need to identify, region by region, what are Europe's areas of comparative advantage and disadvantage in the forest/timber field, and how they should be developed. Examples of advantages are good infrastructure and closeness to markets, high quality of products and processes, access to capital, ability to optimise processes to reduce costs, good skills in design and marketing. Examples of disadvantages are high costs, slow economic growth, relatively unfavourable growing conditions, inflexibility of wood supply and institutions. Companies should develop their own competitive strategies, but it is almost inevitable that governments should be involved, given the long term nature of the decisions and the fact that many millions of hectares of forest are owned and/or managed by public agencies.

5.9.14 The European forest sector in the global context (all stakeholders)

In a period of general globalisation of companies, NGOs, economic, social and environmental agreements and processes, one of the principal questions is: How can forest policy making - still focused at the national level - respond to the changing global environment? European forest sector stakeholders should strengthen their efforts on an international level. The European experiences in sustainable forest management needs to be promoted more actively on a global level (e.g. in discussions and activities concerning certification of forests and forest products).

6 REFERENCES

Aldrian, A, Bauer, A, Eberl, W, Rametsteiner, E, Sekot, W, Wagner, S, and Weiss, G, 2004, Austria country report, report for EC COST E30 Project.

Baruffol, U, Baur, P, Dürrenmatt, R, Kammerhofer, A, Zimmermann, W, Schmithüsen, F, 2003, EU-project evaluating financing of forestry in Europe: Country report Switzerland, Swiss Federal Institute of Technology, Zürich, Switzerland.

Bauer, J, Kniivilä, M, and Schmithüsen, F, 2004, Forest Legislation in Europe, Geneva Timber and Forest Discussion Paper ECE/TIM/DP/37, United Nations, Geneva, Switzerland.

Blombäck, P, Poschen, P, and Lövgren, M, 2003, Employment trends and prospects in the European forest sector, Geneva Timber and Forest Discussion Paper ECE/TIM/DP/29, United Nations, Geneva, Switzerland.

Broadhead, J, Bahdon, J, and Whiteman, A, in prep, Past trends and future prospects for the utilisation of wood for energy, Global Forest Products Outlook Study Working Paper No. GFPOS/WP/05, Food and Agriculture Organization of the United Nations, Rome, Italy.

Bromhead, A, 2000, Timber and wood products, Timber Trades Journal, 29th January 2000, pp 10-11.

Brown, C, 2000, The outlook for future wood supply from forest plantations, Global Forest Products Outlook Study Working Paper No. GFPOS/WP/03, Food and Agriculture Organization of the United Nations, Rome, Italy.

Bouriaud, L, Nichiforel, L, Nastase, C, Dragoi, S, Padureanu, L, and Borlea, G F, 2004, Romania country report, report for EC COST E30 Project.

Carvalho Mendes, A M S, 2004, Portugal country report, report for EC COST E30 Project.

Chobanova, R, Mihova, K, Ivanova, D, Koleva, V, Hristova, G, Doichinova, H, Bonev, K, Tzolova, R, and Terzieva, T, 2004, Bulgaria country report, report for EC COST E30 Project.

Ciesla, W M, 2002, Non-wood forest products from temperate broadleaved trees, Non-wood Forest Products Paper No. 15, Food and Agriculture Organization of the United Nations, Rome, Italy.

Clinch, P, 1999, The economics of Irish forestry, COFORD, Dublin, Ireland.

Collier, P, Short, I, and Dorgan, J, 2004, Markets for non-wood forest products, COFORD, Dublin, Ireland.

Cooper, R, Ingram, J, Martin, S, Slee, B, and Wong, J, 2004, United Kingdom country report, report for EC COST E30 Project.

Cork Information Bureau, 2002, Cork stoppers quality backgrounder, Cork Information Bureau, Portuguese Cork Association (APCOR), Santa Maria de Lamas, Portugal, also available at: http://www.corkmasters.com.

CPI, 2004, Fact sheet: Recovery and recycling of paper and board, Confederation of Paper Industries, Swindon, United Kingdom.

Dengg, J, Hillring, B, Ilavsky, J, Ince, P, Stolp, J, and Perez-Latorre, M, 2000, Recycling, energy and market interactions, Geneva Timber and Forest Discussion Paper ECE/TIM/DP/15, United Nations, Geneva, Switzerland.

Dubé, Y, Schmithüsen, F, Eds., 2003: Cross-Sectoral Policy Impacts Between Forestry and Other Sectors. Forestry Paper No 142; FAO, Rome, Italy

EFFE, 2003, EFFE-Project draft research report, European Forest Institute, Joensuu, Finland.

Erkkonen, J, and Sievänen, T, 2003, Visitor information - surveys and countings in Finland, METLA, Finland, available at: http://www.metla.fi/metinfo/monikaytto/lvvi/index-en.htm.

Ernst, M L, 1978, Some implications of current social, economic and technological trends, A D Little, Copely Plaza, United States of America.

FAO, 1988, Forestry policies in Europe, Forestry Paper 86, Food and Agriculture Organization of the United Nations, Rome, Italy.

FAO, 1999, Towards a harmonized definition of non-wood forest products, Unasylva No. 198, Volume 50, pp 63-64.

Forestry Commission, 2002, British timber statistics 2001, Forestry Commission, Edinburgh, United Kingdom, also available at: http://www.forestry.gov.uk/statistics.

Fraser, A I, 2004, Making forest policy work, Forestry Sciences Volume 73, Kluwer Academic Publishers, Dordrecht, The Netherlands.

Gerkens, M et Gérard, E, 2004, Évolution des prix de l'épicea, du chêne et du hêtre entre 1960 et 2003, Forêt Wallonne, No 68, Jan-Fév 2004

Gold, S, 2003, The development of European forest resources, 1950 to 2000: a better information base, Geneva Timber and Forest Discussion Paper ECE/TIM/DP/31, United Nations, Geneva, Switzerland.

Helles, F, and Thorsen, B J, 2004, Denmark country report, report for EC COST E30 Project.

Hoekman, B, English, P, and Matoo, A (editors), 2003, Development, trade and the WTO: a handbook, World Bank, Washington DC, United States of America.

ILO, 2000, Public participation in forestry in Europe and North America, Sectoral Activities Department Working Paper No. 163, International Labour Organization, Geneva, Switzerland.

Iqbal, M, 1993, International trade in non-wood forest products: an overview, FO Working Paper No. Misc/93/11, Food and Agriculture Organization of the United Nations, Rome, Italy, also available at: http://www.fao.org/docrep/x5326e/x5326e00.htm#Contents.

IRF, 1990, World road statistics: 1963 - 1989, International Road Federation, Geneva, Switzerland, available at: http://econ.worldbank.org/resource.php?topic=14&type=18.

Italian State Forest Service, 1990, Proceedings from the seminar on products from the Mediterranean forest, Collana Verde 79/1990, Italian State Forest Service, Firenze, Italy.

Kangas, K, and Baudin, A, 2003, Modelling and projections of forest products demand, supply and trade in Europe, Geneva Timber and Forest Discussion Paper ECE/TIM/DP/30, United Nations, Geneva, Switzerland.

Lawson, G, Hyttinen, P, and Thomas, T, 1998, Policy makers decisions on farm and community forestry in Europe, presentation to ECTF Workshop on Decision Trees, 25 September 1998, Edinburgh, Scotland.

Lebedys, A, in prep, Trends and current status of the contribution of the forest sector to national economies, Food and Agriculture Organization of the United Nations, Rome, Italy.

Lorenz, M, Becher, G, Mues, V, Fischer, R, Ulrich, E, Dobbertin, M, and Stofer, S, 2004, Forest Condition in Europe - 2004 technical report of ICP Forests, Institute for World Forestry, Hamburg, Germany.

MCPFE, 2003a, State of Europe's forests 2003 - The MCPFE report on sustainable forest management in Europe, Ministerial Conference on the Protection of Forests in Europe, Vienna, Austria.

MCPFE, 2003b, Vienna Resolution 4 - conserving and enhancing forest biological diversity in Europe, Fourth Ministerial Conference on the Protection of Forests in Europe, 28-30 April 2003, Vienna, Austria.

METLA, 2003, Finland - average stumpage in non-industrial private forests, Statistical Yearbook of Forestry (Metsätilastollinen vuosikirja) 2003, METLA, Finland.

NOBE, 2002, Forecasts of economic growth in OECD and Central and Eastern European countries for the period 2000-2040, Geneva Timber and Forest Discussion Paper ECE/TIM/DP/24, United Nations, Geneva, Switzerland.

OAO NIPIEIlesprom, 2003, Russian Federation forest sector outlook study, Geneva Timber and Forest Discussion Paper ECE/TIM/DP/27, United Nations, Geneva, Switzerland.

Ollmann, H, 2001, Holzbilanzen für die EU und ihre Mitgliedsländer, Institut für Ökonomie, Bundesforschungsanstalt für Forst und Holzwirtschaft, Hamburg, Germany.

Pajuoja, H, 1995, The outlook for the European forest resources and roundwood supply, Geneva Timber and Forest Discussion Paper ECE/TIM/DP/4, United Nations, Geneva, Switzerland.

Peck, T J, and Descargues, J, 1997, The policy context for the development of the forest and forest industries sector in Europe, Geneva Timber and Forest Discussion Paper ECE/TIM/DP/11, United Nations, Geneva, Switzerland.

PEFC, 2004, PEFC Newsletter - May 2004, Pan-European Forest Certification Council, Luxembourg. Also available at: http://www.pefc.org.

Pettennela, D, Klohn, S, Brun, F, Carbone, F, Venzi, L, Cesaro, L, Ciccarese, L, 2004, Italy country report, report for EC COST E30 Project.

Rametsteiner, E, and Kraxner, F, 2003, Europeans and their forests: what do Europeans think about forests and sustainable forest management? - A review of representative public opinion surveys in Europe. Ministerial Conference on the Protection of Forests in Europe, Vienna, Austria.

Remade Scotland, 2004, Woodwaste arisings in Scotland: assessment of available data on Scottish woodwaste arisings, Remade Scotland, Glasgow Caledonian University, Glasgow, United Kingdom.

Rennel, J, 1984, Future of paper in the telematic World: a Jaakko Pöyry review, Jaakko Pöyry, Helsinki, Finland.

RMK, 2004, Estonia - state forest standing sales auction prices, State Forest Management Board (RMK), available at: http://www.rmk.ee.

Roos, J, 2000, Technological change in Japan's residential construction market and its effect on forest products demand, report to FAO, Food and Agriculture Organization of the United Nations, Rome, Italy.

Schelhaas, M, van Brusselen, J, Pussinen, A, Pesonen, E, Schuck, A, Nabuurs, G and Sasse, V, in prep, Outlook for the development of European forest resources, Geneva Timber and Forest Discussion Paper, United Nations, Geneva, Switzerland.

Schmithüsen, F, 2000, The Expanding Framework of Law and Public Policies Governing Sustainable Uses and Management in European Forests: IUFRO World Series Volume 10 (2000): 1-27, Secretariat, Vienna, Austria.

Schmithüsen, F, 2004, European Forest Policy Developments in Changing Societies - Political Trends and Challenges to Research: EFI Proceedings (2004) 49: 87-99, European Forest Institute, Joensuu, Finland.

Schmithüsen, F; Wild-Eck, S, 2000, Uses and Perceptions of Forests by People living in Urban Areas – Findings from selected Empirical Studies. Forstw. Cbl. 119, (2000), 395-408, Blackwell, Berlin, Germany.

Schuler, A, 2002, Innovative uses of wood promotes market development and supports forest sustainability: a win-win situation for society, forest products industry and forest owners, presentation to the UNECE Timber Committee 60th Session, 24-27 September 2002, Geneva, Switzerland.

Sedjo, R, and Sohngen, B, 1998, Impacts of climate change on forests, RFF Climate Issue Brief No. 9 (Second Edition), Resources for the Future, Washington DC, United States of America, available at: http://www.rff.org/Documents/RFF-CCIB-09.pdf.

Seoane, I, 2002, European Community aid schemes, presentation to ECCP Working Group on Forest Carbon Sinks, 18 October 2002, Brussels, Belgium.

Simula, M, 2003, Forest sector reforms in Eastern European countries - overview and lessons learnt, in proceedings of the workshop: *"Institutional changes in forest management in countries with transition economies: problems and solutions"*, 25 February 2003, Moscow, Russian Federation.

Skogsstyrelsen, 2004, Sweden - average standing sales price, Skogsstatistisk årsbok 2004, Skogsstyrelsen, Stockholm, Sweden.

Solberg, B, in prep, Historical trends in forest products markets in Europe, Geneva Timber and Forest Discussion Paper, United Nations, Geneva, Switzerland.

Thoroe, C, Peck, T, Guarin Corredor, H, and Schmithüsen, F, 2004, The policy context of the European forest sector, Geneva Timber and Forest Discussion Paper ECE/TIM/DP/34, United Nations, Geneva, Switzerland.

UN, 1993, The forest resources of the temperate zones: the UNECE/FAO 1990 forest resource assessment, United Nations, Geneva, Switzerland.

UN, 1998, Non-wood goods and services of the forest, Geneva Timber and Forest Study Paper ECE/TIM/SP/15, United Nations, Geneva, Switzerland.

UN, 1999, Forest Fire Statistics 1996-1998, Timber Bulletin - Volume LII (1999), No. 4, United Nations, Geneva, Switzerland.

UN, 2000, Forest Resources of Europe, CIS, North America, Australia, Japan and New Zealand, United Nations, Geneva, Switzerland.

UN, 2001a, Forest policies and institutions of Europe - 1998-2000, Geneva Timber and Forest Study Paper ECE/TIM/SP/19, United Nations, Geneva, Switzerland.

UN, 2001b, World urbanization prospects: the 2001 revision, Department of Economic and Social Affairs, United Nations, New York, United States of America.

UN, 2002, World population prospects: the 2002 revision, Department of Economic and Social Affairs, United Nations, New York, United States of America.

UN, 2003, Forest products annual market analysis 2002-2004, Timber Bulletin - Volume LVI (2003), No. 3, United Nations, Geneva, Switzerland.

UN, 2004, The condition of forests in Europe - 2004 executive report, Convention on Long-range Transboundary Air Pollution: International Co-operative Programme on Assessment and Monitoring of Air Pollution Effects on Forests, United Nations Economic Commission for Europe, Geneva, Switzerland

Whiteman, A, Broadhead, J, and Bahdon, J, 2002, The revision of woodfuel estimates in FAOSTAT, Unasylva No. 211, Volume 53, pp 41-45.

World Bank, 2004, World development indicators 2003, World Bank, Washington DC, United States of America, available at: http://www.worldbank.org/data/wdi2003/index.htm.

Wibe, S, 1994, Non-wood benefits in forestry - survey of valuation studies, Working Paper No. 199, Department of Forest Economics, SLU-Umea, Umea, Sweden.

Wine Business Monthly, 2001, Cork statistics, Wine Business Monthly - 28 June 2001, available at: http://winebusiness.com/html/MonthlyArticle.cfm?AId=38030&issueId=37997.

WRI, 2004, EarthTrends - the environmental information portal, World Resources Institute, available at: http://earthtrends.wri.org.

Zajac, S, Golos, P, Laskowska, K, Adamczyk, W, Czemko, B, Jodlowski, K, Kalinowski, M, Lis, W, Staniszewski, P, Zastocki, D, and Janeczko, E, 2004, Poland country report, report for EC COST E30 Project.

Some facts about the Timber Committee

The Timber Committee is a principal subsidiary body of the UNECE (United Nations Economic Commission for Europe) based in Geneva. It constitutes a forum for cooperation and consultation between member countries on forestry, forest industry and forest product matters. All countries of Europe; the former USSR; United States, of America, Canada and Israel are members of the UNECE and participate in its work.

The UNECE Timber Committee shall, within the context of sustainable development, provide member countries with the information and services needed for policy- and decision-making regarding their forest and forest industry sector ("the sector"), including the trade and use of forest products and, when appropriate, formulate recommendations addressed to member Governments and interested organisations. To this end, it shall:

1. With the active participation of member countries, undertake short-, medium- and long-term analyses of developments in, and having an impact on, the sector, including those offering possibilities for the facilitation of international trade and for enhancing the protection of the environment;

2. In support of these analyses, collect, store and disseminate statistics relating to the sector, and carry out activities to improve their quality and comparability;

3. Provide the framework for cooperation e.g. by organizing seminars, workshops and ad hoc meetings and setting up time-limited ad hoc groups, for the exchange of economic, environmental and technical information between governments and other institutions of member countries that is needed for the development and implementation of policies leading to the sustainable development of the sector and to the protection of the environment in their respective countries;

4. Carry out tasks identified by the UNECE or the Timber Committee as being of priority, including the facilitation of subregional cooperation and activities in support of the economies in transition of central and eastern Europe and of the countries of the region that are developing from an economic point of view;

5. It should also keep under review its structure and priorities and cooperate with other international and intergovernmental organisations active in the sector, and in particular with the FAO (Food and Agriculture Organization of the United Nations) and its European Forestry Commission and with the ILO (International Labour Organisation), in order to ensure complementarities and to avoid duplication, thereby optimizing the use of resources.

More information about the Committee's work may be obtained by writing to:

Timber Branch
Trade Development and Timber Division
UN Economic Commission for Europe
Palais des Nations
CH - 1211 Geneva 10, Switzerland
Fax: + 41 22 917 0041
E-mail: info.timber@unece.org

http://www.unece.org/trade/timber

UNECE/FAO
Publications

Timber Bulletin* Volume LVI (2003)   ECE/TIM/BULL/2003/...

1. Forest Products Prices, 2000-2002 (tables available on web, no hard copy available).
2. Forest Products Statistics, 1998-2002.
3. Forest Products Annual Market Analysis, 2002-2004.
4. Forest Fire Statistics, 2000-2002 (web data release expected October 2004, hard copy available December 2004).
5. Forest Products Trade Flow Data, 2000-2001 (tables available on web, no hard copy available).
6. Forest Products Markets: Prospects for 2004.

*Timber Bulletin series is currently under review

Geneva Timber and Forest Study Papers

Forest policies and institutions of Europe, 1998-2000   ECE/TIM/SP/19

Forest and Forest Products Country Profile: Russian Federation   ECE/TIM/SP/18

(Country profiles also exist on Albania, Armenia, Belarus, Bulgaria, former Czech and

Slovak Federal Republic, Estonia, Georgia, Hungary, Lithuania, Poland, Romania,

Republic of Moldova, Slovenia and Ukraine)

Forest resources of Europe, CIS, North America, Australia, Japan and New Zealand   ECE/TIM/SP/17

State of European forests and forestry, 1999   ECE/TIM/SP/16

Non-wood goods and services of the forest   ECE/TIM/SP/15

The above series of sales publications and subscriptions are available through United Nations Publications Offices as follows:

Orders from Africa, Europe and the Middle East should be sent to:

Orders from North America, Latin America and the Caribbean, Asia and the Pacific should be sent to:

Sales and Marketing Section, Room C-113
United Nations
Palais des Nations
CH - 1211 Geneva 10, Switzerland
Fax: + 41 22 917 0027
E-mail: unpubli@unog.ch

Sales and Marketing Section, Room DC2-853
United Nations
2 United Nations Plaza
New York, N.Y. 10017, United States, of America
Fax: + 1 212 963 3489
E-mail: publications@un.org

Web site: http://www.un.org/Pubs/sales.htm

* * * * *

Geneva Timber and Forest Discussion Papers *(original language only)*

Forest Certification Update for the UNECE Region, 2003	ECE/TIM/DP/39
Forest and Forest Products Country Profile: Republic of Bulgaria	ECE/TIM/DP/38
Forest Legislation in Europe	ECE/TIM/DP/37
Value-Added Wood Products Markets, 2001-2003	ECE/TIM/DP/36
Trends in the Tropical Timber Trade, 2002-2003	ECE/TIM/DP/35
The Policy Context of the European Forest Sector	ECE/TIM/DP/34
Biological Diversity, Tree Species Composition and Environmental Protection in the Regional FRA-2000	ECE/TIM/DP/33
Forestry and Forest Products Country Profile: Ukraine	ECE/TIM/DP/32
The Development Of European Forest Resources, 1950 To 2000: A Better Information Base	ECE/TIM/DP/31
Modelling and Projections of Forest Products Demand, Supply and Trade in Europe	ECE/TIM/DP/30
Employment Trends and Prospects in the European Forest Sector	ECE/TIM/DP/29
Forestry Cooperation with Countries in Transition	ECE/TIM/DP/28
Russian Federation Forest Sector Outlook Study	ECE/TIM/DP/27
Forest and Forest Products Country Profile: Georgia	ECE/TIM/DP/26
Forest certification update for the UNECE region, summer 2002	ECE/TIM/DP/25
Forecasts of economic growth in OECD and central and eastern European countries for the period 2000-2040	ECE/TIM/DP/24
Forest Certification update for the UNECE Region, summer 2001	ECE/TIM/DP/23
Structural, Compositional and Functional Aspects of Forest Biodiversity in Europe	ECE/TIM/DP/22
Markets for secondary processed wood products, 1990-2000	ECE/TIM/DP/21
Forest certification update for the UNECE Region, summer 2000	ECE/TIM/DP/20
Trade and environment issues in the forest and forest products sector	ECE/TIM/DP/19
Multiple use forestry	ECE/TIM/DP/18
Forest certification update for the UNECE Region, summer 1999	ECE/TIM/DP/17
A summary of "The competitive climate for wood products and paper packaging: the factors causing substitution with emphasis on environmental promotions"	ECE/TIM/DP/16
Recycling, energy and market interactions	ECE/TIM/DP/15
The status of forest certification in the UNECE region	ECE/TIM/DP/14
The role of women on forest properties in Haute-Savoie (France): Initial researches	ECE/TIM/DP/13
Interim report on the Implementation of Resolution H3 of the Helsinki Ministerial Conference on the protection of forests in Europe (Results of the second enquiry)	ECE/TIM/DP/12
Manual on acute forest damage	ECE/TIM/DP/7

International Forest Fire News *(two issues per year)*

Timber and Forest Information Series

Timber Committee Yearbook 2004	ECE/TIM/INF/11

The above series of publications may be requested free of charge through:
UNECE/FAO Timber Branch
UNECE Trade Development and Timber Division
United Nations
Palais des Nations
CH - 1211 Geneva 10, Switzerland
Fax: + 41 22 917 0041
E-mail: info.timber@unece.org

Downloads are available at http://www.unece.org/trade/timber